MICROSOFT CERTIFIED DATABASE ADMINISTRATOR

Test Yourself

MCDBA SQL Server 2000 Administration, Second Edition

(Exam 70-228)

MICROSOFT CERTIFIED DATABASE ADMINISTRATOR

TEST YOURSELF

MCDBA SQL Server 2000 Administration, Second Edition

(Exam 70-228)

Stephen Giles
Glen Martin

Osborne/**McGraw-Hill**

New York Chicago San Francisco Lisbon London
Madrid Mexico City Milan New Delhi San Juan
Seoul Singapore Sydney Toronto

Osborne/**McGraw-Hill**
2600 Tenth Street
Berkeley, California 94710
U.S.A.

To arrange bulk purchase discounts for sales promotions, premiums, or fund-raisers, please contact Osborne/**McGraw-Hill** at the above address. For information on translations or book distributors outside the U.S.A., please see the International Contact Information page immediately following the index.

Test Yourself MCDBA SQL Server 2000 Administration (Exam 70-228), Second Edition

1234567890 DOC DOC 01987654321

ISBN 0-07-213443-7

Publisher	**Project Manager**	**Illustrator**
Brandon A. Nordin	Deidre Dolce	Maureen Forys, Happenstance Type-O-Rama
Vice President & Associate Publisher	**Freelance Project Manager**	
Scott Rogers	Laurie Stewart	**Computer Designer**
	Acquisitions Coordinator	Maureen Forys, Happenstance Type-O-Rama
Editorial Director	Jessica Wilson	
Gareth Hancock		**Series Design**
	Technical Editor	Maureen Forys, Happenstance Type-O-Rama
Acquistions Editor	Rob Scrimger	
Nancy Maragioglio		
	Copy Editor	
	Kelly Marshall	

This book was composed with QuarkXPress 4.11 on a Macintosh G4.

ABOUT THE CONTRIBUTORS

Authors

Stephen Giles (MCSE, MCDBA, MCT, CTT) is a Microsoft Certified Trainer from Toronto, Canada. He has spent the last three years teaching, writing about, and working with SQL Server and Oracle. When not submerged in databases, he spends his time trying to keep up with his daughter Olivia.

Glen Martin (MCSE, MCDBA, CCNA, MCT) is a Microsoft Certified Trainer from Ottawa, Canada. In addition to SQL Server, he also delivers training on many of the other Microsoft server products.

Technical Editor

Rob Scrimger has worked as a computer operator, a programmer, a trainer, a network administrator, and a network manager for various companies for the past 20 years. He has helped write several TCP/IP books, including *Networking with Microsoft TCP/IP: Certified Administrator's Resource Edition* and *MCSE Training Guide: TCP/IP 2nd Edition*. Rob has three MCSEs to his credit: NT 3.5, NT 4.0, and Windows 2000 (Charter Member). In addition, he is an MCT, MCDBA, MCSE+I, MCP+SB, CTT, A+ Certified Technician, and Network + Certified.

ACKNOWLEDGMENTS

I would like to thank Nancy Maragioglio for her encouragement and willingness to answer silly questions (not to mention the odd "tread-mill" extension). Thanks to Rob Scrimger for keeping me honest and providing helpful suggestions on the flow and structure of this book. I want to especially thank my daughter Olivia Rose for being the only 6 month old I know who sleeps through the night. Most of all, I would like to thank my wife Antonella for her support and willingness to put up with the long hours at the keyboard and the lost weekends.

—Stephen Giles

CONTENTS

PREFACE

This book's primary objective is to help you prepare for the MCDBA Installing, Configuring, and Administering Microsoft® SQL Server™ 2000 Enterprise Edition exam (70-228) under the new Windows 2000/Microsoft Windows® XP/Microsoft Windows® .NET MCDBA certification track. As the Microsoft program transitions to these new versions of Microsoft Windows®, it will become increasingly important that current and aspiring IT professionals have multiple resources available to assist them in increasing their knowledge and building their skills.

Microsoft has announced its commitment to measuring real-world skills. This book is designed with that premise in mind; its authors have practical experience in the field, using SQL Server Enterprise Edition in hands-on situations and have followed the development of the product since early beta versions.

In This Book

This book is organized in such a way as to serve as a review for the MCDBA Installing, Configuring, and Administering Microsoft® SQL Server™ 2000 Enterprise Edition exam for experienced SQL Server administrators. Each chapter covers a major aspect of the exam, with an emphasis on the "why" as well as the "how to" of implementing and administering Microsoft SQL Server™ databases.

In Every Chapter

We've created a set of chapter components that call your attention to important items, reinforce important points, and provide helpful exam-taking hints. Take a look at what you'll find in every chapter.

Test Yourself Objectives

Every chapter begins with a list of Test Yourself Objectives—what you need to know in order to pass the section on the exam dealing with the chapter topic. Each objective in this list will be discussed in the chapter and can be easily identified by the clear headings that give the name and corresponding number of the objective, so you'll always know an objective when you see it! Objectives are drilled down to the most important details—essentially what you need to know about the objectives and what to expect from the exam in relation to them.

Exam Watch Notes

Exam Watch notes call attention to information about, and potential pitfalls in, the exam. These helpful hints are written by authors who have taken the exams and received their certification; who better to tell you what to worry about? They know what you're about to go through!

Practice Questions and Answers

In each chapter you will find detailed practice questions for the exam, followed by a Quick Answer Key where you can quickly check your answers. The In-Depth Answers section contains full explanations of both the correct and incorrect choices.

The Practice Exam

If you have had your fill of explanations, review questions, and answers, the time has come to test your knowledge. Turn toward the end of this book to the Test Yourself Practice Exam where you'll find a simulation exam. Lock yourself in your office or clear the kitchen table, set a timer, and jump in.

MCDBA/MCSE CERTIFICATION

This book is designed to help you prepare for the Installing, Configuring, and Administering Microsoft® SQL Server™ 2000 Enterprise Edition Exam (Exam 70-228). This book was written to give you an opportunity to review all the important topics that are targeted for the exam.

The nature of the Information Technology industry is changing rapidly, and the requirements and specifications for certification can change just as quickly without notice. Microsoft expects you to regularly visit their Website at http://www.microsoft .com/trainingandservices.com to get the most up to date information on the entire MCDBA program.

TABLE I	Core Exams	
Windows 2000 MCDBA Certification Track	**Microsoft Windows® 2000 Exams**	**Microsoft Windows® XP/Microsoft Windows® .NET Server Exams**
	Exam 70-028: Administering Microsoft SQL Server 7.0™ Or **Exam 70-228**: Installing, Configuring, and Administering Microsoft SQL Server™ Enterprise Edition	
	Exam 70-029: Designing and Implementing Databases with Microsoft SQL Server 7.0™ Or **Exam 70-229:** Designing and Implementing Databases with Microsoft SQL Server™ 2000 Enterprise Edition	
	Exam 70-215: Installing, Configuring, and Administering Microsoft Windows® 2000 Server	**Exam 70-275:** Installing, Configuring, and Administering Microsoft Windows® .NET Server (Available 2002)

TABLE I (cont.)	ONE REQUIRED ELECTIVE EXAMS
Windows 2000 MCDBA Certification Track	Choose one exam from the list below:

Exam 70-015: Designing and Implementing Distributed Applications with Microsoft Visual C++® 6.0

Exam 70-019: Designing and Implementing Data Warehouses with Microsoft SQL Server™ 7.0

Exam 70-155: Designing and Implementing Distributed Applications with Microsoft Visual FoxPro® 6.0

Exam 70-175: Designing and Implementing Distributed Applications with Microsoft Visual Basic® 6.0

Exam 70-216: Implementing and Administering a Microsoft Windows® 2000Network Infrastructure

Exam 70-276: Implementing and Administering a Microsoft Windows® .NET Server Network Infrastructure (Available 2002)

*Candidates who have passed accelerated Exam 70-240 by December 31, 2001 will receive credit for it as both a core exam and an elective exam in the MCDBA track. Generally, an exam that can be used as either a core or an elective counts only once toward a certification. Exam 70-240 in the MCDBA track is an exception.

HOW TO TAKE A MICROSOFT CERTIFICATION EXAM

If you have taken a Microsoft Certification exam before, we have some good news and some bad news. The good news is that the new testing formats will be a true measure of your ability and knowledge. Microsoft has "raised the bar" for its latest certification exams. If you are an expert in the Windows 2000 operating system, and can implement and administer a Microsoft SQL Server™ database, you will have no difficulty with the new exams.

The bad news is that if you have used resources such as "brain-dumps," boot-camps, or exam specific practice tests as your only method of test preparation, you will undoubtedly fail your Windows 2000 exams. The new Windows 2000 MCDBA exams will test your knowledge, and your ability to apply that knowledge in more sophisticated and accurate ways than was expected for the previous exams.

In the Windows 2000 exams, Microsoft will use a variety of testing formats that include product simulations, adaptive testing, drag-and-drop matching, and possibly even "fill in the blank" questions (also called "free response" questions). The test-taking process will measure the examinee's fundamental knowledge of the Windows 2000 operating system rather than the ability to memorize a few facts and then answer a few simple multiple-choice questions.

In addition, the "pool" of questions for each exam will significantly increase. The greater number of questions combined with the adaptive testing techniques will enhance the validity and security of the certification process.

We will begin by looking at the purpose, focus, and structure of Microsoft certification tests, and examine the effect that these factors have on the kinds of questions you will face on your certification exams. We will define the structure of exam questions and investigate some common formats. Next, we will present a strategy for answering these questions. Finally, we will give some specific guidelines on what you should do on the day of your test.

Why Vendor Certification?

The Microsoft Certified Professional program, like the certification programs from Cisco, Novell, Oracle, and other software vendors, is maintained for the ultimate purpose of increasing the corporation's profits. A successful vendor certification program accomplishes this goal by helping to create a pool of experts in regard to a company's software and by "branding" these experts so companies using the software can identify them.

We know that vendor certification has become increasingly popular in the last few years because it helps employers find qualified workers and because it helps software vendors like Microsoft sell their products. But why vendor certification rather than a more traditional approach like a college degree in computer science? A college education is a broadening and enriching experience, but a degree in computer science does not prepare students for most jobs in the IT industry.

A common truism in our business states, "If you are out of the IT industry for three years and want to return, you have to start over." The problem, of course, is *timeliness*; if a first-year student learns about a specific computer program, it probably will no longer be in wide use when he or she graduates. Although some colleges are trying to integrate Microsoft certification into their curriculum, the problem is not really a flaw in higher education, but a characteristic of the IT industry. Computer software is changing so rapidly that a four-year college just can't keep up.

A marked characteristic of the Microsoft certification program is an emphasis on performing specific job tasks rather than merely gathering knowledge. It may come as a shock, but most potential employers do not care how much you know about the theory of operating systems, networking, or database design. As one IT manager put it, "I don't really care what my employees know about the theory of our network. We don't need someone to sit at a desk and think about it. We need people who can actually do something to make it work better."

You should not think that this attitude is some kind of anti-intellectual revolt against "book learning." Knowledge is a necessary prerequisite, but it is not enough. More than one company has hired a computer science graduate as a network administrator, only to learn that the new employee has no idea how to add users, assign permissions, or perform the other day-to-day tasks necessary to maintain a network. This brings us to the second major characteristic of Microsoft certification that affects the questions you must be prepared to answer. In addition to timeliness, Microsoft certification is also job-task oriented.

The timeliness of Microsoft's certification program is obvious and is inherent in the fact that you will be tested on current versions of software in wide use today. The job task orientation of Microsoft certification is almost as obvious, but testing real-world job skills using a computer-based test is not easy.

Computerized Testing

Considering the popularity of Microsoft certification, and the fact that certification candidates are spread around the world, the only practical way to administer tests for the certification program is through Sylvan Prometric or Vue testing centers, which operate internationally. Sylvan Prometric and Vue provide proctor testing services for Microsoft, Oracle, Novell, Lotus, and the A+ computer technician certification. Although the IT industry accounts for much of Sylvan's revenue, the company provides services for a number of other businesses and organizations, such as FAA pre-flight pilot tests. Historically, several hundred questions were developed for a new Microsoft certification exam. The Windows 2000 MCSE exam pool is expected to contain hundreds of new questions. Microsoft is aware that many new MCSE candidates have been able to access information on test questions via the Internet or other resources. The company is very concerned about maintaining the MCSE as a "premium" certification. The significant increase in the number of test questions, together with stronger enforcement of the NDA (Non-disclosure agreement) will ensure that a higher standard for certification is attained.

Microsoft treats the test-building process very seriously. Test questions are first reviewed by a number of subject matter experts for technical accuracy and then are presented in a beta test. Taking the beta test may require several hours, due to the large number of questions. After a few weeks, Microsoft Certification uses the statistical feedback from Sylvan to check the performance of the beta questions. The beta test group for the Windows 2000 certification series included MCTs, MCSEs, and members of Microsoft's rapid deployment partners groups. Because the exams will be normalized based on this population, you can be sure that the passing scores will be difficult to achieve without detailed product knowledge.

Questions are discarded if most test takers get them right (too easy) or wrong (too difficult), and a number of other statistical measures are taken of each question. Although the scope of our discussion precludes a rigorous treatment of question analysis, you should be aware that Microsoft and other vendors spend a great deal of time and effort making sure their exam questions are valid.

The questions that survive statistical analysis form the pool of questions for the final certification exam.

Test Structure

The questions in a Microsoft form test will not be equally weighted. From what we can tell at the present time, different questions are given a value based on the level of difficulty. You will get more credit for getting a difficult question correct, than if you got an easy one correct. Because the questions are weighted differently, and because the exams will likely use the adapter method of testing, your score will not bear any relationship to how many questions you answered correctly.

Microsoft has implemented *adaptive* testing. When an adaptive test begins, the candidate is first given a level three question. If it is answered correctly, a question from the next higher level is presented, and an incorrect response results in a question from the next lower level. When 15 to 20 questions have been answered in this manner, the scoring algorithm is able to predict, with a high degree of statistical certainty, whether the candidate would pass or fail if all the questions in the form were answered. When the required degree of certainty is attained, the test ends and the candidate receives a pass/fail grade.

Adaptive testing has some definite advantages for everyone involved in the certification process. Adaptive tests allow Sylvan Prometric or Vue to deliver more tests with the same resources, as certification candidates often are in and out in 30 minutes or less. For candidates, the "fatigue factor" is reduced due to the shortened testing time. For Microsoft, adaptive testing means that fewer test questions are exposed to each candidate, and this can enhance the security, and therefore the overall validity, of certification tests.

One possible problem you may have with adaptive testing is that you are not allowed to mark and revisit questions. Since the adaptive algorithm is interactive, and all questions but the first are selected on the basis of your response to the previous question, it is not possible to skip a particular question or change an answer.

Question Types

Computerized test questions can be presented in a number of ways. Some of the possible formats are used on Microsoft certification exams and some are not.

True/False

We are all familiar with True/False questions, but because of the inherent 50 percent chance of guessing the correct answer, you will not see questions of this type on Microsoft certification exams.

Multiple Choice

The majority of Microsoft certification questions are in the multiple-choice format, with either a single correct answer or multiple correct answers. One interesting variation on multiple-choice questions with multiple correct answers is whether or not the candidate is told how many answers are correct.

EXAMPLE:

Which two files can be altered to configure the MS-DOS environment? (Choose two.)

or

Which files can be altered to configure the MS-DOS environment? (Choose all that apply.)

You may see both variations on Microsoft certification exams, but the trend seems to be toward the first type, where candidates are told explicitly how many answers are correct. Questions of the "choose all that apply" variety are more difficult and can be merely confusing.

Graphical Questions

One or more graphical elements are sometimes used as exhibits to help present or clarify an exam question. These elements may take the form of a network diagram, pictures of networking components, or screen shots from the software on which you are being tested. It is often easier to present the concepts required for a complex performance-based scenario with a graphic than with words.

Test questions known as *hotspots* actually incorporate graphics as part of the answer. These questions ask the certification candidate to click on a location or graphical element to answer the question. For example, you might be shown the diagram of a network and asked to click on an appropriate location for a router. The answer is correct if the candidate clicks within the *hotspot* that defines the correct location.

Free Response Questions

Another kind of question you sometimes see on Microsoft certification exams requires a *free response* or type-in answer. An example of this type of question might present a TCP/IP network scenario and ask the candidate to calculate and enter the correct subnet mask in dotted decimal notation.

Simulation Questions

Simulation questions provide a method for Microsoft to test how familiar the test taker is with the actual product interface and the candidate's ability to quickly implement a task using the interface. These questions will present an actual Windows 2000 interface that you must work with to solve a problem or implement a solution. If you are familiar with the product, you will be able to answer these questions quickly, and they will be the easiest questions on the exam. However, if you are not accustomed to working with Windows 2000, these questions will be difficult for you to answer. This is why actual hands-on practice with Windows 2000 is so important!

Knowledge-Based and Performance-Based Questions

Microsoft Certification develops a blueprint for each Microsoft certification exam with input from subject matter experts. This blueprint defines the content areas and objectives for each test, and each test question is created to test a specific objective. The basic information from the examination blueprint can be found on Microsoft's Web site in the Exam Prep Guide for each test.

Psychometricians (psychologists who specialize in designing and analyzing tests) categorize test questions as knowledge-based or performance-based. As the names imply, knowledge-based questions are designed to test knowledge, while performance-based questions are designed to test performance.

Some objectives demand a knowledge-based question. For example, objectives that use verbs like *list* and *identify* tend to test only what you know, not what you can do.

EXAMPLE:

Objective: Identify the MS-DOS configuration files.

Which two files can be altered to configure the MS-DOS environment? (Choose two.)

A. COMMAND.COM

B. AUTOEXEC.BAT

C. IO.SYS

D. CONFIG.SYS

Correct answers: B, D

Other objectives use action verbs like *install*, *configure*, and *troubleshoot* to define job tasks. These objectives can often be tested with either a knowledge-based question or a performance-based question.

EXAMPLE:

Objective: Configure an MS-DOS installation appropriately using the PATH statement in AUTOEXEC.BAT.

Knowledge-based question:

What is the correct syntax to set a path to the D: directory in AUTOEXEC.BAT?

A. SET PATH EQUAL TO D:

B. PATH D:

C. SETPATH D:

D. D:EQUALS PATH

Correct answer: B

Performance-based question:

Your company uses several DOS accounting applications that access a group of common utility programs. What is the best strategy for configuring the computers in the accounting department so that the accounting applications will always be able to access the utility programs?

A. Store all the utilities on a single floppy disk and make a copy of the disk for each computer in the accounting department.

B. Copy all the utilities to a directory on the C drive of each computer in the accounting department and add a PATH statement pointing to this directory in the AUTOEXEC.BAT files.

C. Copy all the utilities to all application directories on each computer in the accounting department.

D. Place all the utilities in the C directory on each computer, because the C directory is automatically included in the PATH statement when AUTOEXEC.BAT is executed.

Correct answer: B

Even in this simple example, the superiority of the performance-based question is obvious. Whereas the knowledge-based question asks for a single fact, the performance-based question presents a real-life situation and requires that you make a decision based on this scenario. Thus, performance-based questions give more bang (validity) for the test author's buck (individual question).

Testing Job Performance

We have said that Microsoft certification focuses on timeliness and the ability to perform job tasks. We have also introduced the concept of performance-based questions, but even performance-based multiple-choice questions do not really measure performance. Another strategy is needed to test job skills.

Given unlimited resources, it is not difficult to test job skills. In an ideal world, Microsoft would fly MCP candidates to Redmond, place them in a controlled environment with a team of experts, and ask them to plan, install, maintain, and troubleshoot a Windows network. In a few days at most, the experts could reach a valid decision as to whether each candidate should or should not be granted MCDBA or MCSE status. Needless to say, this is not likely to happen.

Closer to reality, another way to test performance is by using the actual software and creating a testing program to present tasks and automatically grade a candidate's performance when the tasks are completed. This *cooperative* approach would be practical in some testing situations, but the same test that is presented to MCP candidates in Boston must also be available in Bahrain and Botswana. The most workable solution for measuring performance in today's testing environment is a *simulation* program. When the program is launched during a test, the candidate sees a simulation of the actual software that looks, and behaves, just like the real thing. When the testing software presents a task, the simulation program is launched and the candidate performs the required task. The testing software then grades the candidate's performance on the required task and moves to the next question. Microsoft has introduced simulation questions on the certification exam for Internet Information Server 4.0. Simulation questions provide many advantages over other testing methodologies, and simulations are expected to become increasingly important in the Microsoft certification program. For example, studies have shown that there is a very high correlation between the ability to perform simulated tasks on a computer-based test and the ability to perform the actual job tasks. Thus, simulations enhance the validity of the certification process.

Another truly wonderful benefit of simulations is in the area of test security. It is just not possible to cheat on a simulation question. In fact, you will be told exactly what tasks you are expected to perform on the test. How can a certification candidate cheat? By learning to perform the tasks? What a concept!

Study Strategies

There are appropriate ways to study for the different types of questions you will see on a Microsoft certification exam.

Knowledge-Based Questions

Knowledge-based questions require that you memorize facts. There are hundreds of facts inherent in every content area of every Microsoft certification exam. There are several keys to memorizing facts:

Repetition   The more times your brain is exposed to a fact, the more likely you are to remember it.

Association   Connecting facts within a logical framework makes them easier to remember.

Motor Association   It is often easier to remember something if you write it down or perform some other physical act, like clicking on a practice test answer.

We have said that the emphasis of Microsoft certification is job performance, and that there are very few knowledge-based questions on Microsoft certification exams. Why should you waste a lot of time learning filenames, IP address formulas, and other minutiae? Read on.

Performance-Based Questions

Most of the questions you will face on a Microsoft certification exam are performance-based scenario questions. We have discussed the superiority of these questions over simple knowledge-based questions, but you should remember that the job task orientation of Microsoft certification extends the knowledge you need to pass the exams; it does not replace this knowledge. Therefore, the first step in preparing for scenario questions is to absorb as many facts relating to the exam content areas as you can. In other words, go back to the previous section and follow the steps to prepare for an exam composed of knowledge-based questions.

The second step is to familiarize yourself with the format of the questions you are likely to see on the exam. You can do this by answering the questions in this book, or by using Microsoft assessment tests. The day of your test is not the time to be surprised by the construction of Microsoft exam questions.

At best, performance-based scenario questions really do test certification candidates at a higher cognitive level than knowledge-based questions. At worst, these questions can test your reading comprehension and test-taking ability rather than your ability to use Microsoft products. Be sure to get in the habit of reading the question carefully to determine what is being asked.

The third step in preparing for Microsoft scenario questions is to adopt the following attitude: Multiple-choice questions aren't really performance-based. It is all a cruel lie.

These scenario questions are just knowledge-based questions with a story wrapped around them.

To answer a scenario question, you have to sift through the story to the underlying facts of the situation and apply your knowledge to determine the correct answer. This may sound silly at first, but the process we go through in solving real-life problems is quite similar. The key concept is that every scenario question (and every real-life problem) has a fact at its center, and if we can identify that fact, we can answer the question.

Simulations

Simulation questions really do measure your ability to perform job tasks. You must be able to perform the specified tasks. One of the ways to prepare for simulation questions is to get experience with the actual software. If you have the resources, this is a great way to prepare for simulation questions.

SIGNING UP

Signing up to take a Microsoft certification exam is easy. Sylvan Prometric or Vue operators in each country can schedule tests at any testing center. There are, however, a few things you should know:

- If you call Sylvan Prometric or Vue during a busy time, get a cup of coffee first, because you may be in for a long wait. The exam providers do an excellent job, but everyone in the world seems to want to sign up for a test on Monday morning.

- You will need your social security number or some other unique identifier to sign up for a test, so have it at hand.

- Pay for your test by credit card if at all possible. This makes things easier, and you can even schedule tests for the same day you call, if space is available at your local testing center.

- Know the number and title of the test you want to take before you call. This is not essential, and the Sylvan operators will help you if they can. Having this information in advance, however, speeds up and improves the accuracy of the registration process.

TAKING THE TEST

Teachers have always told you not to try to cram for exams because it does no good. If you are faced with a knowledge-based test requiring only that you regurgitate facts, cramming can mean the difference between passing and failing. This is not the case, however, with Microsoft certification exams. If you don't know it the night before, don't bother to stay up and cram.

Instead, create a schedule and stick to it. Plan your study time carefully, and do not schedule your test until you think you are ready to succeed. Follow these guidelines on the day of your exam:

- Get a good night's sleep. The scenario questions you will face on a Microsoft certification exam require a clear head.

- Remember to take two forms of identification—at least one with a picture. A driver's license with your picture and social security or credit card is acceptable.

- Leave home in time to arrive at your testing center a few minutes early. It is not a good idea to feel rushed as you begin your exam.

- Do not spend too much time on any one question. You cannot mark and revisit questions on an adaptive test, so you must do your best on each question as you go.

- If you do not know the answer to a question, try to eliminate the obviously wrong answers and guess from the rest. If you can eliminate two out of four options, you have a 50 percent chance of guessing the correct answer.

- For scenario questions, follow the steps we outlined earlier. Read the question carefully and try to identify the facts at the center of the story.

Finally, we would advise anyone attempting to earn Microsoft MCDBA and MCSE certification to adopt a philosophical attitude. The current Windows MCDBA will be the most difficult MCDBA ever to be offered. The questions will be at a higher cognitive level than seen on all previous MCDBA exams. Therefore, even if you are the kind of person who never fails a test, you are likely to fail at least one certification test somewhere along the way. Do not get discouraged. Microsoft wants to ensure the value of your certification. Moreover, it will attempt to so by keeping the standard as high as possible. If Microsoft certification were easy to obtain, more people would have it, and it would not be so respected and so valuable to your future in the IT industry.

MICROSOFT CERTIFIED DATABASE ADMINISTRATOR

Installing SQL Server 2000

TEST YOURSELF OBJECTIVES

W hether you are upgrading to Microsoft SQL Server 2000 from an earlier version of SQL Server or performing a clean install, proper planning is an essential part of a successful implementation of SQL Server. In the course of the installation you must make decisions that will affect how SQL Server will behave. Some of these decisions cannot be reversed after installation. Careful consideration must be given to these decisions as part of the installation process.

To install SQL Server 2000 successfully, you must be aware of the decisions you will be asked to make during the installation process. You will need to know which operating system you can use to install SQL Server and which editions of the product you should install. You will also be expected to understand all of the elements of the installation process and the effect of your decisions on the outcome of the installation. You are expected to understand how to install SQL Server on a Windows Cluster. You need to understand collations options. In addition, you will have to demonstrate a full understanding of how to install multiple instances of SQL Server. You will have to know the implications of choosing default path and your choice of security context for the SQL services. Finally, you are expected to understand how to upgrade to SQL 2000 from both SQL 6.5 and 7.0.

TEST YOURSELF OBJECTIVE 1.01

Installing SQL Server

SQL Server 2000 can be installed on a number of Windows platforms. It will install on Windows 98/ME, Windows NT 4.0 (Workstation and Server), and Windows 2000 (Professional Server, Advanced Server, and Enterprise Server). There is also a version of SQL Server 2000 that will run on Windows CE. When you install SQL Server on Windows 98/ME it will run as an application. When it is installed on NT or Windows 2000 it will run as a service. This means that in order to run SQL Server on a Windows 98/ME computer, a user must be logged on to the computer. When the user logs out, SQL Server will stop running. However, on Windows 2000 and NT, SQL Server can run independent of any logged-on users.

SQL Server also ships in multiple editions:

- Personal
- Developer

- Standard

- Enterprise

- CE

- Enterprise Evaluation

The edition you will choose to install is determined by the operating system and required functionality. The Personal edition of SQL Server is the only edition that will install on Windows 98/ME. It provides a SQL Server engine and the administrative tools, but is limited in functionality and number of available connections. It is used most often for mobile users (such as outside sales people) who need to take a copy of the database with them on their Windows 98/ME notebooks. This edition also installs on Windows NT Workstation and Professional edition. The Developer edition will install on all versions of Windows NT and Windows 2000. It has all of the functionality of the Enterprise edition but is only licensed for development purposes. It is ideal for database developers testing SQL Server tools on a Windows NT Workstation or Windows 2000 Professional computer. The Standard edition will install on Windows NT Server or Windows 2000 Server. It is meant for departmental-sized databases. If you need more advanced features, such as failover clustering, you will require the Enterprise edition. This edition requires Windows 2000 Advanced Server, Datacenter Server or Windows NT 4.0 Enterprise edition. Obviously, SQL Server CE will require a Pocket PC running Windows CE. The Enterprise Evaluation edition of SQL Server has all of the features of the Enterprise edition, however, it will stop functioning after 120 days.

QUESTIONS

1.01: Installing SQL Server

1. Jim is the administrator for the sales department. He is responsible for managing 200 outside sales people. The sales staff covers a wide area, and is often away from the office for up to a week. Jim has been asked to install a new sales automation tool on the notebooks of all the sales staff that require access to SQL Server 2000 to function. They are running a mixture of Windows 98, NT 4.0 Workstation, and Windows 2000 Professional. Because the users are

often not connected to the network, Jim has decided to install SQL Server on each of the notebooks. Which edition should he install?

A. Personal

B. Developer

C. Desktop

D. Standard

E. Enterprise

2. Your web developers have asked you to install SQL 2000 on their notebooks. Many of them are developing data-aware Active Server pages and need access to a database to test their code (even when they are disconnected from the network). A few of these Active Server pages will access a data warehouse using the Analysis Services. Some of the developers are running Windows 2000 Professional and the rest are running a mixture of Windows 95, Windows 98, and Windows ME. What must you do to configure all of these users to allow them to run SQL Server on their notebooks? (Choose all that apply.)

A. Upgrade all of the Windows 9*x* computers to Windows 2000 Professional.

B. Install the Developer edition of SQL Server 2000 on all of the notebooks.

C. Upgrade all of the Windows 95 computers to Windows 98.

D. Install the Personal edition of SQL Server 2000 on all of the notebooks.

E. Install the Standard edition of SQL Server 2000 on all of the notebooks.

TEST YOURSELF OBJECTIVE 1.02

Failover Clustering

SQL Server 2000 can be installed on a Windows Cluster to provide failover clustering. Clustering allows companies who need high availability (such as online retailers, or manufacturers running 24 hours a day) to maintain a redundant copy of the SQL services. With failover clustering the redundant copy is automatically brought online if the primary server fails (such as a failed power supply or hard drive).

SQL failover clustering runs on top of the Windows Cluster service. Windows Clustering requires at least two computers linked by a network link. These two servers are both linked to an external SCSI or hardware RAID device. Windows will be installed locally, and any applications will be installed on both servers in the cluster. Any data that must be available to all members of the cluster will be placed on the external storage device. One of the two servers (or nodes) will be designated as the primary node and the other will be the secondary node. When you install the Windows Clustering Service, the service creates a "virtual server." This server has a name and a network address that is separate from the names of the other servers in the cluster. The network clients connect to the virtual server. However, when a user connects to the virtual server address or name, he is redirected to one member of the cluster that has been made the primary server. If the primary server becomes unavailable, the virtual server automatically "fails over" to the secondary server, which steps in to take the primary server's place. Because the clients connect to the virtual server, they do not notice any interruption of service. In Windows 2000 it is actually possible to have more than 2 nodes in a cluster. A cluster can contain up to 32 nodes.

Installing SQL failover clustering requires NT 4.0 Enterprise edition, Windows 2000 Advanced Server, or Datacenter Server and the Enterprise edition of SQL Server. Before installing SQL you must configure the cluster service on Windows 2000 and create the virtual server. You will then install SQL Server on the virtual server. To install SQL on a virtual server, you must choose Virtual Server on the Computer Name form in the Installation program as shown in the following illustration, and specify the name of the virtual server (rather than the name of the primary or secondary server).

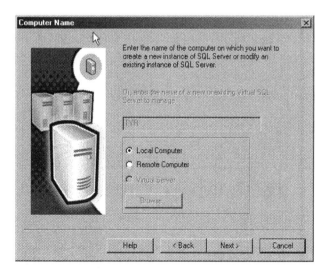

If you install SQL Server directly onto either the primary or secondary server, the installation will not support failover clustering. The Windows 2000 Cluster Service will create a copy of the SQL server on both the primary and secondary server. If you are not using the Enterprise edition of SQL Server or if the cluster service is not configured, this option will be grayed out (as in the previous illustration). If you have a Windows 2000 server that is not cluster-aware, it is possible to "upgrade" the server to a cluster server.

Windows Clustering can be divided into two configurations:

- Active-Passive
- Active-Active

The Active-Passive model is the one described above. In this model, the secondary node does nothing except test to see if the primary node is available, and process and update changes. This provides full redundancy, but also means that twice the amount of hardware is used as is required to run the server. This makes the Active-Passive model very costly in terms of hardware.

In the Active-Active model, each server is primary for one virtual server and secondary for the other. This means that there will be two virtual servers on the network—one for each member of the node. If one of the nodes fails, the other node will continue to be primary for its virtual server, but it will also take the place of the failed server as a new primary. This means that both servers are used as part of production, however, if one of the nodes fails, the second server must have enough resources to run both virtual servers.

Make sure you are aware which versions of SQL Server and which versions of Windows are required to install SQL Server on a failover clustering.

QUESTIONS

1.02: Failover Clustering

3. You have been asked to install SQL Server 2000 to support your corporate web site. You will require high availability for this server and you have decided to install SQL Server with failover clustering. You have configured a cluster between two Windows NT 4.0 Enterprise servers. However, when you run the

installation, you are not given the option to install SQL on a virtual server. What is the most likely reason that this option is not available when you install SQL Server?

A. You are not installing the Enterprise edition of SQL Server.

B. You cannot install a cluster-aware version of SQL Server 2000 on a Windows NT 4.0 server.

C. You must first install a default instance of SQL Server and then make it cluster-aware.

D. You must install the cluster on a Windows 2000 Datacenter server.

4. You have installed a cluster-aware version of SQL Server 2000 on a virtual server called AppsSrv1. The cluster is comprised of two Windows 2000 Advanced servers called Apps1 (the primary node) and Apps2 (the secondary node). When you install SQL Server, where do the application files for the SQL server *physically* reside?

A. On the primary node only

B. On the secondary node only

C. On the virtual server

D. On both the primary and secondary nodes

5. You currently have two SQL servers running in your environment. Both of these servers are installed on Windows 2000 Advanced Server. Each server is running at approximately 50% of the total capacity for the hardware. Both of these SQL servers contain critical data for your company. Your managers are concerned that these databases may be susceptible to failure. You have been asked to establish failover cluster on both servers. What must you do to configure clustering? (Choose all that apply.)

A. Add the cluster service to both servers.

B. Add two more Windows 2000 Advanced servers and install cluster services on all four servers.

C. Configure the servers in an Active-Passive configuration.

D. Configure the servers in an Active-Active configuration.

E. Upgrade all of the servers to Windows 2000 Datacenter Server.

F. Upgrade all of the servers to SQL 2000 Enterprise Server.

TEST YOURSELF OBJECTIVE 1.03

Default Collation

When you install SQL Server you are given the option to modify the default collation. The default collation controls how SQL Server stores and retrieves character data (char, varchar, text) and Unicode data (nchar, nvarchar, ntext). Basic character data is 8-bit values (providing 256 characters with 128 standard characters and 128 extended characters). Unicode uses a 16-bit character set (providing 65,536 possible characters). Unicode is used to support multinational databases that require non-western European characters. The collation consists of three elements:

- Sort order for non-Unicode data
- Code page for non-Unicode data
- Sort order for Unicode data

When choosing the default collation you will also have to choose case sensitivity (either sensitive or non-sensitive) for both Unicode and non-Unicode data. The SQL default collation is SQL_Latin1_General_CP1_CL_AS. Latin1_General is the standard code page for most western European languages. It uses the dictionary sort order, and is case insensitive.

If you require a collation that is different than the default, you are given the option to change it. Once you set a default collation for the server it cannot be changed without re-creating the Master database. In SQL 2000, this collation will be the default for all databases unless you choose an alternate collation when you create your database. In earlier versions of SQL Server, all databases and database objects were required to use the server's default collation. However, in SQL Server 2000 you can set a different collation at the database and at the column level. You can also create multiple instances of SQL Server on the same computer and give each instance a different collation (named instances will be discussed in section 1.04). If you require a collation other than the default, you choose it from the list of possible collations in the SQL Collations box of the Collation Settings form. The illustration on the following page shows the Collation Settings form with the default collation setting highlighted in the SQL Collations box. In order to see the SQL Collation Settings form, you must choose a custom install. If you do not choose custom as the installation type, SQL Server installs the default collation and does not show you this form.

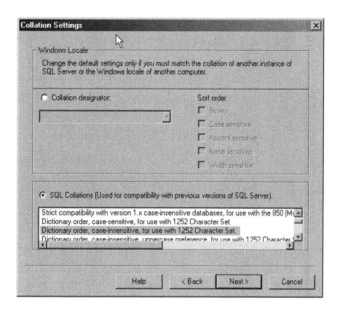

If you require an alternate collation than the ones provided, you can also create your own collation using the Collation Designator as shown in the preceding illustration. When you click the pull-down menu, you are presented with all of the various collations. You can then modify your Unicode settings with the check boxes to the right of the pull-down box.

Note: With this tool it is possible to set a different case sensitivity to your Unicode and non-Unicode character data. You should use the same degree of sensitivity with both character types.

exam
Watch

Remember that unlike SQL Server 7.0, it is also possible to set the collation at the database and the column level. This means that it is possible to have a database (or even a table) that uses a collation that is different than the default.

QUESTIONS

1.03: Default Collation

6. Sally has installed a Microsoft SQL server using the default collation. One of her users needs to add a database to the server that requires a non-standard character set and sort order. Sally's budget does not have provisions for a second server. What can Sally do to support the new collation for this database? (Choose all that apply.)

   A. Use sp_configure to change the collation on the server.

   B. Install a new instance of SQL Server with a different collation on the same server.

   C. Create the new database with a different collation than the default.

   D. You cannot support this database on the server.

   E. Change the default collations settings in HKEY_Local_Machine\Software\ Microsoft\SQL Server\default settings.

7. Jake is a SQL Server administrator for a multinational fast food chain. He has just installed the server called ArchData1 using the default collation. This server will be used to hold archival data from several other servers on the company's global network. After importing some test data, he notices that some imported rows contain textual errors. Other rows (imported from different servers) do not contain these errors. What is the most likely cause of this problem?

   A. Some of servers are using a different code page.

   B. Some of the servers are using Unicode datatypes.

   C. Some of the servers are using different Unicode code pages.

   D. Some of the servers are configured to be case sensitive.

Number of Instances

Earlier versions of SQL Server only allowed one installation (or instance) of SQL on a server. Now, SQL Server 2000 has the ability to support multiple instances on the same computer. Each instance is an independent installation of SQL Server. Each instance has its own:

- System databases (Master, Model, Msdb, and Tempdb)
- Files (located in a separate file path)
- Services (with individual security contexts)

The first instance on a SQL server is the default instance. It has the same name as the NetBIOS name of the server. By default, it is installed in the path c:\Program Files\Microsoft SQL Server\mssql\. It has a SQL Server service (mssqlserver) and a SQL Agent service (sqlserveragent).

When you install a second instance, you are prompted to provide a name for the instance. When the instance is created, it will have the name <server name>\<instance name>. For example, if the Windows server was called Corp1 and you installed a second instance on the server called TestServer, the full name of the instance would be Corp1\TestServer. The default path will be c:\Program Files\Microsoft SQL Server\mssql$<instance name>\. The SQL services will also contain the name of the instance. The SQL Server service will be called mssql$<instance name> and the agent service will be called sqlagent$<instance name> accounts. For obvious reasons you cannot have two instances with the same name on a server.

Each instance is independent of the others. The only files shared between all of the instances are those that belong to client tools (Enterprise Manager, Query Analyzer, etc.). It is possible to start or stop one instance without affecting the other. And each instance can have its own service account, and therefore run under a different security context than the others. You can have up to 16 named instances on a server. You can also remove an instance without affecting any of the other instances on the server.

QUESTIONS

1.04: Number of Instances

8. Two different groups share a SQL server named TestData1. The first group uses the default instance and the second group uses a named instance called RDTest. The manager of the R&D group is concerned that members of the other group will get access to the R&D group databases because the instances are installed on the same server. What can you tell her about having multiple instances that would help to put her mind at ease?

    A. Each instance has its own Master database, and logon accounts from one instance are not added to the other instance.

    B. SQL 2000 implements an instance-dependent version of Enterprise Manager and Query Analyzer for each instance.

    C. Each instance has its own services with its own security contexts.

    D. You are using the local system account for each instance.

9. You have created three named instances on your server. A business unit that was sold to another company used the default instance. The data was migrated to the new company and your users no longer access this instance. The two named instances are still in production. Your server is running short of resources (both memory and disk) and you do not have any budget to increase the hardware. What can you do to recover resources? (Choose all that apply.)

    A. Stop the services for the default instance.

    B. Uninstall the default instance using the Add\Remove Programs utility in the Control Panel.

    C. Use sp_serveroption to give some of the default instance free space to the other two instances.

    D. You cannot recover resources from the default instance once they have been allocated.

10. Your company hosts web sites for corporate clients. As part of the service you provide for your clients, you also make SQL Server available for those clients who want to run e-commerce sites. Each client requires their own server, with their own Master database. You currently have 40 clients who have subscribed to this e-commerce server. What is the minimum number of physical computers you will require to host these clients?

   A. 40

   B. 3

   C. 4

   D. 1

TEST YOURSELF OBJECTIVE 1.05

File Location

As you saw in the last section, the default install path for all instances is: c:\Program files\Microsoft SQL server\mssql\ (or c:\Program files\Microsoft SQL server\ mssql$<instance name>\ for a named instance). The file path is also the default location for the SQL application files (in a folder called Binn). This path is also the default location for the physical files used by the system databases. They are stored in a file called Data. The Data folder is also the default location for all user databases (including the Northwind and Pubs databases). There is also a folder called Backup which is the default location for all SQL Server backups.

In the installation process, you are given the option to change the default path for the Program files (all of the files in the Binn folder) and the Data files (the location for the physical files for the system databases as well as the default location for your user databases). You want to make sure that these folders will have enough space for continued growth—particularly with system databases. If you do not have enough space in the default path, you should change the location of one or both default file locations. If you choose to install the SQL Server tools (such as Enterprise Manager or the Query Analyzer), they are also installed in the default path under a folder called c:\Program files\Microsoft SQL server\80\Tools\.

QUESTIONS

1.05: File Location

11. You are the administrator of a database called TestSrv. You used the Create A Database Wizard on a named instance called take2. You selected the default file location when you ran the wizard. You now want to copy the data files for this database to another server. Assuming SQL Server was installed on the C: partition, where would you go to find the data files?

    A. c:\mssql8\Take2\Data

    B. c:\Program Files\Microsoft SQL Server\mssql$take2\Database

    C. c:\Program Files\Microsoft SQL Server\mssql\Take2\Data

    D. c:\Program Files\Microsoft SQL Server\mssql$take2\Data

12. You are the administrator of a SQL Server 2000 with only the default instance. One of the .dll files needed by Enterprise Manager was damaged. You have received a new copy of the .dll and all you have to do is overwrite the corrupt file with new file. Assuming SQL Server is installed on the C: partition, where would you go to find the files for Enterprise Manager?

    A. c:\Program Files\Microsoft SQL Server\mssql\tools

    B. c:\Program Files\Microsoft SQL Server\80\Tools\Binn

    C. c:\Program Files\Microsoft SQL Server\mssql\Binn\ClientTools

    D. c:\Program Files\Microsoft SQL Server\80\ClientTools

13. Sam is installing SQL Server 2000 on a Windows 2000 Advanced server. The server has two physical disks. Each disk is partitioned with a single volume. The first disk is running a bit short of space. He wants to install the SQL Server program files on the first disk, but install the database files on the second disk.

He also wants to make this new path the default path for all data files. How can Sam install the data files on a different disk from the program files?

A. In the destination folder section of the Setup Type form, click the Browse button next to Data File and select a folder on the second disk.

B. Perform a default installation and use sp_movedbfile to move the database files to the second disk. Use sp_configure and alter the Default Data File Path parameter to point to the new data file on the second disk.

C. Perform a default installation and use the ALTER DATABASE statement to move the database files to the second disk. Edit the Registry to point the default data file path to the new location.

D. Backup all of the databases and restore them onto a folder on the second disk. Use sp_configure and alter the Default Data File Path parameter to point to the new data file on the second disk.

TEST YOURSELF OBJECTIVE 1.06

Service Account

SQL Server runs as a service on Windows NT and 2000. It actually runs as two services: the SQL Server services (mssqlserver), which runs the server engine, and the SQL Server Agent services (SQLAgent), which controls monitoring, and automation. Like all other services, these services run under their own security context. This means that the services can be running on the server even when no other user is logged on. When you install SQL Server, you must decide what security context these services will use. You are given two options:

■ Use the local system account

■ Use a domain user account

Which option you choose depends on the role this SQL server will play on your network. The local system account will allow the services to start and will give the services local administrative rights. However, the local system account is not a domain account, and therefore cannot authenticate itself outside of the local server. If you choose the local system account, SQL Server will not be able to interact with any other computers on the network. This includes mail servers and other SQL servers. If your SQL server will need to use the SQL Mail or SQL Agent Mail, or interact with other SQL servers for such activities as replication, linked queries, and data transfer, you must use a domain user account.

Domain user accounts exist on a domain controller, rather than the local server, and can be used to authenticate the server to any other member computer in the domain. For example, to allow mail services, you are able to create a mailbox and a login on your Exchange server using the SQL service accounts. To allow the SQL services to access other network resources, you must grant the appropriate rights to the account to the remote systems. If you use a domain user account, you must assign the account the necessary rights required to act as a service on the local server. The service account will require certain Windows and SQL Server administrative rights. The easiest way to give the service account these rights is to add the account to the local administrator account for the server where you are installing SQL Server. If you choose not to use the local service account, you must perform the following manually:

- Grant the account logon as a service right.
- Give the service the permissions to read and modify SQL server files.
- Alter the Registry to access several registry keys.
- Give the account permission to modify .mdf, .ndf, and .ldf files (the SQL server database files).

SQL Server gives you the ability to use a different account for each service, however, to avoid complexity you should use a common domain account for both services. You should use a dedicated user account for the SQL services (as opposed to using your account or one of your other administrative accounts). This will allow you to audit your service account. Because this is a domain user account it is possible to log on interactively as that account. You should also make sure to enable the Password Never Expires option for this account. If the service password expires, the service will fail to start until you manually change the service password. Finally, you must ensure that the User Must Change Password At Next Logon option is not selected. The SQL Server services are not able to change their own passwords and if you select the option, the services will not be able to logon to Windows and the SQL server will not start.

QUESTIONS

1.06: Service Account

14. Fred has just installed SQL 2000 Server on a fresh install of Windows 2000 Server. He has configured both services to use a domain user account. However, when the installation is complete, both the SQL Server service and the SQL Server Agent service fail to start. He tries several times with both the service manager and the net start command but the services fail each time. He can ping an Active Directory Domain Controller and he has confirmed that the password for the service has been typed correctly. What else might cause this failure? (Choose all that apply.)

   A. He has not given the domain user account the appropriate rights.

   B. He has not used the Windows local system account.

   C. He has checked the User Must Change Password At Next Logon password option in the Properties sheet for the domain user account.

   D. He must register the server in the Enterprise Manager.

15. You have installed two instances of SQL Server 2000 on a Windows 2000 Advanced server called Tor_Corp1. You installed the first instance as the default instance, and called the second instance HRData. You have made a change to the configuration settings on the HRData instances and must stop and restart this instance. You open the Windows 2000 services utility. Which service must you restart?

   A. mssqlserver

   B. Tor_Corp1\HRData

   C. mssql$HRData

   D. HRData$mssqlservice

Performing a Custom Upgrade to SQL Server 2000

With multiple instances, there are some options for upgrading from earlier versions of SQL Server to SQL Server 2000. In some cases, it is possible to install SQL Server 2000 as a second instance and then migrate data from the earlier version to the new instance. This can be easier and safer than performing a direct upgrade. Safer in the sense that if there are problems with the install, the original database is unchanged and you can uninstall the secondary instance and start over again with worrying about data loss or extended down time.

SQL Server supports a direct upgrade path from SQL Server 6.5 and SQL Server 7.0. There is no direct path from SQL Server 6.0 and earlier. To upgrade from these versions of SQL Server, you must first upgrade to either SQL 6.5 or 7.0 Server. The details of how to upgrade are specific to the version of the original database.

QUESTIONS

1.07: Performing a Custom Upgrade to SQL Server 2000

16. Sally is the administrator for the Human Resources department of a large insurance company. One of the groups has been running their applications for several years on a SQL 6.0 server. They have been upgrading their hardware regularly to keep up with the demands of their users. They have purchased a new application for tracking employee training paths. This application requires support for user-defined functions. For this, they will require SQL Server 2000. The manager of this group has asked Sally to upgrade all of their current databases to SQL Server 2000. They have tested their other applications and all

of them will run under SQL Server 2000. The current hardware will support an installation of SQL Server 2000. What must Sally do to upgrade this server?

A. Install SQL Server 2000 as the default instance and run the SQL Server Upgrade Wizard to upgrade the databases.

B. Install SQL Server 2000 as the default instance and use the Copy Database Wizard to move the SQL 6.0 databases to the SQL 2000 server.

C. Install SQL Server 2000 into the same path as the SQL 6.0 server

D. Upgrade the SQL 6.0 server to SQL 6.5 or 7.0. Then upgrade the SQL 6.5 or 7.0 databases to SQL 2000.

TEST YOURSELF OBJECTIVE 1.08

Upgrading to SQL Server 2000 from SQL Server 6.5

There is a direct upgrade path from SQL Server 6.5 to SQL 2000. When you upgrade a SQL 6.5 database to SQL 2000, all databases, and users are migrated to the SQL 2000 server. After the installation, the SQL 6.5 server is not deleted from the server. SQL 6.5 and SQL 2000 cannot run on the server at the same time. When you install SQL 2000 on the server, SQL 6.5 will be unavailable. However, SQL will install a utility that allows you to change between SQL 6.5 and SQL 2000. When you activate the switch utility, it stops the services belonging to whichever version of SQL Server is running and starts the other version's services. It also switches the short cuts to all of the administrative tools on the Start menu to the current version.

Because the two versions cannot run at the same time, you must use the SQL Server Upgrade Wizard to perform an upgrade from SQL 6.5 to SQL 2000. To run the wizard you first must have SQL 2000 installed on the server as the default instance. The SQL Server Upgrade Wizard will migrate all objects and data from the SQL 6.5 server to SQL 2000. Remember that the Upgrade Wizard will not remove the objects from the original 6.5 server. This is important to remember because it means that the server must have enough space to hold two complete sets of the databases including all of the data. If the server does not have sufficient space to maintain two complete copies of the SQL 6.5 server, the upgrade will fail. You can also run the SQL Server Upgrade Wizard on a second server. In this case you will be migrating the data from one server to the other. The SQL 6.5 server will remain intact and active, but all of the databases and users will be moved to the new server.

When you upgrade either on the same server or on different servers using the SQL Server Upgrade Wizard, SQL will establish a Named-Pipe connection between the two servers. However, if you have a tape drive installed on the server, you can also perform the upgrade using tape. In a tape upgrade, SQL performs a backup of all of the databases to be upgraded to tape and then migrates the databases from the tape to the SQL 2000 server. When you do an upgrade from tape, you are given the option to drop the databases that you have upgraded. This is a useful solution to the problem of performing an upgrade on a single server when you do not have enough drive space. Be careful when selecting this option. The Upgrade Wizard will delete all devices— not just those of the databases being upgraded. Before you perform any upgrade, make sure that you have a full backup of all of the databases on the SQL 6.5 server.

QUESTIONS

1.07: Upgrading to SQL Server 2000 from SQL Server 6.5

17. Your company has recently acquired one of its competitors. You have been asked to integrate all of their databases into your system, and upgrade all databases to SQL 2000. One of the servers is a SQL 6.5 server called SalesHistory. It contains a 20GB device that contains historical data from the sales group. The server meets the minimum hardware requirements for SQL Server 2000 and it has a 30GB hard drive with 8GB free. It has a local tape drive installed. You manager has told you that there is currently no budget to purchase new hardware. You install SQL Server 2000 on the server and run the SQL Server Upgrade Wizard. However, the wizard informs you that there is not enough space to perform the upgrade. How can you upgrade this server without purchasing new hardware?

   A. Select the Delete On Upgrade option in the Upgrade Wizard, to delete the devices from SQL 6.5 as they are upgraded.

   B. Choose to backup to tape, and select the Delete option in the SQL Server Upgrade Wizard.

C. It is not possible to upgrade from SQL Server 6.5 to SQL Server 2000 without sufficient disk space.

D. Perform an overwriting upgrade that replaces the SQL 6.5 server with SQL 2000.

18. You are administering a test server in your environment. The server is currently running SQL Server 6.5. You are evaluating several programs that will run on SQL Server 2000. You want to run SQL 2000 on the test server, but you also need to be able to test other applications against the 6.5 server. What must you do to install SQL 2000 on the server but still have access to the SQL 6.5 server?

A. Simply install SQL 2000 on the test server.

B. Run the SQL Server Upgrade Wizard, and select the Leave SQL 6.5 On Server option.

C. Leave the SQL 6.5 server as the default instance and install SQL 2000 as a secondary instance.

D. Install SQL Server 2000 into a different partition on the same server.

TEST YOURSELF OBJECTIVE 1.09

Upgrading to SQL Server 2000 from SQL Server 7.0

When upgrading from SQL 7.0 to SQL 2000 you have more options than you have when upgrading from 6.5. First, you can install SQL 2000 over the top of SQL 7.0. When you do this, SQL Server 2000 replaces the SQL 7.0 server. This new server maintains all logins, configuration settings, and user databases. This is a one-way upgrade. If you want to revert to the SQL 7.0 server, you will have to uninstall SQL Server 2000, re-install SQL 7.0 and then restore your users and databases from backups (assuming you have up-to-date backups). There is, however, another option.

Unlike SQL 6.5 Server, it is possible to run both SQL 7.0 and SQL 2000 at the same time on a server. SQL 7.0 must run as the default instance. You then must install SQL Server 2000 as a named instance. Both databases will be fully accessible and the SQL 7.0 databases will not be upgraded. What will be upgraded are the SQL administration tools. However, you can use the new version of Enterprise Manager and Query Analyzer to access the SQL 7.0 server. The only tool not upgraded is the Books Online. SQL Server 2000 installs a copy of the SQL 2000 Books Online, but leaves the SQL 7.0 Books Online unchanged. If you look at the start menu, you will see both a SQL Server 7.0 and SQL Server folder. When SQL installs the first SQL 2000 instance, it will redirect to the SQL Server 7.0 folder to point to the new tools.

Once the second instance is installed, you can use the Copy Database Wizard (or the DTS tools) to migrate the users and databases from the SQL 7.0 server to SQL Server 2000. Performing a migration rather than a complete overwriting upgrade allows you to have more control over when you move data. It also leaves the SQL 7.0 server intact and accessible while you migrate the data. When you use the Copy Database Wizard, you get more than just the data. This wizard will also migrate related metadata, such as user logons, automation jobs, triggers, and stored procedures. Essentially, you are migrating all objects from the SQL 7.0 server to SQL 2000; however, you can do so at your own pace without altering the SQL 7.0 server (or even taking it offline).

exam
ⓌＡＴＣＨ

Remember that if you choose to upgrade SQL 7.0 rather than install SQL 2000 as a second instance, it will overwrite the SQL 7.0 server. If there are any errors with the upgrade, you must uninstall SQL and restore the SQL 7.0 server from a backup. If you do not have a backup, the data will be lost.

QUESTIONS

1.09: Upgrading to SQL Server 2000 from SQL Server 7.0

19. Jane is the administrator of a SQL 7.0 server. The company has acquired an upgraded version of a third party software package that requires SQL Server 2000. The original application runs off of a database called RecData on the SQL 7.0 server. However, there are other applications running against databases on the same server that will not run under SQL Server 2000. You do not have the budget to buy a second server. How can you run the new software package without losing support for the legacy applications?

   A. Install SQL Server 2000 on the server, use the SQL Server Switch to switch between SQL 7.0 and SQL 2000 server.

    B. Leave the SQL 7.0 server running as the default instance. Install SQL Server 2000 as a second named instance, use bcp.exe to move the data from the SQL 7.0 to SQL 2000 instances. Manually recreate all of the users' other objects.

    C. Leave the SQL 7.0 server running as the default instance. Install SQL Server 2000 as a second named instance; use the Copy Database Wizard to move the RecData database to SQL 2000.

    D. You cannot have SQL 7.0 and SQL 2000 running on the same server.

20. Stewart is the administrator for a Microsoft SQL 7.0 server named Corpsrv1. He has recently performed a version upgrade of Corpsrv1 and upgraded it to SQL Server 2000. However, he discovered after the version update that some of his applications would not function. He wants to undo the upgrade and revert to a SQL 7.0 server. How can he undo the upgrade?

    A. Rerun the SQL 7.0 setup from a SQL 7.0 server CD.

    B. Use rebuildm.exe to switch the server back to its pre-upgrade state.

    C. Use the SQL Server Uninstaller to remove the upgraded version of SQL Server 2000.

    D. Uninstall SQL 2000 using the Add/Remove Software Wizard. Reinstall SQL 7.0 and restore the database from a full backup.

21. John is the administrator for a company that develops sales automation software. He needs to test his software under SQL Server 6.5, SQL Server 7.0, and SQL Server 2000. However, due to budget constraints he has only been given one test server. How can he configure his server so that it will run all three versions of SQL Server?

    A. Install SQL 6.5 as the default instance. Install SQL 7.0 as a named instance and install SQL 2000 as a second named instance.

    B. First Install SQL 6.5 on the server. Next, install SQL 7.0. Leave SQL 7.0 as the default instance and install SQL 2000 as a named instance. Use the SQL Switch tool to access the SQL 6.5 server.

    C. You cannot install SQL 6.5 and SQL 7.0 on the same server.

    D. First Install SQL 6.5 on the server. Next, install SQL 7.0. Finally install SQL 2000 and use the SQL Switch utility to switch between the three versions of SQL Server.

LAB QUESTION

Objectives 1.01–1.09

Jane has just been hired as the chief DBA for a multinational manufacturing company. The network consists of a single Active Directory domain. She has been instructed to move all of her SQL servers to SQL 2000. In her environment she currently has eight SQL 7.0 servers, two SQL 6.5 servers and one SQL 6.0. All of these servers meet the minimum hardware requirements to install SQL Server 2000. All of these servers must be available while the upgrade is taking place. She also will need to add three new SQL 2000 servers to meet the growing needs of the various groups throughout the company. Each one of these servers has a hardware RAID array to hold the data files for all of the databases.

One of the new SQL 2000 servers will be a central reporting server that will need to draw data from most of the other servers. This server will be installed on a Windows 2000 Datacenter server. Two of the SQL 7.0 servers are located in Europe and one is located in Hong Kong. All of these servers will also need to communicate with the central reporting server.

Because major business decisions about ordering and sales will be made based on information from this reporting server, Jane's managers want her to configure this server for high availability. There is another Windows 2000 Datacenter server available with an external SCSI RAID array. When the report server is fully loaded it will consume 75% of the available resources on the server.

Based on the this scenario, answer the following questions:

1. Will Jane have any problems upgrading all of the existing SQL servers to SQL Server 2000? If so, what would she have to do to deal with this problem?

2. What security context should she use for the SQL Server and SQL Agent services?

3. What should she do to place the data files for the new SQL Server databases onto the RAID arrays? How can she make this the default data file location?

4. Will the operating system and hardware allow the report server to be clustered? What type of cluster must she implement?

5. What must she do to ensure that the multilingual databases can be combined without data corruption?

QUICK ANSWER KEY

Objective 1.01
1. A
2. A and B

Objective 1.02
3. A
4. D
5. A, D, and F

Objective 1.03
6. B and C
7. A

Objective 1.04
8. A
9. A and B
10. B

Objective 1.05
11. D
12. B
13. A

Objective 1.06
14. A and C
15. C

Objective 1.07
16. D

Objective 1.08
17. B
18. A

Objective 1.09
19. C
20. D
21. B

IN-DEPTH ANSWERS

1.01: Installing SQL Server

1. ☑ **A** is correct because the only edition that will install on all of the operating systems used by the sales staff is the Personal edition. This provides a fully functional SQL Server engine. It will act as a suitable data source for the sales automation tool.

   ☒ **B** is incorrect because the Developer edition is only licensed for development work. Installing the Developer edition would allow the application to function, but would violate the license agreement. **C** is incorrect because it no longer exists in SQL Server 2000. In SQL 7.0, you were given the option of installing the Server or Desktop editions of SQL. In SQL Server 2000, the Personal edition has replaced the Desktop edition. **D** and **E** are incorrect because both the Standard edition and the Enterprise edition will not install on any of the operating systems used by the sales staff. Both of these are server versions of SQL Server 2000.

2. ☑ **A** and **B** are correct because the Developer edition of SQL Server 2000 provides the users with all of the same database services as the Enterprise editions. The only difference is that it is licensed solely for development purposes. Using this edition will allow your developers to test their Active Server pages against a fully functional database. However, the Developer edition will not run on Windows 9x (including Windows ME) so you will have to upgrade all users to Windows NT 4.0 Workstation or Windows 2000.

   ☒ **C** is incorrect because the Developer edition will not install on Windows 98, therefore the upgrade will not help you implement SQL Server on the notebooks. **D** is technically correct in the sense that the Personal edition will provide access to a simple database engine. However, it will not give the developers a full database with all of the other services (like the analysis services) so the Developer edition is the only choice. **E** is incorrect because it would require that you upgrade all of the notebooks to Windows 2000 or Windows NT 4.0 Server.

1.02: Failover Clustering

3. ☑ **A.** is correct because failover clustering is only available on SQL Server 2000 Enterprise edition. If you install the standard version of SQL Server, you are not given the option to install SQL Server on a virtual server. You will still be able to install SQL Server on one member of the cluster. But this installation will not be part of the cluster and will not provide high availability.

☒ **B, C,** and **D** are incorrect because you can install SQL Server failover clustering on a Windows NT 4.0 cluster. You will require Windows NT 4.0 Enterprise edition to create the cluster. There is no way to upgrade SQL Server to a cluster-aware version after it has been installed. If you have installed SQL Server and want to make it cluster-aware, you must reinstall SQL Server. In Windows 2000, clustering is supported on both Windows 2000 Advanced Server and Windows 2000 Datacenter Server.

4. ☑ **D** is correct because the primary benefit of failover clustering is redundancy. The clients connect to the virtual server but it is one of the nodes in the cluster that responds to that request. If one server fails, a redundant copy takes its place. For this reason, SQL Server must physically exist on both servers. When you choose to install SQL Server on the virtual server, the Windows Clustering service maintains a duplicate copy of SQL Server on both servers. You do not have to maintain the duplicate copies because the Windows Cluster service will maintain them for you.

☒ **A** and **B** are incorrect because you would have nothing to failover to if SQL was only installed in one place. **C** is incorrect because the virtual server does not physically exist and therefore, has no place to install the files.

5. ☑ **A, D,** and **F** are correct because since the servers are not running at the full capacity of the server, it is possible to configure these two servers to run in an Active-Active cluster. Both servers are already running Windows 2000 Advanced Server so all you would have to do is enable the Cluster service and configure two virtual servers (one for each actual server). It is possible to upgrade SQL Server 2000 from a local server to a cluster-aware server by re-running the setup utility. You would also need to add an external SCSI device to each server, and link them together. Finally, you must upgrade to SQL 2000 Enterprise edition to install a failover SQL server.

☒ **B** and **C** are incorrect because you would only need the extra server if you were going to implement an Active-Passive cluster. Since you already have two servers, and these servers have the capacity to act as a secondary node for each other, it would be more efficient to use an Active-Active cluster. **E** is incorrect because the minimum requirement for clustering is Windows 2000 Advanced Server. Since SQL Server is already running on an Advanced server, there would be no benefit in upgrading to a Windows 2000 Datacenter server.

1.03: Default Collation

6. ☑ **B** and **C** are correct because each installation of SQL Server can only have a single default collation. However, each named instance on a server can have its own collation. Therefore, Sally could install another named instance on the same physical server and install a second SQL server that uses the correct collation for the new database. SQL Server now also provides the ability to create a database with a different collation than the default. So she could create the new database on the current configuration of SQL Server.

   ☒ **A** is incorrect because you cannot change the default collation using sp_configure. sp_configure is a stored procedure that allows you to alter some server settings. However, the only way to alter the default collation is to rebuild the Master database using a utility called **rebuildm.exe**, or reinstall the database. However, when you use either method, you will loose all of your user logons and databases. **D** is incorrect because SQL 2000 allows you to set the collation at the database level. **E** is incorrect because collation information is stored in the Master database, not the Registry. It is not possible to alter to default collation from within the Registry (this key also does not exist).

7. ☑ **A** is correct because the code page determines how SQL Server will interpret the extended character sets of non-Unicode character data (char, varchar, and text columns). When you transfer data, the binary values for the characters from the source are sent. How those characters are interpreted depends on the code page of the destination. If the code pages are different, it is possible that meaningless characters will appear in the data or destination server.

   ☒ **B** and **C** are incorrect because there is only one Unicode character set. This problem would not occur if all of the character columns were using

Unicode datatypes (nchar, nvarchar, ntext). Unicode characters are actually best suited for this kind of multilingual database. **D** is incorrect because case sensitivity would not cause data corruption in character data. The only impact of mixing case sensitivity is that WHERE clause conditions on text columns will also become case sensitive and all of the expected data may not be returned from some servers.

1.04: Number of Instances

8. ☑ **A** is correct. Because each instance has its own system databases, users who log on to one instance have no contact with the other database. There is no way for a user to log on to the default instance and then try and access data in RDTest databases. The user would have to log in to the RDTEST instance before there was any chance of accessing the databases.

☒ **B** is incorrect because SQL Server 2000 installs a common set of administrative tools. These tools are not instance independent. **C** is incorrect because, while it is true that each instance has its own security context, this has no bearing on internal security. The only way a user could use the service accounts to gain access to data would be to find the password and name of the account used by RDTest and logon to the server as that account. This would connect the user with the same rights as the service account. **D** is incorrect again, because the service accounts have no direct bearing on user access.

9. ☑ **A** and **B** are correct because when you stop the services for one instance, you free up any memory held by that instance for the other instances running. Therefore, stopping the services for the default instance will free up memory resources for the other two instances. Uninstalling the default instance, is the preferable solution. You can uninstall any instance (including the default instance) without affecting the others. By uninstalling the default instance you free up both the memory resources and the disk space occupied by this instance.

☒ **C** is incorrect because you cannot reallocate resources using sp_serveroption. Shrinking the databases on the default instance would free up some disk space, but instances are not given a set amount of disk resources to be re-distributed. In any event, the sp_serveroption stored procedure is used to change settings for linked servers. **D** is incorrect because it is possible to uninstall any one instance, include the default instance. There is no special importance placed on this instance except that it has the same name as the server.

10. ☑ **B** is correct because assuming you have sufficient hardware resources, you can install a maximum of 16 named instances on a physical server. If you have 40 clients you will require a minimum of three computers (with room on the third server for eight more instances). Remember, however, that all instances will share the same system resources (such as memory, disk I/O, and processors). It is likely that you will maximize your system resources before you reach the maximum number of instances.

    ☒ **A** is incorrect because each of the instances will share a Master database. Each instance will have its own Master database, so a named instance will satisfy the client requirements. **C** is incorrect because four servers could support 64 instances. Since you only need 40 instances, this is not the minimum required number of servers. However, in the real world, you would most likely want to spread your instances across more than the minimum number of servers. **D** is incorrect because one server will only support 16 instances and each one of you 40 clients will need their own named instance.

1.05: File Location

11. ☑ **D** is the correct answer because by default all database files for a named instance are stored in c:\Program Files\Microsoft SQL Server\mssql$<instance name>\Data. The default location of data files on the default instance is c:\Program Files\Microsoft SQL Server\mssql\Data.

    ☒ **A** is incorrect because SQL Server does not, by default, create a c:\mssql8 folder (unlike SQL Server 7.0, which was installed by default under the c:\mssql7 folder). **B** is incorrect because there is not a database folder under either root. **C** is incorrect because it places the named instance data as a subfolder under the default instance path. The named instance has its own path under c:\Program Files\Microsoft SQL Server.

12. ☑ **B** is correct because all instances of SQL Server share a common set of administrative tools. These tools are stored in c:\Program Files\Microsoft SQL Server\80\Tools\Binn.

    ☒ **A** and **C** are incorrect because both reference the file location for the default instance. The client tools are instance independent and under their own path. **D** is incorrect because there is no client tools folder under the c:\Program Files\Microsoft SQL Server\80\ folder.

13. ☑ **A** is correct because, by default, SQL Server installs the program files in a folder called Binn and stores the data files in a folder called Data under the default root (c:\Program Files\Microsoft SQL Server\mssql\). However, you are given a chance to change one or both paths, as shown in the following illustration. If you change the program file path, all of the files used by SQL Server are moved to the new path. If you change the data file path, SQL Server will place the data files for the system databases (Master, Model, Msdb, Tempdb) in the new path. It will also set the new path as the default data file path. The default path is where all user databases will be placed if you don't specify another location.

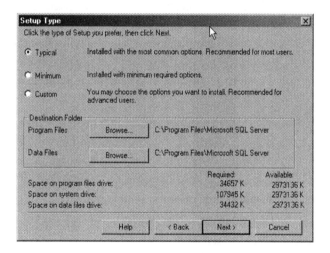

☒ **B** is incorrect because there is no sp_movedbfile stored procedure in SQL Server 2000. The sp_configure stored procedure is used to change server settings, however, there is no Default Data File Path parameter for this procedure. The default path is not a configurable parameter; rather, it is established when you install SQL Server. **C** is incorrect because you cannot move data files with the ALTER DATABASE statement. There also is no registry key to alter to reset the default data file location. **D** is partially correct. It is possible to backup a database from one location and restore it into a new location. However, it is not a good solution. In order to restore the Master database, you will have to start the server in single user mode. This makes this method awkward to implement. Moving these files does not alter the default file path. As you saw in the explanation for **B**, the sp_configure cannot be used to alter the default file path.

1.06: Service Account

14. ☑ **A** and **C** are correct. Because Fred is able to connect to an Active Directory Domain Controller, and has confirmed the password, the problem must be with the account itself. If the domain user account supplied for the SQL services does not have the appropriate rights, the service account will not be able to logon to Windows and the service will fail. Also, if Fred has accidentally selected the User Must Change Password At Next Logon option, the service will fail because SQL Server does not have the ability to change its own password.

    ☒ **B** is incorrect because the local system account is not necessary to start SQL Server. As long as the domain user account information is correct and the service has the correct rights, it will allow the SQL services to start. **D** is incorrect because the services are not affected by being registered in the Enterprise Manager. The Enterprise Manager will automatically register both instances.

15. ☑ **C** is the correct answer because the name of the SQL Server service for a named instance is always mssql$<instance name>. The SQL Server Agent account will be called SQLAgent$<instance name>. No two named instances can have the same name on the same server; all instances will follow the same naming convention for their services.

    ☒ **A** is incorrect because it is the name of the SQL Server service for the default instance. **B** is incorrect because it is the default name for the instance itself. All named instances on a SQL server are given a name in the form of <server name>\<instance name>. **D** is incorrect because it inverts the order of the elements in the service name.

1.07: Performing a Custom Upgrade to SQL Server 2000

16. ☑ **D** is correct because there is no direct upgrade path from SQL 6.0 databases to SQL 2000. In order to upgrade any SQL server earlier that SQL 6.5 you must first upgrade the server to a version of SQL Server that does have a direct upgrade path with SQL Server 2000 (SQL 6.5 or 7.0). This upgrade

will be performed using the upgrade tools provided by these earlier versions of SQL Server. SQL Server 2000 does not provide any tools for updating earlier versions of SQL Server with SQL 6.5 or 7.0 Server.

☒ **A** is incorrect because the SQL Server Upgrade Wizard is unable to upgrade SQL 6.0 databases. The SQL Server Upgrade Wizard is the tool you would use to upgrade SQL 6.5 to SQL 2000. **B** is incorrect because the Copy Database Wizard can only be used to move database objects between SQL 7.0 and SQL 2000. This wizard will not even copy database objects from a SQL 6.5 database. **C** is incorrect because overwriting a database will not upgrade it. This solution will not migrate any objects or data to the SQL 2000 server but will must likely corrupt the SQL 6.0 installation.

1.08: Upgrading to SQL Server 2000 from SQL Server 6.5

17. ☑ **B** is correct because the only way you can upgrade this server without purchasing more hardware is to perform a tape upgrade. With a tape upgrade, the Upgrade Wizard creates a tape backup of all SQL 6.5 databases. You are given the option of dropping the databases once they are backed up. SQL 2000 then migrates the database from tape to an installed version of SQL Server. For this to work, the tape drive must be installed locally.

☒ **A** is incorrect because there is no option to Delete On Upgrade when you perform a Named-Pipe upgrade. This option is only available when you perform an upgrade from tape. **C** is incorrect because you have the upgrade to tape option available. **D** is incorrect because you cannot perform an overwriting upgrade in SQL 6.5. In order for this to work, SQL 6.5 and SQL 2000 would have to running at the same time. Because the two versions cannot run at the same time, you cannot upgrade one over the other.

18. ☑ **A** is correct because SQL 6.5 and 2000 can exist on the same server; they just cannot both run at the same time. When you install SQL Server 2000 it does not alter the SQL 6.5 server. When you want to test applications on SQL 6.5, all you have to do is use the SQL Switch to change from SQL 2000 to SQL 6.5. You must make sure, however, that you have enough disk space for both databases.

☒ **B** is incorrect because there is no special option to leave SQL 6.5 on the server—this is the default behavior of the Upgrade Wizard. You are also not performing an upgrade; your only requirement is to have SQL 6.5 and SQL 2000 installed on the same server. **C** is incorrect because SQL 6.5 cannot be a default instance for SQL 2000. This would imply that they are running at the same time. **D** is incorrect because the physical paths for the installation do not have any bearing on the co-existence of the two versions of SQL Server.

1.09: Upgrading to SQL Server 2000 from SQL Server 7.0

19. ☑ **C** is correct because if you install SQL 2000 as a named instance on the SQL 7.0 server, SQL 7.0 becomes the default instance for that server. It is still accessible and none of its databases are affected. You can then migrate any databases to the SQL 2000 instance. In this way, the new application can access SQL 2000 while the older applications still access their databases in SQL 7.0.

☒ **A** is incorrect because when you use the SQL Switch, it does not apply to SQL 7.0 databases. It is used to switch between SQL 6.5 and either 7.0 or 2000. Even if you could use the Switch with SQL 7.0, it would be a poor solution because only one of the servers would be available at any given time. This means that one of the applications would always be unavailable. Answer **B** is technically correct, but not the best answer. The bcp.exe utility is used to import and export data between SQL tables and delimited text files. Unlike the Copy Database Wizard, it does not migrate any other objects, so you would have to script everything manually. **D** is incorrect because it is possible to have SQL 7.0 and 2000 instances running simultaneously, provided that SQL 7.0 is the default instance.

20. ☑ **D** is correct because it is not possible to undo a version upgrade. Once you have upgraded a SQL Server 7.0 database to SQL Server 2000, you must uninstall SQL 2000 and reinstall SQL 7.0. When you uninstall the SQL 2000 server, all users and databases will be lost. To return your databases to the state they were in prior to the upgrade, you must restore them from a full backup. If you do not have a full backup then there is no way to return to a pre-update state. For this reason, you should always backup all of your databases (including

Master and Msdb) before you perform a version upgrade. The permanence of these upgrades is another argument in favor of performing a migration to a named instance rather than a version upgrade.

☒ **A** is incorrect because you cannot install SQL 7.0 over a SQL 2000 server. Attempting this will only result in an error. **B** is incorrect because the rebuildm.exe utility is not able to change installation versions. This utility is used to rebuild the Master database if it has become corrupt. **C** is incorrect because the SQL Server no longer includes an uninstall utility (it has been replaced by the Windows 2000 Add/Remove Programs Wizard). The uninstaller in SQL 7.0 could only remove the server, not undo upgrades.

21. ☑ **B** is correct because SQL Server 7.0 and SQL Server 2000 can run together on the same server. When the two are installed together, SQL Server 7.0 must be the default instance. SQL Server 6.5 cannot run with either SQL Server 7.0 or SQL Server 2000. The SQL Switch tool will allow you to switch between SQL 6.5 and SQL 7.0/SQL 2000. When you click the Switch, it stops one service and starts the other. It also changes the shortcuts in the Start menu so that the appropriate administrative tools are present.

☒ **A** is incorrect because SQL Server 6.5 cannot be the default instance when installing SQL Server 2000 on the same server and SQL Server 7.0 must be the default instance. **C** is incorrect because there is nothing to prevent any of these versions from being installed on the same server as any other. The only restriction is that SQL Server 6.5 cannot run at the same time as the other two databases. **D** is incorrect because the SQL Switch is only used to switch between SQL Server 6.5 and SQL Server 7.0/2000. You do not need the Switch to alternate between SQL Server 7.0 and SQL Server 2000. They can both co-exist provided that SQL 7.0 is the default instance.

LAB ANSWER

Objectives 1.01–1.09

1. Jane will not have any problems upgrading the SQL 7.0 servers. She can install SQL 2000 as a second instance on each of these computers and migrate data across while the SQL 7.0 server is still available. It will not, however, be possible to perform this type of migration with SQL 6.5. There is a direct update path, so performing the upgrade won't be a problem. However, she can run either SQL 6.5 or SQL 2000 on a server, but not at the same time. An active migration requires that both servers are running. Therefore, she will be able to upgrade the SQL 6.5 server to SQL 2000, but the SQL 6.5 server will be unavailable while the migration is taking place. The only way to keep the 6.5 server active during the upgrade would be to upgrade these servers across the network to SQL 2000 servers running on different computers. If she wants to upgrade these servers on the same computer, this is not an option. There is not a direct upgrade path from SQL 6.0 to SQL 2000. In order to upgrade this server, Jane will first have to upgrade it to either SQL 6.5 or SQL 7.0 (in this case SQL 7.0 would be a better choice because it will allow for a migration while the database is still active).

2. Because all of the servers must be able to communicate with each other, they will require a common security context. All of the computers are part of a single domain; therefore, Jane can use a domain user account for the SQL Server and SQL Agent services. If she uses a domain user account, Jane must ensure that the account has the appropriate rights on all of the servers that must communicate with each other. The easiest way to achieve this is to use the same domain user account for the services on all of the servers and add that account to the administrators local group for each computer. If she does not want to add this account to the administrators group, Jane will have to make sure that she gives the account the appropriate rights on all servers. By using a common account for all of the servers, Jane does not have to worry about adding permissions for a number of different accounts to other servers so that they can all communicate.

3. To place the data files on the RAID array of the new servers, Jane simply needs to set a different path location for the data files in the destination folder box on the Setup Type form. When she uses this tool to change the location of the data files, it will also set the new location as the default location.

4. The operating system and hardware for the report server will support failover clustering. In order to enable failover clustering for a SQL server, the server must be running Windows 2000 Advanced Server, Windows 2000 Datacenter Server, or Windows NT 4.0 Enterprise edition. The server is running Windows 2000 Datacenter Server so the clustering service is supported. She also has a secondary server with an external SCSI RAID device. This will provide the necessary hardware requirements for a SQL 2000 failover clustering installation. She will also need to use the Enterprise edition of SQL Server to install SQL Server on the cluster. In this scenario she will be limited to using Active-Passive clustering. Active-Active clustering would not be advisable because the server is at 75% capacity without the cluster. This means that if the second server fails, there would be insufficient resources to run both the reporting server and whatever she installed on the second server (unless it is very small). In the Active-Passive model, the secondary node will monitor the state of the primary node and will step into its place as necessary. The Active-Passive will not place any extra overhead on the primary node if the secondary node fails.

5. To reduce data corruption in her character data, Jane should use the same default collation for all servers. If she has special language character needs (which is most likely in Hong Kong), she can use the Unicode datatypes (nchar, nvarchar, and ntext) to give her support for any non-western character sets. She can use these datatypes without altering the default collation. If she uses different collations on the various servers and uses the character data types (char, varchar, and text), she may experience data corruption as data from one code page is copied to another. The Unicode characters will always be interpreted the same way, regardless of what code page has been selected.

MICROSOFT CERTIFIED DATABASE ADMINISTRATOR

2

Configuring SQL Server 2000

TEST YOURSELF OBJECTIVES

I nstallation is only the first step in implementing a Microsoft SQL Server. Once the server is installed, it must be configured. Proper configuration will insure that the server is able to perform as expected. In addition to configuring the server, you must also be prepared to deal with errors and problems, both during and after the installation.

You will need to have a firm grasp of some of the post-installation configuration options. You should understand, and be able to implement linked servers. You will also need to understand how to configure the security context for a linked server. You will need to know how to do this both in the Enterprise Manager and using stored procedures.

SQL Server 2000 has the ability to send email from both the SQL Server service and the SQL Agent service. You will be expected to understand how to enable mail support for both services. In addition, you must be familiar with the SQL Server 2000 network libraries. You will need to know how to add and configure these libraries and which libraries to use under different conditions. Finally, you will be expected to troubleshoot and solve problems both during and post installation.

TEST YOURSELF OBJECTIVE 2.01

Creating a Linked Server

A linked server is simply a named link to another OLE DB data source. Any data source that is accessible through OLE DB (such as SQL Server, Oracle, DB2, or Access) can be configured in a linked server relationship. If you want to write distributed statements such as a SELECT, INSERT, UPDATE, or DELETE statement from you local server, you must configure a linked server. A distributed statement is a Data Manipulation Language statement (DML) that deals with data from more than just the local server. When you create a linked server, you add information about the remote data source such as its name and how to connect to it. Your SQL server will add this information into the sysservers table in the Master database. Once this connection information has been registered, you can reference any object on the remote server using its fully qualified object name (which is server.database.owner.object).

You can add a linked server with either Enterprise Manager, or the SQL stored procedure sp_addlinkedserver. With both methods you will establish the name

and the OLE DB connection information for a remote data source. When using
`sp_addlinkedserver`, the syntax looks like this:

```
EXEC sp_addlinkedserver @server = 'name of server',

@srvproduct = 'name of product',

@provider = 'OLE DB Provider',

@datascr = 'data source', @location = 'location'

@provstr = 'provider string', @catalogue = 'catalogue'
```

For example, to create a link to SQL Server called London, you would execute the
following statement:

```
EXEC sp_addlinkedserver  @server = 'London',

                         @srvproduct = 'SQL Server'
```

If the OLE DB data source is a SQL 7.0 or a SQL 2000 Server database, you only
need to supply the `@srvproduct` parameter; SQL Server will configure the rest of the
connection information. If you are connecting to any other data source, you must
include additional connection information. The information you must supply will
differ depending on what type of database you are connecting to. You should consult
the SQL Server Books Online for these additional options. If you are connecting to a
SQL 2000 named instance you must supply both the server name and the instance
name (for example, `sp_addlinkedserver 'myserver\newinstance', 'SQL
Server'`).

exam
ⓦatch

*Most administrative tasks in SQL Server can be performed either in Enterprise
Manager or with Transact-SQL statements (such as system stored procedures
or DBCC statements). In the real world you may choose to use Enterprise
Manager for your administration, however, make sure you are fully comfortable
with both methods. The exams often focus on Transact-SQL administration
(mostly through the use of stored procedures). You must have an understanding
of how Transact-SQL works because the exam may present you with several
sample scripts and ask you to determine which one will correctly resolve a
particular problem. See question numbers 1 and 3 in this section for examples
of these types of questions.*

To add a linked server from the Enterprise Manager, right-click the Linked Server icon in the Security folder and click Add Linked Server. On the Linked Server Properties sheet, shown in the following illustration, enter the name of the server that you want to link to and add the necessary connection information. Notice again that if you select SQL Server as the server type, the rest of the options are not required.

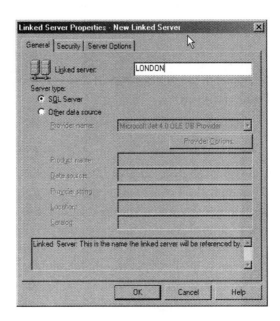

Once you have added the linked server, you must configure the security context for the connection. In Transact-SQL, you configure this context with the sp_addlinkedsrvlogin system stored procedure. The syntax for sp_addlinkedsrvlogin is:

```
exec sp_addlinkedsrvlogin @rmtservername = 'name of linked
server',

@useself = {'true' | 'false'},

[@locallogin = '{NULL, 'local login name',

@rmtuser = 'remote login',

@rmtpassword = 'remote login password']
```

The @locallogin parameter allows you to specify which logins are able to connect to the remote server across the link. If this value is NULL, all users will be allowed to use

the link. If you set the @useself value to false, you must specify a remote user account for
SQL Server to use when authenticating to the remote server. If you do not use this stored
procedure you will not have permission to connect to the linked server. If you are using
Enterprise Manager, you will configure the security context by clicking the Security
tab and adding the security information on the form, as shown in the next illustration.
You can configure the linked server settings by either using sp_serveroption or by
clicking the Server Options tab on the Linked Server Properties sheet. The syntax for
sp_serveroption is:

```
exec sp_serveroption @servername = 'server name',

@optname = 'server option',

@optvalue= 'value for options'
```

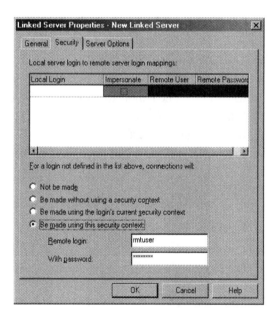

When using a linked server, the following applies:

▩ You can submit queries that reference tables and views from the remote data
   sources in the FROM clause of a SELECT statement.

▩ You can include remote data sources in JOIN operations.

▩ You can modify data on a remote data source using Data Manipulation
   Language statements—INSERT, UPDATE, and DELETE.

■ You can execute stored procedures on remote data sources (note that the procedures will run on the remote data source, rather than on your local server).

■ You cannot issue Data Control Language (DCL) statements: GRANT, REVOKE, or DENY.

■ You cannot issue any Data Definition Language (DDL) statements: CREATE, ALTER, DROP, etc.

QUESTIONS

2.01: Creating a Linked Server

1. You have installed SQL 2000 Server on a computer called London. You want to connect to a remote data source so that you can run remote queries on that data source. The remote data source is a SQL 2000 Server named instance called Salesdata on a Windows 2000 Advanced server called Bombay. Bombay also has a default SQL 2000 server instance. Which of the following Transact-SQL statements will allow you to connect to the Bombay server?

A. `EXEC sp_addlinkedserver 'Bombay\salesdata', 'SQL Server'`

B. `EXEC sp_addlinkedserver 'Bombay', 'salesdata', 'SQL Server'`

C. `EXEC sp_addlinkedserver 'Bombay\salesdata', 'SQL Server',`
   `'SQLOLEDB', 'Bombay'`

D. `EXEC sp_addlinkedsrvlogin 'Bombay\salesdata', 'SQL Server'`

2. You have added a linked server to an Oracle database in your environment. However, when you try to access this database with a distributed query, the query fails. You have confirmed that you are using the correct OLE DB provider and that you have entered the name of the server correctly. You have also confirmed that you can ping the Oracle server both by DNS name and IP address. What else might be causing your connection to fail?

A. You are not logged on as **sa**.

B. You need to use `sp_addlinkedsrvlogin` to configure how you will authenticate to the Oracle database.

    C. You have not correctly configured an ODBC dsn.

    D. You must set the Allow Heterogeneous Queries setting to 1 using `sp_serveroption`.

3. Jane is the administrator for several SQL Server 2000 servers. She has 50 users who access the sales database on one of her servers. These users need to run queries that draw information from another SQL server. To provide access to this data, she has created a linked server. Jane wants to give these users access to this data, but she does not want to give the users the ability to connect to the remote server except through the linked server connection. She also wants to limit user access to those tables that contain the information they need. What is the best way for Jane to give these users access to the remote server?

    A. Create a login for each user on the remote server. Give each user the rights to only those tables that they need.

    B. Create a login for each server on the remote server. Create a role and add all 50 users to the role. Assign the appropriate permissions to the role.

    C. Create a single logon account on the remote server and assign it the appropriate rights on the necessary tables. Map all of the user accounts to that login using `sp_addlinkedsrvlogin`.

    D Use `sp_addlinkedsrvlogin` to create local logins for the 50 users on the remote server.

    E. Use `sp_configure` to have the linked server pass the local logon RS.

TEST YOURSELF OBJECTIVE 2.02

Configuring SQL Mail and SQL Agent Mail

Both the SQL Server service and the SQL Server Agent have the capability to send email. However before you can use email, you must configure the mail service. The first part of configuring the mail service is to configure a profile for the SQL service accounts. If you are not using a domain user account to authenticate the SQL Server and SQL Agent service accounts you will not be able to configure the mail service. Before you begin, you must also create a mailbox on your mail server for the SQL service account before configuring the profile.

To configure the mail profile:

1. Log on to Windows using the domain user account that you have assigned to the SQL services.

2. Double-click the Mail icon in Control Panel. (For some mail servers, like Lotus Notes, you might want to start a mail client to configure the profile. Not all mail servers will allow you to create a profile usable by SQL Mail.)

3. Configure the mail profile using the appropriate mail services to communicate with your mail server.

4. Stop and restart the SQL Server and SQL Agent service.

Once you have configured the profile, you can use this profile to configure the mail services.

To configure the mail service for the SQL Server service:

1. Open the Support Services folder in Enterprise Manager.

2. Right-click the SQL Mail icon and select Properties.

3. Choose the correct profile from the Profile Name list box on the Properties sheet, as shown in the following illustration.

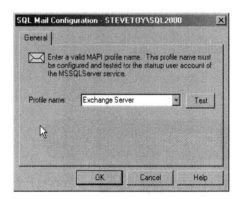

4. Click the Test button to test the connection and click OK.

To configure the SQL Agent Mail, open the Management folder:

1. Right-click the SQL Server Agent icon and choose Properties.

2. On the General tab, choose the correct profile in the Mail Session list box, as shown in the next illustration.

3. Click the Test button to test the connection and click OK.

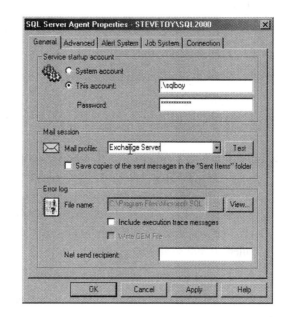

Once you have configured the mail for both services, you can use xp_sendmail to send mail from the SQL Server service and you can configure the SQL Server Agent service to send email to operators through automation jobs and alerts. If you use different service accounts for the SQL Server service and the SQL Agent service, you may have two mailboxes (and two profiles). Make sure you use the correct mail profile for each account.

QUESTIONS

2.02: Configuring SQL Mail and SQL Agent Mail

4. You are attempting to configure the SQL Agent Mail to allow the SQL Server Agent service to email operators when errors occur. You open the Agent Properties sheet and click the Profile list box but there are no profiles listed.

Which of the following may explain why there are no profiles listed? (Choose all that apply.)

A. The SQL Agent service is not started.

B. You are using the local system account to authorize the SQL Agent service.

C. SQL Mail service is not started.

D. You have not configured a profile for the mail service.

E. The mail server is not accessible.

5. Jim wants to configure the SQL Server service for SQL Mail. He has written several triggers that will send emails to different users using the xp_sendmail procedure. His SQL server is using a domain user account and he has configured a mail profile for this account. However, when he tests the connection, it fails. His mail server is a UNIX Sendmail server. What may explain why the connection failed? (Choose all that apply.)

A. He has incorrectly configured the profile.

B. A network connection to the mail server is unavailable

C. He has not configured the SQL Agent Mail service.

D. He is not using Microsoft Exchange.

E. He is not using the local system account.

6. Phil has configured his SQL server to contact a local Exchange server. He has created a domain user account and configured a mail profile for that account. Both the SQL Server and SQL Agent services are using that account. He has configured SQL Mail and selected the correct profile. When he tests the connection in SQL Mail, it is successful. He has also configured the SQL Agent Mail in the Properties sheet for the agent. When he tests that connection it is also successful. Phil has added several alerts on this server and has configured SQL Server to email him when certain errors occur. Later on, Phil notices that the error has occurred several times but he has not been sent an email. When he uses xp_sendmail he is able send himself an email. What is the most likely reason that the SQL Agent failed to send an email?

A. The SQL Server Agent service is not started.

B. The SQL Mail service is not started.

C. SQL service and the SQL Agent service cannot run at the same time if they share the same mail profile.

D. The Exchange server is not available.

E. The mailbox used by the SQL Server Agent service has not been configured correctly.

TEST YOURSELF OBJECTIVE 2.03

Configuring Network Libraries

SQL Server uses network libraries to allow communication between the server and the client applications on the network. Network libraries allow processes to communicate with each other. SQL Server "listens" on all of the installed network libraries for communication requests from the clients. You can have multiple network libraries installed on a SQL server. The network libraries you choose will depend on how your clients are connecting to the network and the operating system used by the client. Your client applications must be using one of the network libraries bound to the server. If your client uses a network library that is not installed on the server, that client will be unable to connect to the server (even if it is able to establish a network connection). The network libraries available to SQL Server 2000 are:

Named Pipes   One of the two default network libraries installed on SQL Server 2000. Named Pipes allow connection between client and server over any of the Microsoft network protocols. Named Pipes will also allow SQL Server to connect with an Active Directory Domain Controller to allow Windows authentication.

TCP/IP Sockets   The second default network library. It allows TCP/IP communication using Windows Sockets. TCP/IP Sockets will also enable SQL Server to connect with an Active Directory Domain Controller to allow Windows authentication. TCP/IP Sockets use a default port number of 1433, but you have the option of changing the port assignment in the Properties sheet for this library.

Multiprotocol   Uses Windows Remote Procedure Calls (RPC). It allows Windows authentication and works over all supported protocols. It also has its own encryption for data and passwords. Multiprotocol will also enable SQL Server to connect with an Active Directory Domain Controller to allow Windows authentication.

NWLink IPX/SPX   The library needed to allow NetWare clients to connect using IPX\SPX. To use this library, the server must also have NWLink protocol installed.

Appletalk   Allows Apple Macintosh computers to connect to the SQL server using the Apple Talk protocol. The server must also have AppleTalk installed to use this library.

Banyan Vines   Allows Banyan Vines clients to connect to the SQL server on the Vines IP network protocol.

VIA ServerNet II SAN   Allows clients to use a ServerNet II System Area Network (SAN). A SAN is a reliable high-speed network designed for linking groups of servers, using the Virtual Interface Architecture (VIA). They are designed for high-speed traffic between servers (such as SQL servers working with distributed queries).

VIA GigaNet SAN   Allows connection on a GigaNet SAN using VIA.

When you install SQL Server you are given an option of which network libraries to install. After the installation, you can add and modify the network libraries using the Server Network utility.

You can also use the Server Network utility to change the properties of the network libraries. When choosing which libraries to install there are a few factors you should bear in mind:

- If you plan to connect to the SQL server from Internet Information Server (IIS)—especially if you are using a Secure Socket Layer (SSL) connection—you must use the TCP/IP Sockets library or the Multiprotocol library. If you are using Multiprotocol to connect to IIS you must make sure that the TCP/IP network protocol is running on the server.

- In order to permit Windows authentication (in Windows only or Mixed mode) to take place, one of your libraries must be TCP/IP Sockets, Named Pipes, or Multiprotocol. Only these libraries are able to connect to an Active Directory Domain Control to verify the user.

- If SQL Server is installed with failover clustering, only Named Pipes and TCP/IP Sockets are supported.

Make sure you know when to use a particular network library. For example, you should know which libraries are required for Windows authentication and which network protocols the different libraries support. You may have scenario questions that require you to choose the appropriate protocol.

QUESTIONS

2.03: Configuring Network Libraries

7. You have several clients that will need to connect to your SQL server. Your clients are running a mixture of Windows 2000 Professional, Windows 95, and Windows NT 4.0 Workstation. All of these clients are part of a Windows 2000 domain. Your Windows clients will be connecting to the SQL server through Internet Information Server. You also have a number of NetWare clients. The Windows clients are all running TCP/IP as their network protocol. Which network clients would allow all clients to connect to the server? (Choose all that apply.)

    A. Named Pipes

    B. NWLink IPX/SPX

    C. Appletalk

    D. Multiprotocol

    E. TCP/IP Sockets

8. Jen is the administrator for a SQL Server 2000 server. The server uses TCP/IP Sockets as its only network library. This server is used by several Active Server pages and is accessible from a web server outside the company's firewall. Jen is concerned that hackers may be able to access her network through the Internet. She is using the default IP port number for SQL Server. What can Jen do to make this connection more secure?

    A. Select Use IP Encryption on the TCP/IP Sockets Properties sheet in the Server Network utility.

    B. Close port 1433 on the SQL server.

    C. Change the default port number on the TCP/IP Sockets Properties sheet in the Server Network utility from 1433 to another value.

    D. Change the default port number on the TCP/IP Sockets Properties sheet in the Server Network utility from 80 to another value.

    E. Close port 80 on the SQL server.

9. Stewart is trying to configure a SQL Server 2000 server to act as a data source for an Active Server page application on his corporate Intranet. He is having difficulty establishing a connection to the server. He is running Multiprotocol over TCP/IP so that he can encrypt the communication. He has SSL enabled, but after removing it, he still cannot connect. The SQL server and the IIS server are on the same side of the firewall and he is able to ping the SQL server from the IIS server by both IP address and DNS name. The SQL server is also running the NWLink IPX/SPX library to allow some NetWare clients to connect directly. What is the most likely reason that he cannot connect from his web server?

    A. You cannot run Multiprotocol over TCP/IP. It only supports NetBEUI.

    B. The ASP is not configured to use Multiprotocol.

    C. You must run the TCP/IP Sockets library to connect a SQL server to an IIS server.

    D. You cannot have the Multiprotocol and NWLink IPX/SPX network libraries installed at the same time.

    E. Multiprotocol will not allow him to connect to an Active Directory Domain Controller.

TEST YOURSELF OBJECTIVE 2.04

Troubleshooting Failed Installations

Sometimes installations do not go smoothly. You are expected to have an understanding of how to identify and resolve common installation problems. The first part of troubleshooting is being able to identify the problem. The best way to begin troubleshooting an installation is by verifying the installation. As part of the verification process you will perform the following:

- Confirm that the SQL Server service and the SQL Agent service have been installed and properly configured. This includes ensuring that the services are able to start and that they have the correct default settings (like Autostart).

- Verify all system databases have been properly installed.

- Verify all files have been correctly installed. By default, SQL Server 2000 program files are installed in c:\Program Files\Microsoft SQL Server\ Mssql\Binn (or c:\Program Files\Microsoft SQL Server\mssql$<instance name>\Binn for a named instance).

- Verify that the administrative tools have been added.

- Ensure that the correct security mode has been chosen. SQL 2000 allows you to place the server in two modes: Windows authentication mode and Mixed mode. Mixed mode will allow both Windows authentication and SQL Server authentication. You will need Mixed mode to use the **sa** account. When you install SQL Server, Windows authentication mode is the default security mode.

Verifying the installation will reveal any installation problems.
If you discover problems, there are several places you can go to begin troubleshooting:

- Check in the SQLstp.log file. If the error occurred during the actual installation, this should be the first place you look to troubleshoot the problem. This file is the spooled output of the installation process. If the installation failed before completion, the last line in the log will be the last step SQL Server was working on when it failed. This file is placed in the c:\winnt folder (or whatever you have called your Windows system root folder).

- Check the Application log in the Windows Event Viewer. SQL Server writes its program errors to this log. If you cannot connect to databases or if you have problems with the administrative tools, you can use this log to attempt to identify the source of any errors.

- Check the system log in the Windows Event Viewer. Errors with SQL Server service and the SQL Agent service are written into the system log. If you are having trouble starting any of the services, this is where to look for the source of the problem.

- Use the SQL Server error logs. SQL Server starts a new log each time the SQL Server service starts. This log records the startup process and then logs subsequent activity on the server.

■ Check the SQL Server Agent error log to find errors with the SQL Server Agent. This log is found by right-clicking the SQL Server Agent icon in the Management folder of Enterprise Manager as shown in the next illustration, or by viewing the SQLAgent.out file in the log folder of your server installation path.

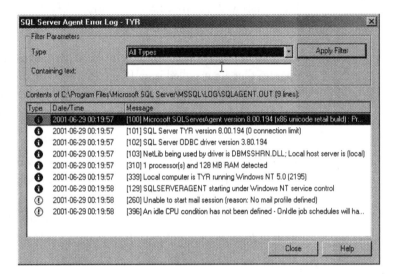

On the exam, you may get questions asking you to deal with specific scenarios. There are a number of common problems that you may experience after an installation. They can be broken down into two broad categories:

■ Service errors

■ Connection errors

Service errors show themselves in an inability to start the SQL Server and SQL Agent Services. There are a number of factors that can cause a service error:

Incorrect logon information   If you have installed the SQL services using a domain user account, you must enter the correct information for that user. If you have typed an incorrect user name or an incorrect password, the SQL services will not be able to authenticate themselves to Windows. If they cannot log into Windows, the service will not start.

Lack of user rights   If you do not give the domain user account sufficient rights, it will not be able to start the SQL server. The service account must have the right to log in locally and will need administrative rights over several registry keys and the SQL server. (See Chapter 1, section 1.06 for more information.) In addition to these rights, the SQL Server Agent requires administrative rights on the Windows server. It is possible, therefore, that the SQL Server service may start, but the SQL Agent Service will fail.

The Domain Controller is not available   If there is no available Domain Controller, SQL Server will not start. Windows must be able to authenticate the logon information passed to it by the SQL Server services. To authenticate this information, Windows needs to access the Domain Controller.

The Registry is corrupt   If the Registry is corrupt, SQL Server will not start, even if the service is able to authenticate properly. This indicates a faulty installation.

Connection errors reveal themselves in the inability for a client to communicate with the server   They can have several causes:

Networking errors   These are problems with the physical network. Often they will show up in the inability to connect to a domain controller. If the client is unable to make a network connection to the server, obviously, they will be unable to connect.

Network library issues   Both the client and the server must be using the same network libraries. If the client is running a library that is not supported on the server, the connection will fail.

Permissions   Some client tools require administrative privileges to connect to the SQL server. If a user does not have the appropriate rights, the connection may fail because the user cannot authenticate to the server.

QUESTIONS

2.04: Troubleshooting Failed Installations

10. Jim is the administrator for several SQL servers. He has just installed a SQL Server 2000 server and configured it to auto start, however, when he restarted the server, the SQL Server service would not start. He has tried starting the service manually with the net start command, but it still will not start. Where can he go to find the possible reason for the service failure?

  A. The system log in Event Viewer

  B. The SQLstp.log file

    C. The application log in Event Viewer

    D. The services log in Event Viewer

    E. The confgsql.out log file

11. Sam has just finished installing a SQL Server 2000 server. He has just rebooted the server and is attempting to connect to the server for the first time using Query Analyzer when he receives the message shown in the following illustration.

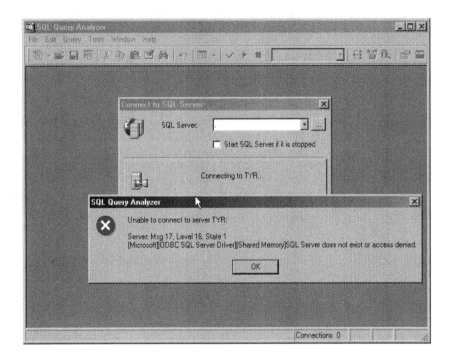

He has configured the server to use the local system account to authenticate the SQL Server service. What is the most likely reason for this message?

    A. There is no Domain Controller available.

    B. The SQL Agent service has not started.

    C. The SQL Server service is not started.

    D. When configuring the server during installation, he has entered an incorrect password for the local system account.

    E. Sam does not have administrative rights on the server.

LAB QUESTION

Objectives 2.01–2.04

You are the senior administrator for a number of Microsoft SQL servers. One of your junior administrators has asked you to help him troubleshoot an installation that is not going well. He is installing a second instance called Taketwo on a SQL 2000 server called Tyr. He has installed the services to use an account that you added for him in the Windows 2000 Active Directory. You also configured the local server so that this account would have the appropriate rights. Your network is using TCP/IP as its primary network protocol.

He has installed the server but he cannot get the service to start. When you look in the system log in Event Viewer, you see the error shown in the next illustration.

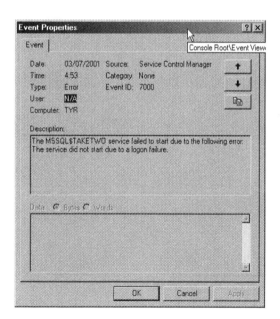

You suspect that SQL server is unable to contact the Domain Controller.

1. What is the first thing you should check when troubleshooting this service error?

2. You have confirmed that the service is using the correct logon and password but the server still does not start. What should you test next? How would you test this step?

3. Are there any other error logs that you could use for further help?

4. You change the service login to use the local system account and the service still fails to start. What would you suspect is the problem? How would you resolve it?

QUICK ANSWER KEY

Objective 2.01
1. A
2. B
3   C

Objective 2.02
4. B and D
5. A and B
6. A

Objective 2.03
7   B, D, and E
8. C
9. B

Objective 2.04
10. A
11. C

IN-DEPTH ANSWERS

2.01: Creating a Linked Server

1. ☑ **A** is correct because if the source is a SQL 7.0 or SQL 2000 server you do not have to provide any connection information. All you need to provide is the name of the server and SQL Server as the product type. However, because you are connecting to a named instance, you must provide the full instance name (<server name>\<instance name>) for the SQL server.

   ☒ **B** is incorrect because it includes too many parameters. If you present the server name and the instance name as two separate parameters, it will place the first value in the server name parameter (@server), it will read the second value as the server product (@srvproduct) and will read the server name as the OLE DB provider values (@provider). This will cause a syntax error. Always remember with stored procedures that the order of the supplied parameters is very important, because SQL Server will take each value supplied and insert them into the parameters in the order they appeared in the CREATE PROCEDURE statement. The SQL Server Books Online lists the system procedures parameters in this order. **C** is incorrect because you do not need to include provider information when you link to a SQL server. If you were to run this statement you would receive the following error:

   ```
   Server: Msg 15428, Level 16, State 1, Procedure
   sp_addlinkedserver, Line 67
   ```

   ```
   You cannot specify a provider or any properties for product
   'SQL Server'
   ```

   ☒ **D** is incorrect because sp_addlinkedsrvlogin is used to add logon options for connecting to a linked server. It cannot be used to create the linked server.

2. ☑   **B** is correct because in order to execute a distributed query, you must establish both the linked server connection information and the security context under which connections will be made. The `sp_addlinkedsrvlogin` stored procedure maps the local security context to one that SQL Server will use when connecting to the remote data source. In this example, your local SQL server can find and connect to the Oracle server, however the connection information does not provide valid login information for the Oracle server. By default, if you do not run `sp_addlinkedsrvlogin`, SQL Server will attempt to authenticate you using whatever credentials you used to log on to the local SQL server. If this login does not have rights on the remote server, the connection will fail.

   ☒   **A** is incorrect because you do not have to be **sa** to issue a distributed query. You must be an administrator to create a linked server, but in this example, the problem arises from the connection—not configuration—so this is not the solution. The **sa** account is a local SQL Server login account and would have no rights on the Oracle server. **C** is incorrect because the linked server is using an OLE DB provider to connect to the Oracle server, not ODBC. This would only be a consideration if you were connecting to an ODBC data source using the OLE DB provider for ODBC. **D** is incorrect because this parameter does not exist. All linked server data sources will allow distributed queries.

3. ☑   **C** is the correct answer because you can use the `sp_addlinkedsrvlogin` stored procedure to delegate a single login account on a remote server. The default behavior is to try to authenticate the local user on the remote server using the same credentials that the user used to connect to the local server. However, you can point all users towards a default login. This allows you to create a single logon on the remote server and only assign permissions once. Also, the users are not aware of how they are authenticating to the remote data source. This means that they are only able to log on to the remote server when they execute a distributed query through the linked server. This can also be set using the Security tab of the Linked Server Properties sheet in Enterprise Manager, as shown in the next illustration. You can assign login mappings individually or

as a default. The illustration shows that the server will authenticate all users as a user called linked_account and will supply a password for that account if necessary.

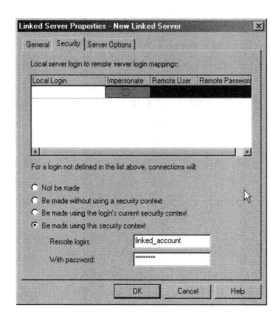

☒ **A** and **B** are both incorrect because it will give each user a local logon on the remote data source. Answer **B** makes it easier to assign user rights, but you actually do not want user rights assigned to individuals. **D** is incorrect because `sp_addlinkedsrvlogn` is not used to create logins on the remote servers. Rather, it establishes the security context that local users will use on the remote server. Any accounts used by `sp_addlinkedsrvlogon` on the remote server must exist before they can be referenced by the procedure. **E** is incorrect because this is already the default behavior of a linked server. There is no option under `sp_configure` for logins. Even if this were possible, the answer would still be wrong because it would require all of the users to be able to logon to the remote server using their current credentials. Jane does not want the users to be able to access the data except through the linked server. Adding logon rights for the users to the remote server would negate this requirement.

2.02: Configuring SQL Mail and SQL Agent Mail

4. ☑ **B** and **D** are the correct answers. **B** is the correct answer because you cannot configure SQL Agent Mail if you are using the local system account. This account only exists on the local server and cannot be used to access remote servers (such as the mail server) because it cannot authenticate on the remote server. You also could not create a mail profile for this account because it is not possible to logon interactively as the local system account. **D** is correct because even if you have configured SQL Server to authenticate the SQL Agent service using a domain user account, you still must configure a mail profile for this account before you can configure the SQL Agent Mail. This profile tells SQL which mail server to use when receiving mail, and which server to use when sending mail. It also determines how the service should authenticate itself to the mail server.

    ☒ **A** is incorrect because you can configure the mail even if the agent is not started. You will not be able to send alerts without the agent running, but the configuration only requires that the mail profile is accessible. **C** is incorrect because the SQL Mail and the SQL Agent Mail services are completely independent of each other. It is possible to configure the SQL Agent Mail without configuring SQL Mail and vice versa. **E** is incorrect because when you configure the SQL Agent Mail in the SQL Server Agent Properties sheet it does not check the mail server; it only looks for a mail profile on the local machine. If you click the Test button, SQL Server will then try to connect to the mail server, but prior to testing the connection, the mail server does not have to be available to configure mail support for the SQL Agent.

5. ☑ **A** and **B** are the correct answers. **A** is correct because SQL Server relies on the profile to instruct it on how to contact the mail server. If you have incorrectly typed the server name or entered incorrect authentication information, the connection to the server will fail. SQL Server will allow you to configure the SQL Mail service with the incorrect profile because it does not test the profile until it tries to contact the mail server. **B** is correct because the connection will fail if the mail server does not respond to a messaging request. This also will not prevent you from configuring SQL Mail.

☒ **C** is incorrect because the configuration of the SQL Server Agent service has no effect on the configuration of the SQL Server service; both services run independent of each other. **D** is incorrect because the SQL Mail service does not require Microsoft Exchange Server to function. The SQL Mail and SQL Agent Mail will connect to any MAPI compliant mail server (including UNIX Sendmail). As long as the profile is correctly configured, SQL Mail will connect to the Sendmail server. In this case you will most likely have to configure your security account and password as part of the profile. Microsoft Exchange will validate the users based on the Windows domain account information. **E** is incorrect because you cannot configure SQL Mail if you are using the local system account.

6. ☑ **A** is the correct answer because the SQL Agent service must be running in order for SQL Server to send email through alerts or jobs. The mail service seems to be running properly. Phil has configured a single domain user account for both the SQL Server and SQL Server Agent services. Furthermore, because he is able to use the `xp_sendmail` successfully, it is clear that the service is configured correctly. The `xp_sendmail` stored procedure uses the SQL Mail account rather than the SQL Agent Mail, so it will function properly even if the SQL Agent services are stopped.

☒ **B** is incorrect because it is the SQL Agent Mail service that is required in this scenario. This service is started with the SQL Agent service. The SQL Mail service is started when the SQL Server service is started. You are not required to manually start the service. **C** is incorrect because the SQL Agent Mail and SQL Mail services are independent. Sharing the same mail profile simply means that both services look to the same mailbox and the same mail server when performing any mail-related activities. There is no restriction that prevents both services from using the same mail profile. **D** is incorrect because if the mail server were unavailable, `xp_sendmail` would not function. It uses the same mail service that the SQL Agent service uses so any interruption in access to the mail server would affect both services. **E** is incorrect because, again, the two services are sharing the same profile. This means that they are sharing the same mailbox configuration. If the configuration were incorrect, it would affect both the SQL Agent Mail and SQL Mail equally. This would also prevent `xp_sendmail` from functioning properly.

2.03: Configuring Network Libraries

7. ☑ **B**, **D**, and **E** are the correct answers. **B** is the correct answer because the NetWare clients will require the NWLink IPX\SPX. NWLink is Microsoft's implementation of the Novell IPX/SPX. Without this library installed, the NetWare clients will not connect. **D** is correct because you can use the Multiprotocol library to connect to the IIS server as long as TCP/IP is installed as a network protocol. **E** is correct because the Microsoft clients are all using TCP/IP as their network protocol and connecting through IIS. The TCP/IP Sockets library will allow users to connect to IIS. It can only be installed if the computer is running the TCP/IP networking protocol.

   ☒ **A** is incorrect because although some of the Microsoft clients could connect directly with Named Pipes over TCP/IP, Named Pipes cannot be used to connect users from an IIS server. In addition, the Windows 9*x* clients do not support Named Pipes. **C** is incorrect because the Appletalk library is only used for clients running the Appletalk network protocol.

8. ☑ **C** is the correct answer because the default port number assigned to SQL Server is 1433. If anyone wanted to connect to the SQL server from the Internet they would be running TCP/IP and would try to connect on the default port. If you change the port number for the TCP/IP socket to a non-standard port, the hacker would have to know the new port number and the IP address. In your Active Server pages, you will have to code the new port information to allow them to connect.

   ☒ **A** is incorrect because the TCP/IP Socket library does not have any encryption capabilities. If you want to encrypt TCP/IP communication in Windows 2000 you must use the Windows 2000 Internet Protocol Security (IPSec). Alternately, you could use Multiprotocol, which has is own built-in encryption capability. You enable Multiprotocol encryption by checking the Enable Encryption check box on the Multiprotocol Properties sheet in the Server Network Utility dialog box, as shown in the next illustration. **B** is incorrect because closing port 1433 without changing the default port will block all communication between the Active Server pages and the SQL server. While this will definitely increase security, it will also break all of the web applications. **D** is incorrect because port 80 is the default port number reserved for the WWW service (that is, by web pages). If anything, changing the port number might make Jen's server more susceptible because someone attempting to contact a web server will find the SQL server instead. **E** is incorrect because SQL Server does not use port 80 for its IP communication. Instead, it uses port 1433. Therefore, closing port 80 will not have any effect on the security of the SQL server.

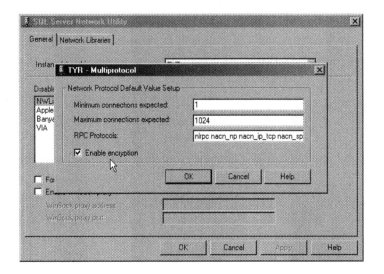

9. ☑ **B** is the correct answer because both the client and the server must be using the same network library. SQL Server can have multiple network libraries running at the same time and respond to multiple clients. However if the client is using a library not installed on the server, no connection is possible (even if you can establish a network connection). This is why Stewart is able to ping the SQL server, but not connect to it with his Active Server page.

☒ **A** is incorrect because it is possible to run Multiprotocol on the TCP/IP network protocol. Multiprotocol will run on top of any of the Microsoft networking protocols (TCP/IP, NetBEUI, and NWLink). This will allow you to connect to the server in a networking sense. This is why Stewart is able to ping the SQL server. However, Multiprotocol will not allow you to establish an Inter Process Communication (IPC) channel between the web server and the SQL server. IPCs allow two applications to communicate with each other. Therefore the two Windows servers will be able to communicate but the applications running on those servers will not. **C** is incorrect because

Multiprotocol over IP will allow SQL Server to connect to IIS. However, the Multiprotocol library must be used on the client; otherwise connecting will not be possible. **D** is incorrect because it is possible to bind multiple network libraries to the same SQL server. Each one listens for network traffic sent to the server by a client that is using the same network library. These libraries are not connected to each other and there is no way for the presence of one library to interfere with the functioning of another library. **E** is incorrect because Multiprotocol will allow the SQL server to connect to an Active Directory Domain Controller. If Stewart is using Windows authentication he will need the ability to connect to an Active Directory Domain Controller. However the underlying connection problem has to do with IPCs—not with authentication.

2.04: Troubleshooting Failed Installations

10. ☑ **A** is the correct answer because Windows writes all errors involving services into the system log in Event Viewer. This includes errors with the SQL Server and SQL Agent services. If a service fails to start, this is the best place to start troubleshooting the failure.

☒ **B** is incorrect because the installation seemed to run without error. The SQLstp.log file only records the process of installation. When the system restarts, this log will not record any further. **C** is incorrect because the application log in Event Viewer does not store service errors. Instead, it stores those errors raised by SQL Server itself. This is the best place to look for errors with the running of SQL Server, however, until the SQL Server service starts, there will be no entries made in this log. **D** is incorrect because there is no services log in the Event Viewer. This is the task of the system log. **E** is incorrect because there is no file called confgsql.out.

11. ☑ **C** is the correct answer. If the server is not started, connecting is not possible. Sam most likely did not select auto start as one of the service options and when he rebooted the server, he failed to manually start the server.

☒ **A** is incorrect because Windows only needs access to a Domain Controller if the SQL Server service is authenticating with a domain user account. Since Sam has configured the server to use the local system account, the Windows 2000 server authenticates it locally. **B** is incorrect because the SQL Agent service does not have to be running in order for the SQL Server service to start. However, the SQL Server service must be running in order for the SQL Agent service to start. **D** is not correct because you do not enter login information for the local system account. This account is controlled entirely by the local Security Access Manager on the Windows 2000 server where SQL Server is installed. **E** is incorrect because you do not need administrative rights to run Query Analyzer. However you do require logon rights to the SQL server. If he does not have the appropriate rights, he would receive a different error message. The next illustration shows the error message that is raised if you do not have the correct logon rights.

LAB ANSWER

Objectives 2.01–2.04

1. Since you are able to log on to the server, the domain controller is most likely available. You should begin troubleshooting the connection by ensuring that the junior operator has supplied the correct user id and password for the service. In either the Properties sheet for the server in Enterprise Manager or in the Windows Services tool, confirm that you are using the correct user id and password. Note that user id's should include the name of the domain (for example bigcorp\sqlsuer). If you have misspelled or omitted the domain name, Windows cannot authenticate the account.

2. If you suspect that your server cannot contact a Domain Controller, you should begin by testing the network. Since you are using TCP/IP, you can try pinging the server by name and by IP address. If you are unable to do so, you must isolate the network problem. You should also make sure you are using Named Pipes, Multiprotocol or TCP/IP Sockets as one of your network libraries. If you are not, this will prevent SQL Server from connecting to the Domain Controller (even if there is a network connection).

3. There are no other logs that will provide more information. The application log in Event View and the SQL logs both record errors raised by SQL Server. If the server services are not started, these logs do not contain any information. The system log in Event View is your only source of information.

4. If you have changed to the local system account, you can rule out any login or networking errors (because all authentication takes place internally to the local Windows server). In this case it is most likely a corruption in the Registry that is preventing the service from starting. If this is the case, you can attempt to repair the corruption using the advanced options in the SQL Server Setup utility. If this fails, you will have to reinstall the server. It is quite likely, however, that if the problem were this server, it would not show up as a login failure.

MICROSOFT CERTIFIED DATABASE ADMINISTRATOR

3

Creating SQL 2000 Databases

TEST YOURSELF OBJECTIVES

T he primary object in SQL Server 2000 is the database. The database is the container that logically groups all other objects on the server. If you plan to administer SQL Server you must have a detailed understanding of how to create, modify, and configure your databases to get the most out of SQL Server.

You are expected to have a thorough understanding of how a database is created and modified. You will need to be aware of the various database options and how they affect the database. You should be comfortable with the creation and placement of filegroups and their effects on maintenance and performance. You must be familiar with the process of expanding and shrinking databases. You will be expected to understand the proper sizing and placement of transaction logs. You will also be expected to understand how the configuration of a database can affect its performance. Finally, you will be expected to know how to detach and reattach an existing database.

TEST YOURSELF OBJECTIVE 3.01

Creating and Altering Databases

The database is simply the logical and physical container for your data. When you access data in your database in SQL Server, you don't connect to the data on the hard drive directly. Instead, you contact the server engine and it manipulates the data on the physical hard drive. It is the database that determines where the physical data resides. A SQL server can contain multiple databases and each one is considered a separate unit of storage and security.

A database requires a minimum of two files:

The data file   This file contains the actual data and other database objects (such as indexes, user-defined functions and stored procedures).

The log file   This file contains the transaction log. This log is used to maintain transactional consistency in the event of a system failure.

Physically, the data file can be placed on any local disk. It is not possible to place a data file on a network share. A local disk can, however, include external storage devices (such as an external SCSI drive or a hardware RAID array). A database can actually have multiple data files and these files can be on more than one disk. When you create a database with more than one data file, SQL Server treats all of the files as a single logical space. Objects are created on any file in the database. And SQL Server will spread the data from an individual table evenly across all files.

When creating a database, you need to know what you want to name the database, where on the server you want to place the database's physical files, and what the initial creation size of the database will be. Database names must be unique to the SQL server where they are created. It is possible to have databases with the same name on different servers (including different instances of SQL Server 2000 on the same computer). When you create the physical data files, you must give them a logical name and a physical name. The logical name is used to refer to the data files within SQL Server. SQL Server assigns a default extension of .mdf to the primary data file and .ndf to all secondary data files. It also assigns an .ldf extension to the log file(s).

When you create a database, SQL Server will populate the primary data file with metadata tables (formerly referred to as system tables). Metadata is simply SQL Server keeping information about itself and the data it contains. All database objects, users and permissions are stored in the metadata tables in the primary filegroup. SQL Server populates the primary data file with metadata by copying the Model database into the new database. The Model database contains all of the necessary metadata tables. The behavior is useful to be aware of, because anything you add to the Model database will be replicated to all subsequently created databases. New to SQL Server 2000, you can also choose a different collation for the database than the server default collation. For more on the default collation see Chapter 1, section 1.03.

You can create a database either in Enterprise Manager or using Transact-SQL. You can create a database in Enterprise Manager by right-clicking the Database folder and then selecting New Database. This will open the Database Properties sheet. From here you can configure all elements of the database as shown in the next illustration. You can also run the Create Database Wizard.

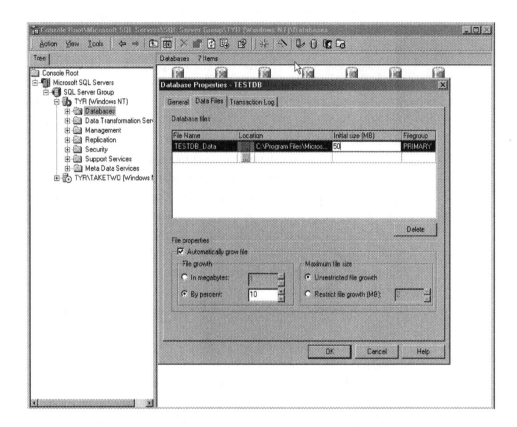

The basic syntax for creating a new database in Transact-SQL is:

```
CREATE DATABASE database_name

ON PRIMARY

(NAME = logical_file_name,

 FILENAME = 'physical_path_to_data_file',

 SIZE = size,

 [MAXSIZE = maximum_size,

 FILEGROWTH = growth_increment]

 )

[, secondary data file options]

 [LOG ON
```

```
(NAME = logical_file_name,

FILENAME = 'physical_path_to_data_file',

SIZE = size,

[MAXSIZE = maximum_size,

FILEGROWTH = growth_increment])]
```

The primary keyword indicates which file will be the primary data file. The primary data file contains all of the system tables copied from the Model database. This file should be given an .mdf extension to identify it as the primary data file. The MAXSIZE and FILEGROWTH options are not required values. SQL Server will apply defaults if these values are not set. In fact, there are defaults for most values. The only value absolutely required in a CREATE DATABASE statement is the database name. The default logical name of the primary data file is dbname_data. The default size will be the size of the Model database, and the default filename is the database name with an .mdf extension in the default path. Maxsize and Filegrowth are discussed in more detail in section 3.04.

It is also possible to omit the transaction log information. However, all databases must have a transaction log and SQL Server will create one by default if you don't specify how and where to create the log. This is discussed in more detail in section 3.05. To create a database you must be granted the CREATE DATABASE permission. If you are a member of the system administrators or database creators groups, you are automatically granted this permission.

Once you create a database, you can modify it either by going into the Properties sheet for the database in Enterprise Manager or with the ALTER DATABASE statement.

With the ALTER DATABASE statement you can add and remove data files and filegroups and modify existing files. For example, if you wanted to add a new 5GB data file to a database called Sales in a folder called Data on the d: drive, you could use the following syntax:

```
ALTER DATABASE sales

ADD FILE

 (NAME = sales_data2,

  FILENAME = 'd:\data\sales_data.ndf',

  SIZE = 5000MB)
```

For the exam you will be expected to know all of the options for the CREATE DATABASE and ALTER DATABASE statements. Many of these options are discussed in the remaining sections of this chapter, but it is a good idea to use the Books Online to familiarize yourself with all of the options.

QUESTIONS

3.01: Creating and Altering Databases

1. You are the administrator for your company's SQL 2000 server. You have just installed the server and are in the process of creating several databases. In each database, you want to include the same set of user-defined functions and some stored procedures used to track database usage. You also want two log tables to be included in all databases. What is the easiest way to add these objects to all of your databases?

    A. Create an insert trigger on the sysobjects table in the Master database. Have this trigger add all of the objects to each new database.

    B. Create a job in the Msdb database that creates the new objects. Modify and run the job after creating each new database.

    C. Write a vbscript that will add all of the objects. Run the script after creating each new database.

    D. Add the objects to the Model database.

    E. Write a script that creates all of the objects. Include the RUN AFTER option in the CREATE DATABASE command to run the script for each database.

2. Which of the following roles have permission to create a database? (Choose all that apply.)

    A. Database Administrators

    B. System Administrators

    C. Setup Administrators

    D. Database Creator

    E. Disk Administrator

3. Jan is the administrator for several SQL 2000 servers. One of her databases, rdtests, is growing faster than expected. She has added a second 30GB disk to the server and wants to add a second data file on the new disk for that database, 20GB in size. She issues the following Transact-SQL statement:

```
ALTER DATBASE rdtests

    ADD FILE

    (NAME = rdtest2_data,

    FILENAME = 'redtest2.ndf',

    SIZE = 20)
```

However, when she runs the script she gets an error telling her that there is a Device Activation error. What is the most likely cause for this error?

A. The new disk has not been formatted with NTFS.

B. She has not specified the full path name for the physical file.

C. She has not specified the size in GBs.

D. She cannot add a file to a different disk from the data file.

E. Users are accessing the database.

4. You have created a table in a database that consists of three files on three separate disks. Over time, the table has been populated with 200,000 rows of data. When you created the table there were only two disks. The third disk was added when the table was at 100,000 rows. Which of the following statements best describes the location of the data in this table?

A. SQL server will create the table on one of the two original disks and place all data for that table on the same data file.

B. SQL server will spread the data evenly between the two files that were present when the table was created.

C. SQL server will place all data on the primary data file until it becomes full and will then start filling the second file.

D. SQL server will create the table on one of the data files and then store data evenly on all of the disks in the database.

E. SQL server will create the table on the file that you specify in the CREATE TABLE statement. If you do not specify, it will create the table on the primary data file.

Setting Database Options

Once you have created a database, you can alter the default options set on the database. The options will determine the behavior of your database. There are a number of options that can be configured. The following table explains some of the more commonly set options. The database options include the recovery options, which will be discussed in detail in Chapter 6.

Option Name	Behavior When Option Is TRUE
AUTOCLOSE	Allows SQL Server to automatically close a database when the last user logs off to free system resources.
AUTO_CREATE_STATISTICS	Allows SQL Server to automatically create any missing statistics needed by the query optimizer.
AUTO_UPDATE_STATISTICS	Allows SQL Server to automatically update any out-of-date statistics.
AUTOSHRINK	Instructs SQL Server to periodically shrink data files (see section 3.04).
DBO_USE_ONLY	Allows only users who are members of the System Administrators or db_owner role to access the database.
READ_ONLY	Sets the database so that data can only be viewed, not modified.
QUOTED_IDENTIFIERS	Allows double quotes to be used as object delimiters in addition to the square brackets.

Option Name	Behavior When Option Is TRUE
RECURSIVE_TRIGGERS	Allows a table to contain a trigger that is able to loop back on itself directly. For example, if this value is set to true you could create an Insert trigger that generates a value for one of the columns in the row being inserted. If this is set to false it will not prevent indirect recursion. An example of indirect recursion would be an update trigger on table A that updates table B and in turn fires a trigger on table B that updates table A.
SELECT INTO BULK COPY	Allows certain non-logged operations, including the creation of a permanent table using SELECT … INTO and fast bulk copy.
TORN_PAGE_DETECTION	Allows SQL Server to detect incomplete write operations because of power failures or other system interruptions.
TRUNC. LOG ON CHKPT	Truncates all committed transactions from the log each time a checkpoint occurs. This option is still available for backwards compatibility. You can set this option by choosing the simple recovery model.
ANSI_NULL_DEFAULT	Changes the default behavior of SQL Server. When a table is created, the null behavior of the columns in that table is set to NOT NULL unless specified otherwise.

Some of these options can be configured in the Options tab of the Database Properties sheet in Enterprise Manager, as shown in the following illustration:

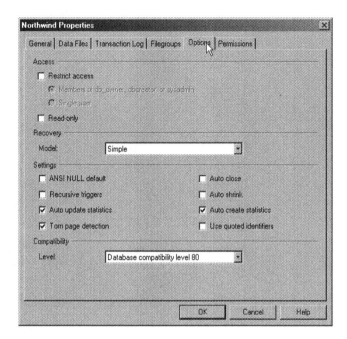

However there are some options that can only be set using the sp_dboption stored procedure. The syntax for this procedure is:

```
EXEC sp_dboption 'database name', 'option' {true | false}
```

You set an option to true to enable it and to false to disable it. You can also set database options using the SET argument of the ALTER DATABASE statement. The syntax for using this argument is:

```
ATLER DATABASE database name
```

```
SET option {ON | OFF}
```

Just as with sp_dboption, you can use the method to set all available options.

If you want to see which options have been set on a particular database you can use sp_helpdb, sp_dboption or the Databasepropertyex() functions. The Databasepropertyex function returns a 1 if the option is set or a 0 if it is not. For example, to see if the AUTO_UPDATE_STATISTICS option was set on a database you use the following query:

```
SELECT DatabasePropertyex('northwind', 'isAutoUpdateStatistics')
```

To use `sp_dboption` to find which options have been set on a database, you simply type the database name as a parameter of the procedure. For example, to find which options have been set on the Northwind database, you would type:

```
EXEC sp_dboption northwind
```

When you execute `sp_helpdb` and specify a database name, the options that are turned on will show up in the status column returned by the procedure.

QUESTIONS

3.02: Setting Database Options

5. You are the administrator for a SQL server named RDTest2. One of the developers in the R&D group wants to write a recursive trigger on one of the tables but the option has not been set. The table is in a database called systemtests. Which of the following statements will enable the recursive trigger option on this database?

   A. `EXEC sp_dboption systemtests , 'recursive trigger', true`

   B. `EXEC sp_dboption 'recursive trigger', ' systemtests', true`

   C. `EXEC sp_dboption ' systemtests' , 'recursive trigger', true`

   D. `EXEC sp_dboption ' systemtests' , 'recursive trigger', on`

   E. `EXEC sp_dboption ' systemtests' , 'recursive trigger', 1`

6. Sam is responsible for the SQL servers in a test lab for several application developers. They are migrating a database from test into a production environment. The developers want to move the database to a live server on the corporate network but allow only the development team to access the database.

All of the developers are members of the db_owner role for this database. How can Sam restrict access to the database to only members of the development team? (Choose all that apply.)

A. Use the Options tab on the Database Properties sheet in Enterprise Manager to set the database to read only.

B. Use the Options tab on the Database Properties sheet in Enterprise Manager to set the database to dbo_use_only.

C. Use `sp_dboption` to set the dbo_use_only option to true.

D. Use the Options tab on the Database Properties sheet in Enterprise Manager to restrict access to Members of db_owner, dbcreator, or Sysadmin.

E. Use `sp_dboption` to set the database to offline.

7. Jim is the administrator for a SQL 2000 server. He has been experiencing problems with the power supply on his server. He has ordered a new power supply, but it will take several days for the component to arrive. He is concerned that the power failures are causing data corruption on the physical files. What can he do to determine if data corruption has occurred because of a power failure?

A. Create an automation job to recover each database whenever the server is started.

B. Enable the Torn Page Detection option.

C. Enable the Autoclose option.

D. Enable the Auto Update Statistics option.

E. Run DBCC SHOWCONTIG on each database every time the server starts.

TEST YOURSELF OBJECTIVE 3.03

Adding/Configuring Filegroups

As you saw in section 3.01, if you have a database with multiple files, objects in that database will be spread across all files. You can control this behavior with filegroups. A filegroup is a logical grouping of one or more data files. A database can contain multiple filegroups. All databases contain at least one filegroup, the primary filegroup. The primary filegroup is created when you create the primary data file. If you do not create any other filegroups all files will be part of the primary filegroup. However, once you place a file in a filegroup, you can now deal with that file as a logically separate unit. With a filegroup you can:

- Place the physical pages for a table or an index on the data files belonging to a specific filegroup
- Backup only one filegroup on a database
- Assign a single highly accessed table to its own filegroup (using the ON filegroup option in the CREATE TABLE statement)
- Store the data from text and image data in a table using the TEXTIMAGE ON filegroup statement in the CREATE TABLE statement

The database, however, still considers all filegroups as part of itself. For example, if you had a database with two data files, each 20GB in two separate filegroups, SQL Server would still see the database as a 40GB in size. However, if you create a table on one of the two filegroups, SQL Server will not spread objects and data across both files. If you added a second data file to one of the two file groups, any object you create on that filegroup will be placed evenly on the two files within the filegroup.

To create a filegroup you use either the CREATE DATABASE or ALTER DATABASE statements. With the CREATE DATABASE statement you simply include the keyword **filegroup** and the name of the filegroup before defining the data file properties. The following example creates a database called Test with one file on the primary filegroup and another file in a filegroup called FG1:

```
CREATE DATABASE Test

ON PRIMARY

(NAME = test_data1,
```

```
FILENAME = 'c:\sqldata\testdata.mdf',

SIZE = 20GB),

FILEGROUP FG1

(NAME = test_data2,

FILENAME = 'd:\sqldata\testdata.ndf',

SIZE = 20GB)
```

Each filegroup will have a 20GB data file on a different disk. You can now create objects in either Primary or FG1. You can also add filegroups and files to filegroups using the ALTER DATABASE statement. When you use this statement to add a filegroup, you must first create the filegroup and then add a file to that filegroup. This must be done as two separate statements. Since filegroups are entirely logical, it is possible to create a filegroup without adding any files to it. The following example creates a third filegroup in Test and adds a file to it:

```
ALTER DATABASE Test

ADD FILEGROUP FG2

GO

ALTER DATABASE Test

ADD FILE

(NAME = test_data3,

FILENAME = 'f:\sqldata\testdata2.ndf',

SIZE = 20GB)

TO FILEGROUP FG2
```

When you create user-defined filegroups you must decide which filegroup will be the default filegroup. If you create tables and indexes without referencing a particular filegroup they will be added to the default filegroup. When you first create a database it will create a filegroup called Primary and set it as the default. You can change the default filegroup either with the ALTER DATABASE statement or with Enterprise Manager. With Enterprise Manager, open the Properties sheet for the database and click the Filegroups tab. To change the default, simply click the default check box that corresponds with the filegroup that you want to make primary as shown in the following illustration.

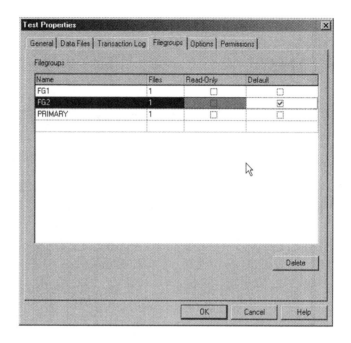

Here the default filegroup is changing from Primary to FG2. In the ALTER DATABASE statement, you would use the following syntax to make FG2 the default filegroup:

```
ALTER DATABASE Test

MODFIY FILEGROUP FG2 DEFAULT
```

After executing this statement, all objects will be created on this filegroup unless you specify an alternate location.

exam
⚠atch

Filegroups form a major part of Microsoft's strategy for dealing with very large databases. Expect to see questions on dividing large databases onto different filegroups. Filegroups can be used to ease maintenance and improve performance. Microsoft's focus leans more towards ease of maintenance (particularly with the ability to backup individual filegroups rather than the whole database).

QUESTIONS

3.03: Adding/Configuring Filegroups

8. You are the administrator for a large manufacturing plant. You are responsible for a SQL server that consists of three filegroups on three separate disks. One of the filegroups called BOM contains a single table. This table is the bill of materials table for all of the products that your company builds. This table consists of hundreds of thousands of records. It has filled 90% of the disk and you anticipate that it will grow another 30% before the end of the year. How can you make enough space for the table to continue growing? (Choose the best answer.)

   A. Use the ALTER DATABASE statement to merge the BOM filegroup with another filegroup on the server.

   B. Add another disk to the server and create a new data file. Add that data file to the BOM filegroup.

   C. Purchase a larger hard drive and move the data file belonging to the BOM filegroup to the new disk.

   D. Change the BOM filegroup to DEFAULT. This will allow it to take space from other filegroups.

   E. Add another disk to the server and create a new filegroup on that disk. Expand the table onto the new filegroup.

9. You are the database administrator for a magazine distribution company. You have been asked to create a database for the nationwide subscription system. There are millions of records in this system. You have an external hardware RAID array with 10–50GB hard drives. The database will be approximately 400GB in size. With your current tape drive, a complete backup of this database will take approximately 20 hours. Your managers want the database backed up frequently. How would you configure the database to provide better backup performance? (Choose the best answer.)

   A. Create five filegroups with two files in each filegroup. Place all the data files on the RAID array.

   B. Separate the RAID array into ten independent disks and create one filegroup on each disk.

   C. Separate the RAID array into ten independent disks and create one data file for each disk.

   D. Create ten data files on the RAID array.

   E. Compress the data files using NTFS compression to make the backup set smaller.

TEST YOURSELF OBJECTIVE 3.04

Expanding and Shrinking Databases

When you create a database, you set an initial size. However, this size is not static. It is possible to both increase and decrease the size of a database. You can also modify the size of individual data files. Changes in database and file size can be performed manually or automatically. Auto growth is a default behavior of all data files. In section 3.01 you saw that one of the properties you could configure for a data file is FILEGROWTH. Along with FILEGROWTH you can also specify a MAXSIZE property. By default, when a data file becomes full it will grow by its FILEGROWTH size until it reaches the MAXSIZE value. You can set FILEGROWTH to a static amount (for example 100MB) or by a percentage. If you do not specify values for these two properties, SQL Server automatically sets the FILEGROWTH value to 20% and the MAXSIZE to unlimited. This means that the file will grow until it fills the physical volume. For this reason you should always set a MAXSIZE property on your data files.

   If you want to manually change the size of a data file, you use the MODIFY FILE option of the ALTER DATABASE statement. For example, if you wanted to expand a data file called testdata from the test database from 20GB to 30GB, you would use the following syntax:

```
ALTER DATABASE test
MODIFY FILE (NAME = testdata,
SIZE = 30GB)
```

The value you place in the SIZE parameter should be the new size of the data file after it has been expanded. If the disk containing the data file is getting full you can expand the database by adding another database file on another disk using the ADD FILE option of the ALTER DATABASE statement.

You can also configure databases and data files to shrink automatically. By default, a data file expands when it becomes full. However, it does not shrink by default when the amount of data is reduced. If you had a 50MB data file and you placed 60MB of data into that file it would expand by its filegrowth size until it had room for all the data. If you then delete 30MB of data, the data file will be at least 60MB in size (although much of that space is "free space"). If you want to have your data files shrink automatically you must enable the AUTOSHRINK database option (see section 3.02 for information on how to enable this option). When the AUTOSHRINK option is set, SQL Server periodically checks the amount of free space in the database (that is the combined free space of all data files in a database). If the amount of free space is greater than 30%, it will shrink the database to 30% free space.

You can also manually shrink either an individual data file or the entire database using the DBCC SHRINKDATABASE or DBCC SHRINKFILE commands. When you use the DBCC SHRINKDATABASE, it will shrink all data files in the database and may even rearrange data. For example, if one data file was 50% full and the other file was 70% full and you instructed SQL Server to shrink to 40% free space, it would move 10% from file B to file A. You cannot shrink a file smaller than the size of data or the stated file size (the last value of the SIZE parameter from either a CREATE DATABASE or ALTER DATABASE statement). The syntax for the DBCC SHRINKDATABASE statement is:

```
DBCC SHRINKDATABASE (database, target percentage)
```

The target percentage value is the amount of free space remaining after the database is shrunk. For example, suppose you were to issue the following statement:

```
DBCC SHRINKDATABASE (Test, 20)
```

You would shrink all of the files in the test database so that they contain the physical data plus 20% free space. This can cause some confusion with the DBCC SHRINKFILE command.

With the DBCC SHRINKFILE command you can shrink a specific file rather than shrinking the database as a whole. The syntax for DBCC SHRINKFILE is:

```
DBCC SHRINKFILE (data file, target size)
```

Unlike the DBCC SHRINKDATABASE command, rather than specifying a percentage size, you actually specify the physical size of the file after it is shrunk. The target size is listed in Megabytes (MB). You must switch the context to the database in which the file resides before you can execute this statement. You can switch context with the USE command. For example:

```
USE Test

GO

DBCC SHRINKFILE (testdata, 15)
```

This command will change the context to the test database and shrink the data file to 15MB. If you attempt to shrink a file smaller than the amount of data it contains, SQL Server will raise an error. However, if there are multiple data files, you can use the EMPTYFILE option to move all data in a data file to other data files in the database. This will only work if there is enough free space in the other data files to hold all data on the data file being emptied. This is useful if you want to remove a data file from a database. You should run this command before dropping the file.

QUESTIONS

3.04: Expanding and Shrinking Databases

10. Frank is the administrator of a SQL 2000 server used in a test environment. For testing purposes, large volumes of data are periodically dumped into the various databases on the server. This data is usually deleted after the test has been run. As a result of this behavior, the data files are continually filling the physical disks. Frank finds that he is continually shrinking the data files manually. What can Frank do to eliminate the need to manually truncate the databases on this server? (Choose the best answer.)

    A. Place a trigger on each database to automatically shrink the database using DBCC SHRINKDATABASE every time a table is truncated.

    B. Create an automation job that runs DBCC SHRINKDATABASE on each database every 30 minutes.

C.   Use the SQL Server Profiler to monitor for DELETE and TRUNCATE statements and program it to run DBCC SHRINKDATABASE whenever these events occur.

D.   Place a trigger on each table that raises an error every time the table is truncated. Create a job that runs DBCC SHRINKTABLE every time the error is raised.

E.   Use `sp_dboption` to enable the autoshrink option on each database.

11.   You are the administrator of a SQL 2000 server called CorpSales. CorpSales contains a number of small databases that store historical sales data. Recently one of the disks in the server failed. It contained one of the two data files that belong to a database called 1999Sales. When the database was created the server had two 5GB hard drives allocated for this database. You have replaced the 5GB disk with a 40GB disk and restored the data file from a backup. You are concerned that the second disk may soon fail. How would you move the second data file onto the new disk? (Choose the best answer.)

A.   Use the `sp_detach_file` stored procedure to detach the file and `sp_attach_file` to attach it to the new disk.

B.   Backup the data file of the 5GB disk and restore it onto the 40GB disk.

C.   Stop the server. Use xcopy to move the data file from the 5GB disk to the 40GB disk.

D.   Use the ALTER DATABASE statement to expand the data file on the 40GB drive to hold all of the data on the 5GB disk. Run DBCC SHRINKFILE with the EMPTYFILE option on the data file on the 5GB disk. Drop the data file on the 5GB disk using the ALTER DATABASE statement with the REMOVE FILE argument.

E.   Use the ALTER DATABASE statement to expand the data file on the 40GB drive to hold all of the data on the 5GB disk. Use the ALTER DATABASE statement with the REMOVE FILE option to remove the file on the 5GB disk. SQL Server will automatically migrate all data to the data file on the 40GB disk before dropping the file.

TEST YOURSELF OBJECTIVE 3.05

Sizing and Placing the Transaction Log

All databases must have at least one transaction log file. When creating a database, you need to give consideration to both size and the placement of the transaction log file. In order to determine the size of the log file, you must first have some idea of how the database is going to be used. The transaction log stores transactions so that, in the event of a system failure, data loss is minimized. A transaction is a collection of one or more statements that must complete entirely or not at all. Transactions modify data or the schema of the database itself. All INSERT, UPDATE, and DELETE statements (SQL DML statements); all CREATE, ALTER, and DROP statements (SQL DDL Statements); and all GRANT, DENY, and REVOKE statements (SQL DCL statements) will be recorded in the transaction log. If the transaction log becomes full, no further transactions will be allowed until the transaction log is expanded or cleared. SELECT statements are not considered part of a transaction and are not recorded in the transaction log.

If the database will be used to process a large number of transactions, you will want a larger log. This type of database is often referred to as an Online Transaction Processing (OLTP) database. If your database will be used almost exclusively for running queries, you will not require as much log space. This type of database is often referred to as a Decision Support System (DSS) database. There is no absolute rule to the size of a transaction log; it will depend on the usage. However, as a general rule of thumb, an OLTP database should have a transaction log that is approximately 25% of the size of the data file(s). A DSS database will require a transaction log that is approximately 10% of the data file(s).

exam
🕅 *atch*   *You may get questions asking you to estimate a size for the transaction log. Remember that OLTP databases require more log space than DSS servers. The 25% and 10% ranges are a good guideline. You might also see references to OLAP databases or Data warehouses. These are DSS servers that are running the SQL Server Analysis services. For the purpose of calculating log size, treat them as DSS servers.*

The placement of transaction log files is important both for performance and recoverability. You should avoid placing the data file and the transaction log file on the same physical disk. From a performance standpoint, SQL Server accesses the hard drive differently for data files and log files. Data files tend to be accessed in a sporadic manner as data is written to and read from the disk. Log files, on the other hand, are accessed in a series of sequential write operations. Log files are only read during the recovery process and during checkpoints so most of the activity is a constant series of write operations. If these two files are accessed simultaneously on the same disk, there will be a high degree of contention as SQL Server tries to access and modify the data file and write those changes to the transaction log. Placing these files on separate disks will remove this contention.

From a recoverability standpoint, if you place the log file and the data file on the same disk, you will lose much more data if the hard drive fails. If you place the data file and log file on separate disks, and the disk containing the data file fails, you can still access the transaction log and save all changes since the last backup. If the files are on the same disk and that disk fails, all of those changes will be lost. You will only be able to recover the database up to the point of the last backup. If you are able to save the changes, they can then be restored in addition to the last backup. This will allow you to return the database to the state it was in just prior to the failure.

It is possible to have multiple transaction log files, and, like data files, these can be placed on separate disks. However, unlike data files, SQL Server will fill these files in a sequential order. It will fill the first log file before moving on to the next. Transaction log files cannot be placed in filegroups. Like data files, they must be created on the local server. It is not possible to place a transaction log on a mapped network drive or a removable storage device (like a Zip drive or a CD-RW drive). Because transaction logs write in a sequential manner, they do not get any benefit from being placed on a striped volume (such as a RAID-0 or RAID-5 array).

QUESTIONS

3.05: Sizing and Placing the Transaction Log

12. You have been asked to create a database that will store a large volume of archival data. The data in this database will be static and users will run complex

queries against the data. The server contains two internal disks and an external RAID-5 Array (as shown in the illustration that follows). The data files for this database will be 50GB in size. Which of the following statements would you include in the CREATE DATABASE statement to create the best placement for the transaction log? (Choose the best answer.)

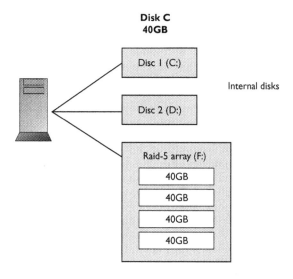

A. LOG ON

    (NAME = tlog1,

     FILENAME = 'c:\Logs\tlog.ldf',

     SIZE = 5GB,

     MAXSIZE = 8GB)

B. LOG ON

    (NAME = tlog1,

     FILENAME = 'd:\Logs\tlog.ldf',

     SIZE = 5GB,

     MAXSIZE = 8GB

C. LOG ON

    (NAME = tlog1,

      FILENAME = 'f:\Logs\tlog.ldf',

      SIZE = 5GB,

      MAXSIZE = 8GB)

D. LOG ON

    (NAME = tlog1,

      FILENAME = 'f:\Logs\tlog.ldf',

      SIZE = 13GB,

      MAXSIZE = 14GB)

E. LOG ON

    (NAME = tlog1,

     FILENAME = 'd:\Logs\tlog.ldf',

     SIZE = 13GB,

     MAXSIZE = 14GB)

13. Which of the following SQL statements will be recorded in the transaction log? (Choose all that apply.)

A. SELECT p.productname, p.orderno, p.unitcost * p.amtsold AS total_sale, t.avgsale

   FROM orderlist p INNER JOIN

   (SELECT productno, AVG(unitcost * amtsold) as avgsale FROM orderlist GROUP BY unitcost) t

B. GRANT select, insert, delete

   ON membertable

   TO fred, dave, sam

C. CREATE VIEW dept10

   AS

   SELECT e.emp_id, e.fname, e.lname , d.city

   FROM employee e JOIN department d

   ON e.deptid = d.deptid

   WHERE d.deptid = 10

D. UPDATE products

   SET price = price * 1.1

E. EXEC sp_helpdb 'Northwind'

TEST YOURSELF OBJECTIVE 3.06

Configuring Database Options for Performance

When you configure your database, there are certain steps that can be taken to improve its overall performance. The biggest cost in accessing data in a database is disk I/O, the physical reads and writes to and from the data files. You should take steps to improve I/O and minimize disk contention. Disk contention is when more than one processes attempt to access the hard drive at the same time. The following steps can improve disk I/O and reduce disk contention.

- Avoid placing the data files and operating system files or SQL Server files on the same disk (which is interesting, considering the default data file location is under c:\Program files, which is the same default volume location as the WINNT folder).

- If possible, avoid placing multiple data files on the same physical disk (particularly from the same database). If both files are accessed simultaneously, it will cause disk contention.

- Place the log file and the data file on separate disks. This will also improve recoverability and reduce data loss if the disk containing the data file fails.

- Use filegroups to place heavily modified tables on their own disk.

You can also improve the performance of you system with RAID. RAID stands for Redundant Array of Independent Disks. Windows supports four levels of RAID:

RAID-0   Disk Striping. RAID-0 writes data across two or more disks in 64KB stripes. This spreads the I/O across the disks. RAID-0 is very fast, however it does not provide any redundancy and should be avoided for data and log files.

RAID-1   Disk Mirroring. In RAID-1, data is written simultaneously to two disks. One disk is the active disk and the other is the mirrored copy. RAID-1 is best suited to protect transaction logs. Since logs write sequentially there is no benefit in putting them on a striped array.

RAID-5   Disk Striping with Parity. RAID-5 writes data across three or more disks. However, on each stripe, one of the disks will contain the parity bit. This is redundant data that will allow the array to continue functioning if one of the disks in the set fails. RAID-5 is the best choice for data files. It provides redundancy but also provides improved I/O performance. There is, however, some overhead added when using RAID-5 because the parity information must be calculated for each stripe. This overhead can be negated by the I/O performance increase. Normally you would need five or six disks in the array before the I/O benefit outweighs the cost of the parity calculation.

RAID-1&0   This is sometimes referred to as RAID-10. In this configuration, a RAID-0 array is mirrored. This provides all of the I/O performance of RAID-0 with the protection of RAID-1. This is the best configuration in terms of performance, but it also has the highest cost. Windows cannot create RAID 1&0 arrays. To implement this option, you will need a hardware RAID solution that supports this configuration.

When planning your database, it is important to determine the initial creation size. If you make your initial database too small, you will be forced to expand it, or allow auto growth to increase the size of the file. If you make the initial creation size too large, you will waste space on the hard drive (since you cannot shrink a data file smaller than its initial creation size). When determining the initial creation size of the database, you need to have some idea of how SQL Server stores data. SQL Server logically subdivides the data file into 8KB blocks or pages. Each page contains some header information and is able to store 8060 bytes of data. The page size is relevant because it is used to determine how much space is allocated for any object. A data page can only store data from one table or index on a page. Furthermore, one row in a table cannot exceed one page. When calculating space requirements:

- Calculate the size of a row for each table in the database. To calculate row size, simply add up the length of the datatypes for each column. For variable length columns (for example the varchar) take an average value based on the expected length of values in a column—in other words make an educated guess at an average length).

- Divide 8060 by the row size. This will tell you how many rows will fit on a page.

- Estimate the expected number of rows and divide this number by the number of rows per page. This will tell you how many pages this table will require.

- Repeat these steps for all tables. Total the number of pages.

- Convert the resulting total to MB and this will give you your initial creation size.

exam
Watch

You may be asked to perform a calculation like this on the exam. Make sure you are comfortable with the formula.

QUESTIONS

3.06: Configuring Database Options for Performance

14. You are planning to install SQL 2000 Server on a computer that has three internal EIDE disks and a RAID-5 controller with four 40GB SCSI disks (as shown in the illustration that follows). Windows 2000 is installed on the first internal disk, and SQL Server is installed on the second disk. Your database will

be used for a parts tracking system. The data will be updated frequently. Where would you place your data files? (Choose all that apply.)

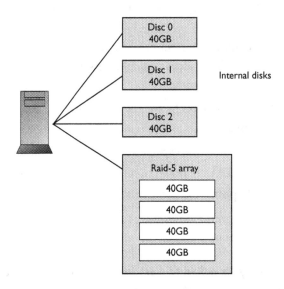

A. Place the transaction log file in the default file location.

B. Place the transaction log on the third disk.

C. Place the data file on the third disk.

D. Place the transaction log on the RAID-5 array.

E. Place the data file on the RAID-5 array.

15. You are the administrator for a SQL 2000 server. This server contains two production databases: Sales and Accounting. The Sales database consists of two 30GB data files and one log file 15GB in size. The Accounting database consists of one 20GB log file and three 40GB data files. The server is configured with three internal disks and a RAID array consisting of five 30GB drives (as shown in the illustration that follows). Windows 2000 and SQL Server are installed on Disk 0. How would you place these files to get the best performance? (Choose all that apply.)

A. Place both transaction logs on Disk 1. Mirror the disk with Disk 2.

B. Place one data file on each disk of the external array.

C. Place the Sales transaction log on Disk 1 and the Accounting transaction log on Disk 2.

D. Create a RAID-0 set on the external array and place all of the data files from both databases on the array.

E. Create a RAID-5 set on the external array and place all of the data files from both databases on the array.

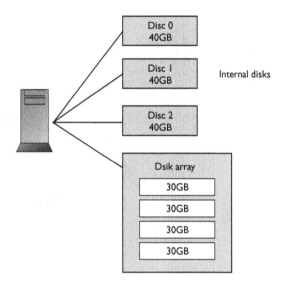

TEST YOURSELF OBJECTIVE 3.07

Attaching and Detaching Databases

It is also possible to take a database from one server and add it to another server. In order to do this you must first detach the database from its source. Detaching a database removes all records of the database from the Master database. However, unlike dropping the database, detaching does not delete the physical data and log files for the database. Once the database is detached you can copy it to the new location. You can detach a database either through the Enterprise Manager or by using the `sp_detach_db` stored procedure. In Enterprise Manager, right-click your database and click All Tasks | Detach Database, as shown in the following illustration.

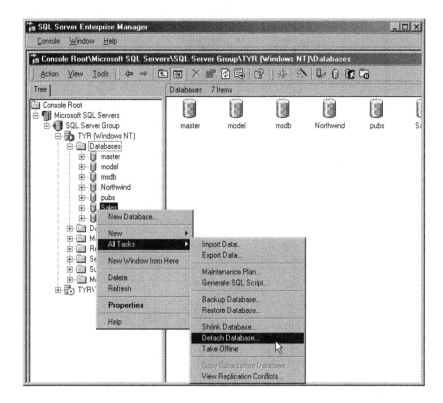

The syntax for the `sp_detach_db` is:

```
sp_detach_db [@dbname = ]'database name',
             [ [@skipchecks = ] {'true' | 'false' | null}]
```

The skipchecks option will skip issuing an UPDATE STATISTICS statement if set to true.

Once you have detached the data files, any locks held by SQL Server are removed and you can move the file freely. The file can be reattached on the same server or on a different server. Detaching and reattaching a data file is one way of moving a data file to a different disk location. You might also want to move a file from one named instance to another. When you attach a database, you make all of the relevant entries into the Master database and point to the new file location. To reattach the data file you can use either Enterprise Manager or the sp_attach_db stored procedure. In Enterprise Manager, right-click the Databases folder and select All Tasks | Attach Database.

The syntax for sp_attach_db is:

```
sp_attach_db [@dbname = ] 'Database name',
             [@filename1 = ] '<physical file path>'[, …
[@filename16 = ]'
             <'physical file path'> ]
```

You can list up to 16 database files with this procedure. You must include the full path to the location of the file including a drive letter. This must be enclosed in single quotes. If you enter an incorrect path or omit the quotes, the procedure will fail. You only need to point to the primary data file. This file contains the sysfiles table that lists all of the other files in the database.

QUESTIONS

3.07: Attaching and Detaching Databases

16. You have just detached a database using sp_detach_db and have copied the database to another server on the network. The destination volume is formatted with NTFS. You are trying to attach the database using Enterprise Manager; however, when you browse for the .MDF file and click OK you receive the following error message, as shown in the next illustration. What is the most likely reason for the connection failure?

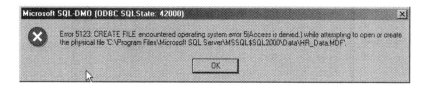

A. You did not detach the database using Enterprise Manager.

B. You do not have administrative rights on the local Windows server.

C. The SQL Server service account does not have administrative rights on the local Windows server.

D. The NTFS permissions on the data file prevent the SQL Server service from accessing the file.

E. The file was corrupted when you detached it.

17. Bob has copied the database and log files from a database called HR_Info to his server. The database is made up of a data file called HRInfo_data.mdf and a log file called HRInfo_log.ldf. They are in a folder called Newdb on the d:\ drive. He also wants to rename the database HRInfo_copy. Which of the following statements will allow him to attach the database?

A. ```
sp_attach_db "HRInfo_copy", "d:\Newdb\ HRInfo_data.mdf",
"d:\Newdb\ HRInfo_log.ldf".
```

B. ```
sp_attach_db HRInfo_copy,  'd:\Newdb\ HRInfo_data.mdf',
                          'd:\Newdb\HRInfo_log.ldf'.
```

C. ```
sp_attach_db 'HRInfo_copy', 'd:\Newdb\HRInfo_data.mdf'
                'd:\Newdb\HRInfo_log.ldf'.
```

D. ```
sp_attach_db 'HRInfo_copy', 'HRInfo_data.mdf',
                'HRInfo_log.ldf'.
```

E. ```
sp_attach_db 'HR_Info'\'HRInfo_copy',
                'd:\Newdb\HRInfo_data.mdf',
                'd:\Newdb\HRInfo_log.ldf'.
```
```

LAB QUESTION

Objectives 3.01–3.07

You have been asked to plan and implement a database for a small law firm. The database will be used to track billable hours. When built, the database will contain the following four tables, as shown in the following illustration.

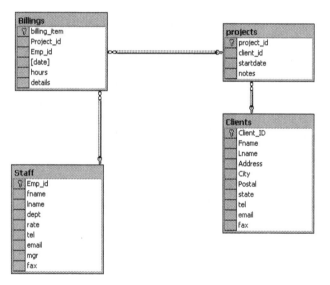

The billing table will be updated regularly, but the other three tables will only be updated infrequently. SQL Server has been installed on a server that contains four internal 40GB disks. Windows and SQL Server are installed on the first disk.

The four tables are expected to have the following sizes:

Table Name	Row Size	Expected number of rows
Billing	900 bytes	100,000
Clients	600 bytes	2000
Projects	800 bytes	5000
Staff	600 bytes	200

1. How big should the data file be?

2. Where would you place the transaction log?

3. How could you improve the performance of the billing table in your database design?

4. If the law firm were to acquire another firm and increased systems requirements, beyond the current two disks, how would you increase the size of the database to accommodate growth?

5. Assuming the disks each contain one volume (lettered C:–F:) and the data files would be placed under a folder called data and the logs would be placed under a folder called log, what would the CREATE DATABASE statement look like for this database? (Assume that you will include a filegroup for the billing table and place the transaction log on drive D:.)

QUICK ANSWER KEY

Objective 3.01

1. D
2. B and D
3. B
4. D

Objective 3.02

5. C
6. C and D
7. B

Objective 3.03

8. B
9. A

Objective 3.04

10. E
11. D

Objective 3.05

12. B
13. B, C, and D

Objective 3.06

14. B and E
15. B and E

Objective 3.07

16. D
17. C

IN-DEPTH ANSWERS

3.01: Creating and Altering Databases

1. ☑ **D** is the correct answer. When you create a new database, SQL Server copies the Model database, renames it, and expands it to the initial creation size specified for the primary data file. The Model database can be updated and any changes made to the Model database will be reflected in subsequent database creations. Changing the Model database has no effect on databases that you have already created. User-defined datatypes, functions and stored procedures are all stored in the metadata tables in the Model database. Because of this copying behavior, the size of the Model database is the smallest possible size for a user database.

   ☒ **A** is incorrect for two reasons. First, when you create a new database, a record of that database is inserted into the sysdatabases table in Master rather than the sysobjects table. Second, it is not possible to place a trigger on a table object in the Master databases. **B** is incorrect because the job would have to be edited each time you ran it. This is because you would have to specify manually which database the job should run against. You must also manually run the job. Updating the Model database requires no further intervention on your part to add the objects. **C** is incorrect because it also requires manual intervention. It is possible to write a vbscript to create all of these objects, but it will require a strong understanding of how to program the SQL Distributed Management Objects (DMO). **E** is incorrect because there is no RUN AFTER option in the CREATE DATABASE statement. You would have to manually run the script in each database.

2. ☑ **B** and **D** are the correct answers. Only members of the System Administrators and Database Creator roles have permission to create new databases.

   ☒ **A** is incorrect because there is not a Database Administrator role in SQL 2000 Server. **C** is incorrect because the Setup Admin is only able to configure linked servers. **E** is incorrect because the Disk Administrator is only able to manipulate the physical disk.

3. ☑   **B** is correct because you must include the full path name. Without the full path name, SQL Server does not know where to find the file and returns a device error. You will get the same error if you misspell any part of the path.

    ☒   **A** is incorrect because you can create a SQL Server data file on both NTFS and FAT/FAT32 partitions. If the partition is NTFS, you must make sure that the SQL Server service account can access the partition and that it is not compressed. SQL Server will not allow you to create a data file in a compressed folder. **C** is incorrect because SQL Server will default to MB. This means that the new data file will only be 20MB (instead of 20GB) but this will not cause a syntax error. You can specify the size in Kilobytes (KB), Megabytes (MB), Gigabytes (GB), and Terrabytes (TB). **D** is incorrect because you can have multiple data files associated with a single database, and these files can be on different disks as long as all of the disks are local to the same server. **E** is incorrect because it is possible to add files to a database while users are accessing the databases. However, you cannot drop a file on a database while the database is in use.

4. ☑   **D** is correct because SQL Server treats all of the data files as a single logical space. It will store data and objects within the available space. It tries to place this evenly so that no one data file fills ahead of the others. It will create the initial table on one data file (chosen randomly) and then the data will be placed on any file in the database.

    ☒   **A** is incorrect because data in tables will be placed across all available disks, not just the disk that the table is originally created on. **B** is incorrect because SQL Server does not keep track of when data files are added. In this scenario, the table would have been spread across the two original files until the third file was added, then it would be stored on all three files. **C** is incorrect because it assumes that SQL Server fills the file in order. In reality, SQL spreads the data in the heap across all data files. **E** is incorrect because it is not possible to specify where you want to create a table. The only way to do this is with the use of filegroups. Filegroups are discussed in section 3.03.

3.02: Setting Database Options

5. ☑   **C** is the correct answer. The correct syntax is to list the name of the database enclosed in single quotes, then the option (also enclosed in single quotes), and finally true or false (without quotes) to turn the option on or off.

☒ **A** is incorrect because the database name is not enclosed in single quotes. **B** is incorrect because the order of the parameters is reversed. When SQL executes this procedure it will attempt to set the systemtests option on database recursive trigger. It will return an error telling you that this database does not exist. Remember with all stored procedures unless you include the parameter name and an equal sign, you must supply parameters in the order they are listed in the procedure. **D** is incorrect because it uses ON as a third parameter instead of true. The `sp_dboption` stored procedure will only accept true or false as values for the third parameter. You use ON and OFF when you change options using the ALTER TABLE statement. **E** is incorrect, because, like answer D it does not use true or false to set the database state. The `sp_dboption` stored procedure will not accept 1 and 0 in place of true and false.

6. ☑ **C** and **D** are the correct answers. The dbo_use_only option will only allow those users mapped to the database owner (dbo) account to access the database. By default, members of the System Administrators, Database Creators, and db_owner roles are mapped to dbo. Since the developers are members of the db_owner role, they will be able to access the database on the live system. However, any user who is not one of these groups will be denied access to the database (even if a login has been created for them). In Enterprise Manager, you must click the Restrict Access check box and then select Members Of db_owner, dbcreator, Or sysadmin, as shown in the following illustration.

☒   **A** is incorrect because setting the database would not restrict access to non-developers. It would simply prevent anyone with a user account on the database from making changes to the data. **B** is incorrect because there is no dbo_use_only option in the Options tab. Instead you must select Restrict Access | Members OF DB_owner, DBcreator, OR SYsadmin. **E** is incorrect because setting the database offline would prevent all users from accessing the database, including the developers.

7.   ☑   **B** is correct. The TORN_PAGE_DETECTION option allows SQL Server to detect incomplete write operations when the system recovers. SQL Server recovers each database every time the server starts. Torn pages occur when there is an interruption on the server while it is in the middle of writing a page back to the hard drive. The SQL server page is 8KB in size, but it performs writes in 16–512 byte sectors. As soon as the first sector is updated, the page is marked as updated. Therefore, if the failure occurs after the first sector is updated, the page will appear updated even though it is incomplete. The TORN_PAGE_DETECTION will mark a database as suspect when it is recovered. You will have to recover from backup and reapply the transaction log (if possible) to repair the data file. You can also avoid torn pages by installing a disk controller with a battery backup for is disk caching. This battery backup will allow writes to be completed or rolled back in the event of a power outage.

☒   **A** is incorrect because all databases will be recovered automatically every time the database is started. If the Torn Page Detection option is set to false, recovery will not detect torn pages. **C** is incorrect because the Autoclose option has nothing to do with recovery. The Autoclose option will close a database when the last user disconnects from the database. This frees up any system resources (such as physical RAM) used by the database. SQL Server will reopen the database when a user reconnects. This option is only useful for personal SQL Server installations, when you will generally only be working with one database at a time. It is not recommended on databases with a large number of users that disconnect and reconnect, because of the overhead involved in constantly closing and reopening the database. **D** is incorrect because the statistics are used to optimize queries. The SQL Query Analyzer uses statistics to find the least expensive execution plan for a SQL statement. **E** is incorrect because the DBCC SHOWCONTIG statement is used to determine the degree of fragmentation on indexes and tables. It does not provide any information on torn pages.

3.03: Adding/Configuring Filegroups

8. ☑ **B** is the correct answer because a filegroup can contain more that one physical data file. By expanding the BOM filegroup onto a second disk, SQL Server will only place data from the bill of materials table on that new data file.

   ☒ **A** is incorrect because you cannot merge filegroups together. Filegroups are separate logical entities. Once they are created they cannot be collapsed into each other. **C** is technically correct, but it is not the best answer. It is much easier to add additional files than it is to keep moving the data file to a larger hard drive. When you add a second file, the filegroup maintains all the space allocated to the first data file and adds the space allocated to the second data file. In addition, when the second data file becomes full, you can simply add a third. **D** is incorrect because the default setting does not give the filegroup any special rights to space occupied by other filegroups. The only change in the properties of the new default filegroup is that if an object is created without specifying a filegroup, that object will be added to the default filegroup. Keeping this in mind, changing BOM to the default filegroup will most likely speed up the rate in which the data file fills. **E** is incorrect because a table object can only belong to one filegroup. It is not possible to extend the table onto another filegroup.

9. ☑ **A** is the correct answer because it is possible to backup filegroups individually. By separating the database into five filegroups, each backup should take approximately four hours. With this method you should be able to backup one filegroup per day. Placing all of the data files on the RAID array will also give you increased I/O performance. While you should only place one data file per disk in a normal system, with a RAID array you can place one data file per spindle in the array.

   ☒ **B** is incorrect because you will lose all of the I/O performance gained by using the RAID array. It will, however allow you to backup the database more frequently. **C** and **D** are incorrect because you do not get any logical divisions if all of the files are part of one filegroup—even if they are divided across multiple disks. In answer **D**, you maintain the I/O performance of the RAID array, but do not solve your backup problem. **E** is incorrect because SQL Server will not allow you compress data files using NTFS compression.

3.04: Expanding and Shrinking Databases

10. ☑   **E** is the correct answer. When you enable the Autoshrink option on a database it periodically checks the amount of free space in the database (5 minutes after the option is first set and then every 30 minutes after that). If the total free space across all of the databases is greater that 30%, it runs the DBCC SHRINKDATABASE to bring the database back to 30% free space. Once you set this option, it requires no further intervention on the part of the administrator.

    ☒   **A** is incorrect because you cannot set a trigger at the database level. Triggers can only be set on tables or views. **B** is incorrect because it is a waste of resources to run the DBCC SHRINKDATABASE every half hour. If a large dump has taken place, but the tables have not yet been truncated with the job runs, SQL Server will expend I/O and process resources executing the job, but it will not have any effect on the server. When you enable the Autoshrink option it only runs DBCC SHRINKDATABASE if it detects that the database contains greater than 30% free space. **C** is incorrect because you cannot set alerts in the Profiler. The Profiler is an excellent tool for monitoring activity on a database, but it does not have any automation capability. **D** is incorrect because the triggers are much more expensive than the Autoshrink option and they must also be set for each table. Technically, this answer will solve the problem. However, it would be very costly in terms of system resources to implement (because of the cost of maintaining all of the triggers) and would be much more difficult to administer.

11. ☑   **D** is the correct answer. When you use the EMPTYFILE option, it migrates all data from the file being emptied into the other data files in the database (or filegroup if you are using user defined filegroups). This will only work if there is enough space in the other files to hold all data in the file being emptied. Once the file has been emptied, you can use the ALTER DATABASE statement to remove the file. You cannot drop a file while it has data in it.

    ☒   **A** is incorrect because there is no `sp_detach_file` stored procedure. There is an `sp_detach_db` procedure but this removes the entire database (see section 3.07). It is not possible to detach and move a single data file on the database. **B** is technically correct because you can use the RESTORE command to restore a data file to a new location. However, this solution places two data files on the same disk. There is no advantage to having two data files on the same disk. In fact, the two files will compete for disk resources as SQL Server tries to spread data evenly between the two data files. **C** is incorrect because SQL Server is not able to detect when data files are moved. If you were to stop the server and move one of the data files to a new location, the database would appear as suspect when the server is restarted. This occurs because SQL Server stores the paths to the data files in the sysdatabases system table in the Master database. If SQL Server cannot find all of the files listed in sysdatabases, it cannot recover the database and leaves it as suspect (and therefore inaccessible). **E** is incorrect because you cannot drop a file while it has data in it. If you were to try to drop this file you would receive the following message:

```
Server: Msg 5042, Level 16, State 1, Line 1

The file 'datafile' cannot be removed because it is not empty.
```

3.05: Sizing and Placing the Transaction Log

12. ☑ **B** is the correct answer. Because this is a DSS server you will not need more than 10% of the data file. Since the data file in this case is 50GB you do not want it to be any larger than 5GB. In fact, because the data is static you can probably make the log even smaller. You will mostly likely place the data files on the F: drive because data access will be improved by the RAID array, whereas there is no benefit to placing the transaction log on a striped array. Since the operating system files and the SQL server files are on drive C, drive D is the best choice.

☒ **A** is incorrect because it places the log file on the same volume as both Windows and SQL Server files. This would create disk contention between the log file and other I/O intensive operations (like writing to the Windows Page file). **C** is incorrect because it places the log file on the RAID array. The sequential nature of the transaction logs means that there is no performance benefit to placing the log file on that drive. **D** is incorrect because it places the log on the RAID array and makes it 25% of the size of the data file. This is an appropriate ratio for an OLTP system, but this database will serve a DSS function. **E** is also incorrect because it assigns 25% of the data file to the log.

13. ☑ **B, C,** and **D** are the correct answers. **B** is correct because all Data Control Language statements (GRANT, DENY, REVOKE) are logged. **C** is correct because all Data Definition Language (CREATE, ALTER, DROP) statements are logged. **D** is correct because all Data Manipulation Language statements (INSERT, UPDATE, DELETE) are written to the transaction log. This particular query is one to watch for. UPDATE statements will make one log entry for each row that is updated. Because there is no WHERE clause in this UPDATE statement, it will update all rows in the table. If there are 50,000 products that will be 50,000 entries in the log! This type of statement will fill a transaction log if you are not careful.

☒ **A** is incorrect because queries, no matter how complex, are not logged. Only those statements which in some way modify data in the database are written to the transaction log. **E** is incorrect because this stored procedure is used to query the metadata tables in the Master database. It is considered a query operation and, like answer **A**, is not written to the transaction log.

3.06: Configuring Database Options for Performance

14. ☑ **B** and **E** are the correct answers. It is best to place the transaction log and data file on separate disks. This will reduce data loss if the disk containing the data file fails because the log can be backed up and restored in addition to the last backup. Transaction logs primarily deal with sequential write operations. That is, the transaction log is constantly writing in order from the beginning to the end of the data file. RAID stands for Redundant Array of Independent Disks. RAID-5 is known as Disk Striping with Parity. In RAID-5, data is written in 64KB stripes across all of the disks in the set. Sequential operations do not benefit from RAID-5. However, I/O intensive operations will benefit from RAID-5. Because the data is striped, it is possible for one process to be writing to one disk in the array while another process is reading from another disk. Because of this, it is best to place the data file on the RAID array and place the transaction log by itself on the third disk.

☒ **A** is incorrect because the default file location is in a subfolder called Data in the SQL Server install path. By placing the log in the default location you are placing the log on the same disk as SQL Server. The log will perform much faster if it is not sharing disk resources with the rest of the processes running on the server. **C** is incorrect because you do not want to place the data file and the transaction log on the same disk. Since you are placing the log on this disk, it is a poor choice. **D** is incorrect because this would also be placing the transaction log on the same disk as the data file. Technically, placing both files on the RAID array is not as dangerous as placing both files on one disk, because the data file is actually striped across several disks and the data is protected from disk failure by the redundancy built into RAID. However, the sequential nature of writes to the transaction log negates any I/O performance gained through the RAID array.

15. ☑ **B** and **E** are correct. **B** is correct because to avoid disk contention, you should place each transaction log on its own disk. Both of these files will require continuous sequential writes. Placing each one on its own disk will avoid these write operations from conflicting with other write operations to other files. **E** is correct because creating a RAID-5 array will provide both fault tolerance and improved I/O. You could only place one file per disk, but since the array is striped across several disks you should place one file per disk in the array. There are five disks and you have five data files. The total size of all the files is 180GB and the total usable space in the RAID array is 240GB (5 × 30GB - 30GB for the parity information). Therefore, there is enough room to fit all of the data files on the single RAID-5 array.

   ☒ **A** is incorrect because if you place the two log files on the same disk it will create contention on the disk as both databases try to write to the disk at the same time. Mirroring the disks will not break up this contention. **C** is incorrect because you loose all the I/O performance benefit of the RAID array by placing all of the files on separate disks. **D** is incorrect because RAID-0 provides no redundancy and greatly increases the risk of disk failure and data loss on the system.

3.07: Attaching and Detaching Databases

16. ☑ **D** is the correct answer because the SQL Server service must be able to access the file in order to attach it. If the data files are in an NTFS folder that the server service account cannot access, an error will be raised.

⊠   **A** is incorrect because there is no difference between files detached using Enterprise Manager and those detached using the `sp_detach_db` stored procedure. Both methods simply remove the file from the Master database and release any locks; they do not alter the files. **B** is incorrect because this is an object access issue rather than a user rights issue. Even as an administrator you can be locked out of an NTFS resource if you are not assigned permission. You would need the appropriate rights just to access this tool in Enterprise Manager. **C** is incorrect because, just as with answer **B**, this is a question of the file access permission of the service account. Even if you added the service account to the local administrators group, the connection would still fail if that group or the domain user account had not been given NTFS read permission. **E** is incorrect because you would receive a different message if the file was unreadable due to corruption.

17.   ☑   **C** is the correct answer because it is the only one that is syntactically correct. For the procedure to run without generating a syntax error you must place single quotes (') around all of the parameters. Furthermore, you must include the full path to the file location. Finally, the database will be called whatever value you place in the first parameter. If you want to change the database name, simply enter the new name.

⊠   **A** is incorrect because it has surrounded all of the parameter values with double quotes. Double quotes are only used as object delimiters. Object delimiters allow you to use object names that violate SQL Server standard naming rules. **B** is incorrect because you have omitted the single quotes around the database name. **D** is incorrect because you have not entered the full path to the database files. If you omit this information, SQL Server is not able to find the files to attach. **E** is incorrect because there is no special syntax to changing the database name. This particular script will raise an error because the back-slash is an illegal character in database object names.

LAB ANSWER

Objectives 3.01–3.07

1. The data file should be approximately 107MB. The Billings table would need 2,500 pages (8060 / 900 = 8 rows per page. 100000 rows / 8 = 12,500 pages). The client table would need 154 pages (8060 / 600 = 13 rows per page. 2000 / 13 = 154 pages). The Project table would need 500 pages (8060 / 800 = 10 rows per page. 5000 / 10 = 500 pages). The Staff table would need 16 pages (8060 / 600 = 13 rows per page. 200 rows / 13 = 16 pages). This gives a total of 13,170 pages. If you multiply the total number of pages by 8060, you get 106,150, 200 bytes or roughly 107MB.

2. The transaction log should be on its own disk. Since you have four disks, but Windows and SQL Server are installed on C:, you should place it on one of the other disks.

3. Since you have four disks, you could create a second file group on the fourth disk and place the billing table on this filegroup. Because the database is currently quite small you may not notice a huge improvement, but as the database continues to grow, having the active billing table on its own disk will improve the I/O for the whole database.

4. You would have to add more disks and use the ALTER DATABASE statement to create new data files on these disks. If you purchased an external RAID device, you could create this extra data file across the RAID set.

5. It might look something like this:

```
CREATE DATABASE billtracking

ON

PRIMARY

(

NAME = billtracking_data,
```

```
FILENAME = 'e:\data\billtracking.mdf',

SIZE = 100MB

)

FILEGROUP Billing

(

NAME = billtracking_data2,

FILENAME = 'f:\data\billtracking2.ndf',

SIZE = 100MB

)

LOG ON

(

NAME = billtracking_log,

FILENAME = 'd:\log\billtracking.ldf',

SIZE = 50MB

)
```

MICROSOFT CERTIFIED DATABASE ADMINISTRATOR

4

Creating and Managing Database Objects

T

he database is only one object that must be administered in a SQL 2000 server. You must have some understanding of the objects that reside within a database, particularly those objects that improve performance and create stability within the database.

You will be expected to have an understanding of how to create and manage the various constraints, both within and between tables. You will be expected to understand how to implement, and how to maintain indexes to improve the performance of your database. You will need to have some understanding of stored procedures. You will also be expected to understand how and when to use triggers. Finally, you should understand how views are created and modified.

TEST YOURSELF OBJECTIVE 4.01

Creating and Managing Basic Database Objects

Although you won't be tested directly on certain objects, it is important to have some understanding of all of the database objects. In particular, you should know how to create and modify a table, you should know what a data type is, and you should be aware of rules and defaults.

The table is the most basic object in a database. It is where data is stored. Tables consist of rows and columns. A column contains one particular piece of information (such as a name or a fax number); a row contains one record. All columns have a data type. SQL Server has number of predefined data types. Data types dictate what type of data can be placed in a column. For example the int datatype will allow only integer values and a char(10) will contain a fixed-length character value 10 characters long.

You can also create your own data types. These user-defined data types actually map to system data types. User-defined data types are used to standardize the datatype for a particular column. For example, if you were the primary administrator for a database and you wanted all of your developers to use a char(10) for phone and fax numbers, you could create a data type called phone_no and map it to a char(10) data.

This data type can then be used when you create tables. To create a user-defined datatype, you use the `sp_addtype` stored procedure. The syntax is:

```
EXEC sp_addtype @typename = 'data type name',

@phystype = 'SQL Server data type [,  @nulltype = {NULL |
NOTNULL}

 @owner = 'owner name']
```

User-defined data types are created at the database level. Once you have created a data type you can use it in any table in the database. However if you move a table containing user-defined data types to another database, you must create the data types in the second database. Because they involve extra system resources to look up the mapping, you should minimize the use of these data types.

To create a table, you use the CREATE TABLE statement. The syntax for CREATE TABLE is:

```
CREATE TABLE tablename

(

column_name    data type [{NULL | NOT NULL}],

col2 …

)
```

The name of the table must be unique to the database and owner; the column names must be unique to the table. All names must meet the SQL Server naming rules (for example, they cannot be SQL Server keywords, they must start with an alphabetic character and they cannot contain embedded spaces). You can use delimited names if you must include spaces or reserved words, by surrounding them with square brackets "[]" (like "[order details]" which contains both a space and a reserved word). You should, however, avoid using delimited names. To create a table you must have the CREATE TABLE permission.

The final objects you should be aware of are defaults and rules. These are older objects that have been mostly replaced by constraints (see section 4.02). They still exist in SQL 2000 for backwards compatibility. Both are independent objects within a database and can be reused on multiple tables.

A default object is like a default constraint. If a value is not supplied for a column, the default value will be inserted in its place. You create a default with the CREATE DEFAULT statement. Once you have created a default, you can associate it with a particular column or user-defined data type using the sp_bindefault stored procedure.

A rule object is like a check constraint. It specifies what values are permitted in a column. The conditions of a rule are similar to the conditions in a WHERE clause. For example, you could create a rule that required data to be part of a list of values using an IN operator or require that data in a column fall within a certain range of values using the BETWEEN operator. You create a rule using the CREATE RULE statement and bind rules to columns using the sp_bindrule stored procedure.

exam
ⓦatch

You will not need to know how to create rules and defaults, but they often show up as incorrect answers. If you are given a choice between a DEFAULT or RULE and a CHECK or DEFAULT constraint, the constraint is generally the correct choice.

TEST YOURSELF OBJECTIVE 4.02

Creating and Managing Constraints

Constraints are used to control what data is allowed in a table. Constraints are also a key element in building a relational database.

There are five main constraints you need to be aware of, as listed in the following table.

Constraint	Description
Primary Key	Used to uniquely identify each row in a table. When a table has a Primary Key constraint, values in the column cannot be duplicated and cannot be NULL. A primary key can contain one or more columns. Uniqueness is maintained by a unique index, which is created automatically when the constraint is created. The index cannot be dropped without removing the constraint.

Constraint	Description
Foreign Key	Used to enforce referential integrity between tables. A foreign key must reference a primary key or a unique column. A foreign key column will allow duplicates but any value entered in the column must first exist in the primary key column. Once a foreign key value has been added, you cannot modify or delete the primary value, without first deleting or modifying the foreign key value. The primary or unique column can be on the same table as the foreign key or on a different table.
Check	The check constraint is used to qualify data that is entered into a column by either an INSERT or UPDATE statement. It checks all values against a certain criteria (much like a WHERE clause). It can use all WHERE clause operators.
Unique	A unique constraint requires that all values in a column are unique. However unlike the primary key, the unique constraint will allow a NULL to be entered into the column. Like the primary key, the unique constraint automatically creates a unique index on the column. This index cannot be dropped without dropping the constraint.
Default	Defaults only apply to INSERT statements. If an INSERT statement does not supply a value for a column with a default constraint the default value is entered instead of the NULL. However, if you explicitly place a NULL in a column (using the NULL operator) the default will not be applied.

Constraints are bound to the tables on which they are created. You can create and modify constraints with either Transact-SQL or the Enterprise Manager. To add a constraint in Enterprise Manager, you need to use the Design Table sheet. To access this Properties sheet, right-click any table and select Design Table. In the Design Table Properties sheet, click the Manage Relationships button (with the exception of the Primary Key constraint, which has its own button). The following illustration shows the Manage Relationships Properties sheet open. The mouse pointer is on the Manage Relationships button.

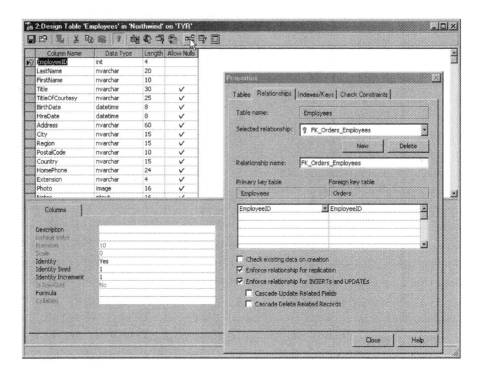

To add and modify constraints using Transact-SQL you must use either a CREATE TABLE or ALTER TABLE statement. You can add constraints as part of the column definition or after the column definitions. Just to make things more confusing, if you create a constraint on a single column it is referred to as a column constraint and if you create a constraint on multiple columns it is called a table level constraint. For example, this CREATE TABLE statement places a column-level, Primary Key constraint, and a table-level, Foreign Key constraint.

```
CREATE TABLE ConstraintExample
( Productid int CONSTRAINT pk_prod_prodid PRIMARY KEY
NONCLUSTERED,
   Productname varchar(40),
   Price money,
   ProductClass int   CONSTRAINT fk_class_productclass FOREIGN
KEY (productClass, category) REFERENCES
   class(productclass, category)
)
```

Each constraint is introduced with the CONSTRAINT keyword. They are each given a name and then the type of constraint is listed. The constraint names must be unique to the database. This code assumes that product class and category form the primary key of the class table.

Constraints are checked whenever an INSERT, UPDATE, or DELETE statement is submitted against a table (with the exception of DEFAULT, which is only checked on INSERT). DELETE statements are only checked on foreign key columns when you delete a value from the primary key column. If the operation violates the condition of the constraint, SQL Server cancels the operation and returns an error before the statement is executed. This makes check constraints very fast. This behavior is automatic.

exam
ⓦatch

Make sure you know when to use each type of constraint (particularly Primary and Foreign Keys). Also, remember that because constraints are checked before an operation is executed, they are more efficient than triggers. Triggers should only be used if you require more functionality than a constraint is able to provide.

QUESTIONS

4.02: Creating and Managing Constraints

1. You have created a table with the following script:

```
CREATE TABLE contacts

(ContactID int CONSTRAINT pk_contid PRIMARY KEY CLUSTERED,

FirstName varchar(20) NOT NULL,

LastName varchar(30) NOT NULL,

CompanyID int NOT NULL REFERENCES company(companyid)

City varchar(30) )
```

When you execute this statement, you get the following error:

```
Server: Msg 1767, Level 16, State 1, Line 1

Foreign key 'FK__contacts__Compan__3E52440B' references
invalid table 'company'.
```

```
Server: Msg 1750, Level 16, State 1, Line 1
Could not create constraint. See previous errors.
```

When you check, you find that the company table already exists and it has a companyid column. What is the most likely cause for this error? (Choose the best answer.)

A. The companyid column does not have a Primary Key constraint or a unique constraint.

B. You did not include the CONSTRAINT keyword in the creation of the foreign key.

C. You cannot have a NOT NULL foreign key column.

D. You cannot create a Foreign Key as a column level constraint.

E. You have to enable the Allow Referential Linking option on the database.

2. You are the administrator for a small retail company. You have several order entry people who must enter customer records into the same database. The majority of the customers are from the same city. Your order entry people are complaining that they must retype the same values repeatedly. What can you do to make it easier for the order entry people to add the customer records? (Select the best answer.)

A. Create a trigger that automatically enters the city.

B. Create a DEFAULT constraint.

C. Create a stored procedure that will automatically enter the city.

D. Create a check constraint that will replace the value of the city column if it is left null.

TEST YOURSELF OBJECTIVE 4.03

Creating and Managing Indexes

Indexes are used to improve the speed of queries. Like an index at the back of a textbook, you can use an index to quickly locate where a particular piece of information is stored in a database. If you are querying for one row from a table and do not have a valid index, SQL Server must perform a full table scan. That is, it must read all of the rows in a table to locate the value. Table scans involve a large amount of I/O and tend to be very slow. SQL Server stores indexes in the data file. Indexes are stored in a B-tree (B for Balanced) structure (see the illustration that follows). The B-tree structure has three levels:

Root level   This is the top of the tree. All index queries start at the root level.

Intermediate level   If large numbers of values are indexed, there may be one or more intermediate levels. These are like sub-root pages. They are sometimes referred to as non-leaf level index pages.

Leaf level   The leaf level is the bottom of the B-tree. It contains the actual data list for the index. All indexed values will appear in the leaf level.

B-tree index structure

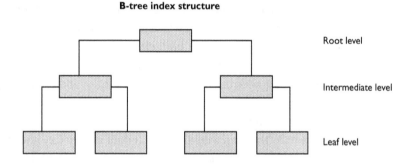

Root level

Intermediate level

Leaf level

There are two types of indexes in SQL Server: clustered and non-clustered. A non-clustered index stores a list of indexed values and pointers to where the row can be found in the table's data pages (the heap). In a clustered index, the leaf level contains the actual data. A clustered index will physically rearrange the data in a table and sort it according to the column that it indexed. A non-clustered index is like the index at the back of a textbook. It does not contain the data you are looking for; rather it contains a reference to where that data can be found. A clustered index is more like a phone book. The data in a phone book is physically ordered by last name. When you find a value in the phonebook, you also find the rest of the data for that record.

When you place non-clustered indexes on a table that already has a clustered index, SQL Server will use the clustered key instead of the row id pointer. The clustered key is simply the column(s) used by the clustered index. When you search this non-clustered index, its leaf level values contain a matching value that can be referenced in the clustered index. For example, if you had a clustered index on last name and a non-clustered index on first name, the leaf level of the non-clustered index would match each first name with a corresponding last name. It would then search the clustered index, based on that last name value, to find the rest of the data in the row. If you create a clustered index on a table that already contains non-clustered indexes, it will force SQL Server to rebuild the non-clustered indexes. For this reason, you should create clustered indexes before creating non-clustered indexes.

You create an index using the CREATE INDEX statement. The syntax of this statement is:

```
CREATE [UNIQUE][CLUSTERED | NONCLUSTERED] INDEX index_name
ON table(column(s))
```

If you do not specify which type of index to create, SQL Server will create a non-clustered index. You can create clustered and non-clustered indexes on multiple columns. This is known as a concatenated key. If you concatenate two columns together, SQL Server considers both elements as part of one value. For example, if you created an index on the first name and last name columns, it would treat Bob Smith as one value (which was different from Robert Smith and Jane Smith). This can be a useful way of creating unique values for primary keys. It is also useful when creating a unique index. Unique indexes can be either clustered or non-clustered. They are used to enforce uniqueness in a column. Both the Primary Key and unique constraints automatically create unique indexes to maintain uniqueness in a column.

SQL Server maintains the contents of indexes dynamically. When you add or delete a row or modify a value in an indexed column, SQL Server automatically updates the index to reflect the change. This is important to remember from a performance perspective. Indexes will speed up queries, but they tend to slow down data modifications (inserts, updates, and deletes). You should avoid placing a large number of indexes on tables that will be heavily modified.

Because indexes store data in a sorted order, adding and modifying data causes the indexes to fragment. Just like tables, indexes store their data in pages in the data file. However, unlike tables, all of the data in the index is stored in sorted order. When you add data to an index and the page where the value should be inserted is full, SQL Server "splits" the page. SQL Server takes half of the data and copies it to another page. Splitting will fragment the index, causing it to take up more pages than may be necessary to hold all of the data. Also, as the pages split, the B-tree structure of the index is unbalanced (particularly if you add a number of rows that all have a similar value—like 60 users all named Smith). As an administrator you will have to monitor and maintain indexes. To detect the fragmentation of an index you use the DBCC SHOWCONTIG statement. This statement shows the degree of fragmentation on a table or index. For example, the following statement shows the degree of fragmentation to the product name index on the products table:

```
DBCC SHOWCONTIG ([Order Details], Orderid)


DBCC SHOWCONTIG scanning 'Order Details' table...
Table: 'Order Details' (325576198); index ID: 3, database ID:
6
LEAF level scan performed.
- Pages Scanned...............................: 4
- Extents Scanned............................: 3
- Extent Switches............................: 2
- Avg. Pages per Extent......................: 1.3
- Scan Density [Best Count:Actual Count].......: 33.33% [1:3]
- Logical Scan Fragmentation .................: 0.00%
- Extent Scan Fragmentation ...................: 0.00%
- Avg. Bytes Free per Page...................: 2169.8
- Avg. Page Density (full)...................: 73.19%
DBCC execution completed. If DBCC printed error messages,
contact your system administrator.
```

The output of this statement shows how fragmented an index is, and how full each index page is. The Scan Density [Best Count:Actual Count] value shows what percentage of pages are contiguous. There are four pages on three extents so there are no more than two pages out of eight on each extent dedicated to the index. The values in square brackets show the optimum number of extent switches and the actual number of extent switches. If the index was unfragmented, the ratio would be 1:1 (since all four pages would fit in one extent). The Avg. Page Density shows what percentage of the page is full.

For the exam, make sure you are familiar with reading the output of the DBCC SHOWCONTIG statement.

When an index is too fragmented, you must re-index it to rebalance the tree. You can re-index one of two ways: you can use the DBCC DBREINDEX statement, or you can run the CREATE INDEX statement with the DROP_EXISTING option. When you re-index you can also set a FILLFACTOR value. The fill factor leaves a percentage of free space on each leaf level index page. If the table being indexed is heavily modified, the fill factor will reduce the amount of splitting in the index (since room has been left on each page for data to be inserted). The amount of fill factor will depend on the expected amount of activity and the size of the table. If a table is heavily modified you will want to leave an appropriate amount of space. However, leaving 10% of a 10,000-row table is much different than leaving 10% of 10,000,000 rows. The fill factor value represents what percent of the page to fill with data. For example, suppose you issued the following statement:

```
DBCC DBREINDEX ([Order Details], Orderid, 60)
```

SQL would rebuild the Orderid index on the Order Details table but would only fill each page to 60% (leaving 40% free space). If you set a fill factor to 0, SQL Server will interpret this as no fill factor (or the same as fill factor 100%). It is impossible to fill each page with 100% free space, as this would prevent any data from being stored. The fill factor is not dynamically maintained, and as data is added to the underlying tables, the amount of free space will get smaller. The Avg. Page Density (full) value in the DBCC SHOWCONTIG statement shows the current fill amount for each index.

Using the CREATE INDEX statement with the DROP_EXISTING option is also how you would alter an index after it has been created. There is no ALTER INDEX statement in Transact-SQL.

SQL Server 2000 has added the ability to place indexes on views. When you do this, you place the actual data in view into the leaf level of the index. This allows you to examine the contents of the view without running the underlying query. You should avoid these indexes if the underlying tables are modified heavily, as the overhead required to maintain these indexes will be very high. In order to create an index on a view, you must include the WITH SCHEMABINDING option in the CREATE VIEW statement. This option prevents the underlying tables from being modified unless the view is first dropped.

QUESTIONS

4.03: Creating and Managing Indexes

3. Some of the application developers in your department have noticed that one of the queries in their application runs very slowly. The query returns all sales for a given week that has a price that falls within a particular range of values. The query returns all values ordered from highest to lowest. This table is heavily modified throughout the week. Currently there are no indexes on the table. What could you do to make this query perform faster? (Choose the best answer.)

   A. Create a non-clustered index with a fill factor of 60.

   B. Create a clustered index with a fill factor of 10.

   C. Create a clustered index with a fill factor of 60.

   D. Create a non-clustered index with no fill factor.

   E. Create a clustered index with a fill factor of 0.

4. You have created a non-clustered index on the lastname column of a table called customers. The name of the index is cust_lastname. The customers table is updated frequently, as new customers are added and modifications are made to the records for your existing customers. For a while, queries which reference lastname have run quickly, however, your users report that these queries are starting to run much slower. You decide to re-index the column. You also want to leave 30% free space on each index page. Which of the following statements could you use to re-index the column? (Choose all that apply.)

   A. `DBCC DBREINDEX ('customers', 'cust_lastname', 30)`

   B. `CREATE INDEX cust_lastname ON customers(lastname)`
      `WITH FILLFACTOR = 70, DROP_EXISTING`

   C. `ALTER INDEX cust_lastname`
      `ADD FILLFACTOR = 70`

   D. `DBCC DBREINDEX ('customers', 'lastname', 70)`

   E. `DBCC DBREINDEX ('customers', 'cust_lastname', 70)`

TEST YOURSELF OBJECTIVE 4.04

Creating and Managing Stored Procedures

Stored procedures are simply blocks of SQL code that reside on the server. These blocks of code are named and can be executed by name. Stored procedures have several advantages:

- Since they are parsed when they are created, they do not have to be parsed again when they are executed. This makes subsequent executions faster.

- They can contain parameters that are passed to the procedure when it is executed.

- Because the SQL code resides on the server, you do not have to send large amounts of text across the network.

- Because the stored procedures reside on the same server as the databases, they do not need to cross the network to lookup metadata.

- When a stored procedure is first executed, its execution plan is cached and can be reused the next time the procedure is called.

- SQL Server may maintain several cached execution plans to allow parallel execution.

- You can centralize your application logic by having all applications call the same procedure rather than submitting the same SQL statements independently.

You can create a stored procedure either with the CREATE PROCEDURE statement or with Enterprise Manager. In Enterprise Manager, expand Databases, right-click the Stored Procedure folder and chose New Stored Procedure, as shown in the next illustration. In the window, type the code for the procedure. The syntax for the procedure is:

```
CREATE PROC[EDURE] owner.name

[@input_variable datatype, [@var2 …]]

AS

SQL statement.
```

You must give the procedure a unique name within the database. The statement after the "AS" can contain any valid SQL code.

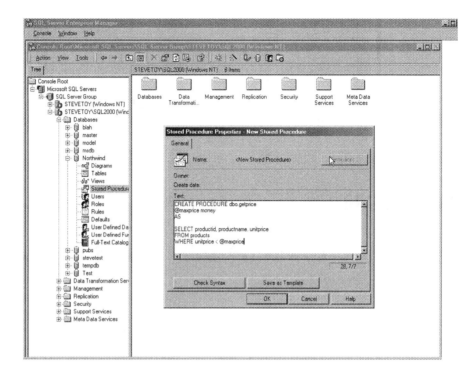

Stored procedures are contained in a particular database and must be executed from that database. For example, the following will execute the procedure shown in the previous illustration:

```
EXEC northwind.dbo.getprice 15
```

This procedure will return all products that cost less than $15.00. However, if you created the stored procedure in any database other than Northwind, this statement would return an error. The exception to this rule is the system-stored procedures. These procedures are created in the Master database and are identifiable by the sp_ prefix. When you execute a procedure beginning with sp_, SQL Server first looks for the procedure in the Master database and then looks locally if it does not find it in Master. This works for any database. For this reason, you should avoid use the sp_ prefix when creating your own stored procedures. The EXEC statement indicates to SQL Server that this is a stored procedure. If the stored procedure is called in the first line of a batch, this statement can be omitted. However, it is a good practice to include the EXEC statement whenever you call a stored procedure (including system stored procedures).

If you want to modify a stored procedure, you simply need to edit the text. You can do this by double-clicking the procedure in Enterprise Manager or using the ALTER PROCEDURE statement. With either of these methods you can completely alter the text of the procedure without changing its permissions. If you want to see the text of a stored procedure you can view it in the Enterprise Manager by right-clicking the procedure and selecting the Properties sheet, or you can execute the sp_helptext system stored procedure.

QUESTIONS

4.04: Creating and Managing Stored Procedures

5. You have recently been hired as the administrator for a SQL 2000 server. The person who was administering the server before you created several stored procedures to handle repetitive administrative tasks. However, he failed to document the procedures properly. How can you examine each stored procedure to see what it does? (Choose all that apply.)

   A. Use the sp_helptext system stored procedure.

   B. Use the sp_showproc system stored procedure.

   C. In Enterprise Manager, right-click each procedure and choose Properties.

   D. Use the Open button to open each procedure in Query Analyzer.

   E. Use the DBCC SHOWPROC statement.

6. You have written a script that rebuilds all indexes on a table. You want to place this script in a stored procedure so that you can easily run the script. You want to be able to execute this procedure from any database on your server. What would be the easiest way to create this procedure? (Choose the best answer.)

   A. Save the CREATE PROCEDURE statement to a script and run it in each database.

   B. Create the stored procedure in the Model database.

C. Create the stored procedure in one database and then use the Enterprise Manager to copy the procedure to all of the other databases.

D. Create it in the msdb database with an sp_ prefix.

E. Create it in the Master database with an sp_ prefix.

TEST YOURSELF OBJECTIVE 4.05

Creating and Managing Triggers

Like stored procedures, triggers are blocks of Transact-SQL code that reside on the server. However, unlike stored procedures, triggers cannot be executed directly by name. Rather, triggers are created on a table or view and are invoked by an action against that table or view (either INSERT, UPDATE, or DELETE). The trigger action can be one or all three of these activities. SQL 2000 Server has two types of triggers:

INSTEAD OF triggers   In an INSTEAD OF trigger, the trigger code executes in place of the INSERT, UPDATE, or DELETE statement that executed the trigger SQL Server will allow you to create instead of triggers on views. This is the only type of trigger that can be placed on a view.

AFTER triggers   These triggers execute their SQL blocks after the triggering activity has occurred. These triggers are part of the same transaction that invoked them. As the name of this trigger implies, the modification actually takes place and I/O and processing time are expended; however the transaction is not committed. The trigger is fired after this modification is complete and it commits the transaction. Therefore, if the trigger issues a ROLLBACK, it undoes both the code of the trigger and the operation(s) that fired the trigger.

You create a trigger with the CREATE TRIGGER statement:

```
CREATE TRIGGER trigger_name

ON {table | view}

{FOR | AFTER | INSTEAD OF}{[INSERT][,][UPDATE][,][DELETE]}

AS

SQL statemet
```

For example, if you wanted to create a trigger that sent the sales manager an email every time a customer was deleted, you could create a trigger like this:

```
CREATE TRIGGER mail_mgr

ON customers

AFTER DELETE

AS

RAISERROR (50001, 10, 1),'/*error message: A customer has
been deleted from the customers table*/'
```

This trigger will only fire if a delete has taken place and will execute the script after the delete has been processed. Once you have created a trigger, you can modify it with the ALTER TRIGGER statement. As with the ALTER PROCEDURE statement, you can completely rewrite the SQL statements associated with the trigger using this statement. You can drop a trigger with the DROP TRIGGER statement. Dropping a trigger does not affect the table or any of its data.

exam
Ⓦatch

Microsoft's position is to move away from triggers. If you encounter a question that offers the choice of using a stored procedure or constraint instead of a trigger, that is most likely the correct answer (provided that the constraint or procedure is able to perform the required action).

QUESTIONS

4.05: Creating and Managing Triggers

7. Jim has created a view called supply_list. This view joins supplier information from the supplier table and product information from the product table. He wants users to be able to add data to both of these tables through the view (because he does not want to give the users direct access to the underlying tables). However, every time he tries to execute an INSERT statement he receives an error. How can you allow an INSERT statement to execute successfully against the view? (Choose the best answer.)

   A. Create an INSTEAD OF trigger on the view that executes two INSERT statements—one against each of the underlying tables.

    B. Create a FOR trigger on the view that executes two INSERT statements—one against each of the underlying tables.

    C. Create an INSTEAD OF trigger on each of the underlying tables. Have these triggers perform the INSERTS.

    D. Create an AFTER trigger on each of the underlying tables. Have these triggers perform the INSERTS.

    E. It is not possible to perform an INSERT on a view that is based on joined tables.

8. You are the database administrator for a manufacturing company. You have a table that requires some complex calculations to validate the data in a column. This validation must derive data from several other tables and perform a complex calculation on the data. The production manager wants the system to automatically rollback any updates that do not pass this test. How can you test data inserted into the table and rollback all rows that do not meet the requirements? (Choose all that apply. Each element will only reflect part of the solution.)

    A. Create an INSTEAD OF trigger that tests the values.

    B. Have the trigger only insert those rows that meet the criteria.

    C. In the body of the text, issue a ROLLBACK statement if the insert does not meet the criteria.

    D. Use a CHECK constraint to test the data before it is inserted.

    E. In the body of the trigger, issue a COMMIT statement only for those inserts that meet the insert condition.

TEST YOURSELF OBJECTIVE 4.06

Creating and Managing Views

Views are used to simplify access to data. A view is a SQL query that is named and can be used as if it was a table object. It can be used in the FROM clause of queries and can, in some cases, be used as the destination in INSERT, UPDATE, and DELETE statements. The purpose of a view is to present a subset of data from the underlying tables. This subset can limit rows or columns and can have multiple table sources. The syntax to create a view is as follows:

```
Create View name

AS

SQL query
```

The SQL queries can be simple or complex. A view is created with any legal SQL query. The following two views demonstrate the difference between a simple and complex query. The first lists the name and price of all products that are not discontinued. The second lists the total sale for each order and the sales person who placed the order.

```
CREATE VIEW productprice

AS

SELECT productname, unitprice FROM products

WHERE discontinued = 0


CREATE VIEW orderinformation

AS

SELECT e.firstname + ' ' + e.lastname AS Salesperson,
od.orderid, od.productid, od.unitprice * od.quantity as
"Total Sale", a.productavg as "Average Sale"

FROM employees e JOIN orders o

ON e.employeeid = o.employeeid

JOIN [Order Details] od

ON o.orderid = od.orderid

JOIN (SELECT productid, AVG(unitprice * quantity) AS
productavg FROM [Order Details]

GROUP BY productid) AS a

ON a.productid = od.productid
```

In these examples, the first view returns a subset of a single column. In the second example the view will show data from three tables (including the output of an arithmetic expression). Once created you can use both productprice and orderinformation in the FROM clause of the SQL query.

Views have several advantages. Views can help focus data by returning only what is required (such as the first example), and can conceal complex queries (as with the second example). One of the big advantages of views is that you can give a user permission to select from a view without giving them permission to access the underlying table or tables. This is an easy way to limit access to data without having to set permissions at the column level.

Once you have created a view, you can modify it with the ALTER VIEW statement. The ALTER VIEW statement allows you to change the definition of a view by rewriting the query that defines the view. For example, if you wanted to change the productprice view to include the productid column you would use the following:

```
ALTER VIEW productprice

AS

SELECT productid, productname, unitprice FROM products

WHERE discontinued = 0
```

With the ALTER VIEW statement you can completely rewrite the defining query. When you alter a view, any permissions set on the view are maintained. Since views do not actually contain data, the view will be automatically updated the next time it is accessed.

QUESTIONS

4.06: Creating and Managing Views

9. Jane is the administrator for several SQL server databases. One of her users in Human Resources needs access to some information from the employee, department, and payroll tables. The definition for the view is as follows:

```
CREATE VIEW dbo.employeeinfo

AS SELECT e.empno, e.firstname, e.lastname, e.address1,
e.city, e.state, e.zip, d.departmentname, p.jobclass

FROM dbo.employee e JOIN dbo.payroll p

ON e.empno = p.empno

JOIN dbo.department d

ON e.department_no = d. department_no

WHERE p.deptno IN (100, 200, 300) and p.jobclass = 'A'
```

For which object(s) will the user require permissions, in order to select from this view?

A.   Just the employeeinfo view.

B.   The employeeinfo view and all tables referenced in the WHERE clause of the query.

C.   The employeeinfo view and the payroll and department tables.

D.   The employeeinfo view and all of the underlying tables.

E.   Just the underlying tables.

10.   Susan is the administrator for a SQL 2000 server in the payroll department. She had created a view for the payroll staff with the following definition:

```
CREATE VIEW departmentview

AS

SELECT pd.* FROM paydetails pd

JOIN departments d

ON pd.deptid = d.deptid

WHERE dept_location = 'New York'
```

The payroll manager has asked her to add a column to the paydetails table which stores a value indicating whether the employee is paid by direct deposit or by check. She wants the view to include the new column. What must you do to include this new column in the view without changing all of the user permissions? (Choose the best answer.)

A.   Re-run the CREATE VIEW statement with the DROP_EXISTING option.

B.   Run the ALTER VIEW statement and include the same query as the original CREATE VIEW statement.

C.   Execute the `sp_viewrepopulate` to include the new column in the view definition.

D.   Drop and recreate the view using the DROP VIEW and recreate it with the CREATE VIEW statements. Make sure to use the same name and query definition.

E.   Do nothing. The new column will appear next time the view is accessed.

LAB QUESTION

Objectives 4.01–4.06

You are the database administrator for a small mail order company. You have created a database for the sales system and added three tables to help track sales: a product list table, a customer list table and an order-tracking table. (See the following illustration.)

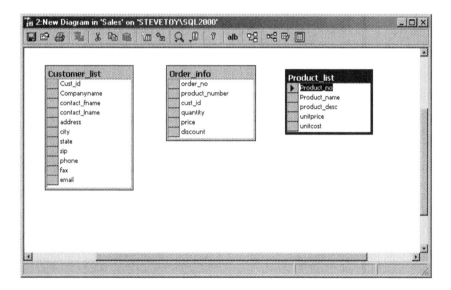

1. How would you link these tables together so that referential integrity is maintained between each of the tables?

2. Your product manager wants the system to make sure that the unit price for all products is at least 20% higher than the unit cost. How would you set this requirement in the table?

3. You want your sales people to be able to change the contact name and telephone number for the customers. However, you do not want to allow them to modify any other columns in the table. How would you achieve this?

4. You would like all of your sales people to be able to see the totals for their orders. Applying the discount to the unit price and then multiplying this value by the quantity sold determines the total. You would also like them to see the company name rather than the customer id of the customer. What would be the easiest way to make this information available to your salespeople?

5. Your users complain that when they look up a particular order, their application is very slow. What could you do to make their application run faster?

A QUICK ANSWER KEY

Objective 4.02
1. A
2. B

Objective 4.03
3. C
4. B and E

Objective 4.04
5. A and C
6. C and E

Objective 4.05
7. A
8. A and B

Objective 4.06
9. A
10. E

IN-DEPTH ANSWERS

4.02: Creating and Managing Constraints

1. ☑ **A** is the correct answer. When you create a foreign key constraint, you must reference a column that has a primary key or unique constraint placed on it.

   ☒ **B** is incorrect because the constraint keyword is not required when you create a column level foreign key constraint. When you place the constraint at the table level you must include the CONSTRAINT keyword. **C** is incorrect because there is no problem having a NOT NULL foreign key. The foreign key constraint itself does not prevent NULL values, so if you don't want the column to contain NULL you must configure it that way. **D** is incorrect because you can have a column level foreign key. **E** is incorrect because there is no option to allow referential linking. SQL Server is a Relational Database Management System (RDBMS). The core of a relational database (and what makes it relational) is the ability to link objects using primary and foreign key constraints. This capability is enabled by default and cannot be disabled.

2. ☑ **B** is the correct answer. When you create a default constraint on a column, the default value will be inserted in place of a NULL. With this default, if the city is the same as the default, the order entry people can simply leave the field blank on their form. The advantage of the default is that if a value is inserted in the column, that value will be recorded instead of the default. This means that the order entry people only have to enter cities that differ from the default.

   ☒ **A** is incorrect because a trigger is more costly than the default and the trigger will fire every time a row is inserted in the table. This includes when the operator intended to insert a city other than the default value. **C** is incorrect because the stored procedure would not allow you to enter a value other than the default. The majority of orders are from one city, but some are not. If you hard code the city into the stored procedure, this will not allow other cities to be inserted. **D** is incorrect because the check constraint is used to validate data; it can't be used to add values to a column.

4.03: Creating and Managing Indexes

3. ☑ **C** is the correct answer. Because the query is returning data in order based on a range, it will benefit from a clustered index. With a clustered index, the data is physically ordered on the index column. This speeds up range searches and ordered returns because SQL Server doesn't have to sort the data to complete the query. Because the table is modified, you want to set some fill factor. If you make the fill factor too large however, make the index larger (because the data will be spread across more pages). A fill factor of 60% will give room for expansion but will not make the index too large.

☒ **A** is incorrect because the clustered index will give more of a performance increase because the data is pre-sorted. If there were already a clustered index on this table then this would be correct (because you can only have one clustered index per table). **B** is incorrect because a fill factor of 10 would leave 90% free space on each page. This would greatly increase the number of pages needed to hold the data and would slow queries (because there are more pages on the leaf level to read through). **D** is incorrect because a clustered index would provide better performance. Also, because the table is heavily modified, setting a fill factor will prevent excessive page splitting. **E** is incorrect because setting a fill factor to 0 is the same as not setting any fill factor. A fill factor of 0 would mean that SQL Server would leave 100% free space on each page. SQL Server will ignore this request and set the fill factor to 100%. (That means it does not leave any free space.)

4. ☑ **B** and **E** are the correct answers. You can only re-create an existing index if you include the DROP_EXISTING option in your CREATE INDEX statement. If you omit this option you will receive an error stating that an index with the same name already exists. The DROP_EXISTING option forces the new index definition to overwrite the original definition. Any aspect of an index can be altered using this method (including the type of index and the columns the index is placed on). You can also re-index with the DBCC DBREINDEX statement.

☒ **A** is incorrect because it will leave 70% free space. The fill factor value will always represent the amount of data each page will hold. **C** is incorrect because there is not an ALTER INDEX statement in Transact-SQL. **D** is incorrect because the second parameter is the index name—not the column containing this index.

4.04: Creating and Managing Stored Procedures

5. ☑ **A** and **C** are the correct answers. Both the sp_helptext stored procedure and the Stored Procedure Properties sheet in Enterprise Manager display the text of the stored procedure. If you want to conceal the text of the procedure, you can include the WITH ENCRYPTION option when you create the procedure. If you choose that option, however, make sure to save a copy of the script because there is no way of decrypting the procedure once it has been encrypted.

   ☒ **B** and **E** are incorrect because these statements do not exist. **D** is incorrect because there is no "open" option in Query Analyzer. To open the text of the procedure you can either open the script that created the procedure, or you can locate the procedure in the object browser and select the Script Object To New Window As option.

6. ☑ **C** and **E** are the correct answers. When you execute a procedure with an sp_ prefix, SQL Server looks in the Master database for the code of the procedure, regardless of which database you execute the procedure in. This allows you to create your own system-stored procedures. You can also use the Object Transfer tool in DTS (accessible through Enterprise Manager) to copy the procedure between databases.

   ☒ **A** is technically correct, however, there are problems with having the same procedure in multiple databases. First, if you want to modify the procedure, you will have to make the modification in each database. Second, if you add a new database, you must remember to create the script. Finally, you will have to set the security for each instance of the procedure independently. **B** is incorrect because adding the procedure to Model will only add it to new databases, it will not update existing databases. **D** is incorrect because the MSDB database is used to store information on jobs and alerts used by the SQL Server Agent. It has no effect on system-stored procedures.

4.05: Creating and Managing Triggers

7. ☑ **A** is the correct answer. It is not possible to add data to more than one table using a single INSERT statement. Because the view is based on a join,

this is what Jim is trying to do when he issues an INSERT against the table. If he uses an INSTEAD OF trigger, he can separate the INSERT into two separate inserts against the underlying tables. With an INSTEAD OF trigger, the INSERT on the view does not actually take place and therefore SQL Server does not raise any errors.

☒ **B** is incorrect because the AFTER trigger will not fire until the INSERT has taken place (and the error has been raised). **C** and **D** are incorrect because if you place the trigger on the underlying tables they will never fire. The INSERT will be applied against the view itself and will fail before anything is inserted into the underlying tables. **E** was correct prior to the introduction of the INSTEAD OF trigger in SQL 2000.

8. ☑ **A** and **B** are the correct answers. With an INSTEAD OF trigger you can choose to insert only those rows that meet the requirements. There is no point in expending the I/O to insert rows that will not be accepted by the trigger. The INSTEAD OF trigger allows you to test first, and only insert those rows that meet the criteria.

☒ **C** is incorrect because a ROLLBACK is not necessary with the INSTEAD OF trigger. The ROLLBACK should be used with the AFTER trigger, but it is not as efficient because SQL Server will perform the update and then undo the update if it does not meet the requirements set by the trigger. **D** is incorrect because the CHECK constraint cannot validate data against values in other tables. This is one example where using a trigger is better than using a constraint. **E** is incorrect because if you do not COMMIT the statements for inserts that do not meet the criteria, SQL will leave these transactions open. This will cause excessive locking and waste resources.

4.06: Creating and Managing Views

9. ☑ **A** is the correct answer because you do not need permission on the underlying tables to select from a view (provided that the owner of view is also the owner of the underlying tables). You only require SELECT permission on the view itself. The creator of the view must have permission to select from the underlying tables. If ownership does not change, the user accessing the view only needs SELECT permission on the view itself. Ownership permissions are discussed in Chapter 8, section 8.06.

☒ **B, C,** and **D** are incorrect because each one includes one of the underlying tables. Access to the underlying tables is not required to access a view. **E** is incorrect because even if you had permission to all of the underlying tables, you would not be able to access the view. To get at this information you would have to query the tables directly.

10. ☑ **E** is the correct answer. Views do not store data. Every time you access a view, SQL Server runs the select statement that defines the view and uses the result set to populate the view. Because the query defining this view includes the * operator in the select list, it will return all columns from the paydetails table. This will include the newly added column.

☒ **A** is incorrect because there is no DROP_EXISTING option for the CREATE VIEW statement. This option is only present in the CREATE INDEX statement. If you were to run CREATE VIEW, you would receive an error stating that the view already exists. If you did need to change the view definition you would use the ALTER VIEW statement. **B** is technically correct, but unnecessary. The view is not physically stored anywhere, so running ALTER VIEW with the same query would not change anything on the server. It would just recreate the view exactly as it is. **C** is incorrect because there is no `sp_viewrepopulate`. Views do not contain data, and therefore don't need to be repopulated. **D** is incorrect because if you drop and recreate the view, you must reset all of the permissions. Object permissions are bound to an object's objectid value. When you drop and recreate the object, SQL Server will give it a new objectid (even if you recreate it with the same name). You must recreate the permissions with the new objectid.

LAB ANSWER

Objectives 4.01–4.06

1. You would maintain referential integrity between these tables by creating primary key\foreign key relationships. The easiest way would be to create a primary key constraint on the Cust_id column in Customer_list and the Product_no column in Product_list. Once you have created the two primary keys, you can then create a foreign key on cust_id in Order_info (referencing Cust_id in Customer_list) and another foreign key on product_number (referencing Product_no on the Product_list table). The column names do not have to be the same in each table. You will identify the correct column name in the CREATE or ALTER TABLE statement.

2. The easiest way enforce this rule is with a check constraint on the unitprice column. This constraint cannot reference other tables, but it can reference other columns in the same row. With this constraint in place, you will have to add data to unitcost before adding data to unitprice. The constraint would look something like this:

```
CONSTRAINT ck_unitprice CHECK (unitprice >= unitcost * 1.2)
```

3. You could to this two ways. The first would be to create a view that only contained the contact information and give the users update permission on the view. As long as this view only references one table this will work. You could also create a stored procedure with input parameters that performed an update based on those parameters. You could then give the users permission to execute the procedure without giving them update permission on the underlying table. The stored procedure gives you more control than the view, but requires more complete programming to deal with possible errors.

4. Again you could achieve this with either a stored procedure or a view. In this case, because you are querying data, a view is probably best. With a view, you can apply a WHERE clause to further limit the data returned by the view. With a stored procedure you would have to make further changes within the

procedure (which your users will not be able to do). The view would look like this:

```
CREATE VIEW orderview

AS

SELECT o.order_no, o.product_number, c.companyname,
(o.quantity * o.discount) * o.quantity AS "Total Sale"

FROM order_info o JOIN customer_list c

ON o.cust_id = c.cust_id
```

5. The easiest way to improve the speed of their queries is to place an index on the Order_no column. Because your users are querying for a specific order number and are not looking for data in ranges, a non-clustered index is probably the best choice. Without an index, SQL Server must perform a table scan (that is, read every row in the table) in order to find a single row.

MICROSOFT CERTIFIED DATABASE ADMINISTRATOR

5

Managing, Monitoring, and Troubleshooting SQL Server 2000 Databases

TEST YOURSELF OBJECTIVES

O nce you have created your database and its objects (such as tables, indexes, and constraints), you must optimize its performance. Optimization involves many factors. You will need to consider not only how to create indexes but when and where to use them. You will also need to be aware of locking in your database as multiple users attempt to access the same data. You will need to optimize the placement of physical data to improve access to the hard drive and you may need to alter your objects after they are created.

Optimizing Database Performance

For this objective, you must be able to plan and manage indexing within a database, pinpoint locking problems, and be aware of strategies that can reduce the likelihood of lock contentions. You must also be familiar with issues related to recompiling stored procedure query plans.

Proper indexing within your databases is critical for maintaining acceptable query response times. However, inappropriate use of indexes can cause transactional throughput to suffer and/or cause poor query performance.

Because clustered indexes require that each row in the table be correctly sorted, inserting a row into a table that has a clustered index can introduce two potential bottlenecks. The first of these issues is referred to as a page split. When a row is inserted into the index, it must be placed on the correct page. If no space is available on the target page, half of the data from that page will be moved to a new page in the index to make room for the incoming row. This can be avoided using the fillfactor and pad_index options when creating the index. These options will specify that as the system builds the index it should leave space on the leaf level (fillfactor) or non-leaf level (pad_index) pages in the index. The pad_index option cannot be used without the fillfactor option. It should only be used when many unique values will be inserted into the table in order to avoid page splitting in the non-leaf level pages of the index. For example, creating a new customer will require adding a new value to the table, but adding a sale on a given date is much less likely to require adding a new value and possibly splitting a non-leaf level page. Both settings are specified as a percentage, generally starting at 80% and increasing or decreasing based on row and table size and expected insert activity.

The second issue related to inserts in a clustered index occurs in RAID disk environments. When a clustered index is created on a RAID set, ideally the system should be able to balance all I/O load across all the disks within the set. When using a column where each newly inserted value will sort at the end of the index, most systems will not be able to balance the work across all the disks, as the amount of data written to the row will be smaller than the RAID interleave size; therefore all work ends up being done by one disk at a time in the set. Depending on the level of activity, this can offset many of the performance gains that you hoped to achieve. Unless you have very large rows and a very small interleave setting on your RAID controller, this will not be very effective and clustered indexes should be avoided on things such as identity columns and other sequentially valued columns.

Non-clustered indexes also suffer from the page split problem, although this is not generally as serious a performance issue as it is for a clustered index. The fillfactor and pad_index settings are only used during index creation and the free space left in data pages will not be maintained during normal index usage. As data is inserted into the index, pages may fill and begin to split again. This behavior can be tracked by watching for an increase in page split activity and then using DBCC SHOWCONTIG to determine how full the index pages are. Although DBCC SHOWCONTIG can be useful for determining whether pages are full, keep in mind that it displays the average free space for all pages in the table or index that you are running it against. Some data pages may be full while others are not, thereby causing page splits, even though the output says that the data pages are not full. DBCC SHOWCONTIG is more useful for determining if an index is fragmented. (For more information on DBCC SHOWCONTIG, see Chapter 4, section 4.03.) Index fragmentation will be discussed later in this chapter.

In addition to selecting the appropriate type of index, it is also important to create indexes on the appropriate columns. Generally, any columns used in JOIN operations, any columns that are referenced in WHERE clauses for your queries, and any columns that you use in ORDER BY clauses are good candidates for indexes. When creating non-clustered indexes for very expensive queries, you may want to "cover" a particular query by creating an index that contains all of the columns referred to by the query. This does lead to rather large indexes but can provide a substantial performance gain if the index is placed on a different disk or RAID set, thereby reducing the activity in the table. This can be done using filegroups, which will be covered later in this chapter. With careful planning you can create an index that will cover multiple queries, reducing the need to create redundant indexes. If all data for a particular query is available within an index, (in cases where all the columns selected in the query are part of the index), SQL

Server can retrieve rows for the query from the index without causing any locking in the table. This can greatly improve performance in databases that are used for both reporting and transaction processing. Performance would be further improved by moving these indexes to filegroups on other disk arrays, reducing the I/O operations against the disks that contain the table itself. When creating clustered indexes, only one clustered index can be created on each table, and as mentioned previously it is important to plan your clustered index carefully to avoid excessive page splits.

Clustered indexes are based on one or more columns from your table. These columns form the clustering key for the index. The clustering key should generally have one or more of the following characteristics:

Narrow   Use of a wide column (or a collection of columns) will require additional storage space for each non-clustered index that you create and will also increase the amount of read I/O operations in the indexes.

Static   It is best to avoid updating the values that form the clustering key, reducing the need to move rows within the index.

Searched in a Range   If queries are run against the clustering key in a range, the structure of the clustered index allows substantial performance gains by allowing the system to scan the index for a starting row and then use pointers in the leaf level pages to retrieve the rows without having to search the index several times.

Used to select specific rows from the table. If you commonly run queries or reports that select single rows of the table, based on a specific column or set of columns, having all of the columns stored in the index will improve lookup performance. This can cause I/O "hot spots" in some scenarios and should be used with caution.

In order to make it easier to select indexes, you can use the Index Tuning Wizard, which is part of the Profiler utility. For purposes of the exam you should be familiar with both these tools, as well as the creation of indexes and the use of DBCC SHOWCONTIG.

Much like indexing, locking can also have a substantial impact on performance. Locking, however is not controlled directly the way that indexing is. Locking can be controlled indirectly using techniques such as locking hints and transaction isolation levels.

Locking within a database ensures that transactions cannot interfere with one another, by controlling access to various data structures within the database. Locks generally are maintained on a row-by-row basis, although the system can lock data pages, tables, extents—even the entire database! Locking at different levels can allow improved performance for operations such as bulk data loads. For example, when loading thousands of rows from a file during a data import process, you can specify that the system should use table level locks. This will improve performance but would prevent other activity in that table. However, if data imports occur when there is no other activity in the table, this should not be a problem. Locks can be either shared or exclusive, although locks can be converted between the two modes, such as with an update lock that can operate in both shared and exclusive mode as appropriate. Shared locks are used to specify that a given page needs to be read by a transaction. Multiple transactions can read the same data structure without interfering with one another. Naturally, this is why the term "shared" was used. Exclusive locks are obtained when a page needs to be modified. An exclusive lock cannot be obtained when any other locks are held on that data structure, hence the term "exclusive." If an exclusive lock needs to be obtained on an object that already has other locks on it, the system will place the lock request into a queue, in order to allow the transactions that are holding locks to release them. The amount of time that the transaction should wait to obtain the locks that it requires can be configured using the SET LOCK_TIMEOUT statement. This can be set independently for different database connections as needed.

In order to provide some control over the locking process, SQL Server does provide the ability to specify the lock strategy that should be used. It is highly recommended that locking hints be avoided and that locking be controlled by the system. In order to ensure proper locking performance, it is recommended that developers and DBAs focus on solid transaction design and proper indexing. These two strategies combined provide the system with the best opportunity to lock effectively. Transactions should be kept as short as possible and indexes should be used to reduce the amount of time that SQL Server requires to accommodate the transactions.

SQL Server offers four transaction isolation levels, which can be used to control the locking behavior of a transaction:

> **READ COMMITTED**   This is the default isolation level. When attempting to read data that is exclusively locked, the system will wait for the exclusive lock to be released.

> **READ UNCOMMITTED**   This isolation level allows you to view data that has been modified, even if the transaction has not been committed. The system does not need to wait for locks to be released when querying data that is exclusively locked.

REPEATABLE READ   This isolation level will force the system to maintain all shared locks acquired during the transaction for the duration of the transaction. This prevents other transactions from modifying or deleting any of the data that was selected. This allows subsequent queries in the same transaction to ensure that no data has been changed or deleted.

SERIALIZABLE   This isolation level also forces the system to maintain shared locks for the duration of the transaction. Furthermore, if indexes are in place on the columns referred to in the WHERE clause of your queries, no new data can be inserted for values that match the conditions of any of the WHERE clauses in that transaction. This ensures that no data will have changed if any data is queried multiple times in the transaction, whereas REPEATABLE READ will allow new data to be inserted while only preventing update and delete activity.

There is one locking scenario, however that requires special attention and consideration. A "deadlock" can occur when two transactions are waiting on one another to complete. Neither transaction can continue until the other has finished and the system must select one of the transactions to be cancelled. Deadlocks can be avoided by applying the general design principles regarding transactions and indexing mentioned earlier, but additional care should be applied when designing transactions to ensure that tables are always updated in the same order to avoid the deadlock situation. Client applications should also be developed to respond gracefully by checking for error number 1205 (which indicates that the transaction was cancelled due to a deadlock). The transaction can then be repeated, and hopefully a new deadlock will not occur. In order to control which transaction will be cancelled in the event of a deadlock, you can use the SET DEADLOCK PRIORITY statement in your Transact-SQL code. To help isolate the cause of deadlocks, you can use the Create Trace Wizard in Profiler. Choose the Deadlock Trace option when asked what type of trace you would like to create. While the trace is running, user activity will be monitored for the cause of the deadlocks.

For purposes of the exam, you should be familiar with the concept of locking, general design principles that should be applied to avoid locking problems and the tools available to monitor locking within SQL Server. General locking concepts and principles have been discussed; the tools available for monitoring locking will be covered in the following section.

SQL Server provides these tools for monitoring locking and blocking within a database:

- Windows 2000 System Monitor (referred to as Performance Monitor on NT)
- SQL Server Profiler
- sp_lock system stored procedure
- sp_who system stored procedure
- Current Activity monitor in the Enterprise Manager

In order to monitor the occurrence of deadlocks and the data such as the average lock wait time, the System Monitor should be used.

To determine if one transaction is blocking another (causing the blocked transaction to wait) you can use either SP_WHO or the Current Activity monitor. See the following illustration to view an example of the Current Activity tool.

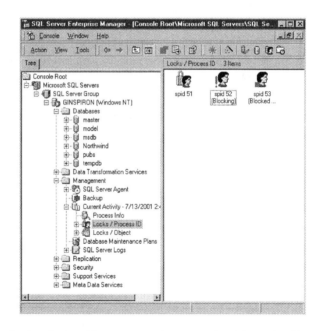

To view the locks obtained by a transaction, you should use the Current Activity monitor or the Profiler.

Recompiling

When a stored procedure is run, the procedure is compiled by the query processor and stored in a system table. On subsequent executions, the stored procedure query plan is retrieved from the table (unless the query plan is already resident in the cache), in order to avoid having to recompile the procedure on subsequent executions.

For most procedures, the compile time is not particularly significant, but if a particular piece of code will be run with heavy frequency or by many users, even small savings can add up to provide a substantial benefit. These benefits do not come without a tradeoff, however. As the underlying conditions within the database (such as indexing) are changed, the stored query plan associated with a procedure may no longer be optimal. As such, one of the considerations when planning the use of stored procedures is determining when a procedure's query plan should be rebuilt and the most appropriate approach to use to accomplish this.

Stored procedures will automatically be recompiled whenever an index on a table referenced by the procedure is dropped, or if the ALTER TABLE statement is run against any tables referenced by the procedure. As of SQL Server 2000, each procedure will be recompiled on the first execution following a restart of the instance.

You would need to recompile the procedure manually when the number of rows or distribution of values in the tables used by the procedure change sufficiently that the system may be able to use different row retrieval and table join strategies for the queries in the procedure.

There are a few ways that we can control the recompile process. A stored procedure can be created using the WITH RECOMPILE option, in which case the procedure will be recompiled on each execution. Generally, this is used with procedures that can be run against any table in the database using a parameter. Each subsequent execution can generate a very different query plan, and therefore even trying to store the query plan may simply be a wasted effort. Stored procedures can also be recompiled when they are executed, using the EXEC statement with the WITH RECOMPILE option. This allows us to force the system to recompile the procedure as needed, but isn't always appropriate, since the procedure will actually be run. The third option, which provides for very good flexibility, is to use the sp_recompile stored procedure to recompile procedures on demand. sp_recompile is used on a table-by-table basis and will force any stored procedures that reference those tables to be recompiled by the system the next time they are executed. This provides for recompilation as necessary but does not execute the procedures. You can easily create a scheduled job to recompile procedures associated with particular tables as needed without the concern of having the procedure do something inappropriate, such as in a case where a procedure may modify the database.

QUESTIONS

5.01: Optimizing Database Performance

1. You're planning the indexes for a table that will contain customer sales data. The script used to create the table is as follows:

```
CREATE TABLE SALES_DATA

(ORDER_ID INT PRIMARY KEY CLUSTERED,

CUST_ID INT FOREIGN KEY REFERENCES CUSTOMERS(CUST_ID),

LOCATION_ID INT FOREIGN KEY REFERENCES LOCATIONS(LOCATION_ID),

REP_ID INT FOREIGN KEY REFERENCES SALES_REPS(REP_ID),

ORDER_DATE DATETIME,

SALES_CODE INT,

TOTAL_VALUE MONEY)
```

This table will be used to store up to three months worth of sales data. Any data older than three months will be removed from the database, but will still be available within the data warehouse.

You anticipate as many as 10,000 new sales records per day. Each week a report will be run to summarize the sales by region. This is the only active reporting that is done in the database; all other user activity is related to transaction processing. The query that will be run is as follows:

```
SELECT LOCATION_ID, SUM(TOTAL_VALUE) FROM SALES_DATA WHERE

ORDER_DATE BETWEEN (GETDATE()-7) AND GETDATE()

GROUP BY LOCATION_ID
```

What index should you create to ensure that this report will run efficiently?

A. Create a non-clustered index on LOCATION_ID.

B. Change the clustered index to the TOTAL_VALUE column.

C. Change the clustered index to the ORDER_DATE column.

D. Create a composite non-clustered index on TOTAL_VALUE, LOCATION_ID, and ORDER_DATE.

2. Your database development team is currently testing a new application against a SQL Server 2000 database. They are concerned that a significant portion of the time, they receive error messages stating that the transaction has been selected as the victim of a deadlock, and they need to re-run the transaction. Upon viewing the Deadlocks/Sec counter in the System Monitor, you notice that as many as 50 deadlocks are occurring per second during heavy system load. What can be done to alleviate this problem?

A. Client applications should be designed to simply resubmit the transaction when this occurs.

B. Indexes should be rebuilt to reduce fragmentation.

C. Transactions should be configured with a lower lock timeout value.

D. Transactions should be redesigned to reduce the occurrence of the deadlocks.

3. Users who need to run reports in the database are complaining that some of the time, the query takes significantly longer to run than normal. Upon further investigation, you suspect that this may be due to other activity in the database interfering with the report. What tool can you use to easily determine which user connections are blocking the report from running?

A. System Monitor

B. Profiler

C. `sp_lock`

D. `sp_who`

4. You are troubleshooting a poorly performing query. The text of the query is as follows:

```
SELECT PLANT_NO, PART_NO, LOT_NO, AVG(FIDELITY)

FROM YIELD_INFO (TABLOCK)

GROUP BY PART_NO, PLANT_NO, LOT_NO

HAVING AVG(FIDELITY) < 4

WHERE PART_NO IN ('14355-780', '13453-770', '34258-760')
```

This query is only run occasionally, and always when no other activity is occurring in the table. How can you improve performance for this query?

A. Create a non-clustered index on the FIDELITY column.

B. Remove the TABLOCK locking hint.

C. Create a non-clustered index on the PART_NO, PLANT_NO, LOT_NO, and FIDELITY columns.

D. Create statistics on the FIDELITY column.

5. You currently use the Database Maintenance Plan Wizard to rebuild all indexes in your database on a twice-weekly basis. Users are complaining that after periods of heavy activity, system performance is poor. Upon further investigation, the problems seem to disappear after the indexes on the table are rebuilt. Using the System Monitor during the peak periods, you determine that the Page Splits/Sec counter and the Disk Write Queue counter seem abnormally high. After the periods of heavy system activity, DBCC SHOWCONTIG indicates that the clustered index for the table is heavily fragmented. How can you alleviate this problem?

A. Create a performance alert to rebuild the clustered index automatically after periods of heavy load.

B. Enable the Auto Update Statistics property for your database.

C. Increase the fill factor setting for the clustered index.

D. Use DBCC INDEXDEFRAG to defragment the clustered index when this occurs.

TEST YOURSELF OBJECTIVE 5.02

Optimizing Data Storage

Managing I/O effectively within SQL Server requires not only an efficient database design, but also a proper storage infrastructure in place to support the differing needs of various portions of your database. Although to many people RAID-5 is "all you'd ever need," this is simply not the case. RAID-5 does provide a fairly good cost/performance ratio, but you would never want to use it for your transaction logs due to the write overhead involved in calculating parity data. (For more information on RAID, see Chapter 3, section 3.06.) Within the actual database, we also have various components competing not only for disk time, but also requiring different types of I/O. Some tables in your database may be very read-intensive, while others may be used exclusively for writing. Not only can this reduce performance while various activities within your database compete with one another, the performance goals for a read-intensive table versus a write-intensive table are not always compatible.

In order to alleviate this, you may want to split part of your database on to another physical disk or a different RAID set. This not only allows the formerly competing activities to proceed without hindering one another, it also provides the opportunity to use different RAID types or take advantage of different speed disks depending on the needs of different tables.

SQL Server allows multiple data files to be created for a database quite easily. By default, when new files are created in the database, SQL Server will add them to the primary filegroup for the database and any objects created will be stored across the various files in that filegroup. This does not provide an opportunity to manually place tables or indexes on the disks that are most appropriate. In order to do that, additional filegroups must be created, one or more data files must be created on the appropriate disks, and then those data files must be added to the new filegroup. From this point, objects may be placed on the new filegroup(s) as appropriate. There are various data structures that can be created this way: tables; indexes; and columns that use the text, ntext or image datatypes.

A good example of using multiple disks in conjunction with filegroups would be to place the indexes for a heavily accessed table on one or more disks separate from the actual table. This would allow reads to occur from the indexes even when the tables are relatively busy.

One major drawback to using filegroups is that an object cannot span multiple groups the way that they can span multiple data files. Space management becomes more complex because you will need to ensure that each filegroup has sufficient space or room for growth to accommodate the objects.

If necessary, filegroups can also be marked read-only to prevent updates to portions of the database. To set a filegroup to read-only, you would use the ALTER DATABASE statement or Enterprise Manager, as shown in the illustration that follows. This option can be changed as often as you like; for example at the end of the quarter you might place certain parts of the database in read-only mode while various fiscal reports are being run, to ensure that the various different reports generated are all based on the same data. For details on how to create filegroups see Chapter 3, section 3.03.

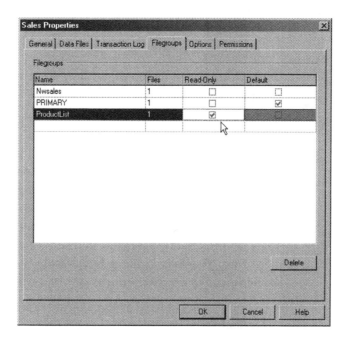

QUESTIONS

Objective 5.02: Optimizing Data Storage

6. You are the administrator of a SQL Server-based data warehouse. About ten very small tables are used for various lookups to cross-reference part numbers with particular manufacturing plants and production lines, as well as for geographic information such as zip and area codes. Users do occasionally update this information, but under very controlled circumstances, to ensure consistency when users do analysis of the data. Due to the restrictions on when these tables can be changed, you want to ensure that none of the users who are responsible for maintaining this data can make changes at inappropriate times. What is the best way to accomplish this? (Choose all that apply.)

   A. Create a scheduled job to grant and remove user permissions to update the tables at the appropriate times.

   B. Place all lookup tables on a new filegroup.

   C. Mark the new filegroup as read-only. Remove this option at the appropriate times using a scheduled task.

   D. Mark the filegroup as DBO Use Only. Remove this option at the appropriate times.

7. You are the administrator of a database that is used for both transaction processing and reporting. Due to user complaints about the length of time required to run various queries, you have deployed a number of new non-clustered indexes. This has caused some transactions to be processed more slowly, and you notice an increase in disk queuing during your performance monitoring. You do not seem to be exhibiting any locking problems. What should you do to improve performance? (Select all that apply.)

   A. Drop all non-clustered indexes. Create a composite clustered index on the columns used by the reports in each table.

   B. Change the fillfactor on the non-clustered indexes to reduce the occurrence of page splits.

   C. Move all clustered and non-clustered indexes to a different disk or RAID set using filegroups.

   D. Move the non-clustered indexes to a different disk or RAID set using filegroups.

8. One of your databases is primarily used for decision support and reporting. After being in production for several months, you notice that performance of some reports is starting to suffer. You review the execution plan for the query using the Query Analyzer, and nothing in the execution plan seems abnormal. The query continues to use the indexes that it was intended to. What could be causing the sudden drop in performance?

   A. Index statistics are out of date.

   B. An inappropriate fillfactor was configured.

   C. The indexes are fragmented and should be rebuilt.

   D. The query plan must be refreshed.

TEST YOURSELF OBJECTIVE 5.03

Managing Database Schema

There are times when you may need to alter the schema of an object after you create it. For this objective, you should be familiar with the use of the ALTER TABLE statement to add, modify, or drop columns from a table; you should also know how to manage constraints associated with tables.

The ALTER TABLE statement can be used to add a column to an existing table using the ADD option. For example, to add a phone number column that will be allowed to contain NULLS to the customers table you would use this syntax:

```
ALTER TABLE SALES
ADD PHONE_NO CHAR(13) NULL
```

The column definition syntax for the ALTER TABLE statement is the same as the CREATE TABLE statement. When adding a column to a table, if the table contains data, it is important that you either allow the new column to be null or provide a default value for the column; failing to do so would prevent the new column from being created.

Removing the column from the table would use this syntax:

```
ALTER TABLE SALES

DROP COLUMN PHONE_NO
```

The ALTER TABLE statement can also be used to change the properties of a column in a table. You can modify the NULL/NOT NULL property and choose a new datatype. When modifying a column, you must ensure that any data already in the table will still be permitted. For example, you cannot change the nullability of a column that contains null values to NOT NULL. Conversely, you cannot change the datatype of a column that contains character data to the INT datatype. Any type of data can be inserted into a character datatype, provided that the length of the character datatype (CHAR, VARCHAR, NVARCHAR) is sufficient to store all the data. You can also convert a character column to a date column, if all the data is in a date format already.

You may also need to add or remove constraints on an existing table. As was discussed in Chapter 4, section 4.02, constraints provide a way to ensure that data in a table is appropriate to various business conditions such as ensuring that an inserted date is not too far in the past or too far in the future. Constraints are added to tables using the ALTER TABLE statement. For example, to add a constraint to check that a provided date is not more than two days in the past you could use this syntax:

```
ALTER TABLE SALESINFO

ADD CONSTRAINT DATE_CHECK CHECK

(ORDER_DATE >= (GETDATE()-2))
```

When adding a constraint to a table you can specify whether the system should validate existing data against the conditions of the new constraint. This is done using the WITH CHECK or WITH NOCHECK option. If the data had already been checked against this condition using another method (such as validation code in a client application), you can save considerable time by specifying that the data does not need to be checked. These options should be specified after the ALTER TABLE statement but before the ADD CONSTRAINT option. For example, to create the DATE_CHECK constraint mentioned earlier, without validating existing data against the new constraint, you would use the following syntax:

```
ALTER TABLE SALESINFO

WITH NO_CHECK

ADD CONSTRAINT DATE_CHECK CHECK

(ORDER_DATE >= (GETDATE()-2))
```

You can enable or disable constraints as needed to allow you to temporarily suspend checking of the constraint without needing to delete and recreate the constraint. This is also done using the ALTER TABLE statement. For example, to disable a constraint named CHECK_BALANCE in the ACCOUNTS table you would use this syntax:

```
ALTER TABLE NOCHECK CONSTRAINT CHECK_BALANCE
```

To re-enable the constraint you would use this syntax:

```
ALTER TABLE CHECK CONSTRAINT CHECK_BALANCE
```

When you are performing an operation that will modify a large number of rows in a table (such as a bulk import of data into the database), you can greatly improve the speed of the operation by temporarily disabling constraints. You can also disable constraint checking in tools such as DTS, allowing the system to import data that has already been validated at a faster pace.

Before you re-enable the constraints, you must check that all of the imported or modified data meets the condition set by the constraint. If any of the data violates the constraint, SQL Server will not allow you to re-enable the constraint. You will notice that the syntax for enabling or disabling a constraint is very similar to the syntax for checking existing data when adding a constraint. Do not get the two operations confused. For performance reasons, you should also remove any constraints that are not necessary. To delete the constraint permanently you would use this syntax:

```
ALTER TABLE DROP CONSTRAINT CHECK_BALANCE
```

Dropping a constraint does not remove or affect the existing data in the table.

QUESTIONS

Objective 5.03: Managing Database Schema

9. You are in the process of migrating data from a legacy system. You need to import four million rows from a flat file using DTS. You would like to ensure that the import can proceed as quickly as possible. All data was already checked against business rules when it was created in the legacy system. Which of these choices could improve import performance? (Choose all that apply.)

   A. Drop indexes on the table that you are importing into.

   B. Use the BCP utility instead of DTS.

   C. Disable all constraints on the table that you are importing into.

   D. Configure DTS to bypass constraint checking.

10. Due to new shipping guidelines, your manager would like you to ensure that users cannot enter orders to be shipped to Alaska or Hawaii. You want to prevent users from inserting the values AK or HI into the state column of the orders table. Which of the following statements will allow this? (Choose all that apply.)

    A. `ALTER TABLE ORDERS WITH NOCHECK ADD CONSTRAINT STATECHECK CHECK (STATE NOT IN ('AK', 'HI'))`

    B. `ALTER TABLE ORDERS ADD CONSTRAINT STATECHECK CHECK (STATE NOT IN (SELECT STATE FROM RESTRICTED_ STATES))`

    C. `ALTER TABLE ORDERS ADD CONSTRAINT STATECHECK CHECK (STATE WHERE STATE <> 'AK' OR STATE <> 'HI')`

    D. `ALTER TABLE ORDERS ADD CONSTRAINT STATECHECK CHECK (STATE NOT REFERENCES ('AK' OR 'HI'))`

11. You need to temporarily disable a constraint on one of your development databases. The constraint is called PART_NUM_FORMAT on a table called PARTS. Which statement can you use to do this?

    A. `ALTER TABLE PARTS WITH NOCHECK CONSTRAINT PART_NUM_FORMAT`

    B. `SP_DISABLECONSTRAINT PARTS(PART_NO_FORMAT)`

    C. `ALTER TABLE PARTS NOCHECK CONSTRAINT PART_NUM_FORMAT`

    D. `SP_UNBINDCONSTRAINT PARTS.PART_NUM_FORMAT`

12. You are attempting to change the nullability property for the primary key of one your tables to allow NULL values. You are unable to get it to work. What could be causing this?

    A. The primary key was designated as unique.

    B. The ANSI NULL setting is turned on.

    C. Primary keys cannot allow NULL values.

    D. A constraint has been created on the column to prevent NULL values.

LAB QUESTION

Objectives 5.01–5.03

You are planning the data file layout for your database. Your server has an external storage unit with six hard drives. Windows and SQL Server are installed on an internal RAID-1 set. Your database will store customer billing information, and will be used primarily for reports. Most of the data in this database is created by loading data from the OLTP databases, which is used for data collection. You will use DTS to transfer the data. When a billing amount is disputed or a payment is made via telephone, the billing tables must be updated. Payments made by mail or electronic means are processed in another database and the data is merged during off-peak hours. Updated activity is expected to account for less than 20% of the overall database usage. Your manager has asked you to design a storage layout with the following characteristics:

Required result:

- Billing data must be well protected to ensure that a hard drive failure does not cause system downtime.

- Transactions must be recoverable in the event of a system failure.

- You would like to ensure that I/O performance does not suffer due to transaction logging.

Desired result:

- Storage overhead should be kept to a minimum to reduce costs without sacrificing recoverability.

Proposed solution:

- Create one large RAID-0&1 set with four of the disks.

- Create a RAID-1 set with the remaining two disks.

- Create one large database file and place it on the RAID-0&1 set.

- Place the database transaction logs on the RAID-1 set.

- Specify the BULK_LOGGED recovery model for the database.

A QUICK ANSWER KEY

QUICK ANSWER KEY

Objective 5.01			Objective 5.02	
1.	C		6.	B and C
2.	D		7.	D
3.	B		8.	C
4.	C			
5.	C		**Objective 5.03**	
			9.	A, C, and D
			10.	A and D
			11.	C
			12.	C

IN-DEPTH ANSWERS

5.01: Optimizing Database Performance

1. ☑ **C** is correct because ORDER_DATE is the search argument. Since we are searching ORDER_DATE based on a range, creating a clustered index on this column provides the best option for this query. Clustered index selection will vary depending on the needs of all your database activity.

   ☒ **A** and **B** are incorrect because even though they are both referred to in the query, they are not used as search arguments and creating an index on either of these columns will not help cut the amount of I/O required for the query. **D** is incorrect because the TOTAL_VALUE and LOCATION_ID are not search arguments and using them in this manner will not be effective.

2. ☑ **D** is correct because although both **A** and **B** can reduce the problem, **D** provides the best option for reducing the heavy occurrence of deadlocks. Deadlocks are common in most databases, but an excessive number such as in this scenario generally indicates a more general design problem.

   ☒ **A** is incorrect because that will not solve the problem and will only cure the symptom. **B** is incorrect because index fragmentation will not directly cause deadlocks. Indirectly, they could be a contributing factor by causing increased transaction durations. In fragmented indexes, the additional pages being read due to fragmentation can cause locking problems within the indexes. This can lead to this type of deadlock behavior in rare instances. **C** is incorrect since the LOCK_TIMEOUT setting is not related to deadlocks but is used for lock wait situations.

3. ☑ **B** is correct. Using Profiler allows activity and locking information to be viewed over a timeline; this can be very helpful in isolating locking problems when many transactions are interacting and competing for locks with one another.

   ☒ **A** is incorrect because the System Monitor will not show information about blocking users. However, it can be used to display statistics such as the average lock wait time. **C** is incorrect because it will not display information about blocking directly. **D** is incorrect. It will probably require several subsequent executions to track locking issues in most scenarios because sp_who will directly display if one SPID is blocking another.

4. ☑ **C** is correct because by creating a covering index for the query you will improve the performance of the operation by reducing the amount of I/O needed to return the data.

   ☒ **A** is incorrect because FIDELITY is not a search argument. **B** is incorrect because in this case, specifying the use of a table lock will improve performance. **D** is incorrect because statistics are used for index and join strategy selection, not for assisting in the calculation of aggregate functions.

5. ☑ **C** is correct because it is the easiest and most effective way to address the problem.

   ☒ **A** and **D** are incorrect because they are very cumbersome solutions and are not very effective from a performance standpoint. They also do not address the cause of the page splits. **B** is incorrect because this issue is not related to the statistics.

5.02: Optimizing Data Storage

6. ☑ **B** and **C** are correct because they allow us to easily enable and disable the ability to change the data without requiring any other intervention.

   ☒ **A** is incorrect because it will require extra administrative effort to keep the scheduled tasks up to date as the permissions may change over time. **D** is incorrect because a filegroup cannot be marked as "DBO Use Only." This setting can only be used on the entire database.

7. ☑ **D** is correct because it allows us to reduce I/O contention by allowing both the table/clustered index to be read while the non-clustered indexes can also be read simultaneously.

   ☒ **A** is incorrect because it is unnecessary. Clustered indexes already contain all the columns in the table. **B** is incorrect because page splits in non-clustered indexes do not substantially affect performance. **C** is incorrect because moving the clustered index to a new filegroup will move the entire table. If the non-clustered indexes are placed there as well, this doesn't change anything and the problem will remain.

8. ☑   **C** is correct because fragmentation in the index would cause performance for data retrieval to suffer, as in this case.

    ☒   **A** is incorrect because if the statistics were causing the problem, the system would generate a different execution plan for the query. **B** is incorrect because an incorrect fill factor will affect transactional as opposed to query performance. **D** is incorrect because the query plan does not need to be recompiled.

5.03: Managing Database Schema

9. ☑   **A, C,** and **D** are correct. **A** is correct because dropping the indexes will reduce the amount of work that must be done during the import. **C** and **D** are correct because bypassing constraint checking will reduce the amount of work that must be done during the import.

    ☒   **B** is incorrect because BCP does not provide any advantage over DTS in this case.

10. ☑   **A** and **D** are correct because they use the correct syntax for the constraint definition.

    ☒   **B** is incorrect because subqueries are not allowed in constraints. **C** is incorrect because although the constraint definition uses the same operators as the WHERE clause, it does not use the WHERE clause itself.

11. ☑   **C** is correct because it uses the correct syntax.

    ☒   **A** is incorrect because the WITH NOCHECK option is used to specify that existing data should not be checked when the constraint is created. **B** and **D** are incorrect because there are no such stored procedures.

12. ☑   **C** is correct because primary keys, unlike unique constraints, do not allow NULL values.

    ☒   **A** is incorrect because primary keys, by definition, MUST be unique. **B** is incorrect because the ANSI NULL setting is designed to control client behavior when dealing with NULLS; it has no effect when explicitly defining the nullability of a column. **D** is incorrect because a constraint would have no effect on the ability to define the setting for the column; it would only affect the data being inserted into the column.

LAB ANSWER

Objectives 5.01–5.03

Separating transaction logging I/O and database I/O will improve performance by isolating transaction logging activity to specific disks. Using RAID for the transaction logs allows the log to be protected in the event of disk failure. RAID-1 incurs little overhead and is fairly cost effective.

Using the BULK_LOGGED recovery model allows the transaction logs to be used for recovery. Transaction log backups will take longer if non-logged operations have occurred, but will reduce the size of the transaction log compared to using the FULL recovery model.

Using RAID-0&1 is the least cost-effective method to protect the data. Although RAID-0&1 performs well, RAID-5 is cheaper due to the use of parity instead of mirroring for redundancy. RAID-0&1 requires twice as many hard drives as would normally be required, whereas RAID-5 only needs one extra drive.

MICROSOFT CERTIFIED DATABASE ADMINISTRATOR

6

Backing Up, Restoring, and Recovering SQL 2000 Databases

TEST YOURSELF OBJECTIVES

O ne of the key roles of a SQL Server administrator is to maintain data integrity in the event of a system failure. You must understand how to backup and restore the data in your databases. You also must maintain transactional integrity in the event of a failure. This chapter looks at all aspects of backing up and restoring data in a SQL Server 2000 database.

You are expected to know how to backup both system and user databases. You will also be expected to understand how to restore these backups. You should have an understanding of the database restoration process. You will need to understand the process of log shipping. You should also understand how to implement integrity checks and how to troubleshoot issues with transactions and logging.

TEST YOURSELF OBJECTIVE 6.01

Recovering System State

SQL Server recovers all databases whenever the SQL Server service is started. Recovery is an automatic process. SQL Server performs this recovery to maintain transactional consistency.

A transaction is one or more Transact -SQL statements that must complete as a single unit.

Consider a money transfer between two accounts. There is no Transact-SQL transfer command, so you must perform two separate UPDATE statements. The first statement would debit the amount from the first account and then credit the same amount to the second account. These are two separate statements, but logically they are inseparable. If the first update occurs, but the second doesn't occur, the transfer does not take place (and you are out the money as well). You avoid these kinds of inconsistencies with the BEGIN TRAN[SACTION] and COMMIT TRAN[SACTION] statement. Any DML operations (Inserts, Updates, or Deletes) between these two statements are read by SQL Server as a single transaction. The transfer statement might look something like this if you were to transfer $100 between account 123 and account 456:

```
BEGIN TRAN

UPDATE accounts

SET balance = balance - 100

WHERE account_no = 123

UPDATE accounts
```

```
SET balance = balance +100

WHERE account_no = 456

COMMIT TRAN
```

When SQL Server executes this statement, either both updates will occur or neither one will occur. SQL Server guarantees transactional consistency in the event of failure through the recovery process.

When you issue a data modification statement (INSERT, UPDATE, or DELETE), SQL Server actually performs the action in an area of memory known as the Buffer Cache. To reduce I/O, changes to the Buffer Cache are not written immediately back to the disk. Because information in cache can be lost if the server fails, SQL Server also makes a note of the changes in the transaction log. If you consider the money transfer example above, the transaction log records the begin transaction statement, each update and the commit statement. If the system stops for any reason, when the SQL Server service restarts, it checks the transaction log to make sure that all committed transactions that had not been written back to disk are recovered. This is known as recovery.

Whenever SQL Server starts, it goes into the transaction log for each database and locates the most recent checkpoint. SQL Server uses checkpoints to write data from the Buffer Cache back to the data files. This speeds up the recovery process because SQL Server does not have to recover from the beginning of the log. After locating the checkpoint, SQL Server then locates the oldest uncommitted transaction from that point and reapplies all committed transactions. It also rolls back any uncommitted transactions. Looking to the previous example, if the server failed between the first and second update statement, when SQL Server recovered the database it would see the begin transaction statement but no corresponding commit. It would then undo (or rollback) the first update. This is why the transaction log is essential for a SQL Server database.

SQL Server recovers every time the server service starts, even if you have stopped the server manually (for example, by using the Service Manager or the `net stop` command). SQL Server does not know why it has stopped so it checks transactional consistency each time. When you stop the server using Enterprise Manager or the Service Manager, SQL Server places a checkpoint at the end of the log. This speeds up the recovery process. Databases cannot be accessed until they have been recovered. If a database cannot be recovered (because of a missing file for example) it will be marked as suspect, as shown in the next illustration. If a database is suspect, it cannot be accessed until it is restored.

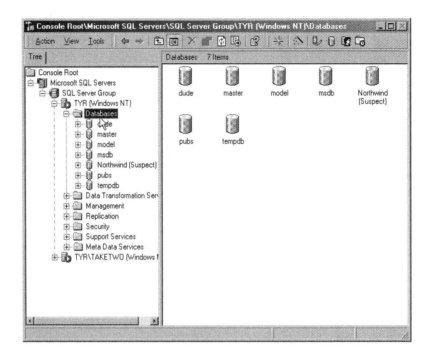

How data is logged, however, is determined by the recovery options you set in the Database Properties sheet. There are three recovery models. Each of these models determines how SQL Server maintains its logs, as shown in Table 6-1.

Regardless of the recovery model, however, SQL Server will go through the automatic recovery process. To set the recovery model, you can either user the Recovery pull-down menu in the Database Properties sheet or you can use the ALTER DATABASE statement:

```
ALTER DATABASE database_name

SET RECOVERY {FULL | SIMPLE | BULK_LOGGED}
```

exam

ⓦatch

If you are presented a choice between the truncate log on checkpoint option and the Simple recovery model choose the Simple recovery model. This model includes the truncate log on checkpoint option, but is the newer, and preferred method of choosing logging.

TABLE 6-1	Option	Description
The SQL Server Recovery Models	Full	When a database is in full recovery mode, all transactions, even transactions generated by a bulk insert or update processes are maintained in the transaction log after a checkpoint. This also includes the output of a CREATE INDEX statement or a bulk insert using bcp.exe or DTS. If one of these activities occurs, each individual insert is logged. The full recovery model allows you to restore the database to a point in time.
	Simple	When a database is in the simple recovery model, SQL Server writes transactions to the transaction log, but deletes committed transactions on checkpoint. When you choose the simple recovery mode, you can only restore to the last full or differential backup. This is similar to the SQL 7.0 option **Trunc. Log on Chkpnt.**
	Bulk-Logged	When a database is in bulk-logged mode, it maintains its transactions (like full recovery); however it does not log transactions resulting form large bulk operations (like a SELECT INTO, a CREATE INDEX statement, or an import of data with bcp.exe or DTS). If you perform one of these operations you will lose the ability to recover to a point in time and will only be able to recover to the most recent full or differential backup.

QUESTIONS

6.01: Recovering System State

1. Susan is the administrator for a SQL 2000 server. After installing an upgrade on her server she was forced to restart the server. Torn page detection has been enabled on the server. When SQL Server restarted, her users complained that one of the database applications was unable to connect to the database. When she checked the database in Enterprise Manager it was suspect. When she

clicked on the database, she could not connect to it. What must Susan do to make the database accessible?

A. Run recover.exe from the command line.

B. Right-click the database and select "connect" in the Enterprise Manager.

C. Restore the database from a backup.

D. Use the xp_restore stored procedure to force recovery.

E. Stop and restart the database using the `net start /forcerecovery:`
    `database_name` command.

2. You are planning the recovery strategy for a database called prod_test. This database will be created on a test server that tests the performance of new database applications. Data will be generated before each test by running a number of scripts to create and populate the tables and indexes. The tests run will normally consist of a large number of INSERT, UPDATE, and DELETE statements. You want to minimize the amount of administration on the database. Which statement would you use to configure your databases? (Choose the best answer.)

A. ```
    ALTER TABLE prod_test
    SET RECOVERY FULL
    ```

B.  ```
    ALTER TABLE prod_test
    SET RECOVERY BULK_INSERT
    ```

C. ```
    sp_dboption 'prod_test', 'trunc. log on chkpt.', true
    ```

D.  ```
    ALTER TABLE prod_test
    SET RECOVERY SIMPLE
    ```

E. ```
    ALTER TABLE prod_test
    SET RECOVERY NONLOGGED
    ```

**TEST YOURSELF OBJECTIVE 6.02**

# Backing Up User Databases

User databases are those databases that you create. They will contain your data and data objects (such as views, functions and stored procedures). It is essential to backup these objects to prevent data loss from both system failure and user corruption. SQL
    ```

Server includes its own backup tool. SQL Server can perform backups while the system is still available to users. Therefore, you do not have to stop the server to perform backups. In order to perform a backup you must be:

- A member of the sysadmin server role
- A member of the db_owner database role
- A member of the db_backupoperator database role
- A user, group or a member of a role that has been granted the BACKUP DATABASE permission

When you perform a backup, you have the option of backing up to a file, tape or to a named pipe. If you backup to a file, that file can be on either a local hard drive or on a network share. However, if you chose to backup to tape, the tape drive (or drives) must be locally installed. A named pipe connection is used to backup to another process (such as a third party backup tool).

There are four types of backups available with the SQL Server backup tool, as shown in Table 6-2.

	Backup Type	Description
TABLE 6-2 Type of Backups Available in SQL Server	Full	A full backup backs up all data files. It also saves the portion of the transaction log that occurred while the backup was running. Full backups record the location from where they backed up their files.
	Differential	A differential backup saves all changes since the last full backup. You cannot perform a differential backup unless you have first performed a full backup.
	Transaction log	A transaction log backup saves all transactions since the last full backup or the last transaction log backup. If you have not performed a full backup, you cannot perform a transaction log backup. Your database must also be in full recovery mode.
	File or filegroup	You can also backup individual files or filegroups. File and Filegroup backups do not require a full backup. If you have created tables on one filegroup and indexes on another, you must backup both filegroups together.

You should backup your user databases in the following conditions:

■ When the database is first created

■ When you add an index

■ Whenever you perform a non-logged operation

■ Whenever you truncate the transaction log using the NO_LOG or TRUNCATE_ONLY option of the BACKUP LOG statement

All of these operations prevent SQL Server from using the transaction log to recover the database. If the transaction log is not available, you will only be able to recover to your last backup. In addition, even if you have chosen the full recovery model, SQL Server will not maintain a transaction log on a user database until you perform a full backup.

For performance reasons, you can backup to multiple database devices. When you backup to multiple devices (for example multiple tapes or multiple devices on a separate disk), SQL Server assigns one thread for each device in the set and backs up to all devices in parallel. Once you backup a database to multiple devices, SQL Server will treat them as a media set. It will not allow you to make subsequent backups unless you include the whole set. You can backup multiple databases to a media set, provided that all members of the set are listed in the backup. All of the media in the media set must be the same. That is, you can create a media stripe with three tape drives or three disk files, but not a mixture of tape drives and hard drive files.

There are certain activities that cannot be performed while a database backup is running. These activities include:

■ Modifying the database with an ALTER DATABASE statement or the Database Properties sheet in Enterprise Manager

■ Creating an Index

■ Shrinking a Database

■ Autogrowth of a database or log file

■ Performing a nonlogged operation

The SQL Server backup process will block all of these operations from occurring while a backup is running. On the other hand, if another administrator is performing one of these activities, you will receive an error when you try to start the backup.

The first step in performing a backup should be to create a backup device. The backup device is simply a named location which is registered in the Master database. The advantage of using a backup device is that it is reusable and you can use it with SQL automation to automate backups. To create a backup device, you can use either

Enterprise Manager or Transact-SQL. In Enterprise Manager, right-click the Backup icon in the Management folder, and select Create New Device. With the Create New Device Wizard, give the device a unique name and a physical filename, including the full file path. You can also use the `sp_addumpdevice` stored procedure. The syntax for this procedure is:

```
sp_addumpdevice {'disk'|'tape'|'pipe}', 'logical
name','physical file'
```

The backup device, however, is not required to perform a backup and you can backup a database directly to the hard drive or to a tape.

To backup the database using Enterprise Manager, you can either right-click the Backup icon in the Management folder and select Backup A Database, or you can right-click any database and choose All Tasks | Backup Database. This will open the SQL Server Backup Wizard, as shown in the illustration that follows. On this form, you need to select the database to back up and the type of backup to perform. If a particular type of backup is not available, the option will be grayed out. For example in the illustration, the Northwind database is in simple recovery mode and has only one data file (and therefore only one filegroup). Because this limits the types of backup possible to full or differential, the File And Filegroup and Transaction Log backup options are not available. You can also choose the backup device (or choose to backup to a file) and whether or not to overwrite any existing backups in the device.

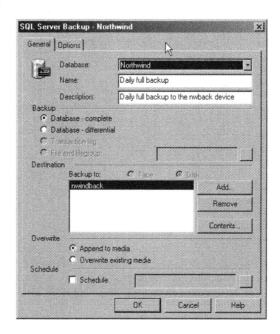

To perform a backup using Transact-SQL you must use the BACKUP DATABASE command. The syntax to perform a full backup of a database is as follows:

```
BACKUP DATABASE name_of_database
[File = 'logical_filename' | FILEGROUP = 'name_of_filegroup']
TO backup_device
[WITH option1, [option2, …]]
```

You can also backup directly to a file location (rather than a backup device) with the following command:

```
BACKUP DATABASE name_of_database
TO {DISK|TAPE|PIPE} = 'full path and filename'
[WITH option1, [option2, …]]
```

If you include the FILE or FILEGROUP options in the backup database statement, only those portions of the database specified will be saved as part of the backup. You can control how your backup saves its information using a number of options after the WITH statement. The options are listed in Table 6-3.

TABLE 6-3	Option	Description
Options for the BACKUP DATABASE Statement	INIT | NOINIT	This option will allow you to overwrite (INIT) or append (NOINIT) the backup to the contents of a database device. The default is NOINIT.
	FORMAT	This option turns off all safety checks. For example, it will allow you to break up a media set by backing up to only one member of the set.
	DIFFERENTIAL	This option will perform a differential backup rather than a full backup. A differential backup only backs up changes that have occurred since the last full backup.

To backup a transaction log, you use the BACKUP LOG statement. When you backup a transaction log, SQL Server performs a checkpoint, backs up the contents of the log and deletes all transactions prior to the last uncommitted transaction. For this reason, performing transaction log backups is the method of controlling log size. The syntax is exactly the same as the BACKUP DATABASE statement (with the exception of specifying BACKUP LOG rather than BACKUP DATABASE). It can include all of the same WITH options used in the BACKUP DATABASE statement, and also includes additional WITH options for specific situations (see Table 6-4).

TABLE 6-4	Option	Description
The BACKUP LOG Options	NO_LOG/TRUNCATE_ONLY	These options flush all transactions prior to the oldest uncommitted transaction from the log. They do not actually perform a backup of the file. They do not write an LSN to the log and can be used to clear the transaction log if it becomes full. In earlier versions of SQL Server, the TRUNCATE_ONLY option placed an LSN in the log and NO_LOG was the only method of clearing the log if it was full. TRUNCATE_ONLY is maintained in SQL 2000 for backwards compatibility.
	NO_TRUNCATE	This option backs up the transaction log without truncating any transactions. It does not force a checkpoint and is used when one of the data files is damaged or missing.

QUESTIONS

6.02: Backing Up User Databases

3. You are the administrator for a SQL 2000 Server. You are implementing a backup strategy for your Mail Order database. This database is currently 10GB

in size. It consists of two data files on different disks and a single transaction log on a third disk. It is accessed between 8 A.M. and 6 P.M. by order entry staff that processes and manually enters the orders. This database handles about 3000 transactions per hour. The server has a locally installed tape drive. You want a strategy that will be able to replace any of the physical files and will also minimize data loss in the event of a failure. What backup strategy would you suggest in this situation? (Choose two answers. Each answer will represent part of the correct answer.)

A. Perform a full backup each night.

B. Perform a filegroup backup each night.

C. Perform a full backup on the weekend.

D. Perform a transaction log backup periodically throughout the day.

E. Perform differential backups periodically throughout the day.

4. You are the administrator for a company that provides equipment manuals to online subscribers. All of the manuals are stored in text columns in the database. The current database is 500GB in size. It consists of four files on a RAID-5 array. There are roughly 200 documents added to the database each day. However the database is heavily queried 24 hours a day, 7 days a week. You want to back up the database to a local tape drive. However, if you were to perform a full backup it would take approximately 25 hours to complete. You have been asked to provide a backup strategy for this database. How would you implement the backup strategy? (Choose the best answer.)

A. Perform a filegroup backup each night. Perform transaction log backups throughout the day.

B. Perform a full backup once per week (at a point when access is normally lighter). Perform several transaction log backups throughout the day.

C. Perform a full backup once per week (at a point when access is normally lighter). Perform a differential backup each night. Perform transaction log backups throughout the day.

D. Perform a differential backup each night and perform transaction log backups throughout the day.

E. Once per week, take the database offline and perform a full disk backup.

5. Jim is the administrator for a SQL server called Corpdata1. One of the disks on Corpdata1 has failed and needs to be replaced. The disk contained one of the data files from a database called HRData. The transaction log file (HRLog.ldf) is still available on another disk. Prior to restoring the database, Jim tries to backup the transaction log with the following statement:

    ```
    BACKUP LOG HRData

    TO Hrlogdevice
    ```

    However, when he runs this backup script, he receives the following error:

    ```
    Server: Msg 945, Level 14, State 2, Line 1

    Database 'HRData' cannot be opened due to inaccessible files
    or insufficient memory or disk space. See the SQL Server
    errorlog for details.

    Server: Msg 3013, Level 16, State 1, Line 1

    BACKUP LOG is terminating abnormally.
    ```

    Why is he unable to backup the transaction log for the HRData database?

    A. He must reference the name of the physical file rather than the name of the database in the BACKUP LOG statement.

    B. He cannot backup a transaction log if one of the data files is not available.

    C. He must manually force a CHECKPOINT before backing up the transaction log.

    D. He must include the WITH FORMAT option in the BACKUP LOG statement.

    E. He must include the WITH NO_TRUNCATE option in the BACKUP LOG statement.

TEST YOURSELF OBJECTIVE 6.03

Backing Up System Databases

The process of backing up system databases is the same as the process used to backup user databases. It is important to know which databases require a proper backup and when they should be backed up. The system databases contain metadata. Metadata is the information that SQL Server requires to function. If SQL Server loses its key system databases, the server will no longer function. The data loss incurred by losing a system database can include losing users, databases or scheduled jobs. The four system databases in all SQL servers are Master, Model, MSDB and Tempdb. Of these four, Tempdb does not require a backup (because it is a space used by SQL Server to store information temporarily). If any of the remaining three databases become corrupt, you could seriously compromise your SQL server. It is also important to have a backup of these databases because the system database restore tool (rebuildm.exe) will drop and recreate all system databases—not just Master.

Of these three, the Master database is most important. It contains all server logons and a listing of all user databases. Without a Master database, SQL Server will not function. An out-of-date Master database can be even more trouble. If you restored Master with an out-of-date backup, you will loose any configuration settings, linked servers, server logins or user databases created since the last backup. You should backup the Master database:

- After modifying the master database using the ALTER DATABASE statement
- After creating or modifying a user database with the CREATE DATABASE or ALTER DATABASE statement
- After modifying the contents of the Master database with a system stored procedure (such as `sp_configure`, `sp_addmessage` or `sp_addlinkedserver`)
- After creating server login accounts
- After adding a user-defined error message using `sp_addmessage`

Physically, the Master database is quite small and can be backed up daily without any serious impact on database performance.

The MSDB database stores automation information. It is the database used by the SQL Server Agent. Tasks can include jobs, alerts, DTS packages and defined operators. Without the MSDB database, the SQL Server Agent service cannot start. You should backup the MSDB database:

- Whenever you add a new job, alert, or operator
- Whenever you modify an existing job, alert or operator
- Whenever you save a DTS package to SQL Server

If the MSDB database fails, the SQL Server service will still start. However, no automation operations will occur. If you do not have a backup of the MSDB database, you will have to manually recreate all automation tasks if this database fails.

The Model database is used as a template for all user databases. When SQL Server processes a CREATE DATABASE statement, it copies Model, renames it and expands the copy to the initial creation size. As was mentioned in Chapter 1, you can modify the Model database and have those modifications appear in all subsequent user databases. Whenever you modify the Model database, you should back it up. If the Model database is not available, both SQL Server and the SQL Server Agent will still function normally. The only thing that will be affected is the ability to create new databases. If you modify Model and don't back it up, all of your changes would be lost if you rebuilt the system tables. This may not seem significant because you will most likely not make a large number of modifications to Model. However keeping a current backup of Model will save you from having to recreate all of the modifications you (or any other administrator) have made to the database. As a general rule for all system databases, you should back them up whenever they change.

QUESTIONS

6.03: Backing Up System Databases

6. After which of the following statements should you perform full backup of the Master database? (Choose all that apply.)

   A. `DROP DATABASE northwind`

   B. `TRUNCATE table pubs..authors`

   C. `sp_addmessage (50001, 10, 'User %s was deleted from the system by operator %s')`

   D. `sp_add_alert @name = 'Notify Accounting Manager', @messageid = 50001, @severity = 10, @notification_message = 'The credit limit for customer %s has been raised to %d by %s'`

   E. `ALTER DATABASE MASTER`
      `MODIFY FILE (name = master.mdf, size =30MB)`

7. Jim is the administrator for a SQL 2000 server. He had made several modifications to the server. One modification requires him to stop and restart the server. When the server restarts, SQL Server detects a torn page in the MSDB database. In Enterprise Manager he notices that the MSDB database is marked as suspect. He does not have a backup for MSDB, but he does have a backup for Master. After he rebuilds the MSDB database, which of the following modifications must he manually recreate? (Choose all that apply.)

A. A job created using the DTS Import/Export Wizard

B. A new user defined error messaged created with `sp_addmessage`

C. A new job created with Enterprise Manager

D. A new backup device created with `sp_addumpdevice`

E. A new linked server created using `sp_addlinkedserver`

TEST YOURSELF OBJECTIVE 6.04

Restoring User Databases

Having an effective backup strategy is only part of protecting the data in your database. You must also be able to restore your backup sets in the event of failure or corruption. There are many reasons why you may need to restore a database. You may have a disk failure or user corruption (such as an unintentional or malicious update). You might also be recovering from a disaster such a theft or fire. How you restore your database depends very much on the cause of the failure. The restore process recreates databases from its own backups. The type of restore you use will depend on the type of backup being restored. With the exception of file or filegroup backups, all restore scenarios begin with the restore of a FULL backup. As with most things in SQL Server, you can restore either by using Enterprise Manager or using Transact-SQL. In Transact-SQL, you restore databases with the RESTORE DATABASE statement. The basic syntax for this statement is:

```
RESTORE {DATABASE | log} database_name

FROM database_device

WITH restore_option [, option2 ...]
```

If your backup is not stored in a backup device , you can restore it by specifying the media type (DISK, TAPE, or PIPE). For example, if you had backed up the

Northwind database to a file called nwback.bak in a folder called c:\sqlbackup, you would restore this backup with the following statement:

```
RESTORE {DATABASE | log} northwind

FROM DISK = 'c:\sqlbackup\nwback.bak'

WITH restore_option [, option2 …]
```

The outcome of both statements is the same, and they share the same options.

When you restore a database, the backup process drops all data and log files from the database and recreates them from the backup. You are not required to manually drop the database before restoring it. Because of this behavior, there are certain steps that must be taken before you perform a restore. First, you cannot restore a backup while users are connected to the database. Therefore, one of the first actions you should take is to limit access to the database. You want to limit users from connecting, but not necessarily administrators. The best way to limit access is to set the Members Of db_owner, dbcreator or sysadmin option to true on the database being restored. You can change this option on the database using the Database Properties sheet in Enterprise Manager, as shown in the following illustration, or by using the following Transact-SQL statement:

```
sp_dboption 'database name', 'dbo use only', true
```

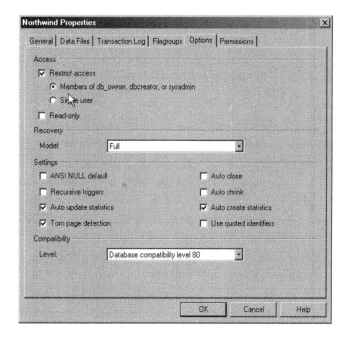

This option limits access to the dbo database user account (for more on the dbo database user account see Chapter 8, section 8.03). If users are still connected, SQL Server will not allow the restore process to drop the database and the restore process will fail.

You should also backup the transaction log before performing a restore. When you restore a full backup, SQL Server drops both the data file and the log file. It replaces the log with the transaction log that it appended to the full backup. This means that any committed transactions since the last backup will be lost. If you backup the log before you restore the database, you will be able to restore the database to the point of failure (or to a point prior to the point of failure, but after the last backup). If the database you are restoring is missing a data file, you may need to use the NO_TRUNCATE option to backup the log (see section 6.01).

One final task you should perform before restoring a backup is to verify the backup set that you are restoring. You need to verify that you have the most current backup and, in the case of multiple backups on the same device, which backup on the device to restore. You also want to verify that the backup device or devices are readable and complete. This is most important in cases where you have backed up a database to multiple devices. SQL Server includes some tools to help verify backups. In Enterprise Manager, the Restore Database sheet lists all recent backups and locates their position within the backup device for you, so you don't need to check this information for yourself. However it does not verify backup sets until you actually run the restore. There are four Transact-SQL restore options that you can use to verify your backup sets. All of them are used in the following manner:

```
RESTORE DATABASE restore_option

FROM device [, device2…]
```

The verify options are listed in Table 6-5.

With all of these options, SQL Server does not actually perform a restore. It only tests the backup set(s) and returns the results of the operation.

When you perform a restore, SQL Server performs certain safety checks. First it checks to see if the database exists on the server. It then attempts to put the files back in the location where it saved them. It also ensures that the database name on the backup set you are using is the same as the name of the database that you are restoring. This ensures that you don't inadvertently restore a database with the wrong backup. There are times, however, when you may want to override some of these security features. The RESTORE statement has a number of WITH options that change the behavior of SQL Server's safety checking. The RESTORE statement also has certain options that control how the restore will take place. The RESTORE options are listed in Table 6-6.

TABLE 6-5	Verify Option	Description
The Transact-SQL Backup Verification Options	HEADERONLY	This option reads the header for a backup device and returns a list of all backups in the device. It returns their names and descriptions and creation data. It also lists which database the backup was taken from and which type of backup each entry represents. You would use this option to find where a particular backup file was located within the device.
	FILELISTONLY	The option returns information about the original database or log files contained in the backup. This option can be used to avoid restoring the wrong file—particularly with file and filegroup backups.
	LABELONLY	The option returns information about the backup media itself, such as when it was created and if it is part of a media set. You can use this option to ensure that you have all of the elements of the backup.
	VERIFYONLY	In some ways this is the most important option. It tests a backup set to determine that it is complete and readable. It will either return an error or a result that the backup set is valid. This option should be used occasionally to check backup media (especially tapes) for physical errors that make the media unreadable.

These options can be used with both database and log restores.

SQL Server also recovers the database after it restores it. The restore process is different than the recovery process. As you saw in section 6.01, recovery occurs automatically each time the server is started. The restore process is the only way for the recovery process to run on a single database. Otherwise you must recover all databases on the server (by stopping and restarting the server service). SQL Server will recover all restored databases by default unless you explicitly instruct it not to recover. This is very important when it comes to restoring differential backups and transaction logs.

TABLE 6-6	Options	Description
The Restore Options	MOVE … TO	This option allows you to restore a data file into a location other than where it was backed up from. When you use this option, the original data file is deleted and a new file is created in the new location. Syntax for this statement is MOVE 'logical file name' TO 'full destination file and path'. You can use this option to move both data and log files.
	FILE	This option is used to specify which file in the backup device to restore. The file is specified using a position number. If you don't specify a FILE value, it will default to the first file in the device. You can find the file position number for the backup you want to restore by using the RESTORE HEADERONLY statement.
	REPLACE	This option is used to turn off safety checking during the restore. The REPLACE option will allow you to overwrite one database with the backup of another database. It will also allow you to backup a database on one server and restore it on another server.
	RESTART	This option is used to restart a restore that has been interrupted before completion. The restart continues the restore from the point of the interruption.

For both the differential and transaction log backups, you must first restore a full backup without recovery. If SQL Server does not find the database in an un-recovered state it will not allow these backups to be restored. You specify recovery using the WITH RECOVERY or WITH NORECOVERY options. The default is WITH RECOVERY. If you are restoring only a full backup, you can omit this option and the database will recover when the restore is complete. However if you have additional differential or transaction log backups to restore, you must specify NORECOVERY on all but the final backup (usually the transaction log backup you made just prior to beginning the restore). There is a third recovery option, WITH STANDBY, which will be covered in section 6.06.

In order to perform a restore from a differential backup, you must first restore a full backup specifying NORECOVERY. Remember that when a full backup runs, it also saves the portion of the transaction log between the start point and end point of the backup. It is this transaction log that you are leaving in an unrecovered state. Once the full backup has been restored, SQL Server will allow a differential backup to be processed. The syntax for restoring a differential backup is exactly the same as the syntax for performing a full backup restore. All you have to do is point to the differential backup in your FROM clause (using the WITH FILE option if necessary).

The full backup that you have restored must be the same as the full backup that was used as the starting point for the differential. If you have restored a different full backup (even if it is from the same database), the differential restore will fail. SQL Server records which full backup is a match for each differential. If you have further transaction log backups to restore, you should also specify NORECOVERY when restoring the differential backup. Remember that differential backups store all changes since the last full backup, so if you have multiple differential backups (one each night for example) you would only have to restore the most recent differential backup. This backup contains all changes stored in the earlier backups.

In order to perform a restore for a transaction log backup you use the RESTORE LOG statement. It has all of the options of the RESTORE DATABASE statement, but has one extra capability—the ability to restore to a specific point in time. Differential backups contain all extents that have changed since the last full backup, however, they only store the state of data at the point that the backup was run. Transaction log backups, on the other hand, contain all changes over a given period of time. That is, if a particular value changes several times over the day, a differential backup will only store the value that was current when the backup ran. The transaction log backup will contain each change to the value since the last full backup or transaction log backup.

This behavior allows you to restore only part of a transaction log. In effect this allows you to roll a database back to a particular point in time. To perform this type of restore you use the WITH STOPAT command. For example, if a malicious update took place at 10:50 A.M., and you noticed it at 11 A.M., you could backup the transaction log and restore it (over an unrecovered full backup restore) using the following statement:

```
RESTORE LOG northwind

FROM nwlog

WITH STOPAT = 'April 3, 2001 10:49 AM'
```

The transactions in the transaction log backup will be appended to the transaction log portion of the unrecovered full backup (since this portion is unrecovered, it still holds partial transactions that may be committed as part of the transaction log backup).

Once it is finished reassembling the parts of the transaction log, it will recover the entire log. The STOPAT command will prevent SQL Server from recovering transactions after 10:49A.M. (just prior to the malicious update). This means that all activity from 10:49 A.M. to 11:00 A.M. will be wiped out. This includes rolling back any transactions that were begun before 10:49 A.M. but not committed until after 10:49 A.M. It is important to remember that this will affect all activity on the database. It is not possible to localize the restore to a single table in SQL Server.

To restore a database using Enterprise Manager, right-click the database and select All Tasks | Restore Database. This will bring up the Restore Database Properties sheet. Any current backups of the database will appear on the form and you can easily select which backups you wish to restore. You can also select additional restore options by clicking the Options tab, as shown in the next illustration. On the Option tab, you can set a number of the WITH recovery options. If you wanted to use the WITH REPLACE option, you would click the Force Restore Of Existing Backup check box. If you wanted to move the database of log files (instead of using the MOVE...TO... option) you complete this information in the Restore Database Files As section. Finally, you specify the RECOVERY option by selecting the Leave Database Operational. No Additional Transaction Logs Can Be Restored radio button. You specify NORECOVERY by selecting the Leave Database Nonoperational But Able To Restore Additional Transaction Logs option.

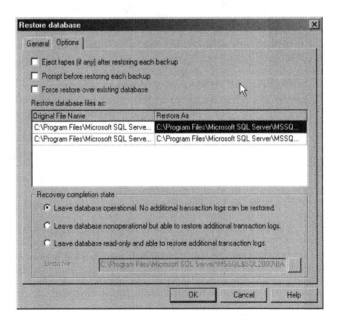

File and filegroup backups are a special case. You do not require a full backup restore to restore a file or filegroup. Instead you can restore just the missing or damaged file or filegroup from a file or filegroup backup or from a full backup (restoring just one file rather than the entire database from the full backup). The syntax for restoring a file or filegroup is:

```
RESTORE DATABASE database_name

{FILE | FILEGROUP} = 'file or filegroup name'

FROM backup device

WITH …\
```

This will restore only the individual file (or the files within a filegroup) specified in the statement. You will require a transaction log to restore a file or filegroup. Because you are only restoring part of the database, you must use transaction logs to bring that part of the database up to the same point in time as the rest of the database. This prevents data inconsistencies. Remember, if you are recovering from a lost or damaged file you may have to use the NO_TRUNCATE option to backup the transaction log. Because you will be performing transaction log restores after restoring the file or filegroup, you must specify NORECOVERY.

QUESTIONS

6.04: Restoring User Databases

8. Susan is the administrator for a SQL 2000 server. She is responsible for a database called WestCost_Inventory. This database consists of one data file, which is 80GB in size, and one transaction log file. Both files are on separate physical disks.

   The disk containing the data file has failed. Susan has a full backup of the database and is able to backup the transaction log. She has replaced the failed disk and formatted the new disk. What must Susan do to restore the database?

   A. Restore the full backup, specifying NORECOVER as one of the restore options. Restore the transaction log backup created prior to the restore and recover the database.

    B.   Restore the full backup specifying the MOVE … TO… option to create the missing data file. Specify NORECOVERY and then restore the transaction log backup created prior to the restore and recover the database.

    C.   Create an empty data file on the new drive with the same name as the missing file. Restore the full backup using the REPLACE option and then restore the transaction log backup.

    D.   Run the DBCC FILEREGEN command before performing the restore to regenerate the missing file.

    E.   Restore the full backup, specifying ADDFILE as one of the restore options. Restore the transaction log backup created prior to the restore and recover the database.

9.   You are the administrator responsible for several small databases. You need to restore a differential backup of the sales database from a backup device called Monday_back. There are several backups stored on this device. When you view the contents of the device using the RESTORE HEADERONLY statement, you receive the output shown in the following illustration.

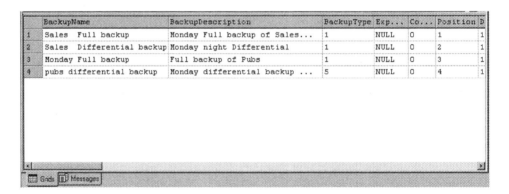

	BackupName	BackupDescription	BackupType	Exp...	Co...	Position	D
1	Sales Full backup	Monday Full backup of Sales...	1	NULL	0	1	1
2	Sales Differential backup	Monday night Differential	1	NULL	0	2	1
3	Monday Full backup	Full backup of Pubs	1	NULL	0	3	1
4	pubs differential backup	Monday differential backup ...	5	NULL	0	4	1

Grids   Messages

Which statement would you use to restore this database?

    A.   RESTORE DATABASE sales

          FILE = 2

          FROM Monday_Back

B. `RESTORE DATABASE sales`
`FROM Monday_Back`
`WITH FILE = 2`

C. `RESTORE DIFFERENTIAL DATABASE sales`
`FROM Monday_Back`
`WITH FILE = 2`

D. `RESTORE DATABASE sales`
`FROM Monday_Back`
`WITH Position = 2`

E. `RESTORE DIFFERENTIAL DATABASE sales`
`FROM Monday_Back`
`WITH FILE = 'Sales Differential Backup'`

10. Jane is the administrator for a SQL 2000 server. This server contains a database that stores technical manuals in text columns. The database is 900GB in size. The database is created on four different filegroups. Each filegroup contains two different files. Jane performs a full backup at the beginning of each month and backs up one filegroup each night. She also backs up the transaction log every four hours. One of the disks in filegroup one has failed. Jane has replaced the disk. What must she now do in order to recover the database? (Choose the best answer.)

A. Restore the full backup and the restore the most recent backup for filegroup one.

B. Back up the current transaction log. Restore the full backup and then restore the most recent backup for filegroup one. Then reapply all transaction log backups since the filegroup backup was made.

C. Restore only the filegroup one backup.

D. Back up the current transaction log. Restore only the current filegroup backup and all of the transaction log backups since the filegroup was backed up.

E. You must restore all of the filegroup backups but not the full backup. Reapply all transaction logs since the oldest filegroup backup was created.

Restoring System Databases

The process for restoring system databases is similar to restoring a user database. There is, however, one significant issue—restoring the Master database. In order for the SQL Server restore process to run, the SQL Server service must be running In order to run, the SQL Server service needs access to the Master database. If the Master database becomes corrupted or fails, therefore, you will be unable to restore the database until you can get the server to start. To get the server started, you need access to the Master database—a Catch-22. Microsoft solves this problem by including a command line utility for rebuilding the Master database—rebuildm.exe. This utility is located by default in the Program Files\Microsoft SQL Server\80\tools\binn folder. When you run this utility, it will drop and recreate all of the system databases. In order to run this utility, you must have a copy of the original source files (the ones used when SQL Server was installed). You can find these files on the SQL Server Installation CD in the x86\data folder. This utility recreates all of the system databases, not just Master, so you will have to restore all system databases once you run the utility. If the Master database fails, you will most likely not be able to backup any of the system databases, so it is important to keep regular backups.

To restore Master there are several steps you must take. The first step is to recreate the Master database using rebuildm.exe, as shown in the next illustration.

In the Rebuild Master tool, enter the full path to the data files. It is best if you copy the files to the local hard drive and remove the read only attribute on the files. You also have the option of changing the default collation. If you have set a non-standard collation, you must reset it by clicking the Settings button. You should be very careful when changing collation settings. The way text data is presented to the user is controlled by the collation. If you change the collation, you may corrupt existing textual data (that is, data in columns with char, varchar, nchar, nvarchar, text, and ntext data types). Once the system databases have been rebuilt, you must restore them to bring the server back to the state it was in before the failure. In order to restore the Master database, however, you must start the server in single use only mode. You accomplish this by running the following command from the command prompt:

```
Sqlservr.exe -c -m
```

This will start the server in single use only mode. If you don't start the database with this command, the SQL Server service will establish a persistent connection to the server and you will not be able to run the restore process. The -c switch prevents SQL server from coming under the control of the Windows Service Control Monitor and the -m switch starts the server in single use only mode. If the server is a named instance (that is, not the default instance), you must use the -s switch to specify the instance name. When you list the instance name, only include the name of named instance and not the name of the default instance. For example if you had a named instance called testsvr\instance2, you would submit the switch "-s instance2" in the sqlservr command.

This is not accurate—this option prevents SQL Server from coming under the controller of the Windows Service Control Monitor.

Once the server has been started in single user mode, you can run the restore on the Master database. Remember that the database devices exist in Master and will be unavailable until you restore. You must therefore reference the backup set by its full path, specifying the media type. For example, if you had a backup device called masterbackup that pointed to the c:\backup\masterbackup.bak file, you would use the following restore:

```
RESTORE DATABASE master

FROM DISK = ' c:\backup\masterbackup.bak'
```

If you referenced the masterback device you would receive an error message stating that the device does not exist. When the restore is complete, you should stop the server and restart it normally. If the restore was successful, you should see all of your user databases, and logins on the server. Once you have restored the Master database, you must now restore MSDB and Model (if you had made any changes to Model). You can restore these databases in the same way that you would restore a user database. Remember that rebuildm.exe will rebuild all of the databases. If you do not have a backup of the Master database, you will have to reestablish all of your user database using `sp_attach_db` and manually recreate all of your user logins. If you do not have a backup of MSDB you will have to recreate all of your alerts and jobs manually.

QUESTIONS

6.05: Restoring System Databases

11. You are the administrator of a SQL server named corpdata2. Your users are complaining that they are unable to establish connections to the server. You check the logs and find that the server rebooted last night because of a power failure. Now the SQL Server service will not start. When you examine the startup logs, you notice that SQL Server is unable to read msdb.mdf. You do not have a backup of the MSDB database. However, you have created a large number of alerts, automation jobs and several complex DTS packages. How can you recover the corpdata2 server? (Choose the best answer.)

   A. Run regrebuild.exe to rebuild the MSDB database.

   B. Rerun the SQL setup program and select Rebuild System Tables on the Advanced tab.

   C. Copy the msdb.mdf file from the SQL server installation disk and use `sp_attach_db` to attach the file.

   D. Run rebuildm.exe and rebuild all of the system database, restoring Master from backup.

   E. Run rebuildm.exe and in the Settings sheet, clear all databases except for MSDB.

12. Your MSDB database has become corrupt. You have rebuilt all of your system databases and restored Master. What must you do to restore the MSDB database form a current backup?

    A. Perform a normal restore just as you would any user database.

    B. Restart the server in single user only mode and restore the MSDB database.

    C. After rebuilding the system databases, restore the Master and MSDB databases together before restarting the server.

    D. Restart SQL Server in read only mode before restoring the MSDB database.

TEST YOURSELF OBJECTIVE 6.06

Configuring, Maintaining, and Troubleshooting Log Shipping

Backups are extremely important to prevent data loss. They are, however, not the only way of protecting data. You can also use backups to create and maintain standby servers. A standby server is a redundant, read only copy of one or more databases. The creation of a standby server is possible because of a third recovery option—WITH STANDBY. In section 6.04 you learned about the RECOVERY and NORECOVERY options. If you restore a database WITH RECOVERY, the database is accessible, but you cannot apply any further transaction log or differential backups. If you restore the database WITH NORECOVERY, it is not accessible, but you can still apply further transaction log or differential backups. The WITH STANDBY option brings a database to a state that makes the database accessible but still able to receive further restores. It rolls back any uncommitted transactions, but saves these transactions in a standby log. When you restore another backup against the standby server, it reapplies the deleted transactions from this log before performing the restore. It allows the database to operate in a read only manner. However, you still apply transaction log backups taken from the original server and apply them against the standby server. SQL Server allows you to automate this process through a method called *log shipping*.

Log shipping is, at the most basic level, a process that allows you to take transaction log backups from one server and use them to update a copy of that database on another server. Log shipping begins with a full backup of the database that is going to be copied. You copy the backup to the target server and restore it using the WITH STANDBY option. Once the initial configuration is complete, you can configure log shipping. Log shipping involves three steps.

1. The primary server backs up the transaction log of the database that is being shipped. The backup must be to a file that has a name containing the current date and time. Before configuring log shipping, you should create a folder to hold the log backups. You must then share the folder on the network to make it accessible to the standby server.

2. The standby server runs a job that copies the file from the primary server to a folder on the standby server.

3. A second job is run on the standby server that restores the transaction log on the standby server using the standby option.

These jobs need to be scheduled together so that they operate in the correct order. Once the process is complete, the standby server will mirror the primary server. Also, because you are backing up and restoring transaction logs, any objects created on the primary server (such as new tables or indexes) will be recreated on the standby server.

All of these jobs run the SQL Server Agents on each computer. Because the services interact, it is important that they share a common security context. This means that the account used by the SQL Server Agent service on the standby server must have permission to access the server containing the primary database. If the agent on the standby server is unable to authenticate to the primary server, log shipping will fail. That means that both agent services should be running under Windows domain user accounts. It is also important that the SQL Agent on the standby server has read permission on the shared folder containing the backup. If the Agent on the standby server is unable to copy the backups from the primary server, log shipping will also fail.

SQL Server 2000 includes a wizard to help you set up log shipping. It is part of the SQL Server Maintenance Plan Wizard. To open this wizard, open the Management folder in Enterprise Manager. Right-click the Database Maintenance Plan icon and select New Maintenance Plan. To enable log shipping with this wizard, you must select the database you are going to use as the primary database and click the Ship The Transaction Logs To Other SQL Servers (Log Shipping) check box below the list of databases, as shown in the next illustration. This wizard will allow you to automatically set up the initial standby server and to schedule and automate the log shipping process.

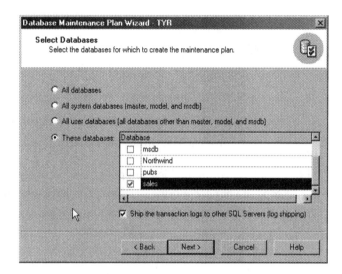

Standby servers are used to maintain a copy of a database that can be brought online in place of the primary server if it fails. It can also be brought in to replace a server when it is taken offline for scheduled maintenance or upgrades. Standby servers do not have failover capability. That is, if the primary server fails, clients must be manually connected to the standby server; it will not automatically switch from the primary server to the standby server.

QUESTIONS

6.06: Configuring, Maintaining, and Troubleshooting Log Shipping

13. You are the database administrator for your company. You have two SQL servers and you want to configure log shipping to maintain a backup copy of your inventory database. You start the Database Maintenance Wizard on the server that contains the inventory database, and select the inventory database

from the list, but the Ship The Transaction Logs To Other SQL Servers (Log Shipping) check box is grayed out. What is the most likely reason this option is not available?

A. The SQL Server Agent service on the standby server does not have the appropriate rights on the primary server.

B. You have not yet performed a full backup on the inventory database.

C. The inventory database is read only.

D. The inventory database is using the simple recovery model.

E. You must run the wizard on the standby server.

14. You have configured log shipping between two servers to maintain a standby copy of your accounting database. You have scheduled log shipping to run once per day. However, when you test the process, log shipping fails. You are able to ping each server by name and IP address. Which of the following may be the cause of failure? (Choose all that apply.)

A. The SQL Server Agent on standby server is using the local system account.

B. The SQL Server Agent on primary server does not have rights to log onto the standby server.

C. The standby server and primary server are on different subnets in the same network.

D. The SQL Server Agent on the standby server does not have write permission on the network share on the primary server.

E. The SQL Server Agent on the standby server does not have read permission on the network share on the primary server.

TEST YOURSELF OBJECTIVE 6.07

Performing Integrity Checks

Backups and log shipping will protect your data in the event of failure. However, you must still monitor the integrity of your data. Remember that SQL Server backups copy the entire data file. If you have integrity errors in your database, those errors will be included in the backup. Integrity errors occur when pages are written incorrectly to the physical disk, or when the link between index pages and data pages is broken. These allocation errors can be detected and dealt with using DBCC statements or the Database Maintenance Plan Wizard.

There are three main DBCC statements that you can use to check database integrity. They are listed in Table 6-7.

TABLE 6-7	DBCC Statement	Explanation
DBCC Statements to Check Data Integrity	DBCC CHECKTABLE	This statement checks the integrity of all pages associated with a particular table or indexed view. This check includes all data, text and image pages, and also the index pages of any indexes associated with the table. It checks for such problems as incorrect linkages between table and index pages, incorrect pointers, and indexes that are not in proper sorted order.
	DBCC CHECKALLOC	This statement checks the integrity of all pages in a specific database. It also returns page usage such as the number of pages used by an object and the number of dedicated extents.
	DBCC CHECKDB	This option performs the tasks of both DBCC CHECKTABLE and DBCC CHECKALLOC. If you run DBCC CHECKDB you do not need to run the other two. DBCC CHECKDB places a schema level lock on the entire database while it is running which prevents any modifications to any object in the database until the statement has run.

For each of these statements, you can avoid checking indexes by using the NOINDEX option. All three have similar syntax:

```
DBCC {CHECKALLOC | CHECKTABLE | CHECKDB} ('table_name' |
'view_name', [NOINDEX])
```

All of these DBCC statements can also be used to repair detected errors. In order for this to occur, however, the database must be in single user mode. There are three repair options as shown in Table 6-8.

	Option	Description
TABLE 6-8 The Repair Options	REPAIR_FAST	Performs minor repairs such as removing extra keys in a non-clustered index. This option will not result in any data loss.
	REPAIR_REBUILD	Performs all repairs done by REPAIR_ FAST but will also perform more resource-expensive tasks (such as rebuilding indexes). This option will not perform any repairs that may result in data loss.
	REPAIR_ALLOW_DATA_LOSS	Performs all repairs that the REPAIR_ REBUILD performs. It will also perform more low-level repairs such as correcting allocation errors. An allocation error occurs when a page is marked in the data file as being used, but is not associated with any index or table. When an allocation error occurs, any data on that page will not be returned if the object is scanned. Selecting this option may result in data loss if it is unable to associate the page with any table or index and de-allocates the page.

You can also schedule integrity checks through the Data Maintenance Plan Wizard. If you select the Check Database Integrity check box on the Database Integrity Check form as shown in the illustration that follows, SQL Server will run a DBCC CHECKDB statement. You can set further options by selecting the other options. If you choose the Exclude Indexes button, SQL Server will include the NOINDEX option to the DBCC CHECKDB statement. If you select the Attempt To Repair Any Minor Problems check box, it will add the repair option. It will also put the database into single user mode every time this portion of the wizard runs. For this reason, you should not schedule this operation while users are connected.

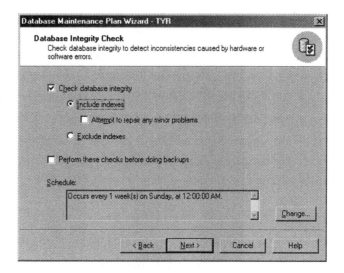

Aside from log shipping and database integrity, the Database Maintenance Plan Wizard also allows you to schedule and automate the following tasks:

- Reorganize indexes pages and reset fill factor using the DBCC REINDEX command
- Remove unused space using DBCC SHRINKDATABASE
- Backup databases
- Backup transaction logs
- Maintain a report of all maintenance activity
- Automate the elements on all databases, all user or system databases, or on specific databases

QUESTIONS

6.07: Performing Integrity Checks

15. You want to run a consistency check on a database called rd_results and all of its tables. You want the check to correct any errors even if it means the possibility of data loss. Which statement would you use to meet all of these requirements?

    A. `DBCC CHECKALLOC ('rd_results', REPAIR_ALLOW_DATA_LOSS)`

    B. `DBCC CHECKDB ('rd_results', REPAIR_REBUILD)`

    C. `DBCC CHECKTABLE ('rd_results', REPAIR_ALLOW_DATA_LOSS)`

    D. `DBCC CHECKTABLE ('rd_results', REPAIR_REBUILD)`

    E. `DBCC CHECKDB ('rd_results', REPAIR_ALLOW_DATA_LOSS)`

16. Which of the following tasks can be automated using the Database Maintenance Wizard? (Choose all that apply.)

    A. Back up the Master database

    B. Autogrow a database

    C. Run the DBCC CHECKTABLE statement

    D. Back up the transaction log for a specific user database

    E. Reorganize indexes with a specific fill factor on all databases

---

TEST YOURSELF OBJECTIVE 6.08

Troubleshooting Transactions and Locking

The concept of the transaction was introduced in section 6.01. A transaction is a collection of one or more Transact-SQL statements that must run entirely or not at all. Transactions are important when you look at backing up transaction logs.

Remember that when you recover a database, uncommitted transactions are rolled back and committed transactions are reapplied. There is one other element of transactions that you need to be aware of, and that is locking. Locks prevent one user from overwriting the changes of another user in the middle of a transaction. SQL Server has two basic types of locking—shared and exclusive. SQL Server can place locks at the row, page, extent, table and database level. It tries to lock at the lowest level, but will escalate locks if the cost of holding lower level locks is inefficient (such as holding row level locks on every row on a page instead of locking the page).

When you retrieve data with a SELECT statement, SQL Server places a shared lock on the resources being affected. If you issue an INSERT, UPDATE, or DELETE statement, SQL Server acquires an exclusive lock on the affected resources.

If a resource has a shared lock and you attempt to select from that resource, SQL Server will allow you to access it. However, if a resource has an exclusive lock on it, no other process can access that resource until the lock is removed. If another process wants to access a resource that has an exclusive lock on it, that process will be blocked until the lock is lifted. It is possible to override this behavior at the session level using the SET ISOLATION LEVEL command. The syntax for this statement is:

```
SET ISOLATION LEVEL {READ COMMITTED| READ UNCOMMITTED
|REPEATABLE READ | SERIALIZABLE}
```

These four isolation levels are described in Table 6-9.

Transactions maintain their locks until the entire transaction is complete. This allows SQL Server to insure transactional consistency between all of the steps in the transaction. It also means that transactions can block each other in a cascading fashion. This behavior is necessary, but can cause performance issues if too many transactions are blocking each other. For this reason, you will need to monitor locking on your servers. There are several tools to help monitor locking. Specifically, you can monitor locking with Transact-SQL stored procedures, with Enterprise Manager and with the SQL Server Profiler.

In Transact-SQL there are two stored procedures that will help you monitor locking—sp_lock and sp_who. The sp_lock stored procedure will return all locks in a particular database. It lists the type of lock, the object ID for the object that is locked and the ID of the process (spid) that has acquired the lock. You can then use the sp_who stored procedure to find out who executed the process and what command was executed. This same information can be displayed graphically in the Current Activity tool in Enterprise Manager. To access the Current Activity tool, open the

TABLE 6-9

Lock Isolation
Levels

Isolation Level	Description
Read Committed	This is the default isolation level. When you access the database in read committed mode, you are unable to read objects while they are locked with an exclusive lock.
Read Uncommitted.	This isolation level allows "dirty reads." These are reads of uncommitted data. This isolation level does not set shared locks and ignores exclusive locks. This is not recommended.
Repeatable Read	This prevents one process from modifying rows while they are being queried by another process. Essentially this level of locking allows SELECT statements to lock rows until the entire query is complete.
Serializable	This is the highest level of locking. It places a lock on the entire range of values covered in a query. It also holds the lock until you issue a commit transaction statement. Essentially this isolation level treats the SELECT statement the same way it would an INSERT, UPDATE, or DELETE statement. Because of the high degree of locking, you should try to avoid this isolation level.

Management folder and click Current Activity. Under Current Activity is a process info icon (which returns information very similar to that returned by sp_who), and an icon that shows locks by process and locks by object. These tools not only show you quickly what locks have been acquired but it will also show you graphically which processes are blocked and which processes are blocking.

The final method of monitoring locking is the SQL Server Profiler. The Profiler captures activity against a particular database. You can specify many activities to trace and one of these is locking. If you are concerned about excessive locking, you can monitor locks being acquired and released. The advantage of the Profiler, unlike Enterprise Manager and the Transact-SQL statements, is that the trace is not static. The other two methods present a real-time snapshot of locking. The Profiler provides a trace over time. You can leave this trace running for a period of time and see if locking is greater at different times during the day.

QUESTIONS

6.08: Troubleshooting Transactions and Locking

17. You are the administrator for several databases on a SQL 2000 server. Several of your order entry people have called to report that sometimes their application appears "frozen" whenever they try to modify data in the customers table. They mention this happens when updating some but not all customers in the table. You suspect that one process is blocking the other users. How would you determine which process is blocking the others? (Choose all that apply.)

    A. Run a Profiler trace. Filter for acquired locks.

    B. Use the Current Activity tool in Enterprise Manager.

    C. Run sp_lock and sp_who.

    D. Run a Profiler trace. Filter for locks released.

LAB QUESTION

Objectives 6.01–6.08

You are the administrator of the sales database for Shady's shirt company. The sales database contains sales activity from all of the retail stores. The database is on a SQL 2000 server called WestCoast2. The sales database is 600GB in size and receives about 2000 transactions per hour during the day. It is split across ten 60GB data files. Each file is on its own disk. The transaction log is also on a separate disk. At night, your sales managers and accountants run reports for the day's activity. You have a tape array with six tape drives on another server. The server that the tape array is attached to is also running third party backup software. These drives are accessible from WestCoast2. A full backup of the database takes about five hours.

1. Your manager has asked you to develop a backup strategy for the server. Minimizing data loss is essential. What recovery model would you suggest for this server?

2. What backup strategy would you suggest to your manager?

3. Where will you back your data up to?

4. What effect will your backup strategy have on the nightly reporting jobs?

5. One Wednesday, one of the data disks fails. When you try to backup the transaction log you receive an error. How can you avoid this error?

6. How would you replace the missing data file?

7. You have decided to perform hourly transaction log backups. At 11:40 A.M. a hacker changes the prices of all your shirts to $1.00. You don't notice the update until 11:50 A.M. How will you restore the table?

8. How much data will be lost?

QUICK ANSWER KEY

Objective 6.01
1.   C
2.   D

Objective 6.02
3.   A and D
4.   C
5.   E

Objective 6.02
6.   A, C, and E
7.   A and C

Objective 6.04
8.   A
9   B
10. D

Objective 6.05
11. D
12. A

Objective 6.06
13. D
14. A and E

Objective 6.07
15. E
16. A, D, and E

Objective 6.08
17. B and C

IN-DEPTH ANSWERS

6.01: Recovering System State

1. ☑ **C** is the correct answer. Because the database became suspect when the server was restarted, SQL Server most likely detected a torn page. SQL Server databases become suspect if SQL Server detects a torn page, or is unable to locate all of the data and log files. If this is the case, the only way to recover the database is to restore it from backup. There is no other way to recover a suspect database.

   ☒ **A**, **D**, and **E** are incorrect because none of these options exist. Recovery is an automatic process and there are no executables or stored procedures that will force it to occur. There is no /forcerecovery option for the net start command. Forcing recovery of a database that has a torn page will override the safety checking of the torn page detection. If you have a torn page, it means that a portion of one page was not written to disk, and the data file is therefore corrupt. Forcing the database to start with a corrupt data file will allow users to work with corrupt data. **B** is incorrect because there is no way to reconnect to a database in Enterprise Manager. This option is only available if you right-click the server object in Enterprise Manager.

2. ☑ **D** is the correct answer. Maintaining a transaction log for this database is unnecessary because the data (including the table and index schema) are recreated before each test. You will not be concerned with restoring the database to a point in time, nor will you need to worry about data loss. However, because the tests involve executing a high volume of transactions, the transaction log may either become full, or greatly expand as the tests proceed. If the log fills, the tests will fail and you will have to manually clear the logs. This will add to the administration cost of the database. By choosing the simple recovery model, the transaction log is cleared of all committed transactions every time a checkpoint occurs. This will prevent the testing from filling the transaction log and failing.

⊠   **A** is incorrect because the FULL recovery model will log all activity (including running the scripts to create the database). This will quickly fill the transaction logs and halt testing. **B** is incorrect because the bulk_logged model will log all transactions except those generated by a bulk operation. That is, it will not log the initial table populations or the index creations, but it will log all of the activity generated by the testing. In this case you have the same problem you would have with the full recovery model. **C** is technically correct because the Truncate Log On Checkpoint option will force the database to behave very similarly to the simple recovery model. All committed transactions will be removed from the log whenever a checkpoint occurs. This option existed in earlier versions of SQL Server. It has been incorporated into the simple recovery model and does not need to be set as a separate database object. It only remains for backwards compatibility. **E** is incorrect because there is no option to turn off logging in SQL Server.

6.02: Backing Up User Databases

3.   ☑   **A** and **D** are the correct answers. A full backup will backup all of the data files. You can use a full backup to restore any missing data files. Because of the high number of transactions throughout the day, you will want to perform transaction log backups periodically throughout the day. This will allow you to minimize data loss by saving activity throughout the day. If the transaction log is unavailable you will only lose transactions that occurred after the last transaction log backup. Also, when you backup the log, it will remove any committed transactions. This will keep the transaction log from filling.

⊠   **B** is incorrect because a filegroup backup is only beneficial in a database with multiple filegroups. Since this database only has one filegroup (the primary filegroup), there is no difference between a filegroup and a full backup in this scenario. It is, however, possible to backup individual files. **C** is incorrect because if you only perform a full backup on the weekend, it will take much more time to recover the database than if you perform a daily full backup. A database of 10GB would take roughly one to two hours to complete (depending on the speed of the local tape drive). It could be easily run overnight. **E** is incorrect because a differential database only saves changes since the last full backup. This backup type would help to minimize data loss, but does not clear the transaction log. It also becomes longer as the day progresses. Differential backups are best used to avoid restoring a large number of transaction log backups. However, since you are performing a full backup each night, the transaction log backup is a much better solution to this scenario.

4.   ☑   **C** is the correct answer. You can perform a full backup while the database is being accessed so there is no restriction. You will need at least one full backup as a starting point. However, due to the length of time the backup requires, it is impractical to run more than once per week. To improve the speed of the backup and to have less impact on users, try to schedule the full backup for a period when activity on the database is lower. Differential backups only save changes since the last full backup. For this reason they are much faster to backup. They are much faster to restore than a long sequence of transaction logs. You can use transaction log backups to improve recoverability of data throughout the day. These backups are quick and will have little impact on users.

☒   **A** is incorrect because, although there are four physical files, there is still only one filegroup. The filegroup backup would take as long as a full backup (if SQL Server allowed you to perform it). It would be possible to backup individual files, but this option was not presented. **B** is incorrect because it would take a long time to restore a week's worth of transaction logs. The differential backup makes this unnecessary. **D** is incorrect because both differential backups and transaction log backups require an initial full backup. SQL Server will not allow you to perform either type of backup unless you have performed a full backup. **E** is incorrect because the SQL Server backup utility will allow you to backup a database while users are connected to it. When you stop the server, it is not available to your users. This violates one of the business rules for this server.

5.   ☑   **E** is the correct answer because you cannot backup a transaction log without the NO_TRUNCATE option if one of the data files is missing. In a normal backup, SQL Server performs a checkpoint before backing up the log. The checkpoint process involves writing committed transactions from the Buffer Cache back into the data files. If any of these files is unavailable, the checkpoint cannot proceed. The NO_TRUNCATE does not perform a checkpoint. When SQL Server performs a checkpoint it attempts to write data from the Buffer Cache back to the data file. If SQL Server cannot locate the data file, the backup will fail.

☒   **A** is incorrect because you reference the database name and not the physical file name in the BACKUP LOG statement. **B** is incorrect because, although it is not possible to perform a normal log backup if one of the data files is missing, the NO_TRUNCATION option makes this possible. **C** is incorrect because it is the checkpoint that is preventing the transaction log backup from occurring. Forcing a checkpoint will only raise an error. **D** is incorrect because the WITH FORMAT option only affects how the backup process manages the backup device. This option will turn off safety checks and allow SQL Server to split up a media set.

6.03: Backing Up System Databases

6.   ☑   **A**, **C**, and **E** are correct. **A** is correct because you should backup the Master database every time a user database is created or dropped. If you were to restore the database with an outdated version of Master after issuing this command, you would receive an error because SQL Server would be unable to find the data file (which was deleted by the DROP statement), but would still register the database. **C** is correct because this stored procedure will update the sysmessages table in the Master database. If you did not have a valid backup you would have to recreate all user-defined messages. **E** is correct because you should backup any database after modifying its size or schema.

☒   **B** is incorrect because the TRUNCATE command only modifies the products table in the Northwind database. It does not have any impact on the Master database. **D** is incorrect because it adds a new alert. Alerts are stored in the MSDB database.

7.   ☑   **A** and **C** are the correct answers. When you choose to save a DTS package as a SQL Server package, it is saved in the MSDB database. All jobs are also stored in a table called sysjobs in the MSDB database.

☒   **B** is incorrect because user-defined error messages are stored in the sysmessages table of the Master database. These messages can be used in SQL Server alerts. The definition for an alert that was triggered by a user-defined error would be in the MSDB database, but not the error itself. **D** is incorrect because backup devices are stored in the sysdevices table of the Master databases. **E** is incorrect because the linked servers are created in a table called sysservers in the Master database.

6.04: Restoring User Databases

8. ☑ **A** is the correct answer. When you restore a full backup, it drops all files and recreates them in the same location where it backed them up. As long as Susan doesn't change the disk structure, she does not have to do anything extra to recreate the missing file. Once the full backup has been restored (in NORECOVERY), she can simply restore the transaction log to bring the database up to the state it was in at the point of failure.

   ☒ **B** is incorrect because the MOVE … TO… option would only be necessary if Susan changed the underlying disk structure (such as creating a second partition on one of the existing disks). **C** is incorrect because these steps are unnecessary. The end result of this answer (assuming she included the NORECOVERY option) would be the same as answer **A**, but it would include extra work that had no bearing on the outcome. **D** is incorrect because this DBCC statement does not exist. **E** is incorrect because there is no ADDFILE option for the RESTORE DATABASE statement.

9. ☑ **B** is the correct answer. The position column in the output of the RESTORE HEADERONLY column shows the position of a particular backup within the backup device. You reference this value using the WITH FILE = option.

   ☒ **A** is incorrect because you have used the wrong FILE option. You use the FILE clause before the FROM clause when you are restoring file backups. When you reference the file clause in this location you must then supply the name of the file that was backed up (enclosed in single-quotes). **C** is incorrect because there is no special syntax that differentiates a full and differential backup restore. **D** is incorrect because the position option does not exist in the RESTORE DATABASE syntax. **E** is incorrect because it lists the name of the backup rather than its position number.

10. ☑ **D** is the correct answer because filegroup backups do not require a full database restore. You must restore the transaction logs (including the most recent log) in order to bring the filegroup up to date with the rest of the database. You must apply the filegroup backup with the NORECOVERY option, and only recover the final transaction log. SQL Server will not allow you to recover the filegroup until you backup the current transaction log.

⊠ **A** and **B** are incorrect because both begin with a full backup restore. If you have restored the full backup, you will not be able to apply the filegroup backups. **C** is incorrect because you must include transaction log restores as part of the filegroup restore. **E** is incorrect because you only have to restore the damaged filegroup. This answer will restore the database, but involves a great deal of unnecessary work.

6.05: Restoring System Databases

11. ☑ **D** is correct because if you do not have a backup of MSDB, you must recreate it using rebuildm.exe. When you run this application it rebuilds all of the system databases. After you build the databases you will have to restore Master from backup to get the server back to the state it was in before the disk failed.

⊠ **A** is incorrect because you cannot use the regrebuild.exe to recreate system databases. Regrebuild.exe was a utility that shipped with previous versions of SQL Server. It was used to make registry repairs. It is not included in SQL Server 2000. **B** is incorrect because this option is not included in the advanced installation of SQL server. **C** is incorrect because you cannot use sp_attach_db to reattach system tables. SQL Server must be running before you can use this procedure and the server won't run until you rebuild Master. **E** is incorrect because the Settings button only allows you to change the collation options. Whenever you run rebuildm.exe, it will rebuild all databases.

12. ☑ **A** is the correct answer because once Master has been rebuilt, there is no difference between restoring MSDB and any user database. Remember that all of the rules governing user database recovery will also govern the restore of MSDB.

⊠ **B** and **C** are incorrect because you do not need to set the database into single use only mode before restoring MSDB. Doing so will not prevent you from recovering the database but it is an unnecessary action. **D** is incorrect because the read only setting has no bearing on backup and restore. Even if users are querying the database, they will block a restore process. The restore cannot take place if any users are connected to the database.

6.06: Configuring, Maintaining, and Troubleshooting Log Shipping

13. ☑ **D** is the correct answer because if the database recovery model is set to simple, there will be no transaction logs to ship. The database must be set to use the full recover model for log shipping to occur. If it not set to full, the wizard will not attempt to configure log shipping.

    ☒ **A** is incorrect because the Database Maintenance Plan Wizard is used to configure log shipping. If the Agent service on the standby server does not have the appropriate permissions, log shipping will fail, but this will not affect the wizard. Permissions are not checked until much later in the configuration process. **B** is incorrect because the wizard will perform the initial full database backup when it configures log shipping. **C** is incorrect because the read only access setting has no bearing on backup and recovery, and therefore no bearing on log shipping. **E** is incorrect because you must run the wizard on the primary server. You do not have to be physically on the server, but you must have it registered in Enterprise Manager and run the wizard on the registration.

14. ☑ **A** and **E** are the correct answers. In order for log shipping to occur, the SQL Agent service on the standby server must be able to connect to the share where the primary server has placed the transaction log backup. In order for it to connect, the Agent service must be running under a domain user account that has rights to access the share. If the standby server is using the local system account it will not have the correct security context to connect to the primary server. The Agent on the standby server will also need read access to the network share in order to retrieve the logs.

    ☒ **B** is incorrect because the primary server does not need to log on locally for log shipping to occur. **C** in incorrect because the servers are not required to be on the same subnet. However, they must be able to connect to each other. If either server has been incorrectly configured and could not communicate with the other, then log shipping would fail. **D** is incorrect because the standby server only needs to retrieve data from the primary server; it does not need the ability to add or modify files on the primary server.

6.07: Performing Integrity Checks

15. ☑ **E** is the correct answer because only the DBCC CHECKDB will check both the database and all of its tables. If you want the lowest level of repair, and you are prepared to accept the possibility of some data loss, you would use the REPAIR_ALLOW_DATA_LOSS option.

    ☒ **A** is incorrect because the DBCC CHECKALLOC statement will not check individual tables. Instead, it checks the database as a whole. **B** is incorrect because the REPAIR_REBUILD option will not attempt repairs if there is a possibility of data loss. Because your requirement clearly states that you want to correct any errors, even if it means data loss, this option is not acceptable. **C** and **D** are incorrect because the DBCC CHECKTABLE will only check individual tables. It does not check the database as a whole.

16. ☑ **A**, **D**, and **E** are the correct answers. You can use the Database Maintenance Plan Wizard to backup both user and system databases and transaction logs. You can also use it to rebuild the indexes for all databases, by selecting the All Databases button on the Select Database form.

    ☒ **B** is incorrect because autogrowth is a database property. If set to true, the data or log file will grow whenever it becomes full. You do not have to schedule this growth. **C** is incorrect because the wizard uses the DBCC CHECKDB statement to check database integrity.

6.08: Troubleshooting Transactions and Locking

17. ☑ **B** and **C** are the correct answers. If you look at the locks by object, and examine the customers table, you will quickly see which process is holding the exclusive locks on the table. If it is a single process, you can go into the Process Info screen and kill the process (or you can issue the Transact-SQL Kill command). You can also use `sp_lock` to find out which process has the exclusive look on the table and then use `sp_who` to find out more about the process.

    ☒ **A** is incorrect because the lock has already presumably been acquired (since it is blocking the other processes). You cannot acquire any other locks on a resource while it has an exclusive lock on it, therefore, nothing will be returned by this trace. **D** is incorrect because it will also return no data in the trace. If the users cannot acquire a lock on the resources they need, they will also not release any locks. If the process causing the backlog is released, then the problem will be solved. **E** is incorrect because a deadlock has nothing to do with this scenario. Deadlocks occur when two processes acquire locks on separate resources as the first step of a transaction and they try to acquire locks on each other's resources as a further step. These two processes literally become deadlocked as neither one can complete until the other completes. SQL Server resolves deadlocks automatically by killing one of the two processes and allowing the other to proceed.

LAB ANSWER

Objectives 6.01–6.08

1. Because preventing data loss is important, you should use the full recovery model. If the transaction log is maintained, it will allow you to restore the database up to the point of failure.

2. Because the database is not divided into file groups. The best strategy would be a full backup once per week and a differential backup each night. The differential will take much less time to run, and is faster to restore than a series of transaction logs. You could also choose to perform individual file backups. Because of the high volume of transactions, you will also want to run periodic transaction log backups throughout the day.

3. You will have to backup to disk. You cannot backup to the remote tape drives. If you want to backup to tape, the tape drive must be locally installed.

4. The backup strategy will have little effect on the nightly reports. The SQL Server backup will run while the database is running. There will be a slight performance reduction if the two processes are running at the same time. You should try to schedule your backups for a time when there will be few concurrent connections.

5. You need to include the NO_TRUNCATE option to backup a transaction log if one of the data files is missing. If you do not, SQL Server tries to run a checkpoint and fails because it cannot write to one of the disks.

6. To replace the missing file you can restore it from either a file backup or a full backup. You will need the most current transaction log backup. If possible you can also backup the current log (that is, the portion between the last transaction log backup and the point of failure). You must begin by restoring the file, making sure to specify the NORECOVERY option. You must then restore the differential from Tuesday night (the most recent differential backup), again with NORECOVERY. You will then restore all transaction logs for the day, ending

with the log backup you made just prior to restoring the database. Only recover the final transaction log.

7. You will have to go through the steps listed in answer 6, but include the WITH STANDBY option to restore to a point in time prior to the malicious update.

8. You will loose all transactions against the database from the point specified in the standby (11:39 A.M.) to the point where you recovered the database (in this case 11:50 A.M.).

MICROSOFT CERTIFIED DATABASE ADMINISTRATOR

7

Extracting and Transforming Data with SQL Server 2000

TEST YOURSELF OBJECTIVES

A s organizations begin to accumulate data during normal business processing, the data generated within the database can be used as the basis for learning about the business model of the organization, and hopefully lead to insights on how to improve business processes or assist in making decisions regarding the business.

The XML standard allows client applications to retrieve data from a database using a very flexible mechanism for handling data than is traditionally provided by the more strict structure of relational data.

In order to facilitate reporting and decision support functionality, data may need to be moved off of systems that are actively processing transactions to ensure that business analysis does not get in the way of actually conducting business! Separating database activity, by moving historical data that no longer needs to be updated, also allows response time for reporting and decision support clients to be improved by optimizing the database structure for querying instead of transactional throughput.

SQL Server provides tools that can be used to make client data available via XML, allowing greater flexibility for client developers when handling data retrieved from the database.

In order to facilitate the migration of data between systems, either for the purposes stated previously or for moving data between test and production systems, SQL Server provides tools such as Data Transformation Services, the Bulk Copy utility and the Bulk Insert statement. These tools are optimized for importing and exporting large amounts of data, and the Data Transformation Services allow extensive scripting and job processing functionality to handle even extremely complex data migration from multiple heterogeneous data sources via OLEDB data sources.

TEST YOURSELF OBJECTIVE 7.01

Using XML Support

XML support in SQL Server 2000 provides the ability to make SQL Server data available to XML client applications via Internet Information Services (IIS). All XML functionality is actually incorporated into IIS, rather than SQL Server itself, thereby providing XML support without the need for extensive architectural changes to SQL Server, and also providing easier integration with other web-centric tools such as Active Server Pages.

In order to enable XML support, IIS must be installed on the local system or on a remote web server. Once you have installed IIS, a wizard is provided to create a virtual directory. This virtual directory provides the basis for HTTP and XML access to SQL Server. By default, this wizard will connect to the local system, but you can connect to a remote IIS system by right-clicking IIS Virtual Directory Management in the wizard and choosing the Connect option. Creating a virtual directory provides a namespace for the URLs to be used by client applications. It also specifies the configuration to be used for XML behavior for a particular database. These virtual directories will be hosted within IIS, and one IIS system can support multiple remote SQL servers. A single virtual directory can only support one remote database. Multiple virtual directories must be created in order to support access to multiple databases.

In order to create a virtual directory to allow XML access to a database, you must use the Configure SQL XML Support option in the IIS utility, located in the SQL Server program group. Each of your web sites will be listed, and you can choose the site in which you will need to create the virtual directory. You must then provide the following information:

- The name of the virtual directory to be created. This will form part of the URL used to access the database.
- The physical path where files such as template queries will be located. This will generally be a subfolder of your web server's root directory.
- What security options should be used to connect to SQL Server.
- The name of the server and the database to be made available to XML.
- What type of XML queries will be permitted.
- Virtual names, if using X-Path or template queries.
- Advanced options such as the location of the XML ISAPI .dll and advanced user settings.
- As the following illustration shows, there are a few security options available to you.

They are:

> **Always Log On As**   This setting allows you to have every XML query run through a single Windows or SQL login.
>
> **Use Windows Integrated Authentication**   This setting will use the user's Windows security credentials to connect to SQL Server. This requires Windows authentication in IIS.
>
> **Use Basic Authentication (Clear Text) To SQL Server Account**   This setting will prompt the user for a valid SQL user name and password. These credentials will then be used to connect to SQL Server. This can be used with anonymous or Windows authentication in IIS.

The following illustration shows the settings that are available to control the behavior of the virtual directory:

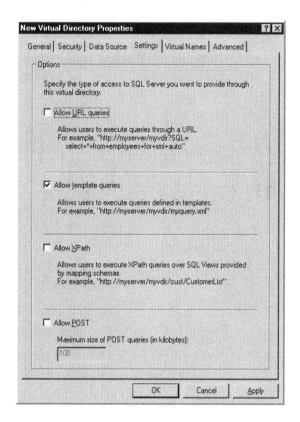

The following options are available:

Allow URL Queries   This option allows XML queries to be formatted as URLs, which allows developers to easily write queries without special configuration tasks. As shown in the previous illustration, queries run this way must include the FOR XML clause.

Allow Template Queries   This option allows XML queries to be stored in a file on the virtual directories' file system location. This allows queries to be generated without displaying query text to users. This also allows queries to be developed independently of the client applications that will be submitting queries. Virtual names must be created in order to map the template files to URL namespaces.

Allow Xpath   Allows queries to be submitted using the X-path query language, designed for more efficient processing of XML data.

Allow Post   Allows database updates via XML templates and queries. The allowable size of uploaded templates can be specified as well.

QUESTIONS

7.01: Using XML Support

1. You would like to configure SQL Server to be accessible via IIS. Your developers want to be able to store XML queries in a file, rather than formatting queries as long URLs. Clients will connect to IIS via Secure Sockets Layer connections. The system needs to be able to support connections from non-Windows clients such as Solaris and OS/2.

    Which of the following must be done to allow this? (Choose all that apply.)

    A. Create a virtual directory for your database.

    B. Configure IIS to support basic authentication over SSL.

    C. Configure the virtual directory to support template queries.

    D. Configure the virtual directory to support URL queries.

    E. Configure a virtual name for the virtual directory used for database access.

    F. Configure the virtual directory to use integrated Windows authentication to connect to SQL Server.

2. You have been asked to enable XML support for one of your databases. Which of the following steps are required to configure database access?

    A. Create a file system folder for the virtual directory.

    B. Create the virtual directory.

    C. Run the `sp_createxmlschema` stored procedure.

    D. Configure the IIS anonymous user account as a SQL user.

TEST YOURSELF OBJECTIVE 7.02

Importing and Exporting Data with Data Transformation Services

Data Transformation Services is designed to extract data from one or more OLE DB data sources, transform data as necessary, and then load the newly prepared data into one or more OLE DB data destinations. ODBC data sources can be accessed via the OLE DB for ODBC provider. Generally, this type of functionality is associated with data warehousing, where source data may need to be migrated to an entirely different table structure due to the different data modeling techniques used in OLTP and OLAP databases.

DTS is not limited to this type of application however, and can be used for moving data between data sources with little or no modification at all. This can be helpful for database migration and integration projects or reorganizing data within the same database. In fact, DTS can be used to create scheduled tasks that do not move data at all, but are used for other database maintenance tasks that can take advantage of the workflow definition features and other task types available. These types of tasks are currently supported by DTS:

File Transfer Protocol   Provides an integrated FTP client to retrieve files from remote systems.

ActiveX Script   Allows scripts written in a COM-compatible scripting language such as VBScript to be run.

Transform Data   This is the basic task for moving and transforming data in DTS. This particular task does not perform as well as the BCP tool or Bulk Insert task (Bulk Insert is also available as a Transact-SQL statement that can be run from a stored procedure or script) for simple data imports. Various options to improve this performance will be discussed later in this chapter.

Execute Process   Allows a program to be run using standard command line syntax.

Execute SQL   Allows a SQL script to be run.

Data Driven Query   Similar to the Transform Data task but can also be used to update or delete existing data, rather than simply inserting new data.

Copy SQL Server Objects   Allows objects such as indexes and constraints to be copied between SQL Server systems. Tables and data can be copied natively by the Transform Data task.

Send Mail   Send Mail via MAPI. This does not require SQL Mail or SQL Agent Mail to have been configured. Multiple MAPI profiles are supported, if needed.

Bulk Insert   This task can be used for data import scenarios where transformation functionality is not required. It allows transaction logging to be bypassed, and does not have the additional overhead of the Transform Data task.

Execute Package   Allows another package to be called from within a package.

Message Queue   Allows messages to be written to or read from Microsoft Message Queue, which allows transactions to be executed against the queue, allowing asynchronous writes to a database that may be offline or under heavy load.

Transfer Error Messages   Allows user-defined message definitions to be copied to another system or instance.

Transfer Databases   Allows entire databases to be copied to another system or instance.

Transfer Master Stored Procedures   Allows system stored procedures to be copied to another system or instance.

Transfer Jobs   Allows SQL Server scheduled jobs to be copied to another database or instance.

Transfer Logins   Allows SQL Server system logins to be copied to another database.

Dynamic Properties   Allows task properties to be changed at run time; for example, to change the properties of an Execute Process task to run it against a different database.

Custom Tasks   Allows COM objects to be called directly from a package.

In order to control the workflow associated with these tasks, precedence constraints can be used to specify that a particular task should only be run after other prerequisite tasks have been completed, or to specify that a task should be run only if another task succeeds or fails. This provides the ability for excellent error handling and conditional logic; this becomes particularly important for more complex data warehouse scenarios.

Clearly, with such a wide variety of functionality, DTS can be quite complex. For relatively simple data movement from one source to one destination, DTS provides an Import/Export Wizard to simplify package development. More complex packages that include multiple sources or destinations or any tasks other than the basic transform can be created or edited using the Package Designer. The following illustration shows an example of a more complex package in the Package Designer. Packages created using the wizard can also be opened using the Package Designer.

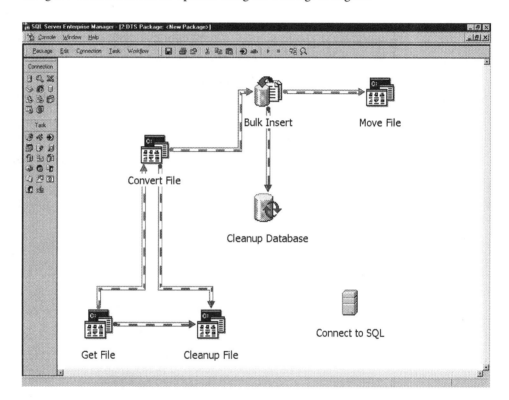

In the designer, green dashed arrows indicate On Success precedence constraints, red dashed arrows indicate On Failure constraints, and blue dashed lines indicate On Completion constraints.

For purposes of this exam objective, you should be familiar with creating simple packages using the wizard and the Package Designer. You should be familiar with the various tasks available and the use of precedence constraints. The next objective will discuss package management and some of the options available for executing packages.

QUESTIONS

7.02: Importing and Exporting Data with Data Transformation Services

3. Your organization is in the midst of migrating data from a legacy database system to SQL Server in order to take advantage of XML and OLAP functionality.

    The legacy system does not have an OLEDB or ODBC driver available, but a third-party utility is available to import and export data via text files.

    You have created a batch file that will retrieve the file from the remote system and convert it to ASCII format. You would like the data import to run as quickly as possible and keep transaction logging overhead to a minimum.

    Which tools can you use? (Choose all that apply.)

    A. Bulk Copy utility

    B. Data Transformation Services Transform Data task

    C. BULK INSERT statement

    D. INSERT FROM statement

4. You are planning to use DTS to extract data from a logging terminal.

    One of your colleagues has written a small program that will extract data from the logging terminal and place it in a comma-delimited text file called RAW_COLLECTOR_DATA.CSV in the DATAGATHER folder.

    You need to create a DTS package that can accomplish the following tasks:

    ■ Import the data from the file RAW_COLLECTOR_DATA.CSV file into a database table.

    ■ If the data load is successful, the file should be moved to the DATAGATHER\ARCHIVE folder.

    ■ A script will need to be run against the data during import in order to reformat the data.

    ■ If the data load is not successful, the file should be e-mailed to an operator.

You take the following actions:

- Create a new DTS package using the DTS Package Designer.
- Add a Text File (Source) data connection for the file.
- Add a SQL Server data connection for the database.
- Configure a transformation to import the data and execute the reformatting script.
- Configure an On Success precedence constraint for the transformation to execute a script to move the file to the DATAGATHER\ARCHIVE folder.
- Configure an On Failure precedence constraint for the Text File data connection object to e-mail the file to an operator using a DTS Send Mail task.

Which of the following conditions are met?

A. Data can be imported into SQL Server from the data file.

B. The data will be reformatted by a script during data loads.

C. The file will be moved if the load is successful.

D. The file will be e-mailed to an operator if the load is not successful.

5. You have been asked to create a development copy of your database.

This new database will be used to test reports and queries before implementing them in production.

Some data in the test database may be modified during tests, and the database will need to be refreshed and brought up-to-date each week.

How should this be implemented?

A. Use the DTS Package Designer to create a workflow that uses `sp_detachdb` and `sp_attachdb` stored procedures to transfer the database.

B. Use replication.

C. Use the DTS Package Designer to create a workflow that uses the Transfer SQL Objects task to copy the database.

D. Use the DTS Import/Export Wizard to create a package that will transfer all database objects and data. Specify that all destination objects should be dropped before the transfer occurs. Schedule the package to run weekly.

Developing and Managing DTS Packages

Generally, developers rather than database administrators will create complex DTS packages, but package execution will normally be within the purview of the DBA. You should be very familiar with the methods available to execute DTS packages and the various options available to control the execution.

Packages can be executed in the following ways:

- From within another DTS package
- From within the Designer or Import/Export Wizard
- Using the DTSRUN utility
- Saving the package as VB code that can be incorporated into another application

In order to ensure the security of your packages, passwords can be used to control who can open the packages in the Designer or execute packages via one of the aforementioned mechanisms. This may be extremely important, considering that the packages may contain usernames and passwords for the databases used by the package.

You have the ability to specify passwords within your package properties to control who can edit or execute the package. The owner password is required to open the package in the Package Designer. The operator password is required to execute the package.

One item of particular importance with regards to DTS security is the use of batch files to execute packages. While this is certainly useful, hard coding database usernames and passwords into a file may well present undesirable security issues. In order to avoid these security issues, DTSRUN can output an encrypted command line. For example, this command will run a package called MYDTSPACKAGE on a system called MYSQLSERVER, logging in using the **sa** user with a password of "SECRET" and a package password of "DTSPASS":

```
DTSRUN /SMYSQLSERVER /NMYDTSPACKAGE /USA /PSECRET /MDTSPASS
```

Adding the /!Y command specifies that the package should not be executed, but that the encrypted version of this command should be generated. Using this switch with the previous command yields the following encrypted output:

```
DTSRun /~Z0x9199CD6BBFE580D96DB5370E53AF3744A1DCC0FF9EB1D11
C324EF4019C4C850392868E554ACCC95616BB8143BA9F31DB368A02FAA6C3
BEEC72B7EB578FE160ADBEF0EEBAE001A6F9DE64B27E033A0424286504E7F
54AC61B321BB698B17D4C8A679794A7FE8CD65F1AE9B3DEA8DFF0FFF4A046
0D1B30D0E21A26FDBE1A0312C935A1D2DB107AD0A38B75D7D0988A42E6ABA
C4F9354AC0103347900 /!Y
```

Make sure that you remove the /!Y switch before copying and pasting this into a batch file, otherwise all subsequent executions will only generate the encrypted output.

With DTS, the Transform Data task can also be configured to provide more throughput in situations where data loads will be run during relatively idle periods, such as at night. These performance-related options are available within the properties of the task, in the Options tab:

Specifying The First And/Or Last Row To Move   This can be useful for testing packages, breaking a large data move into smaller pieces, or skipping a data file header row that simply contains column names.

Fetch Buffer Size   This can be used to specify how many rows should be retrieved from the source at once. This can be used to indirectly control the amount of network bandwidth used by the task.

Use Fast Load   This option can be used against SQL Server data sources to bypass transaction logging, if the database is not running in the FULL recovery mode.

Check Constraints   By default, data loaded through DTS is assumed to have already been validated against business rules and therefore constraints are not checked by default. When using the Fast Load option, this can be enabled to ensure that constraints will be checked against data. This option can degrade data throughput significantly, and should be avoided if it is not needed.

Table Lock   When using the Fast Load option, this will allow DTS to lock the entire table, instead of using row level locks. If packages will be run when users are not active in the database, this can improve performance substantially.

Insert Batch Size   When using the Fast Load option, this allows you to specify the number of rows that should be treated as a batch. Increasing this value can improve performance, but if errors occur, the entire batch will need to be rolled back which can cause substantial overhead.

In addition to DTS, SQL Server also provides tools such as the BCP utility and the BULK INSERT statement. The following table lists the different data load mechanisms available and when to use them.

Data Load Mechanism	Usage Scenario
BCP Utility	Loading data from a single text file from a command prompt or batch file.
BULK INSERT Statement	Loading data from a single text file from within SQL, using scripts or stored procedures.
DTS Import/Export Wizard	Transferring data with or without transformations between two OLEDB data sources.
DTS Package Designer	Transferring data with or without transformations between more than two OLEDB data sources or when more complex workflow must be used to complete prerequisite or additional tasks during package execution.

QUESTIONS

7.03: Developing and Managing DTS Packages

6. You have created a DTS package to collect data from remote franchise and branch locations.

   You have decided to use SQL authentication for the DTS package, as each location is independent and no trust relationships can be created between the locations. Each location is responsible for the costs associated with data reporting, so the DTS package will run on each local server and then a dial-up connection will be initiated with the head office.

Currently, the functionality to run the DTS package and initiate the dial-up connection has been written into a command script. The DTS package will be run via this script on each of the remote systems every night.

You have created a unique login for each remote site, but you do not want users in the remote location to see any usernames or passwords in the command script. How can this be done?

A. Create trust relationships between all locations. Use Windows authentication.

B. Specify that DTSRUN should output an encrypted command line that can be placed in the command script.

C. Configure the package as a Visual Basic file.

D. Configure a new package at the head office to collect the files rather than having a package run on each system.

7. You are running a DTS package that imports data from one of your transaction processing systems and you notice that it runs quite slowly.

There are no users in the database when the package is run.

All business rules and formatting checks have already been validated by the OLTP system.

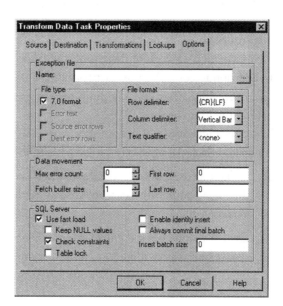

Which of the following properties of the Transform Data task, as shown in the previous illustration, should be turned on to speed up imports into the table? (Choose all that apply.)

A. Use Fast Load

B. Check Constraints

C. Table Lock

D. Enable Identity Insert

TEST YOURSELF OBJECTIVE 7.04

Managing Linked Servers

As you saw in Chapter 2, section 2.01, linked server support provides the ability to use OLEDB to incorporate data from remote systems directly into queries in your system. Once a linked server has been configured, queries such as joins, unions and subqueries can refer to remote tables as easily as one located on the local system. Due to additional overhead and network traffic restrictions, you should not expect the same level of performance that you may be accustomed to with single server queries. Linked servers can be established either through the Enterprise Manager or by using the sp_addlinkedserver stored procedure. You can also configure the security settings for the connection using the sp_addlinkedsrvlogin stored procedure. For more information on both of these procedures see Chapter 2, section 2.01.

In addition to controlling security options, linked server properties can also be used to specify certain compatibility settings between servers such as sort compatibility, as shown on the next page.

These settings allow you to control the behavior of the remote database and various query operations if data needs to be sorted as follows:

- Collation Compatible specifies that both systems use the same sort options and that data comparisons can be executed remotely, conserving resources on the local system.

- Data Access makes the linked server available for user queries. This should always be enabled, unless you need or want to disable queries to the remote system for troubleshooting or other conditions.

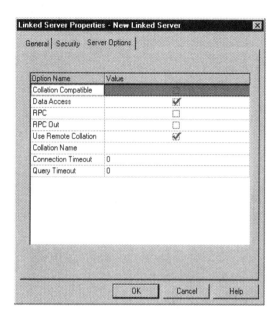

▓ RPC and RPC Out allow stored procedures to be executed. Stored procedures can only be executed remotely against another SQL Server instance.

▓ Use Remote Collation specifies that the remote sort order should be used for data comparisons, rather than the local one. This setting has little effect if the Collation Compatible option is used since both systems will have the same collation. Using Remote Collation will cause sort operations to be run against the remote system, possibly improving performance.

▓ Connection Timeout and Query Timeout allow you to specify how long the system should wait for the remote system before returning an error in the event of delays.

The setting can also be set using the sp_serveroption stored procedure.

Linked servers serve two important functions when dealing with the movement of data. First, it is possible to move data from one table to another either by using a SELECT...INTO statement or by including a subquery from one server in an INSERT statement on another server. More importantly, however, linked servers actually reduce the need to move data. Since you can now write a join statement between two tables on different servers, you do not need to move all of the data to a single server.

QUESTIONS

7.04: Managing Linked Servers

8. You are using SQL authentication due to the design of a custom application that you are running in conjuction with SQL Server, and need to use linked servers to communicate with a remote SQL Server to write a custom report.

    Both servers are running Windows NT Server 4.0 and are members of the same Active Directory forest.

    What authentication schemes can be used for this?

    A. Kerberos Delegation

    B. NTLM Pass-Through Authentication

    C. Impersonation

    D. NULL sessions

9. You have been asked to configure a linked server to a remote SQL server.

    Users who run reports on your system sometimes need to include historic data from another SQL Server system which is being used for long-term data archival.

    This data is publicly available on your web site, therefore security is not any particular concern.

    You would like to ensure that users who run the report can access data from the archive system.

    How should you configure linked server security?

    A. Create a linked server login for each user who needs to run the report. Configure a separate login for each user in the archive system.

    B. Use Kerberos delegation to connect to the archive system with the user's login credentials.

    C. Create one linked server login. Configure the login to be used by all users connecting to the archive system.

    D. Configure a linked server login. Use an XML query to login to the archive system and extract the data.

10. One of your developers is attempting to execute a stored procedure stored in a third party database management system from within a stored procedure in SQL Server. A linked server has been configured and the tables can be queried. You are unable to execute any stored procedures. What must be done to allow this?

    A. Enable the RPC and RPC Out linked server options.

    B. The procedure must be called using the EXEC statement with the REMOTE option.

    C. You must use a remote server instead of a linked server.

    D. This is not possible directly. The OPENROWSET function must be used.

11. You are attempting to execute a linked server query that requires SQL syntax that is not supported by SQL Server, but is supported by the remote system. When attempting to execute the query, you receive an error message and the query does not run. What can be done to resolve this?

    A. Only Transact-SQL syntax can be used.

    B. Only ANSI-SQL syntax can be used.

    C. All non-Transact-SQL syntax must be wholly enclosed in an OPENQUERY statement.

    D. All non-Transact-SQL syntax must be wholly enclosed in a subquery.

TEST YOURSELF OBJECTIVE 7.05

Converting Data Types

When using tools such as DTS, you need to ensure that the data you provide for each column is compatible with the column datatype. If the data types are not directly compatible, you may be able to convert the data to a different datatype, using functions such as CONVERT. Datatype conversion is also an issue when writing T-SQL code that combines data from different columns or attempts to compare variables of different datatypes. Datatypes are used as the basis for creating SQL Server data structures and controlling the potential values of data, therefore, datatype restrictions are very rigidly enforced. You will need to be aware of some of the issues dealing with data of the same datatype with different properties and also datatype compatibility. For example, a character datatype can contain a number (since numbers are characters), but a numeric datatype cannot contain text characters.

There are five basic datatype classes:

Character Data   Character data can be nearly anything, although size and nullability issues will need to be dealt with.

Date and Time Data   Date and Time data can be returned in different formats (such as character format or numeric format) using the convert function. Special functions are also provided to assist in comparisons against date data such as DATEDIFF, which will provide the difference in whichever time measure (such as the number of minutes or the days) between two date/time values.

LOB Data   LOB (Large Object Block) data provides a special class of datatype, used for very large rows that cannot be accommodated with SQL Server's maximum row size of 8060 bytes. The LOB datatypes are TEXT, NTEXT, and IMAGE.

Numeric Data   Numeric data can vary from simple integers to specific precision decimal numbers. The main issues to be aware of when dealing with numeric data are precision, scale and range. Precision specifies the maximum number of digits in a number, scale specifies the number of decimal places allowed in decimal numbers, and range is the minimum and maximum values for a particular datatype. The range for the TINYINT datatype is 0 to 255, whereas the SMALLINT datatype is –32,768 to 32,767.

Variant Data   Variant data can be any of the character or numeric datatypes, and provides very good flexibility. There is only one variant datatype in SQL Server, which is SQL_VARIANT. This datatype generally has high overhead, and should be avoided in most cases. It is designed for use in stored procedures and application code to simplify the use of variables to reduce the need to use CONVERT and CAST.

From these datatype classes, SQL Server provides specific datatypes that will influence the conditions under which data can be entered and how it will be stored. When converting between datatypes of a similar class, where no loss of precision or scale is necessary (such as when converting between integer datatypes such as INT and

TINYINT), conversion is automatic and transparent. In other cases, the CONVERT or CAST functions may need to be used to specify how exactly the data should be converted.

For example, when using the GETDATE() function, the date is returned along with the system time. The CONVERT function allows you to return the date in a specific regional format without the time.

The following query, for example, will retrieve the current date and convert it to CHAR, using style 101:

```
SELECT CONVERT(CHAR, GETDATE(), 101)
```

In this case, you would get the following output on January 1st, 2002: 01/01/2002.

However, the system will not automatically convert the DATETIME datatype to CHAR when attempting to combine these datatypes, such as when attempting to use a variable with the DATETIME datatype to specify a value for a CHAR column. The following error message is produced if the CONVERT or CAST function is not used to explicitly convert the variable value:

```
Server: Msg 241, Level 16, State 1, Line 1

Syntax error converting datetime from character string.
```

QUESTIONS

7.05: Converting Data Types

12. One of your new developers is attempting to write a query to extract the date. When using the GETDATE() function, the date as well as the time is returned. The developer wants to be able to display the date in a specific date format, without including the time. How can this be done most easily?

    A. Use the DATEPART function and specify the date format.

    B. Use the DATEDIFF function and specify the date format.

    C. Use the DATEONLY function and specify the date format.

    D. Use the CONVERT function and specify the date format.

13. One of your developers is trying to write a query using the UNION statement to retrieve data from three tables. He is receiving an error stating that the datatypes are incompatible. What is the solution?

    A. Change the column collation order.

    B. Ensure that all unioned columns have compatible datatypes.

    C. Ensure that all unioned columns have identical datatypes.

    D. Only two tables can be UNIONED in the same query.

14. You are using DTS to extract data from a remote server. Tables in the remote server contain NULL values. When data is retrieved from columns that contain NULL values, you would like NULL values to be replaced with the value NA. Which of the following options will allow you to do this? (Choose all that apply.)

    A. Edit the query used to extract data from the table. Use the ISNULL function to specify the value that should be returned for each column that contains NULL values.

    B. Edit the query used to extract data from the table. Use the NULLIF function to specify the value that should be returned for each column that contains NULL values.

    C. Edit the query used to extract data from the table. Use the CONVERT function to convert the NULL values to the CHAR datatype.

    D. Specify a default value of NA on the destination columns these values will be inserted into. Do not allow NULL values in the destination columns.

15. You are creating the data warehouse for your organization. You have SQL servers running all over the world, and many of them contain multi-lingual data. You are trying to extract a note field that uses a VARCHAR(3000) datatype and put it into an NVARCHAR(3000) datatype. You notice that many rows fail to insert into the table. What should you do?

    A. Specify NVARCHAR(6000).

    B. Specify NTEXT.

    C. Specify NCHAR(6000).

    D. Specify VARCHAR(3000).

Configuring, Maintaining, and Troubleshooting Replication Services

SQL Server replication functionality can be used to distribute copies of your data to or from other databases on SQL Server or remote OLE DB databases such as Access and Oracle. Unlike DTS, replication does not provide the ability to modify data in transit or build extensive workflows, but does provide a much better mechanism for transferring data on a regular basis. Mechanisms are provided within replication to allow data to be replicated as modifications occur or on a scheduled basis. When using replication, it is important to consider the time lapse that will occur between data modifications at the publisher and the replication of that data to the subscribers. This time lapse is referred to as latency. For scenarios that require absolutely no latency, distributed transactions should be used to ensure that data is updated simultaneously across multiple databases. However, this will reduce the autonomy of the databases, as all databases participating in a distributed transaction must be able to commit the work or the update will fail on all systems. Reduced system autonomy is also an issue when using the Immediate Updating Subscribers option, which will be discussed shortly.

Replication can be used to allow data to be collected in retail locations, remote branch offices, manufacturing facilities or any number of other locations and then replicated to a central database. Or, data from a central database can be replicated to those remote locations to provide faster response than using linked servers, reducing network traffic by allowing clients to query a local data store instead of running queries across your WAN, and also providing additional fault tolerance and site autonomy. Microsoft refers to the replication topology of publishers, distributors and subscribers as the replication model. Sites that are connected via RAS or VPN connections will only need to connect long enough to send and/or receive their data. Replicated data can be filtered by column or by row (using a WHERE clause) in order to allow subscribers to receive only the data that is relevant to them.

There are three replication roles:

■ Publishers make their data available for replication.

■ Subscribers receive data from publishers.

- Distributors are responsible for getting the published data to push subscribers and tracking replication status. When using pull subscriptions, the distribution process runs on the subscriber but the subscriber does not need to be configured as an actual distribution server.

All of these roles can be implemented in the same instance of SQL Server, but this is not recommended. Replication can cause substantial overhead due to the tasks involved in distribution, therefore you may want to use a remote distributor to offload much of the replication overhead to another server, freeing up resources on the publisher so that it can accommodate all the data that you are generating.

Subscribers can also act as publishers and make their own data or the data that they have received from other systems available to others. This allows you to take a fan-out approach where data can be replicated strategically to certain systems and then replicated again to additional subscribers to cut the load on the distributor or to reduce network traffic. For example, this could be used in a situation where four servers in a remote location need copies of your data. By using this strategy you can ensure that the same data does not need to be sent across a WAN link four times.

In some cases, subscribers may need to make changes to replicated data and send it back to the publisher. The different replication types have varying levels of support for this type of scenario.

SQL Server provides three replication types:

- Snapshot, which will use the Bulk Copy process to make copies of data. The queued or immediate updating subscribers option can be used to allow subscribers to modify replicated data without causing conflicts with the values stored on the publisher.

- Transactional, which will copy transactions from the source transaction log and apply them to the destination databases. Like snapshot replication, the queued and immediate updating subscribers option can be used to allow changes at the subscriber without causing replication conflicts.

- Merge, which will use an arbitration process to broker updates when conflicts have occurred, providing full two-way replication with extended replication conflict management.

When configuring transactional and merge replication, subscribers must be initialized. This process normally occurs by using a snapshot, in much the same way snapshot replication does, to replicate all current data in a publication to new subscribers. For large publications, the initialization process can be completed manually, such as by sending the publication data on backup tape to the remote location and restoring the data from the tape to the new subscriber.

The queued and immediate updating subscribers options were created to allow subscribers to make changes to data without requiring the full row versioning and update brokering that merge replication requires.

The immediate updating subscribers option specifies that if any replicated data is modified on the subscriber, a distributed transaction should be initiated to immediately update the publisher. In this way, there is little need for conflict management, since the publisher always has the latest data.

The drawback to using the immediate updating subscribers option is that if the publisher is unavailable, replicated data cannot be changed on the subscriber. In order to allow changes to occur locally even if the publisher is unavailable or a network link has failed, the queued updating subscribers options will use MSMQ to write to the subscriber and the message queue, then update the publisher as soon as it is brought back online or communications are re-established.

Although the aforementioned mechanism prevents update conflicts for snapshot and transactional replication, the merge replication type is designed to provide the maximum autonomy for clients. In order to achieve this autonomy, merge replication implements row-level version tracking. When data is replicated, the merge process can detect if an update conflict has occurred. In the event of an update conflict, the system can be configured to automatically resolve conflicts by specifying a higher level of priority for specific systems or by writing custom conflict resolvers using tools such as Visual Basic. If this is not done, replication conflicts must be resolved manually, which can be done by right-clicking the database and using the View Replication Conflicts command on the All Tasks menu.

The Replication Monitor available in the Enterprise Manager can be very helpful for viewing the status of subscribers and reviewing the behavior of the various replication agents. Each agent maintains a history, and it is recommended that you review these histories on a regular basis. The Replication Monitor also provides replication alerts, which are very similar to standard SQL Agent alerts, but are pre-configured for specific replication problems that are likely to occur.

For purposes of the exam you should be familiar with the different types of replication, the intended uses for each type and the various strategies you can leverage when designing your topology and specifying server roles. You should also be familiar with the general process involved in setting up replication. You must:

- Enable your database for publishing.

■ Specify which system and database will be used for distribution.

■ Define what data will be replicated, and the options such as how subscribers will receive their initial synchronization, in which the subscriber initially receives a copy of all the data in the publication so that they are up to date. This can be very network intensive and can be configured to occur manually if needed.

■ Configure subscribers. Subscribers can be configured as push subscriptions, in which case distribution tasks will run on the distributor system, or pull subscriptions, where the distribution tasks will run on the subscriber directly.

QUESTIONS

7.06: Configuring, Maintaining, and Troubleshooting Replication Services

16. You would like to configure replication for your system. You are planning what security context you will use to run SQL Server to ensure that the servers will be able to replicate. How should you configure SQL Server to run? (Choose the best answer.)

A. Run SQL Server on each system with a domain user account. Make the user account an administrator on all SQL systems.

B. Run SQL Server with the local system account.

C. Run SQL Server with a local user account. Create an identical account on each system.

D. Run SQL Server with the **sa** login. Configure the same **sa** password on each system.

LAB QUESTION

Objectives 7.01–7.06

You are the new SQL server administrator for a multinational auto parts manufacturer. The company has locations in Toronto, Chicago, London, and Sydney. Your head office is in Toronto. Each location uses a SQL 2000 server to maintain its inventory lists.

1. Your production manager would like all of the regional offices to report their inventory back to the central server in Toronto every 3 hours during the day. However, he wants to find a way to move the data while minimizing the amount of wide area network traffic. How would you suggest moving this data while reducing the amount of traffic generated by the data transfer?

2. All of the regional sales groups store local sales information in Excel spreadsheets. There are 12 groups in each office. All of the group leaders save their spreadsheets in a file share on the Windows 2000 server running SQL Server in Toronto. The files are updated twice per week. The sales manager would like all of these spreadsheets loaded into a table on the Toronto SQL server. She would like to have the process automated. How would you configure and automate this process?

3. In each city, your company would like to make local inventory available to their customers. They would like this information to be made available on a secure web site. The customers should be able to look up the availability of any item by its part number. How would you provide access to the product inventory list for these customers?

QUICK ANSWER KEY

Objective 7.01

1. **A, B, C, E,** and **F**
2. **A** and **B**

Objective 7.02

3. **A** and **C**
4. **D**
5. **B**

Objective 7.03

6. **A** and **C**
7. **C**

Objective 7.04

8. **C**
9. **D**
10. **C**
11. **D**

Objective 7.05

12. **B**
13. **A** and **D**
14. **A**
15. **A**

Objective 7.06

16. **C**

IN-DEPTH ANSWERS

7.01: Using XML Support

1. ☑ **A, B, C, E**, and **F** are correct. A virtual directory must be created for your database.

   In order to allow client connections to authenticate against IIS, basic authentication must be used since not all clients may be able to use more advanced authentication mechanisms. Due to the inherently insecure nature of basic authentication, it is recommended that SSL be used to prevent usernames and passwords from being intercepted in transit.

   XML queries from files are referred to as template queries, and this must be enabled. X-Path queries are not needed in this case. When using template queries, you must also specify a virtual name for your virtual directory, as this will be used within the template files. Integrated Windows authentication cannot be used to authenticate clients because not all clients will be able to support it. However, IIS is able to authenticate against SQL Server using integrated Windows authentication and this is the recommended configuration.

   ☒ **D** is incorrect because URL queries cannot be submitted from a file template.

2. ☑ **A** and **B** are correct. When specifying the physical path to store the files needed for the virtual directory, the path must already exist.

   Once the filesystem folder has been created, the virtual directory can then be added to allow XML access to the database properly.

   ☒ **C** is incorrect. There is no system stored procedure called `sp_createxmlschema`. All XML functionality, with the exception of some parsing of XML queries, is incorporated into IIS. **D** is incorrect. You do not need to allow the IIS user account to login to SQL Server; you can specify the login method to be used in the virtual directory properties.

7.02: Importing and Exporting Data with Data Transformation Services

3. ☑ **A** and **C** are correct. Both the Bulk Copy and Bulk Insert tools are designed for high-speed data import from a file.

☒ **B** is incorrect. The Transform Data task adds unwanted overhead, with no additional benefits. **D** is incorrect. The INSERT FROM statement does not allow input from a file.

4. ☑ **D** is correct. No data needs to be kept in the development database, so the easiest way to refresh the entire database is to delete and re-copy it each week.

☒ **A** is incorrect. Using sp_detachdb and sp_attachdb is not appropriate, as it would require taking the database offline. This functionality is designed primarily for moving databases and replacing the earlier concept of removable databases in previous versions of SQL Server. **B** is incorrect. Using replication is inappropriate, since it will introduce changes into the database, it is relatively complex to configure, and it will generate additional overhead on the production system. **C** is incorrect. This solution does not include the required execution schedule.

5. ☑ **B** is correct. Simply using an encrypted command line allows the application to work as originally designed and envisioned.

☒ **A** is incorrect. Creating trust relationships is not appropriate as the question specifically states that trust relationships cannot be created. **C** is incorrect. Converting the package to Visual Basic would work, but requires a substantial effort compared to using an encrypted command line for little additional benefit. **D** is incorrect. Configuring packages to run centrally would work, but much like the previous choice, provides additional complexity and effort for little additional value.

7.03: Developing and Managing DTS Packages

6. ☑ **A** and **C** are correct. Using the Fast Load option will allow the system to bypass most transaction logging and using the Table Lock feature can cut memory usage and improve import throughput substantially.

☒   **B** is incorrect. Checking constraints will reduce performance and is not needed since the data has already been validated. **D** is incorrect. Enabling identity insert is not required in this scenario. Enabling identity insert will have little effect on performance and can easily cause more problems than it is worth if you generate non-sequential identity values.

7.   ☑   **C** is correct. In this example, since clients are using SQL authentication, only mapped user accounts or impersonation can be used to authenticate against the remote system.

☒   **A** and **B** are incorrect. Kerberos and NTLM cannot be used with SQL authentication. **D** is incorrect. NULL sessions can be used in Windows for connecting to shared resources, but this is not supported in SQL Server.

7.04: Managing Linked Servers

8.   ☑   **C** is correct. This is by far the easiest solution, and with little need for permission delegation or auditing, losing the ability to uniquely identify users should be an issue.

☒   **A** is incorrect. Creating separate logins for each user is unnecessary in this scenario. **B** is incorrect. Using Kerberos delegation can be somewhat difficult, therefore this solution is not particularly appropriate to the scenario at hand. **D** is incorrect. There is absolutely no need to use XML to query the database in this scenario.

9.   ☑   **D** is correct. Stored procedures can only be run remotely using EXEC on another SQL Server. In order to execute a stored procedure remotely on a non-SQL Server system, you must use the OPENROWSET function.

☒   **A** is incorrect. RPC and RPC Out can be used to permit remote stored procedure execution against another SQL Server. **B** is incorrect. There is no REMOTE option on the EXEC statement. **C** is incorrect. Remote servers are used for replication without remote query support. This feature will not solve the problem.

10.   ☑   **C** is correct. Using the OPENQUERY function will pass the enclosed query directly to the remote system without any pre-parsing by SQL Server.

☒   **A** and **B** are incorrect. Any SQL variant can be used provided it is supported by the remote system when using the OPENQUERY function. **D** is incorrect. Although these types of queries will often be subqueries, this is not required.

11. ☑ **D** is correct. This is quite simple with the CONVERT function.

☒ **A** is incorrect. The DATEPART function can be used for this purpose, but in a very roundabout manner. **B** is incorrect. The DATEDIFF function will provide the amount of time between two dates. **C** is incorrect. There is no DATEONLY function in SQL Server.

7.05: Converting Data Types

12. ☑ **B** is correct. All data types for the columns that will be UNIONED must be compatible.

☒ **A** is incorrect. Changing the column collation would not resolve this problem. **C** is incorrect. The datatypes do not need to be identical. **D** is incorrect. You can UNION as many tables as you need to. There is no hard-coded limit on the UNION operator.

13. ☑ **A** and **D** are correct. The ISNULL function allows you to replace NULL values for a particular column in your result set with another value.

Rather than changing the NULL values, specifying a default on the column and disallowing NULLS will force those values to be replaced with the default. This will not require any changes to existing data or the query.

☒ **B** is incorrect. The NULLIF will replace specified values with NULLS, which is the opposite of the intended solution. **C** is incorrect. The CONVERT function cannot be used to change the value of a NULL. Rather than changing the NULL values, specifying a default on the column and disallowing NULLS will force those values to be replaced with the default. This will not require any changes to existing data or the query.

14. ☑ **A** is correct. The Unicode datatypes (NCHAR, NVARCHAR, and NTEXT) require two bytes of storage per character, instead of one. You must take this into account when planning for use of these columns. The maximum amount of data that can be inserted into the NCHAR and NVARCHAR datatypes is 4,000 instead of 8,0000 characters.

☒ **B** is incorrect. NTEXT is not needed, since we do not need to store more than 4,000 characters. **C** is incorrect. The data should be stored in a varying length datatype as intended originally in this scenario. **D** is incorrect. VARCHAR should not be used as it will not allow non-Latin characters in the database.

15. ☑ **A** is correct. Running all SQL servers under a domain user account with administrative permissions on each system is by far the easiest solution. This may not be appropriate for security conscious environments, and you may want to limit the permission given to the accounts.

☒ **B** is incorrect. Running SQL Server under the local system account will not allow replication to occur. **C** is incorrect. Running SQL Server with a duplicate user account on each system (referred to as pass-through authentication) does not work in a domain environment. **D** is incorrect. SQL Server cannot run under a SQL user account. It must use a valid Windows user account or the local system account.

7.06: Configuring, Maintaining, and Troubleshooting Replication Services

16. ☑ **C** is correct. Merge replication is integrated with the Windows 2000 Synchronization Manager specifically for this reason. You can also configure Synchronization Manager to synchronize when the system is idle, or based on a schedule.

☒ **A** is incorrect. Transactional replication does not support Synchronization Manager. **B** is incorrect. Configuring queued subscribers is not necessary, as the data does not come from the publisher. There is no need to be concerned about conflicting data. This option would be appropriate for updating and deleting data, however. **D** is incorrect. If you are not using queued subscribers, there is no need to install MSMQ.

LAB ANSWER

1. Because you will be transferring data regularly throughout the day, you could complete this task using SQL Server replication. You would configure Toronto as a central subscriber and have each of the other offices publish and distribute their inventories. Because the latency (the period of time between updates) is fairly low and because you want to minimize the amount of traffic sent across the WAN to the Toronto office, you should use transactional replication. This form of replication will only send changes across the network. Using snapshot replication would not make sense because it would involve each office sending their entire inventory list across the network. Merge replication only sends changes, however, because the replication is one way, so there would be no benefit in using merge replication.

2. Because all of the spreadsheets are saved in a central location on the Toronto server, you could create a DTS package that imported all of the spreadsheets into a table. You could create a single package in the DTS designer that would accomplish this task. It would simply require that you standardize the names of each file. You could then use the SQL Agent to execute the package on a set schedule.

3. The easiest way to make this data available on the web would be to configure XML support for SQL Server 2000. Through XML you could provide secure access to your users. And allow them to submit queries against the database.

MICROSOFT CERTIFIED DATABASE ADMINISTRATOR

8

Managing and Monitoring SQL Server 2000 Security

O f all the tasks of the administrator, securing the server is one of the most important. Your SQL server contains data. This data is important to your business and may be sensitive. You need to be able to keep the wrong people from accessing your data. You also need to control which users can access the data. You need to be able to validate your users and determine what level of access they should have. You also need to be able to monitor your database and make sure that your security is working.

You will be expected to know how and when to configure the security mode in SQL Server. You need to know how to create and manage both logons and database user accounts. You must have a solid understanding of the various fixed security roles as well as how to manage security with user-defined security roles. You should understand how to manage security with objects such as views and stored procedures. You must know how to set permissions on SQL Server objects and how to audit your server to detect lapses in your security.

TEST YOURSELF OBJECTIVE 8.01

Configuring Security Modes

Security in SQL Server consists of two parts—authentication and authorization. Authentication is the process that involves having users identify themselves to the server and, in essence, prove that they are who they claim to be. Once SQL Server has verified your identity, it is then able to see what you are allowed to do on the server. This is authorization. The most important part of the authentication process is the validation of users. The security modes in SQL Server 2000 determine how this validation takes place. There are two types of authentication models in SQL Server:

- Windows authentication (or trusted authentication)
- SQL Server authentication

In Windows authentication, the user must establish a session with the operating system using Windows NT challenge response or Kerberos. Once the user has established a session with Windows, they establish a trusted connect between their session and SQL Server. Information about the user (such as their Security Identifier [SID] and the SIDs of any groups that the user is a member) is passed to the SQL Server when the trusted connection is established. Because it is using a trusted connection, SQL Server accepts Windows validation and does not validate the user further. SQL Server then takes their SID information and checks the sysxlogins table in the Master database to see if there is a valid logon for this user, or any group associated with the user. If it finds an entry, the user is authenticated; if not, the user is denied access to the server. Obviously, the user must have a valid Windows login in order to use Windows authentication.

SQL Server authentication uses a different strategy. When the user connects to the server, they offer a user name and a password. Because there is no other service validating the users, SQL Server checks the user name and password against the sysxlogins table. If it finds a matching SQL logon and password, it validates the user. If it cannot find a matching SQL logon and password, the user is denied access to the server. Passwords are only stored for logins using SQL Server authentication. They are stored in encrypted form. A user does not need a Windows login to connect to the server using SQL Server authentication.

SQL Server implements these authentication types in two authentications modes:

- Windows-only authentication mode
- SQL Server and Windows authentication mode or mixed mode

Which mode you choose will depend on the situation of your users. If all users authenticate to a Windows domain, the Windows authentication should be used. If some users do not authenticate to the domain (such as users with other operating systems like Macintosh or Unix), you should use mixed mode. There are some clear advantages to using Windows-only authentication:

- Access is seamless and faster. The user needs to logon to Windows only. Once they are logged on, they are not prompted to logon to the SQL server. The credentials are passed to the SQL Server and validation takes place, but it is invisible to the user.

- You have the ability to add Windows groups as a single logon. If you have groups of users with the same security requirements, you can create a Windows group and create a single logon that will allow all members of the group to access the server. You will first create the group in the Active Directory and add all users who should belong to the group. You will then create a single login for the global group.

- Any advanced security measures you add (such as high encryption, account lockouts, auditing, or strong password policies) will also increase the security of SQL Server since you cannot connect to the server until you logon to Windows.

The disadvantage to Windows-only authentication is that all users must have a valid Windows logon account to access the SQL server.

If this is not the case, you must use mixed mode. You would select mixed mode when:

- You have users that do not logon to the Windows domain, such as Unix, Novell, or Macintosh clients
- You have clients who are connecting from the Internet
- You want to use the **sa** login account

Mixed mode will still allow Windows users to connect using Windows authentication, but it will also give users the option of passing SQL Server a login name and password and authenticating using SQL Server authentication.

You chose an authentication mode when you installed the server, however, you can change your security mode at any time. To change your security mode:

1. Right-click the server and open the Properties sheet for the server.

2. On this Properties sheet, select the mode that you want to set from the Security tab and click OK.

3. Stop and restart the server.

The final step is the most important. The change in the security mode will not take effect until the server is restarted.

QUESTIONS

8.01: Configuring Security Modes

1. You are the administrator for a SQL 2000 server. The manager for the marketing group has approached you because some of her graphic artists need access to one of the databases on the server. These users are connecting from Macintosh workstations. These users are not authenticated by the Windows domain controller. You change the security mode from Windows-only to mixed mode and add logins and passwords for the users. However the users are complaining that they still cannot access the server. You confirm that the required network

libraries are installed. What is the most likely reason that they still cannot access the server?

A. You have not created Windows user accounts for the Macintosh users.

B. SQL Server does not support Macintosh users.

C. You do not have the correct SQL client installed on the server.

D. You have not restarted the SQL Server service.

E. You have not rebooted the server.

2. You are the administrator of a SQL 2000 server. You normally connect using a Windows user account that has been granted administrative rights on the server. Recently a junior Windows administrator accidentally deleted your Windows account. You need to access the server and give your new Windows logon administrative rights. You know the **sa** password and try to logon as **sa**. However you receive the following error:

```
Server: Msg 18452, Level 16, State 1

[Microsoft][ODBC SQL Server Driver][SQL Server] Login failed
for user 'sa'. Reason: Not associated with a trusted SQL
Server connection.
```

You are certain that you have entered the correct password. What is the most likely reason why you cannot connect?

A. The server is in Windows authentication-only mode.

B. You have not added the **sa** account to the Active Directory.

C. The ODBC DSN is not configured to use mixed mode authentication.

D. Someone has deleted the **sa** account.

E. The SQL Server cannot contact a Windows domain controller.

TEST YOURSELF OBJECTIVE 8.02

Creating and Managing Logons

One of the most important elements of the authentication process is the SQL server logon. Regardless of how SQL Server validates users, it checks in the sysxlogins table in the Master database to see if the user has a valid user account. If a user (or possibly a group, if using Windows authentication) does not have a SQL Server login, they will not be allowed to access the server. Just as there are two types of authentication, there are also two types of login accounts: Windows authenticated logon and a SQL Server authenticated logon. As with most things in SQL Server, you can add logons using Enterprise Manager and Transact-SQL.

To create a logon using Enterprise Manager, expand the Security folder, right-click the Logins icon and select New Login. This will bring up the SQL Server Login Properties sheet, as shown in the illustration that follows. To create a Windows authenticated login, click the Windows Authentication button and select the Windows domain where the user account is located. You can only create Windows authenticated logins for existing Windows user and group accounts. Once you select the domain, SQL will automatically place the domain name and a backslash in the Name box. You can then type the name of the user or group to the right of the backslash. All Windows authenticated login names must include the name of the domain (in the form "domain_name\account_name"). You can also click the Browse button next to the Name text box and browse the Active Directory for the account you want to associate with the login. It is possible to create logins for users from any trusted domain. This is why you include the domain name when you enter the user name for Windows authenticated logins.

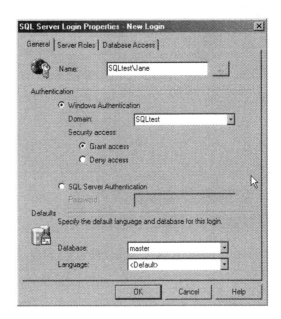

You are not prompted for a password because SQL Server does not validate the user. The SID for the associated login will be stored in the sysxlogins table. Notice as well with the Windows authenticated login in the previous illustration that it is possible to create a granted login or a denied login. In SQL Server, permission (including login permissions) can be either granted or denied. If a permission is denied, the deny will always override any granted permission. When a user connects through Windows authentication, SQL Server considers both the user account and any group associated with the user. The user's login permission is a combination of their personal permissions and any permission inherited from a group. If you add a login for a user, but set it as a denied login, that user will not be allowed to logon to the server even if they have been granted logon permission as a member of group (the same would be true if you granted logon permission to a user but denied login to one of the user's group memberships).

To use the SQL Server Login Properties sheet to create a SQL Server login, you must click the SQL Server Authentication button. You can then give the user a name and a password. When you click OK, SQL Server will prompt you to confirm the password by re-entering it. Both the username and the password will be stored in sysxlogins. Unlike Windows authentication, you do not need to add a domain name next to the user name. There is no association with Windows domains, so you only need the name of the login itself. The password is stored in the sysxlogins in an encrypted format. Not even an administrator can view the password in sysxlogins. If a user forgets their password you can reset it using the Properties sheet for the login, but there is no way of retrieving the password once it is entered. Because there are no other checks, make sure to use a strong password. A strong password should be a mix of numbers, letters, case and special characters. It should also avoid obvious items (like the user ID or the user's first or last name). It should also not be blank. Unfortunately, you have no way of blocking blank passwords for SQL server accounts, but any user with a blank password will show a NULL in the password column in sysxlogins. Because there is nothing similar to group logins with SQL Server authentication, there is no deny login. If you do not create an account for a user, they cannot connect to the server.

There are different Transact-SQL statements for adding each type of login. To add a Windows authenticated login, you use the `sp_grantlogin` stored procedure. The syntax for this procedure is as follows:

```
sp_grantlogin 'domain\{user | group}'
```

When you execute this stored procedure, SQL Server contacts a domain controller and retrieves the SID for the user or group. You can only reference one user or group object with this statement. If you want to create a denied login you can use the `sp_denylogin` stored procedure. The syntax for this procedure is the same as `sp_grantlogin`. You can also remove a Windows authenticated login (either granted or denied) using the `sp_revokelogin` stored procedure. When you issue the `sp_revokelogin` stored procedure, SQL Server deletes the reference to the account in sysxlogins, but does not otherwise affect the Windows account. (That is, it does not delete the group or user, just their login.)

To add a SQL Server authenticated login with Transact-SQL, you use the `sp_addlogin` stored procedure. The syntax for this procedure is as follows:

```
sp_addlogin 'login name', 'password' ['default database',
    'default language', 'sid']
```

Be aware that when you send the text of this stored procedure across the network, it is sent in clear text unless you have encrypted network communication (using IPSEC for example). SQL Server generates a 16-Bit internal SID for each SQL Server login. If you are moving a login from one server to another and want the SID to remain the same, you can specify the value when you create the login. If it has not been assigned, SQL Server will use the SID supplied. Generally you allow SQL Server to generate the SID for you. To remove a SQL authenticated login you use the `sp_droplogin` name. This stored procedure will delete the row from sysxlogions that referred to that login. You cannot drop or revoke a login if that user owns any objects in the database. To drop these accounts you will have to remove them as object owners using the `sp_changeobjectowner` (or `sp_changedbowner`) stored procedure.

A simple way to keep these stored procedures clear in your mind is to remember that with Windows authenticated logins you are granting or denying access to a Windows login account that already exists. When you create a SQL Server login, you are adding or dropping an entry in sysxlogins. The user account has no existence outside of the sysxlogins table.

SQL Server also has certain built-in logins. These logins are created by default when the server is installed. These logins are **sa** and the Builtin\administrators login account. The **sa** account has been in SQL Server since its inception. This account has full administrative control over the server and all databases within the server. In earlier versions of SQL Server, there were some tasks that could only be performed if you connected to the server as **sa**. If you are using Windows authentication-only mode, you will not be able to connect to the server using the **sa** login. The Builtin\Administrators login maps the Windows local administrators group to a SQL Server login. This account is added to the sysadmin role and has the same rights as **sa**. Be aware of this account because it means that anyone who is a member of the administrators local group (like all domain and enterprise administrators on your network) will have full administrative access to your SQL Server. The Builtin\Administrators login can be removed, but the **sa** account cannot be modified or deleted. The only change you can make with **sa** is to reset its password.

QUESTIONS

8.02: Creating and Managing Logons

3. You are the administrator of a SQL 2000 server. You have just added the database for the company order entry system. There are over 200 telephone order takers that need access to the server. In addition, this group has a high turnover rate. In any given month, up to 50 users will quit and be replaced by 50 new workers. All users are members of a Windows 2000 mixed mode domain called Order_entry. They run a combination of Windows 95, Windows 98, NT 4.0 Workstation, and Windows 2000 Professional computers. You want to add these users with the least amount of work. You also want to minimize the administrative overhead of maintaining the logins. How would you configure the logins for these users?

A. Create a Windows authenticated login for each user.

B. Create a SQL Server group login for all the users.

C. Create a global group in the Active Directory and add all of the order entry staff to that group. Create a single SQL Server authenticated login for that group.

D. Create a global group in the Active Directory and add all of the order entry staff to that group. Create a single Windows authenticated login for that group.

E. Create two global groups—one for Windows 9x users and one for Windows NT/2000 users. Add all of the order entry staff into their correct group. Create two Windows authenticated logins, one for each group.

4. You are the administrator of a SQL server called SalesServer in an Active Directory domain called West.Bigcorp.local. The layout of your domain is shown in the illustration that follows. Your server holds all sales information for your domain. There are several sales managers in your domain that need access to the sales database. Sales managers from the East.Bigcorp.local domain also need access to this database. How will you provide access to both groups of sales managers? (Choose all that apply. Each option represents a portion of the solution.)

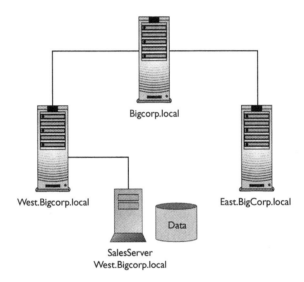

Bigcorp.local

West.Bigcorp.local

East.BigCorp.local

SalesServer
West.Bigcorp.local

Data

A. Create a global group in East.BigCorp.local called sales_mgrs and add all sales managers from that domain into the sales_mgrs group.

B. Create a global group in West.BigCorp.local called sales_mgrs and add the sales managers from both domains into that group.

C. Create a global group called sales_mgrs in the West.Bigcorp.local. Place the sales managers from that domain in the group.

D. Create a single login for the West.Bigcorp.local sales managers group and create SQL Server login accounts for the sales managers in East.Bigcorp.local.

E. Create a separate login for each Sales_mgrs global group.

Creating and Managing Database User Accounts

In section 8.02 you saw how to create a SQL Server login. A login, however, is only half of what is required to access a database. The login simply indicates that you have authenticated yourself to the server and that the server acknowledges that you are who you say you are. Access to a database requires a second piece: a database user account. Authentication is carried out at the server level, but actual authorization (that is, determining what you are allowed to do and not to do) is determined at the database level. There is a logical reason for this two-part security system. A single server may contain multiple databases. All users authenticate to the server, but all users do not necessarily need access to all databases. Moving the majority of the security to the database level makes each database an independent object that can have its own security.

Having a login alone, therefore, does not give you much access on the server. Database user accounts are mapped to individual logins, and it is possible for a login to map to more than one database user account. There are several ways to create a database user account. The first is to click the Database Access tab of the SQL Server Login Properties sheet in Enterprise Manager. This tab lists all available databases and if you click the check box next to a particular database, SQL Server will automatically create a database user account that maps the login. By default, the database user account will have the same name as the login. However you have the option of changing the name if you desire. You can also create a database user account by expanding the database, right-clicking the Users folder and selecting New Database User. This will open the Database User Properties sheet. On this Properties sheet, you simply select the SQL login from the pull-down menu, and if you choose, rename the user account.

You can also create a database user account using Transact-SQL. Database user accounts are created by using the `sp_grantdbaccess` stored procedure. The syntax for this procedure is:

```
USE database

GO

sp_grantdbaccess 'login name'[, 'name in database']
```

You use the same stored procedure to map database user accounts to both Windows and SQL Server logins. Remember that when you reference a Windows authenticated login you must reference both the domain name and the user name. If you only reference the user name, the procedure will return an error. Because database user accounts are database specific, you should include the USE statement to make sure the stored procedure adds the user account to the correct database.

There are two database user accounts that appear in every database: dbo and guest. The dbo accounts appear in the model database and are copied to all databases. The guest account must be added to the database. Guest allows anonymous access to your database. Anyone who has a valid login to the server, but does not have a database user account on a database, is mapped to Guest. This means if you give permission on an object to guest, any user who can login to the server can access that resource. Guest is also a member of the public default role. This means that any permissions granted to the public role will apply to the Guest account (see section 8.04 for more information on the public role). By default, guest has no specific rights on the database. The guest account can be deleted but it is not possible to drop the dbo user account.

The dbo user is very important. The dbo account is the default owner for all databases. As the database owner, the dbo user account has full access to all databases. Members of the sysadmin role are automatically mapped to dbo for all databases (see section 8.04 for information about the sysadmin role). This means that members of this role have full control over all databases controlled by dbo.

QUESTIONS

8.03: Creating and Managing Database User Accounts

5. Jane is the administrator for a SQL 2000 server. Members of the sales, marketing and HR groups will use the server. The members of the sales and marketing groups will each store their own information separately, but will often need to share information between the two groups. The HR group will not share its information with the other groups. Administrators will need access

to all of the data. Due to the sensitive nature of their data, the manager of HR wants to make sure that his staff are the only non-administrative users that can access HR data. What is the minimum number of databases that you would require to meet the security needs of these three groups?

A. Create one large database. Map a database user account to each log in and limit what users can access on a table-by-table basis. Add the administrators to the sysadmin role.

B. Create three databases, one for each group. Create database user accounts in the HR database only for those members of the HR group that need access. For members of the sales and marketing groups, map a database user account for each login in both databases.

C. Create one database for HR and one database for sales and marketing. Create database user accounts in HR for only those users that need access to the HR data. Create user accounts for all other users in the sales and marketing database.

D. Install a named instance and place the HR database on that instance. Create a single database on the default server for the sales and marketing users.

6. Your company is developing a web-based application to allow your customers to check availability of certain products. To do this, the customers will require read permission on the product_inventory table. What is the best way to give your Internet customers access to this table? (Choose the best answer.)

A. Allow the users to connect to the web site with anonymous access. Create a guest login account and map it to the guest account in the database. Give the guest account access to the product_inventory table.

B. Create a SQL Server login account, and map it to a database user account. Give that user account the appropriate permissions. Have the web application connect to the SQL server with that login.

C. Create a SQL server login account and use this login to connect from the web-based application. Add the guest account to the database and give the guest account permissions on the product_inventory table.

D. You cannot give Internet users access to a SQL server.

Adding and Removing Users from Fixed Roles

SQL Server also includes security roles. Roles are essentially groups, but unlike Windows security groups, they have no existence outside of SQL Server. SQL Server uses the term role to avoid confusion with other groups. Like groups, roles can contain users, and any rights assigned to a particular role will be automatically granted to the users who are members of the role.

There are two types roles:

- Fixed roles
- User-defined roles

Fixed roles are created when the server is created. They are fixed in the sense that they cannot be dropped and their permissions cannot be changed. User-defined roles are created in a specific database and can be used to group together database user accounts that have a common security requirement.

There are two types of fixed roles:

- Fixed server roles
- Fixed database roles

The fixed server roles exist at the server level and are independent of any particular user database. They are used to give individual users administrative rights on the server. Fixed server roles contain SQL Server logins (either Windows authenticated or SQL Authenticated). The fixed server roles are listed in the following table.

Fixed Server Role	Description
sysadmin	This role has full administrative control over the server. They can change security and the server settings. In addition, members of this role are mapped to the dbo database user account for all databases on the server. This means that members of sysadmin also have complete access to all tables and all data in all databases.

Fixed Server Role	Description
serveradmin	Members of the serveradmin role can use `sp_configure` and other stored procedures to change server-wide settings. However, unlike members of the sysadmin role, they cannot modify security settings and are not automatically mapped to dbo. This means that they have permission to access the server settings, but not on any specific databases within the server.
setupadmin	Members of this role are able to create linked servers and configure startup procedures.
dbcreator	Members of this role are given the ability to create databases. They become owners for any database that they create. As such they can also alter and drop any database they have created. Members of the dbcreator role are not given any specific control over existing databases.
diskadmin	Members of this role have the ability to create and remove backup devices and modify physical database files. They are not given any specific rights to the data within the databases.
processadmin	Members of this role have the right to issue the KILL statement against any process that is currently running on the server. The KILL statement ends any process and, if the process was part of an open transaction, will also rollback the transaction. It is used mostly to remove any process that has stopped responding and release any locks held by that process.
securityadmin	Members of this role can add, modify and drop logins. They can also give users permission to create databases. Unlike sysadmins, however, they have no other rights on the server.
bulk insert admin	Members of this role are granted the right to perform bulk inserts on a database. A bulk insert is one in which many rows are added through a single operation (such as running bcp, or a DTS package).

All members of a fixed server role also have the ability to add any other user to the role they are member of. There is no way to block this behavior.

To add a user to a fixed server role in Enterprise Manager, click the Server Roles tab of the SQL Server Login Properties sheet for that user. You can also view the Properties sheet for the role in the Security folder to see all users who are a member of a particular role. You can also use the `sp_addsrvrolemember` stored procedure. The syntax for this procedure is as follows:

```
sp_addsrvrolemember 'user name', 'role name'
```

For Windows authenticated users, remember to include the domain name as part of the login name. If you want to remove someone from a fixed server role, you can use the `sp_dropsrvrolemember`. You can also remove a member from a fixed server role using Enterprise Manager. Removing a user from a role will not affect their login in any other way.

The second type of fixed role is the fixed database role. Fixed database roles exist in all databases. The following table lists all the fixed database roles.

Fixed Database Role	Description
db_owner	Members of this role have all rights of the dbo owner user account (although they are not mapped to dbo). They can create objects and access and modify any existing objects in the database.
db_securityadmin	Members of this role can assign statement permissions (such as CREATE TABLE) and object permissions (such as SELECT or INSERT) to any database user. They cannot, however, add new users.
db_accessadmin	Members of this role can add and remove users groups and roles from the database. They cannot, however, assign permissions to these users.
db_ddladmin	Members of this role are able to execute any data definition language statements on the database. DDL statements include all CREATE, ALTER, and DROP statements (except for the CREATE, ALTER, and DROP database statements).

Fixed Database Role	Description
db_backupoperator	Members of this role have permission to backup the database.
db_datareader	Members of this role have permission to SELECT from any table in the database.
db_datawriter	Members of this role have permission to issue INSERT, UPDATE, and DELETE on any table in the database. One thing to note is that db_datawriters are not given SELECT permission on any of the tables. If users do not have SELECT permission, they cannot include a WHERE clause when executing an UPDATE or DELETE statement. This means that they would only be able to affect the table as a whole.
db_denydatareader	This is the opposite of sp_datareader. A member of this role is explicitly denied SELECT permission on all tables in the database.
db_denydatawriter	Members of this group are explicitly denied the right to add, modify or remove any data in the database.
public	This role is given all default permissions. Any member with a database user account in a database is a member of public for that database. This includes the guest account. Therefore, if you give permissions to an object to public, you are granting that permission to anyone with a SQL login, even if that person does not have a database login.

As with the fixed server roles, you cannot alter the permissions of any of the roles. Also, members of any role have the automatic right to give others membership in the role. This behavior cannot be disabled. Fixed database roles are stored in the sysusers table in each database.

To add a database user account to a fixed database role you can use either Enterprise Manager or Transact-SQL. In Enterprise Manager, you can add a user to a role using the Database Access tab of the SQL Server Login Properties sheet, or you can expand the database, click the Roles object and then double-click the role you want to change membership. In the Database Role Properties sheet, you select which users to add to the role. Note that you can only add existing database user accounts to the role. You can also add role membership using the sp_addrolemember stored procedure. The syntax for this procedure is as follows:

```
USE database

GO

sp_addrolemember 'role', 'user name'
```

Because this stored procedure is database specific, it is a good idea to add the USE statement and specify the correct database. Note that the order of arguments for this procedure is the opposite of sp_addsrvrolemember (which is username, role name).

exam
ⓦatch

Security features very highly on this exam. Make sure you know all of the fixed roles and what tasks they are able to perform.

QUESTIONS

8.04: Adding and Removing Users from Fixed Roles

7. You are the administrator for a SQL 2000 server called Production1. This database contains two databases: manufacturing and accounting. You are finding the amount of work required to maintain the server too much for one person. In particular, the manufacturing group undergoes frequent staff changes. The manager for the manufacturing group has appointed someone to assist you. This person needs to be able to create logins, giving users access to the manufacturing database. He should not be able to add users to the accounting database. How would you configure the security for this user? (Choose all that apply. Each selection represents a partial solution.)

    A. Add the user to the sysadmin role

    B. Add the user to the server admin role

    C. Add the user to the security admin role

     D. Add the user to the db_owner role for the manufacturing database

     E. Add the user to the db_ddladmin role for the manufacturing database

     F. Add the user to the db_accessadmin for the manufacturing database role

8. Jim is the primary administrator for a test server in the R&D group. He is configuring access for several database developers. These developers need the ability to create databases and to have full control over the databases they create. They should not have any access to databases created by other developers on the server. What would be the best way to configure the security for these developers?

     A. Add the users to the db_ddladmin role in the Master database

     B. Add them to the dbcreator role

     C. Add them to the dbcreator role and alias them to dbo for all databases they create

     D. Add them to the setupadmin role

     E. Create a server role that grants the developers the CREATE DATABASE permission and maps them to dbo for all databases they create

TEST YOURSELF OBJECTIVE 8.05

Creating Roles to Manage Database Security

SQL Server also gives you the ability to create your own roles. User-defined roles allow you to group together users who have a common security requirement. When you create a user-defined to role, you can assign it permissions just as you would to any other user. You can then add users to that role. Any user you add to the role will get all permissions you have given to the role.

User-defined roles are most useful for grouping SQL Server authenticated logins and grouping Windows logins when a suitable Windows group is not available. It is much easier in Windows authentication to create a group in the Active Directory and manage it as a single login and a single database user account than it is to add multiple logins, create multiple database user accounts, and then add those accounts to a role.

However as a SQL Server administrator you may not have permission to add objects into the Active Directory. If this is the case, using roles is preferable to assigning rights and permissions individually. You should only assign permissions directly to a user if that user has unique requirements not shared by any other user. Assigning permissions will be discussed in section 8.06.

Roles cannot cross databases. If you want to give access to resources in multiple databases to a group of users with a role, you must create a separate role (and separate database user accounts) for each database. You cannot create user-defined server roles. To create a role you must be a member of the Sysadmin, db_owner or db_accessadmin role.

To create a role in Enterprise Manager, expand the database, right-click the Roles object and select New Database Role. The will open an empty Database Role Properties sheet, as shown in the illustration that follows. You must give the role a name that is unique to the database. The form gives you the choice of creating a standard role and an application role. The standard role is the one we have been discussing in this section. (Application roles will be discussed later in this section.) When you select Standard Role, you can then click the Add button to add members to the role (after the role is created you can reopen this property dialog box to modify role membership). When you click Add, SQL Server gives you a list of all database users who are not already members of the role. You can only add valid database user accounts to database roles. You can also make one user-defined role a member of another role.

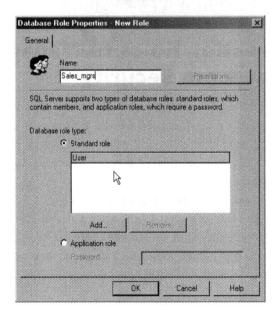

To create a role using Transact-SQL you use the `sp_addrole` procedure. The syntax for this procedure is as follows:

```
sp_addrole 'role name'
```

Once you have created the role you can add users to the role with the `sp_addrolemember` stored procedure. The syntax for this procedure is:

```
sp_addrolemember 'role name', 'user account'
```

As with the Enterprise Manager, you can only add existing database user accounts. If SQL Server cannot find the user account specified on the sysusers table it will return an error. To remove role membership from a user or user-defined role, you use the `sp_droprolemember`. The syntax for using this procedure is the same as `sp_addrolemember`. To remove a user-defined role, you use the `sp_droprole` stored procedure.

SQL Server also includes another type of user-defined role: the application role. Application roles differ from standard user-defined roles because they do not have members. When you create an application role, you give it a password and assign it permissions to resources in a single database. Once it is created you can use the `sp_setapprole` stored procedures (if you know the password for the application role) to change the users security context to that of the application role.

To create an application role you can use the Create Database Role Wizard in Enterprise Manager, or you can use the `sp_addapprole` stored procedure. The syntax for this procedure is:

```
sp_setapprole 'role name', 'password'
```

Once you create the application role, you can assign it permissions on the database the same way you would for any other user or role.

To use the application role, the user must first have a valid login on the server and must have a database user account. Once they have connected to the database, you must execute the `sp_setapprole`. When this stored procedure is executed, the user's security settings are replaced by those assigned to the application role. If the user has access to any other database, they will now connect as guest. This will persist until the user breaks and reestablishes a connection with the server. The syntax for this procedure is:

```
sp_setapprole 'role name', {ENCRYPT(N'password') | 'password'}
```

Because anyone with the correct password can use the `sp_setapprole` procedure, it is possible to send the passwords from the client application to the server in encrypted form using the ENCRYPT option.

The advantage of using application roles is that you can create a login and add it to the db_denydatareader and db_denydatawriter fixed roles. You can then have the application the user is using to connect to the database execute the `sp_setapprole` stored procedure. When the user connects using the application you have created, they will gain access to required resources through the application role's security settings—not their own. If the user connects through any other means (such as an ODBC connection from Excel or Access), they will not be able to access the database resources.

QUESTIONS

8.05: Creating Roles to Manage Database Security

9. Susan has just created a database called RDTest3. Members of the R&D group will access this database. Some of the users in this group are connecting from Windows 2000 computers and use Windows authenticated logins and others are connecting from UNIX workstations using SQL Server logins. The Windows users are not able to log onto the Windows domain. There are two distinct groups of users—researchers and managers. These groups have different security requirements. The users who make up these two groups are mixed between Windows users and UNIX users. Susan wants to give all users the appropriate security with the least amount of administrative overhead. What is the best way for her to assign permissions to these users?

   A. Create two global groups, one for researchers and one for managers. Add all of the Windows users into their proper groups. Create a single logon for each group and assign them the appropriate permissions on the database. Create SQL Server logins for all UNIX users and create two roles in the database for these users. Assign the appropriate permissions to each role or login account.

   B. Create two global groups, one for researchers and one for managers. Add all of the Windows users into their proper groups. Create a single logon for each group and assign them the appropriate permissions on the database. Create two database roles: one for researchers and one for managers. Create a database user account for each of the SQL authenticated logins. Add the two Windows groups and the database user accounts for the UNIX users into the appropriate roles. Assign permission to the roles.

C. Create database user accounts for all of the logins. Create two roles: one for researchers and one for managers. Add all of the database user accounts into their appropriate roles. Assign permissions to the roles.

D. Create database user accounts for all of the logins. Assign each user the appropriate permissions.

E. Add the UNIX users to the Active Directory. Create two global groups: one for researchers and one for managers. Add the users to their proper groups. Create two logins, and map them to two database user accounts. Assign these accounts the appropriate permissions.

10. Sam is developing a database utility that will connect to a SQL 2000 server. He has asked you to create an application role. This role should allow users to query from a table called Pricelist. You create an application role called prod_approle and assign SELECT permission on the Pricelist table. Sam is a member of the db_datareader and db_datawriter role and also has UPDATE and INSERT permissions on the pricelist table. You give Sam the password for the application role and he executes and incorporates the following stored procedure in his application:

```
exec sp_setapprole 'prod_approle', ENCRYPT(N'password')
```

He is able to view the table through his application. He then adds a form that allows users to update a column on the on the table. What will happen when he attempts to connect with his application and why? (Choose the best answer.)

A. He will be able to SELECT from the pricelist table but will not be able to perform the update.

B. He will be able to update the table because he is a member of the db_datawriter database role.

C. He will be able to perform the update because he has been granted the UPDATE permission personally. This overrides any of the roles.

D. He will be able to update because his effective permission is a combination of the application role and his own permissions.

Setting Permissions in a Database

Once you have created logins for all of your users and mapped those logins to database accounts, you can now assign permissions to your users. Permissions dictate what a user is able to do when they connect to the database. There are three levels of permissions in SQL Server:

- Object permissions
- Statement permissions
- Predefined permissions

Statement permissions allow users to create and manipulate objects. They include all of the CREATE, ALTER, and DROP statements. Object permissions will vary between objects. They are listed in the following table:

Permission	Objects Where Permission May Be Set
SELECT	Table, View, Column
INSERT	Table, View
UPDATE	Table, View, Column
DELETE	Table, View
REFERENCES	Table, View, Column
EXEC[UTE]	Stored Procedures

As their name suggests, predefined permissions are a group of object and statement permissions that are set by the system and cannot be modified. These include the permissions assigned to the fixed database and server roles. They also include object owners. If you create an object, you become its owner. As owner, you have full permissions to that object (and in the case of tables, any data within the object).

With the exception of the predefined permissions, users by default have no permission to an object until they are explicitly granted permission. SQL stores permission in a table called sysprotects. Every time you execute a SQL statement, SQL Server queries the sysprotects table to see if you, or any group or role to which you are a member has been given permission to execute the statement. If you have (somehow) been granted the permission, the statement is executed. If you have not been granted the permission, the statement is not executed and an error is returned.

There are actually three states of permission:

GRANT   User|group|role is allowed to perform the action

DENY   User|group|role is explicitly prevented from performing an action

REVOKE   Revoke will simply remove any permissions that have been granted or denied

Both GRANT and DENY place a row in the sysprotects table, while REVOKE will delete an entry from sysprotects. Permissions in SQL Server are cumulative. If you are granted SELECT permission on a table and a role that you are a member of is granted UPDATE permission, then you have both SELECT and UPDATE permissions on that table.

The DENY permission will override a granted permission that is acquired through another source. For example, if you have been granted SELECT on a table, but you are a member of a Windows group that has been denied SELECT on the same table, you will be denied access. There is no hierarchy of permissions (for example, user permissions are not given more weight than group or role permissions). If you are denied permission from any source, that deny will override any other granted permission.

In order to set permissions, you use the GRANT or DENY statement. For example if you wanted to grant the CREATE VIEW statement permission to a database user account called Moe, you would use the following statement:

```
GRANT CREATE VIEW
  TO moe
```

With Object permissions you include the ON clause. For example:

```
GRANT select
ON products
TO moe
```

You can grant and deny multiple permissions to multiple users, but you can only reference one table object. For example, if you wanted to deny the UPDATE and DELETE permissions to Larry, Moe, and Curly you could issue a single statement:

```
DENY update, delete
ON products
TO larry, moe, curly
```

If you were to place a second table object in the ON clause, SQL Server would return an error. If you are granting a user SELECT, INSERT, UPDATE, and

DELETE permissions you can use the GRANT ALL statement rather than listing all of the object permissions.

If you want to undo any of these permission settings, you would use the REVOKE statement. The syntax for this statement is similar to the GRANT and DENY statements except that you reference users in the FROM clause rather than a TO clause. For example, if you wanted to remove the denial from Larry, Moe, and Curly, you would use the following statement:

```
REVOKE update, delete

ON products

FROM larry, moe, curly
```

REVOKE will take either granted or denied permissions back to a neutral state. That is, it will remove the entry from the sysprotects table.

You can also set permissions in Enterprise Manager. You can set them either by clicking the permissions button on the Properties sheet for a particular user or role, or on the Properties sheet for any of the tables, views, or stored procedures. Permissions are set using a tri-state box as shown in the illustration that follows. If the box is clear, this means that the permission is neither granted nor denied. You click a box once and a green check box appears. This is the same as issuing a GRANT statement. If you click that box a second time, a red X will appear. This is the same as issuing a deny statement. If you click the box a third time it will become clear. This is the same as issuing a REVOKE statement.

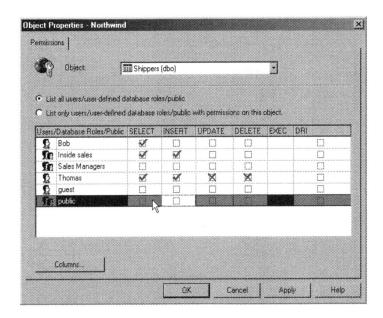

It is also possible to grant and deny permissions at the column level. To do this, you would use the following syntax:

```
{GRANT | DENY} permission(s) ON table(column1 [, column 2...])
TO user(s)
```

You can also revoke column level permission with a REVOKE statement:

```
REVOKE permission(s) ON table(column1 [, column 2...]) FROM
user(s)
```

QUESTIONS

8.06: Setting Permissions in a Database

11. Bob is a manager in your sales group. His account properties appear as follows:

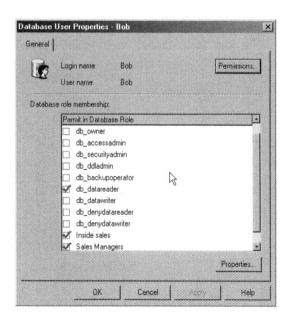

The company does not have a product manager, so as the sales manager, Bob is responsible for maintaining the product list. The current permissions for the product table are as follows:

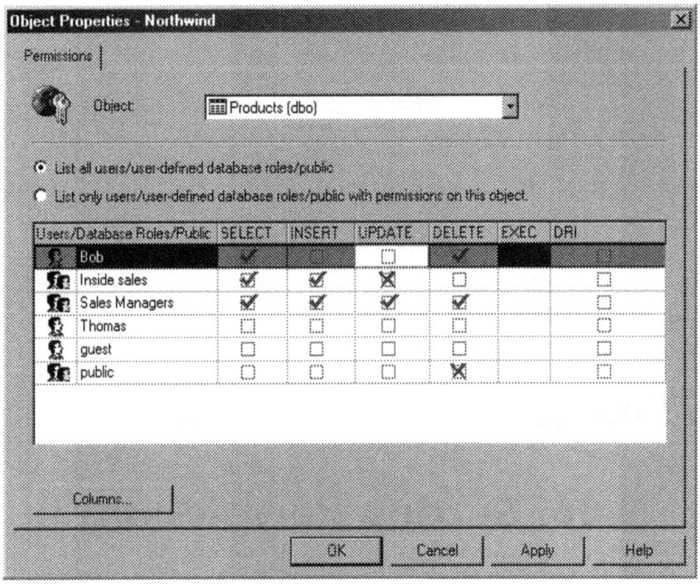

Bob must remain a member of the inside sales role. Which of the following statements must you execute to allow Bob the ability to UPDATE and DELETE rows in the products table? (Choose the best two answers.)

A. `sp_droprolemember 'Public', 'Bob'`

B. `GRANT update`
   `ON products`
   `TO bob`

C. `REVOKE delete`
   `ON products`
   `FROM public`

D. `GRANT delete`
   `ON products`
   `TO public`

E. `REVOKE update`
   `ON products`
   `FROM [inside sales]`

12. The database administrator has granted you permission to execute the
    CREATE TABLE statement on the marketing database. He has also made you
    a member of the db_datareaders role. You have no other permissions on the
    database. You create a table called CallLogs. Which of the following statements
    are you permitted to execute?

    A. ```
       GRANT select
       ON calllogs
       TO public
       ```

    B. ```
       CREATE VIEW vCallcount
       AS
       SELECT salesrep, date, Count(tel_number) AS Number_of_calls
       FROM calllogs
       ```

    C. ```
       UPDATE Calllogs
       SET tel_number = '555-5555'
       WHERE tel_number IS NULL
       ```

    D. ```
       CREATE PROC nonulls
       AS
       UPDATE Calllogs
       SET tel_number = '555-5555'
       WHERE tel_number IS NULL
       ```

    E. ```
       CREATE INDEX ncl_telnumber
       ON CallLog(tel_number)
       ```

## TEST YOURSELF OBJECTIVE 8.07

# Enforcing and Managing Security by Using Stored Procedures, Triggers, Views, and User-Defined Functions

In SQL Server you can give permissions directly to users, groups and roles. However,
you can also use views, stored procedures, triggers, and user-defined functions to help
configure the security in your databases. These are most useful when you want to give
users limited access to table objects.
       ```

View are useful when you want to give users access to some but not all columns and rows in a table. If a view and the underlying table have the same owner, it is possible to give a user SELECT permission on a view, but no access to the underlying table or tables. For example, suppose you have a table called Employees and this table appears as follows:

```
CREATE TABLE employees

(emp_id int,

Fname varchar(20),

Lname varchar(20),

Home_address varchar(60),

City varchar(20),

State char(2),

Zip char(9),

Homephone char(10),

Dept_no smallint,

Ext char(5),

Salary money)
```

And you have a user that needs access only to retrieve the employee's home address to send them pension information. You would not give that user SELECT permission on the table because the table contains confidential information that the user does not need to access. You can set SELECT permissions at the column level, but this would mean granting and maintaining seven different select permissions. Instead, you can create a view that only exposes the necessary columns and give the user permission to select from the view. This means granting and maintaining one permission.

There is one thing to keep in mind in this situation and that is the chain of ownerhip. SQL Server will check for permission every time ownership changes between dependent objects. Consider the following example. A (non-administrative) user named Bob creates a table under his own schema. He gives permission to Jane to SELECT from his table and she creates a view on that table. The table will be referenced as bob.table and the view will be referenced as jane.view. If Jane were to give Stewart select permission on her view, SQL Server would check sysprotects to see if Stewart had select permission on the view and then, because Jane is not the owner of the underlying table, SQL will check sysprotects again to see if Stewart has been granted SELECT permission on the table. Since he has not, he will be unable to access the view. This is known as a broken ownership chain. If you gave Stewart permission to select from the table, he would no longer be limited by the view because he could now access the table directly. To avoid this, you should make sure that all dependant objects have the same owner as the objects that they depend on. Microsoft recommends that you make dbo the owner of all objects to avoid broken ownership chains.

You can achieve the same type of control using programmatic objects like stored procedures, functions, and triggers. Only, unlike views, you can gain more control and functionality. For example, suppose you had a user who needed to update the home address for employees who relocate. You want to give a user the ability to update just those columns that contain address information. You also don't want the user to have access to the sensitive information contained in the table. You could GRANT four column level UPDATE permissions (plus add the SELECT permission on the emp_id column). However, a better option would be to create a stored procedure that takes the new address information as input parameters and performs the update on behalf of the users. It would looks something like this:

```
CREATE PROC update_address

@emp_id int, @address varchar(60), @city varchar(20),

@state char(2), @zip char(9)

AS

UPDATE employee

SET Home_address = @home, city = @city, state = @state,
zip = @zip

WHERE emp_id = @emp_id
```

If the procedure and the employee table have the same owner, SQL Server checks to see if the user has permission to execute the procedure, but does not check again to see if the user has permission to update the table. The same is true of user-defined functions. For example, you could create a function that looks up a value on a table that you own, and give execute permission to another user without giving them direct access to the table. The user could then use that function in a SELECT statement and only the execute permission would be checked.

You can also do this with triggers. For example you could create an update trigger on one table that duplicates the update on a second table. As long as you owned all objects, you could give the user update permission on only the first table and SQL Server will not recheck their permissions when the trigger updates the second table.

QUESTIONS

8.07: Enforcing and Managing Security by Using Stored Procedures, Triggers, Views, and User-Defined Functions

13. The manager of HR has asked you to secure a number of tables in the HRInfo database. There are two tables in particular that she wants managed. The first is a table called PensionInfo, the second is a table called performance_history. She would like all users on the server to be able to view the contents of the PensionInfo and performance_history databases, but only those rows that pertain to the user accessing the tables. Only members of the HR group should be able to modify information in both tables. All your corporate users have access to the database through a global group called Corpusers. How would you give users the required access? (Choose all that apply. Each answer is a partial solution.)

   A. Create a database login for the HR group and grant them SELECT, INSERT, UPDATE, and DELETE permissions on both tables.

   B. Create two views that include a variable for the user's ID in the view definition. Grant the guest account SELECT permission on that view.

   C. CREATE two stored procedures that use the USER system supplied value to determine the user ID of the person executing the procedure. Grant EXEC permission on both procedures to the guest account.

   D. CREATE user-defined functions that use the SUSER_SNAME system supplied value as its input to determine the user ID of the person executing the function. Create a database user account for the Corpusers login and grant that user EXEC permission on both functions.

   E. Create an INSTEAD OF SELECT trigger on both tables that limits the rows returned to those that match the users selecting from the table.

14. You are the database administrator for Bucky's Car Rental. The rental system uses three tables: Rentals, Customers, and Vehicles, as shown in the illustration

that follows. You have a group of users who receive the vehicles when customers drop them off. You want these users to be able to add a value in the dateback column of the rentals table. You also want the value in the available column of the vehicles table changed from "N" to "Y" for the vehicles returned. You do not want these users to be able to change any other values in the tables. You are the owner of all of the tables. How would you give these users the required access? (Choose the correct answer.)

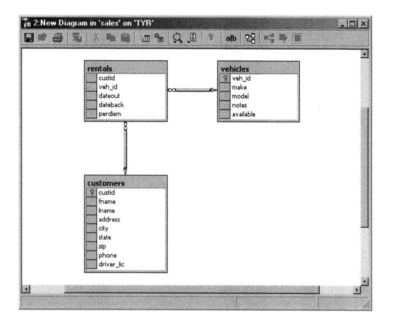

A. Give each user UPDATE and SELECT permissions on only the dateback and available columns.

B. Create a stored procedure that takes input parameters and updates the dateback and available columns. Give the users exec permission on the procedure.

C. Give the user SELECT and update permission on the dateback column. Create a trigger that updates the available column.

D. Create a view that joins the rentals and vehicles tables and only exposes the cust_id, dateback, and available columns. Give the users update permission on this view.

Managing Security Auditing

SQL Server has the ability to audit activity on the server. Auditing allows you to monitor activity on the server so that you can be aware when security settings change or if users are attempting to access databases or database objects without the proper permissions. SQL Server supports C2 level auditing. C2 is a standard for database security set by the U.S. government. One of the requirements for C2 security certification is the ability to audit activity on the server. SQL Server auditing meets this requirement.

In order to use SQL Server auditing you must enable the C2 audit mode. You set this option with the sp_configure stored procedure. This is an advanced option, so in order to set it you must first enable the Show Advanced Options configuration option. Whenever you change an option with sp_configure, you must issue the RECONFIGURE command to update the current configuration. Sometimes you are also required to stop and start the SQL Server service.

The script to enable C2 auditing would look like this:

```
exec sp_configure 'show advanced options', 1

go

RECONFIGURE

exec sp_configure 'c2 audit mode', 1

go
```

With sp_configure, you use the 1 to indicate that the option should be set to true (or on) and 0 to show that it should be set to false (or off). You must be a member of the sysadmin role to enable C2 audit mode. After you have enabled C2 auditing you must restart the SQL Server service for auditing to take effect.

Once the server is restarted, a profiler trace file will be created in the program files\Microsoft SQL Server\{mssql | mssql$instancename}\data folder. The trace will be given a name that includes a timestamp. For example, audittrace_200112084514.trc would be a trace started on August 12, 2001 at 2:45 P.M. This trace file is readable by the SQL Server Profiler. After auditing has been enabled you must decide what to audit. The audit levels are set on the Security tab of the Server Properties sheet shown here:

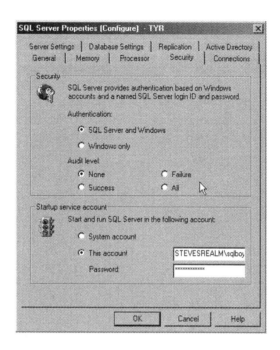

The options are:

- None
- Success
- Failure
- All

The default level is not to audit. The trace file is created, but no activity is recording in the trace. If you set the audit level to Failure, it will capture all events where the activity failed because the user did not have correct permissions or where there was an error. Success will record all activities completed. This is useful when tracking usage on a server. Setting the audit level to All will, obviously, record both successful and failed activity. You should be careful using All because it will cause SQL Server to record all activity on the server to the log. This will have a negative impact on performance. The log will continue to fill until it reaches 200MB. When the log exceeds 200MB, SQL Server will create a new trace file.

QUESTIONS

8.08: Managing Security Auditing

15. Jane is a member of the sysadmin role on a SQL server. She has been asked to audit security on her SQL server. She executes the following stored procedure to enable C2 auditing:

```
sp_configure 'c2 audit mode', 1

GO
```

However she receives the following error:

```
Server: Msg 15123, Level 16, State 1, Procedure sp_configure,
Line 78
```

```
The configuration option 'c2 audit mode' does not exist, or
it may be an advanced option.
```

Why is she unable to enable auditing on this server?

A. She needs to include the EXEC command before the stored procedure.

B. She should have issued the following query:

```
exec sp_configure 'c2 audit mode', true
```

C. She must be a security admin to configure auditing.

D. She did not install the auditing tools when she installed SQL 2000 Server.

E. She must enable the advanced options using `sp_configure`.

16. Jane changes her server to show advanced options and then enables C2 auditing. After enabling C2 auditing, she stops and restarts the server. She confirms that the trace file was created in c:\Program Files\Microsoft SQL Server\MSSQL\Data. After several days, she opens the trace file with the SQL Profiler and discovers that the trace file is empty. What is the most likely reason that the trace file is empty?

    A. Her audit level is set to None.

    B. She has not executed the `xp_starttrace` procedure to begin auditing.

    C. She did not configure the profiler trace using the profiler.

    D. The SQL Server Agent service is not started.

    E. She is not running the Enterprise edition of SQL Server.

LAB QUESTION

Objectives 8.01–8.08

You are the SQL administrator for a mail order bookstore. Your database is called Sales, and contains a number of tables, as shown in the following illustration. Your users fall into three groups: warehouse staff, order entry staff and sales managers. All of your users are part of the same Windows 2000 domain called Norbooks.local. There are 20 accountants, 50 warehouse staff, 60 order entry staff, and 4 sales managers.

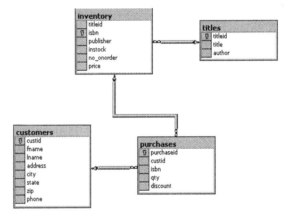

1. How would you authenticate your users to the database? How would you implement your solution using Transact-SQL?

2. One of your publishers needs access to the inventory database to check on the reorder level. You will be making this table available to her across the Internet. How could you allow this user to authenticate? What Transact-SQL statement would you use?

3. Your order entry staff needs to be able to view, add, modify and remove rows from the customers and purchases tables. How many statements would be required to assign all these permissions? What would the statements be?

4. Your sales managers will need to be able to read and modify any table in the database. What would be the easiest way to implement this? How would you implement it using Transact-SQL?

5. Your warehouse staff needs to modify only the instock and no_onorder columns. How would you give them the ability to modify only those columns?

6. You are concerned that someone is trying to gain access to your system. What audit level would you use? What statements would you use to configure auditing?

QUICK ANSWER KEY

Objective 8.01
1. D
2. A

Objective 8.02
3. D
4. A, C, and E

Objective 8.03
5. B
6. B

Objective 8.04
7. C and F
8. B

Objective 8.05
9. B
10. A

Objective 8.06
11. C and E
12. A, C, and E

Objective 8.07
13. A and D
14. B

Objective 8.08
15. E
16. A

IN-DEPTH ANSWERS

8.01: Configuring Security Modes

1. ☑ **D** is the correct answer because you must restart the SQL Server service before any changes in authentication mode will take effect. SQL Server will allow you to create SQL Server login accounts if the server is still configured to use Windows-only authentication. However, it will not allow users to authenticate using these accounts until you change to mixed mode.

   ☒ **A** is incorrect because although it is possible to create Windows login accounts for the Macintosh clients, if these users do not log into the Windows domain they will not be able to connect using Windows authentication. **B** is incorrect because SQL Server 2000 has full support for Macintosh users. **C** in incorrect because you do not need a special client installed on the server to allow non-SQL Server clients to connect. You must, however, make sure that the correct networking components and SQL network libraries are installed to support the operating system of the client. **E** is incorrect because you do not need to completely reboot the server to change modes; you only need to restart the SQL Server service.

2. ☑ **A** is the correct answer. The **sa** account is a built-in SQL Server authenticated user account that has administrative rights on the server. If the server is in Windows authentication-only mode, you cannot use this login.

   ☒ **B** is incorrect because the **sa** login is a SQL authenticated login, so creating a domain user account called **sa** will not allow the login to connect. **C** is incorrect because the ODBC DSN must use whatever authentication mode is set on the server. It does not dictate how users connect. **D** is incorrect because this built-in login cannot be modified or deleted. **E** is incorrect because you do not need to access a domain controller when logging in using SQL Server authentication.

8.02: Creating and Managing Logons

3. ☑ **D** is the correct answer. Because all of the users are members of the same domain, you can create a global group in the Active Directory and create a single Windows authenticated login for that group. Anyone who is a member of that group will be granted the login rights on the server. This is the easiest way to deal with the staffing issue as well. Because authentication is tied to the group, there is no change on SQL Server when staff changes. The only administration required is to add and remove users from the group in the Active Directory.

   ☒ **A** and **B** are incorrect because, regardless of how the users authenticate, dealing with each user individually would add greatly to the administrative workload. Not only would you need to create all of the logins, but also as staffing changes, you will be constantly adding and removing logins on the SQL server. **C** is incorrect because you cannot create a SQL authenticated login based on a group. You can only add individuals. **E** is incorrect because as long as the user has a valid domain user account in the Active Directory and the directory is running in mixed mode, the operating system they are running is irrelevant. If the Windows 2000 domain is in native mode, the Windows 9x clients will not be able to connect unless they first install the Active Directory client on their computers.

4. ☑ **A, C,** and **E** are the correct answers. Because all of these domains are part of the same domain tree, transitive two-way trusts are automatically created between all of the domains. This means that you can create SQL logins for users in any domain in the Active Directory. In this case, creating two global groups is the easiest way to achieve the required results, because you only need to create two logins. You also do not have to make any changes on the SQL server if there are changes in the group membership.

   ☒ **B** is incorrect because a global group cannot contain users from multiple domains. A global group can only contain users and other global groups from the same domain. **D** is incorrect because it is unnecessary to create the SQL Server logins. Because all users are part of a domain, it is much more efficient to take advantage of the Windows 2000 groups. If you created all of the individual user accounts, the sales managers from East.Bigcorp.local would need to log in twice to access the SQL server.

8.03: Creating and Managing Database User Accounts

5. ☑ **B** is the correct answer. Because the sales and marketing staff have a clear separation in tasks, you should create two separate databases. It would be administratively easier to have one database for both, but would limit how you secure the data used by each group. You can still create a database user account for each group in both databases. Because the HR database has a separate security requirement, you should create a separate database. Administrators map to dbo for all databases, so no matter how you configure your database structure, members of the sysadmin role will have full access to all databases.

   ☒ **A** is incorrect because you lose any separate security for the HR users by placing all of the data in one large database. All groups in this example will share a common security context. **C** is incorrect because although they share data, there is a clear separation between the sales and marketing groups, and you will get much better security by having separate databases. You can still map logins for the sales and marketing groups to both databases. **D** is incorrect because it is not necessary to create a separate instance to give the HR database its own security context. Creating a separate database is sufficient in this scenario.

6. ☑ **B** is the correct answer. Because your customers will not log into your Windows domain, you must use a SQL Server login. Once you have created this login, you can then easily map a database user account to that login. When the application connects, it connects as your SQL login and is automatically mapped to the database user account. All of this can be performed through the web applications and the customers will be unaware that they are being authenticated to the server.

   ☒ **A** is incorrect because there is no such thing as a guest login. You can create a guest user account in the database, but the user will still require a valid login to connect to the server. **C** is incorrect because you should avoid using the guest account. If you give access to this account, any other user who connects to the server will be able to view the table. **D** is incorrect because SQL Server logins will allow you to give database access to users connecting from the Internet.

8.04: Adding and Removing Users from Fixed Roles

7. ☑ C and F are the correct answers. When you add the user to the security admin role, that user inherits the right to create new logins. Being a member of the security admin fixed server role does not give you the ability to create or modify database user accounts. By adding the user to the db_accessadmin database role, you give the user the permission to create and modify roles and database user accounts. Because this is a database role, it will only affect the local database. You have not added this user to the db_accessadmin role in the accounting database and he will not be able to create or modify database user accounts in that database.

☒ A is incorrect because adding this user to the sysadmin role will give him full control over the server and full access to all databases. B is incorrect because the server admin does not have security privileges. This role allows the user to change server settings by executing the sp_configure stored procedure and the RECONFIGURE command. D is incorrect because it will give the user full control over the manufacturing database and all objects and data within it. He only needs the ability to add new database use accounts. E is incorrect because the db_ddladmin role gives the user the ability to issue data definition statements (all CREATE, ALTER, DROP statements with the exception of statements that affect databases). DDL statements do not include sp_grantdbaccess or sp_addrole—the procedure needed by this user.

8. ☑ B is the correct answer. Adding the developers to the dbcreator role gives them permission to create new user databases. When they create a database they automatically become the owners of the database. As owners, they have full control over the database. They do not, however, have any control over databases created by other developers.

☒ A is incorrect because the db_ddladmin fixed database role does not have permission to create databases, even if it is in the Master database. C is incorrect because you can no longer add aliases in SQL Server. D is incorrect because the setup admin role does not have permission to create databases; it can only configure linked servers and configure certain stored procedures. E is incorrect because you cannot create server roles. You can only use the existing fixed server roles.

8.05: Creating Roles to Managing Database Security

9. ☑   **B** is the correct answer because it minimizes administration for at least the Windows authenticated user. By grouping all of the Windows users together, you can treat them as one entity. If users leave or join any group, all changes are made at the Domain Controller rather than SQL Server. Because you have SQL Server authenticated logins, you will need to use database user roles to group these users together. By adding the Windows groups and the SQL login into these roles you can centralize the assignment of permissions. This also minimizes the administrator of permissions since permissions only need to be set twice, once for the group login and once for the role containing the SQL Server logins.

   ☒   **A** is incorrect because you are assigning permissions on the object twice for each group (once for each group of Windows users and once for each group of UNIX users). By adding both sets of users to the database role, you eliminate this duplication. **C** is incorrect because you are treating each Windows login individually instead of grouping them together. This means that if users change you will have to make changes on the SQL server, adding more administrative overhead. **D** is incorrect because you want to avoid adding permissions directly to database users. This will greatly add to the administrative overhead of implementing and maintaining security in the database. **E** is incorrect because although you could create login accounts for these users in the Active Directory, the UNIX users are unable to authenticate to Windows. You would need to add services for UNIX (or perhaps SAMBA) to allow these users to use Windows authentication.

10. ☑   **A** is the correct answer because when you execute the `sp_setapprole` stored procedure, it will override your personal permissions. Once this procedure is executed by the application, SQL Server will only check the sysprotects table for which rights the application role possesses. Sam's personal permissions and role membership are never checked.

   ☒   **B** and **D** are incorrect because, although they both presume that Sam's permissions will be tested, in reality only the rights of the application role are tested. **C** is incorrect because there is no hierarchy of permissions. Personal permissions will not override the application role once you have executed the `sp_setapprole` in the database.

8.06: Setting Permissions in a Database

11. ☑ **C** and **E** are the correct answers. **C** is correct because the DENY DELETE permission is preventing Bob from deleting rows from the table. All database user accounts are members of the public role by default. **E** is correct because as a member of the inside sales role, Bob is denied the UPDATE permission on the table. Since he cannot be removed from the role, you must remove the DENY permission to allow him to UPDATE rows. Revoking the DENY returns the value to a neutral state. This will not automatically allow members of the inside sales group to update values in the table; it only removes the explicit denial. You should be careful when removing deny permissions because they may be needed to specifically block certain users. If this was the case you would either have to remove Bob from the insides sales role or he will not be able to perform the update.

☒ **A** is incorrect because you cannot remove a domain user account from the public role. **B** is incorrect because permissions granted personally do not override denied permissions from other sources. There is no hierarchy making user permissions superior to role permissions. **D** is incorrect because you do not need to give read permission to the public role; you only need to remove the DENY to allow Bob access. Since there was an explicit deny placed on this role, you can assume that the public role should not have access to the table.

12. ☑ **A**, **C**, and **E** are the correct answers. **A** is correct because as the owner of the table, you have the right to grant permissions to other users. **C** is correct because ownership also grants you full access to the table and all data in it. **E** is correct because as a table owner, you can also create objects that are bound to the table, including indexes, triggers and constraints.

☒ **B** and **D** are incorrect because they are not considered dependant objects. Even if the view or stored procedure is drawing information solely from the table you own, you will still need CREATE VIEW or CREATE PROC permission to create these objects.

8.07: Enforcing and Managing Security by Using Stored Procedures, Triggers, Views, and User-Defined Functions

13. ☑ **A** and **D** are the correct answers. **A** is correct because members of HR will need full access to the data in these two tables. **D** is correct because the SUSER_SNAME function will return the Windows login name for each user. You can use this function to return values that only matches the user's information.

☒ **B** is incorrect because view definitions cannot accept input values. There would be no way to pass the value into the view when selecting from it. Even if you could, if you authenticated through the guest account, the USER value would always return guest as the username. **C** is also incorrect because if you are using the guest account to authenticate the user, the procedures would function properly but would always return guest as the users login. **E** is incorrect because you cannot create a trigger on a SELECT statement. SQL Server 2000 includes a new kind of trigger that will execute its code instead of performing the calling operation, but this only works on INSERT, UPDATE, and DELETE statements.

14. ☑ **B** is the correct answer. Because stored procedures can take input parameters, you could pass the custid, vehicle_id and databack values into the procedure and have it perform all of the modifications. Because you own all objects, SQL Server will only check to see if your users have EXEC permission on the procedure.

☒ **A** and **C** are incorrect because you would need to give the user SELECT PERMISSION to other columns in the two tables to perform the updates. You should also avoid setting column level permissions.

☒ **D** is incorrect because the users would be able to modify any value exposed by the view.

8.08: Managing Security Auditing

15. ☑ **E** is the correct answer. The C2 audit mode option is an advanced option. Before it can be set you must execute the following statement:

```
exec sp_configure 'show advanced options', 1
```

You will need to include the RECONFIGURE statement. If you don't do this, SQL Server cannot enable auditing.

☒　A is incorrect because the exec command is not necessary when executing system stored procedures if it is the first line of a batch. There is no indication that she is executing this procedure as part of a larger batch. **B** is incorrect because you use 1 and 0, rather than True and False to enable and disable configuration settings with sp_configure. **C** in incorrect because as a member of sysadmin, she has full permissions on the server, including those held by the security admin. The security admin does not have permission to enable auditing. Other than the sysadmin, only members of the server admin role can enable auditing. **D** is incorrect because the auditing function is installed by default when you install SQL Server; it cannot be installed as a separate component.

16. ☑　A is the correct answer. By default the audit level is set to None when you enable auditing. You must change the audit level to Success, Failure or All for the server to begin capturing audit information. Which audit level you choose will depend on why you are auditing. For example, if you were monitoring activity on a particular database you might choose Success, whereas if you were only interested in attempted access from hackers you would choose Failure. You set the audit level in the Security tab of the Server Properties sheet.

☒　B is incorrect because SQL Server does not have an xp_starttrace stored procedure. **C** is incorrect because you do not have to configure the trace file. It is configured automatically when auditing is enabled. You only use the Profiler to view the output of the trace. You can also use the Profiler's filtering capability to restrict searches. **D** is incorrect because the SQL Server Agent has nothing to do with auditing. The SQL Server service is responsible for running auditing. **E** is incorrect because the auditing features are available on all versions of SQL 2000 Server.

A LAB ANSWER

Objectives 8.01–8.08

1. Since all users are Windows users, you would create Warehouse, Orderentry and Salesmanagers global groups in the Active Directory. You can then create a single log for each group and a single database user account. Assuming you used the group names listed previously, the Transact-SQL scripts would look like this:

```
exec sp_grantlogin 'Norbooks\Warehouse'

go

exec sp_grantlogin 'Norbooks\Orderentry'

go

exec sp_grantlogin 'Norbooks\Salesmanagers'

go

use Sales

exec sp_grantdbaccess 'Norbooks\Warehouse'go


exec sp_grantdbaccess 'Norbooks\Orderentry'

go

exec sp_grantdbaccess 'Norbooks\Salesmanagers'

go
```

2. Because this user is connecting from the Internet you must use SQL Server authentication. The syntax would look like this:

```
exec sp_addlogin 'publisher', 'password'

go

sp_grantdbaccess 'publisher'
```

You could also use XML queries and set the access level through the XML virtual directory.

3. You can accomplish this with two statements. It is possible to list multiple permissions and multiple users with the GRANT statement but it can only affect one database per statement. The statements would appear as follows:

```
GRANT select, insert, update, delete

ON customers

TO Norbooks\Orderentry

go

GRANT select, insert, update, delete

ON purchases

TO Norbooks\Orderentry
```

In cases where you are granting all possible permissions for an object you can also use the GRANT ALL statements.

4. The easiest way to give the managers these permissions is to add them to the db_datareader and db_datawriter procedures in the database. You could achieve this with the following code:

```
exec sp_addrolemember 'db_datareader',
'Norbooks\Salesmanagers'

go

exec sp_addrolemember 'db_datawriter',
'Norbooks\Salesmanagers'
```

5. The easiest way to give the warehouse staff the ability to update only these two columns would be to create a stored procedure and give these users EXEC permission on the procedure. As long as the procedure and the table have the same owner, SQL Server will only check to see if the user has EXEC permission on the procedure.

6. To monitor for unauthorized entry attempts, you would set the audit level to failure. This will log failed login attempts and failed object access attempts. The code to enable auditing would look like this:

```
exec sp_configure 'show advanced options' , 1

go

RECONFIGURE

go

exec sp_configure 'c2 audit mode' , 1

go
```

You would have to restart the server at this point and then select Failure from the Security tab in the Server Properties sheet.

MICROSOFT CERTIFIED DATABASE ADMINISTRATOR

9

Managing SQL Server 2000 Automation

S QL Server 2000 includes the ability to automate administrative tasks. The SQL Server Agent service controls automation. You can use SQL Server automation to schedule repetitive tasks, monitor for errors or performance conditions, and notify operators when errors occur or jobs are complete. As an administrator, if you have a full understanding of how automation works, you can use SQL Server to perform repetitive tasks on your behalf.

You need to know how to create jobs and manage automatic jobs. You also need to know how to troubleshoot errors in your jobs. You need to understand how to create alerts to monitor both SQL Server errors and performance conditions. You will also need to understand how to create your own error messages and how to use them in alerts. Finally, you must know how to define operators so that the SQL Server Agent can send notifications to your administrators.

TEST YOURSELF OBJECTIVE 9.01

Creating, Managing, and Troubleshooting SQL Server Agent Jobs

You create jobs to automate repetitive administrative tasks. You can create a job with Enterprise Manager or by using the `sp_add_job` stored procedure. To create a job in Enterprise Manager, expand the SQL Server Agent icon in the Management folder. Right-click the Jobs icon and select New Job. This will bring up the New Job Properties sheet as shown in the following illustration. You must give each job a unique name and ensure that it is enabled. You also need to specify on which computer the job will run and who is the owner.

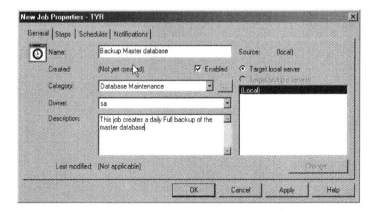

The ownership of a job is important because it will determine how the job runs. If the job executes a Transact-SQL statement, SQL Server impersonates the owner of the job. If the owner has permission to perform the scheduled job, the job will succeed; if not it will fail. For Active Script and operating system jobs, if the job owner is a member of the sysadmin role, the SQL Server Agent will run the task under its own security context. It is important to remember that if the SQL Server Agent service is not running, no automated jobs will run.

If the job owner is not a member of the sysadmin role, the job will fail unless you have created a proxy account. You can define a proxy account with either the `xp_sqlagent_proxy_account` stored procedure or in the Properties sheet for the SQL Server Agent in Enterprise Manager. To access the Properties sheet, right-click the SQL Server Agent icon and select Properties. On the Job Systems tab, clear the Only Users With Sysadmin Privileges Can Execute CmdExec And ActiveScripting Job Steps button and supply the account name and password. By default this option is set on. All of these steps are to prevent users from using SQL Server automation to perform an activity that they do not have rights to perform themselves.

Once you have named the job and sets its owner, you must then create the steps for the job. A job must contain at least one step, but it can contain multiple actions or steps. These steps can include:

- A Transact-SQL statement. These statements can be issued against any database on the server and can include variables and parameters (for functions and stored procedures).

- An Active X script such as VBScript. You can also use scripting languages like Perl if you have the correct language libraries installed.

- An operating system command (an .exe, .bat, .cmd or .com command). You must specify the full physical path name when referencing the command.

- A replication agent job. Several Agents running under the SQL Server Agent service control SQL Server replication activity. You can use SQL Server automation to schedule replication tasks by scheduling the Agents (for more information on replication, see Chapter 7, section 7.06).

Jobs can contain a mixture of all these steps. For example, you could run a job that uses a Transact-SQL script to create a temporary table and then use bcp.exe (an operating system command) to dump the temporary table to a text file. You could then use an Active X script job to FTP this file to another server and restore it in a new location.

You can also control the flow of the steps based on success or failure. In the previous example, if, for some reason SQL Server were unable to create or populate the temporary table, there would be no point in running the bcp.exe or the Active X script steps. For each step, you can specify what happens if the step fails, as shown in the following illustration. You can also set a maximum number of retries before the job fails. If your job steps are dependent on each other, you can have the entire job quit if any of the steps fail. You can also build branching logic into your jobs (for example, on success goto step3, on failure goto step2).

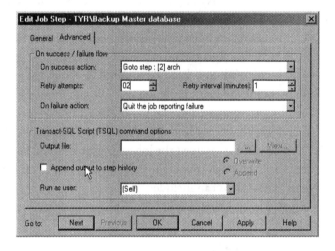

Once you have created the job, you can then schedule it. You add schedules by selecting the Schedules tab of the Edit Job Set Properties sheet and clicking New Schedule. You can schedule a job to run:

- Whenever the Agent starts
- Whenever the CPU becomes idle
- Once at a specific time
- Recurring daily, weekly, or monthly

If you choose to have the job run when the CPU becomes idle, you must define the idle condition. This is set on the Advanced tab of the SQL Server Agent Properties sheet. By default the idle condition is not specified. A server is considered idle when the average CPU usage falls below a certain threshold for a determined length of time seconds (for example, below 10% CPU usage for more than 600 seconds).

When you set the schedule, you must give it a name because SQL Server will allow you to set multiple schedules on the same job. This is useful if the requirements for the job change over time. For example, suppose you want to backup the transaction log of a particular database every two hours during the day, every four hours over night and every eight hours on the weekend. Rather than creating three jobs, you could create a single job and create three different schedules for that job.

Finally, you can notify an operator when the job runs. You can configure the job to notify the operator on job success, fail or completion (success or failure). In order to add the notification you must choose how you want to contact the operator. You have the choice of emailing, paging, or using the NET SEND command to send a pop-up message to the operator in question. When you click the check box next to any of these three options, you can select a single operator. You can select all three methods. However, if you want to email the outcome of a job to more than one person you should create an email distribution list and configure a new operator that uses the distribution list as its email address.

By default most jobs are created locally, however you can configure one of your servers to function as a Multiserver master (or MSX). Make a server a master server and you can then enlist other servers as target servers. Once you have enlisted target servers, you can create jobs on the master server and those jobs will be posted to the target servers. This is important to remember. The job is created on the master server, but it will be run by the local SQL Server Agent services on the target servers. These Agents report the outcome of the job back to the MSX Operator. This operator account is created when you run with the wizard that configures the Multiserver master. Because the job is run locally on the target servers, if the job references an object (such as a backup device or an executable file) that exists on the master but not on the target servers, the job will fail.

Once the target server has completed the job, it will report the outcome of the job back to the master server. To create a Multiserver master, right-click the SQL Server Agent icon in the Management folder and choose Multi Server Administration | Make This A Master. This will start the Make MSX Wizard. In this wizard you will also create the MSX operator account. Once a server is configured as a master server, you can enlist any target server that you have rights to connect. In order to enlist a server as a target server, you must first register them in Enterprise Manager. If you have sufficient rights to register the server in Enterprise Manager, you will also have sufficient permission to enlist the server as a target server. The jobs will appear on the local target servers in the Jobs folder. They can be viewed but not modified on the target server. If you want to make modifications to the job, you must make the changes on the master server.

All jobs record their outcome in a history log. This log is actually stored in the MSDB database in the sysjobhistory table. You can view the outcome of the job by right-clicking the job and selecting View Job History, or you can query the sysjobhistory table.

On the Job History form, you can see the result of each execution of the job. Furthermore, if you click the Show Step Details check box in the top right corner of the form, it will show each step, as shown in the illustration that follows, and the message returned when the step is executed. If a job has failed, this is the best place to look for information because it will tell you exactly why a particular step failed. The illustration shows the output from a failed job. This job has two steps. The first step runs an operating system command to copy an order backup to a different location. The second step backs up a database to that device and over writes it. The .cmd file listed in step 1 is missing and the error for this job step tells you that the file could not be found. It is important to check the log regularly to ensure that all of your automated maintenance activities are running successfully. Because this log is stored in the MSDB database, you need to control its size so that it does not fill the database. SQL Server does this automatically. If you go to the Properties sheet for the SQL Server Agent and click the Job System tab, you can set a limit on the size of the table and the maximum number of rows that will be dedicated to an individual job. If you have space in the MSDB database and want to retain more history information, you can make the history table larger. However, you should still impose a limit on the size of this table to prevent it from filling the database.

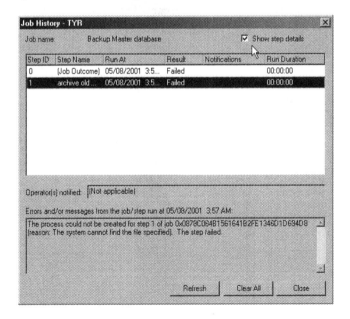

QUESTIONS

9.01: Creating, Managing, and Troubleshooting SQL Server Agent Jobs

1. You are the administrator for a SQL 2000 server. You have been asked to create several jobs for the inventory group. You need to import inventory data from several remote data sources to several holding tables in your database. You have a DTS package that will perform the imports. You then need to run a stored procedure that validates all of the imported data and adds the records to the master inventory list. The job must run every two hours during the day, and every four hours overnight during the week. You also want it to run every eight hours on the weekend. You want to create this job with the least amount of work. How would you automate this process?

   A. Create a single job with multiple steps. Have all of the import jobs run as a separate steps. For each step have the job quit on failure. Set the stored procedure as the last step in the job. Create three schedules for this job for the day, night and weekend periods.

   B. Create one job that imports the data and a second job that runs the stored procedure. Create three schedules for each job for the day, night and weekend periods. Schedule the second job to run ten minutes after the first.

   C. SQL automation cannot run active script jobs. Run the imports using the Windows scheduler and then run the stored procedures from within SQL Server with three schedules for each job for the day, night and weekend periods.

   D. Create three multi-step jobs that execute the active script, and run the stored procedures. Schedule the first one to run during the day, the second one to run at night and the third one to run on the weekend.

2. Jane is the administrator for a SQL 2000 server. She has created a job that imports data into a holding table. Other jobs move this imported data into other tables in the database and mark the rows as moved when they are finished. Sometimes, however, these rows do not get deleted from the holding

table. Jane has created a job that checks the holding table for rows marked as moved and deletes them. This job is not critical and she does not want it interfering with other, more important jobs. She has decided to create a job that runs on CPU idle. A week later she notices that there are several rows in the table that are marked as moved that have not been deleted. The job is enabled and she can run it manually. She checks the job history and finds that the job has never run. She knows that there has been an idle period overnight. What could prevent this job from running? (Choose all that apply.)

A. The SQL Server Agent service is not running on the server.

B. You must be a member of the server admin system role to configure jobs to run on idle.

C. Jane has not defined the idle condition in the SQL Server Agent Properties sheet.

D. Jane must select the Monitor For Idle check box on the Processor tab of the SQL Server Properties sheet.

E. She needs to execute `xp_set_idle_monitor` to begin monitoring for the idle condition.

TEST YOURSELF OBJECTIVE 9.02

Configuring Alerts Using SQL Server Agent

Alerts allow SQL Server to notify operators whenever a predefined event occurs on the server. The SQL Server Agent monitors the server constantly, freeing the administrator from having to monitor error and performance logs. There are two types of alerts in SQL Server:

- Event Alerts
- Performance Condition Alerts

To add an alert, you can either execute the `sp_add_alert` stored procedure, or you can use Enterprise Manager. To create an alert in Enterprise Manager, expand the SQL Server Agent icon, right-click the Alert icon, and select New Alert. This will bring up the New Alert Properties sheet. In the Properties sheet, you must give the alert a name, and then choose the type of alert from the Type pull-down menu. The form will appear different depending on which type of alert you create.

Event alerts monitor for events in the application log of the Windows Event Viewer. The SQL Server Agent parses the application log. If an event of sufficient severity (19 through 25) occurs, or if an error is specifically raised to the log, SQL Server checks in the sysalerts table in the MSDB database to see if alerts have been defined for each event raised. This is important to remember because if an error or event is not written to the Windows application log, any alert based on that event will not be triggered. You also need to remember that if you have configured the SQL Server Agent service to run under a domain user account, that account must have administrative rights not only on the SQL server but also on the Windows 2000 server. If the domain user account used by the Agent does not have Windows administrative rights, it cannot read or write to the event logs.

When you select SQL Server Event Alert you will see the Event Alert Definition section in the Alert Property form, as shown in the illustration that follows. You can set an event alert on either severity or a specific error number. If you choose to create an alert based on a severity, any error with that severity will cause the alert to fire. By default, SQL Server creates alerts for severity 19 through 25. These severity levels represent errors in the system. It is a good idea to assign operators for all of these alerts. You can also specify a specific error number. In the next illustration, an alert has been defined for error 9002. This error message is raised whenever a transaction log becomes full.

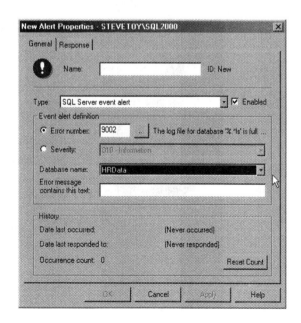

In this form, you can also specify a particular database in conjunction with the error message. Because HRData has been listed in the Database list box, this alert will only be executed if error 9003 applies to the transaction log for HRData. If the log of any other database is filled, SQL Server would raise error 9003 and write it to the application log, but the alert would not fire. You can also limit response based on the text of the error message. If you place a value in the Error Message Contains This Text text box, the SQL Agent will parse the text message returned with a particular error and will only raise the alert if the message contains the value you have typed into that box.

When troubleshooting alerts based on errors, it is important to remember the importance of the event log. If the application event log becomes full, all event-based alerting will end. Windows and SQL Server will both continue to run normally if the application log fills. Errors will still be raised, but will not be recorded in the full log. The alerts still exist, but if the log is full, no new errors will be written to the log. To fix this problem you must clear the application log. By default, the log is 512K in size and overwrites all events older than seven days. You can configure the event log to overwrite as needed but this means that log entries may be overwritten before they are viewed. The size of the log must be monitored.

If you select SQL Performance Condition Alert from the Type pull-down menu, SQL Server alters the Alert Property form. Now instead of listing event numbers and severity, it displays two pull-down menus, one for Object and one for Counters, as shown in the following illustration.

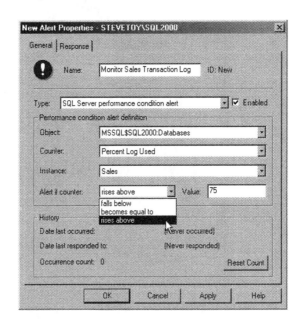

When you configure a Performance Condition Alert, the SQL Agent will use the Performance Monitor counters added by SQL Server to monitor performance and compare the performance against a threshold value. You can only place alerts on SQL Server counters. If you want to place an alert on any of the counters for Windows or any other application, you will have to use the alerts that are part of the Performance tool. You must choose a performance object and then the relevant counter in that object. If the counter has more than one possible instance, you have the choice of choosing which instance to monitor. You can then set the alert to fire when the counter falls below, becomes equal to, or exceeds a particular threshold. In the previous illustration, for example, an alert is configured to execute when the Percent Log Used Counter for the Sales database exceeds 75% full. Again, the SQL Server Agent must have windows administrator privileges to monitor the performance counters. The Agent must also be running.

Regardless of which type of error you raise, you must set a response to that error. To do this, you click the Response tab shown in the previous illustration. In response to an alert you can notify an operator or execute a job. To execute a job, click the Execute Job check box and select the job from the pull-down menu. If the job does not exist, you can select New Job from the pull-down menu and it will call the create Job Properties sheet.

All of the operators that you have defined will appear in the Operators To Notify window. You can choose to notify more than one operator and can add new operators by clicking the New Operator button. You choose how you want to notify the operator(s). Your options are email, pager or the NET SEND command. You can choose more than one notification method for an operator. In the previous illustration, for example, if the transaction log for the sales database exceeds 75%, the alert will run a job that backs up the transaction log for the database. It will also email the SQL admin operator and page the sales admin operator to inform them that the alert has occurred. You can also enter an additional message to be included with the error. For this to work, however, you must configure the mail profile for SQL Agent Mail (see Chapter 2, section 2.02) and the mail server must support paging.

Finally, you can set a delay between responses (see the illustration that follows). This value is important to be aware of with performance condition alerts. If a situation persists, SQL Server will continue to execute the alert whenever the response delay threshold is met. If you set too small a threshold, the alert may be raised several times before you are able to deal with the problem. This will also have an effect on performance. If your server is executing a high number of alerts, this will put stress on your processor. To eliminate this problem, set the delay value to something more reasonable than the default ten minutes.

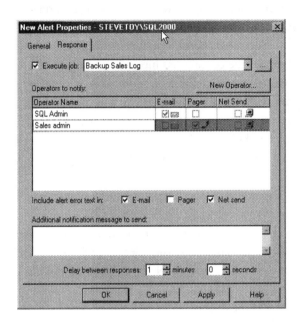

QUESTIONS

9.02: Configuring Alerts Using SQL Server Agent

3. Jamie is the administrator for a SQL 2000 server. The server has two databases: accounting and sales. Jamie is the primary administrator for the server, but there is a separate administrator responsible for sales databases. She wants to configure an alert that will page her if the transaction log for any database

becomes full. She also needs to page the administrator of the sales database only if the log belongs to the sales database. How can Jamie configure her alerts to meet these requirements? (Select the best answer.)

A. Create a single alert that monitors for event 9003 on any database. Configure the alert to always contact her, but only page the sales administrator if the error message contains the word sales.

B. Create two alerts. Have the first alert contact her if the accounting log becomes full. Configure the second alert to contact both her and the sales administrator if the sales transaction log becomes full.

C. Create three alerts. Have the first alert page her if the accounting transaction log becomes full. Have the second alert page her if the sales transaction log becomes full. Configure the third alert to page the sales administrator if the log on sales database becomes full.

D. Create two alerts. Have the first alert page her whenever event 9003 is raised. Configure the second alert to page the sales administrator whenever the transaction log in the sales database becomes full.

4. You have configured an alert to notify you whenever the Percent Log Used value for the westcoast_inventory database exceeds 80%. The database runs normally for several days. Your users are not reporting that they are receiving errors stating the transaction log for the database is full. You examine the database in Enterprise Manager and discover that the log is full. You check the history for the alert and find that the alert has never been raised. Which of the following may explain why this alert was never executed?

A. The application log in Event Viewer is full.

B. The SQL Server Agent service is not started.

C. The Percent Log Used counter is not installed in Windows.

D. You have specified the wrong instance for this counter.

E. The Windows 2000 System Monitor is not running.

Creating and Using User-Defined Event Messages

In section 9.02 you saw how to create alerts based on a SQL Server alert. SQL Server has a large number of predefined error messages, however, it also gives you the ability to create your own error messages. You can use these errors to create user-defined alerts. You can create your own error messages using either Enterprise Manager or the `sp_addmessage` stored procedure. When you create a user-defined error you need to supply a unique number, a severity and the actual text of the message. When you specify the message text you can include placeholders for values that will be passed into the error message when it is raised. You use %s as the placeholder for a string value and %d for a numeric placeholder. You can also specify the message language (for multilingual databases) and whether or not the message should be written to the event log automatically. Microsoft has reserved all error message numbers from 1 to 50,000 so you must assign each error a unique number starting at 50,001. Whenever you create a message, it is added to the sysmessages table in the Master database. Once you add a message to the sysmessages table it can be used by any administrator on the local server.

To create an error with `sp_addmessage`, you would use the following syntax:

```
sp_addmessage 50001, 10, 'The Credit limit of customer %d was
raised to %d by %s'
```

This statement will create message number 50001 with severity of 10 (information) and a message text that takes three parameters (two numeric and one character based). To create a message in Enterprise Manager, right-click the Server icon and select All Tasks | Manage SQL Server Messages. In the Manage SQL Server Messages form, click the Messages tab and click the New button, as shown in the illustration that follows. This form has the same options as `sp_addmessage`. It simply presents them graphically. Once you have created the error message, you can now use it to create an event alert the same way that you created event alerts on SQL Server's errors.

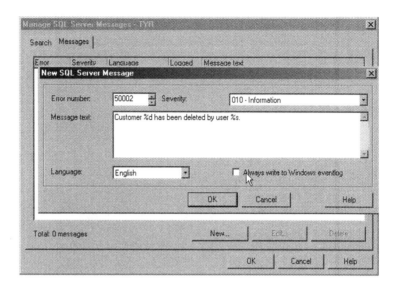

However, in order for you to use a user-defined error in an alert, it must be raised and written to the application log of Event Viewer. You raise user-defined errors programmatically using the RAISERROR statement (for example, in a trigger or stored procedure). There are several ways in which an error can be raised to the Event Viewer. These include:

■ Raise the error using the RAISERROR WITH LOG statement.

■ Configure the error to always write to the Event Viewer by setting the @with_log parameter to true in sp_addmessage or by clicking the Always Write To Windows Event Log check box on the New SQL Server Message form. (You will still need to use the WITH LOG option to prompt the SQL Server Agent to check the sysalerts table.)

■ Set the severity between 19 and 25. Windows automatically writes all events with severity in this range into the Event Viewer. (You will still need to use the WITH LOG option to prompt the SQL Server Agent to check the sysalerts table.)

■ Use the xp_logevent extended stored procedure to raise the error and write it into the Event Viewer log.

An alert defined on this error will never execute unless the error is raised to the application event log. If you have included parameters in the error message, you must include them in the RAISERROR statement. The following statement will raise error 50001 (as defined earlier in this chapter) and write it to the event log:

```
DECLARE @custid int

DECLARE @creditlimit int

DECLARE @employee varchar(15)

SET @custid = 123

SET @creditlimit = 3000

SET @employee = 'Bob Smith'

RAISERROR (50001, 10, 1, @custid, @creditlimit, @employee)
```

The final error message will appear as follows:

```
The Credit limit of customer 123 was raised to 3000 by Bob
Smith
```

This code could be placed in a trigger or a stored procedure and the values of the three parameters could be determined programmatically at runtime.

QUESTIONS

9.03: Creating and Using User-Defined Event Messages

5. Your sales manager has approached you to help him with a problem. He has given his in-house sales staff permission to modify customer records. They need this capability to perform their jobs, but the manager feels that she is losing control of the customer table. She wants an email record of each modification made to customers already in the database. Currently all of the operators update the table using a Visual Basic application that issues UPDATE statements against the database. How would you solve this problem with the least amount of impact on the existing system? (Select the best answer.)

A. Modify the VB application so that it writes a local update log prior to sending the update statement to the server. Run a Windows job that emails the log to the sales manager each day.

B. Create a user-defined event that accepts two parameters. Create an UPDATE trigger on the table that raises a user-defined error using the RAISERROR statement. Create an alert that sends an email to the sales manager.

C. Create a user-defined event that accepts two parameters. Modify the VB application to include a RAISERROR WITH LOG statement. Have the VB application dynamically generate the parameters for the error message. Create an alert that emails the sales manager every time the user-defined error is raised.

D. Create a user-defined event that accepts two parameters. CREATE a stored procedure to include a RAISERROR WITH LOG statement. Within the procedure, programmatically generate the values of the message parameters. Create an alert that emails the sales manager every time the user-defined error is raised.

E. Create a user-defined event that accepts two parameters. Create an UPDATE trigger on the customers table that includes a RAISERROR WITH LOG statement. Within the procedure, programmatically generate the values of the message parameters. Create an alert that emails the sales manager every time the user-defined error is raised.

6. Which of the following methods will write a user-defined error message into the event log? (Choose all that apply.)

A. Set the severity of the error to 18.

B. Use the `xp_logevent` stored procedure.

C. Use the RAISERROR WITH LOG option.

D. Set the @with_log parameter to 1 in `sp_addmessage`.

E. Use the `sp_logevent` stored procedure.

Configuring Operators

In the previous sections you saw how to create alerts and jobs. In each of these you needed to create an operator for notification. When you create an operator, an entry is placed in the sysoperators table in the MSDB database. This entry tells SQL Server how to contact the operators when they are referenced by a job or alert. You will notice that you never specified an operator's email address or pager address in any job or alert. That is because everything is stored in the Operator Properties sheet when you define the operator. Operators do not have to be actual SQL Server administrators; they can be anyone who needs to receive notification of an event from SQL Server.

You can define an operator either using the sp_add_operator stored procedure or by using Enterprise Manager. In Enterprise Manager, right-click the Operators icon under the SQL Server Agent icon and select New Operator. On the General tab, give the operator a name, and then specify how the operator can be contacted, as shown in the following illustration:

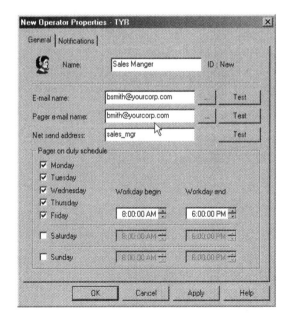

Your choices are:

- Email
- Pager
- A Windows popup using the NET SEND command

In order to use the email and pager options, the SQL Agent Mail must be configured properly. This means that the SQL Server Agent service must be using a domain user account and must have a correctly configured mail profile. If you plan to use the pager option you must already have an email-based pager system installed. Once you configure an operator with a pager, you can also set a duty schedule for that individual. If a job is configured to notify an operator by pager, but completes outside that operator's duty schedule, the page will not be sent.

Because it is possible for an error to occur without anyone scheduled for notification, SQL Server gives you the ability to create a failsafe operator. A failsafe operator is notified every time an alert is raised and the operator assigned to that alert is outside of duty schedule. The failsafe operator is configured on the Alert System tab of the SQL Server Agent Properties sheet. You must first configure the operator and then select that operator form the list box. You are also given the choice of creating a new operator from this list box. An operator can only have one email address and one pager contact. If you want to notify a group of individuals instead of a single person, create an email distribution list and create a single operator with that list as its email address and pager address.

QUESTIONS

9.04: Configuring Operators

7. You are attempting to add an operator for your SQL server. When you attempt to add an email address using the browse button, you receive a MAPI logon error stating that you are unable to logon to the mail server. What may be causing this error to occur? (Choose all that apply.)

   A. The SQL Agent service is not started.

   B. You do not have a mail client running.

    C. You have not configured the SQL Agent profile correctly.

    D. You are not using Exchange as your mail server.

    E. The SQL Agent is running under the local system account.

8. You are configuring an alert that notifies the accounting manager every time an employee changes a customer's credit limit. There are two accounting managers and only one is available at any given moment. You want the email generated by the alert to be sent to both of them at the same time. You have created a user-defined error message and configured the alert to respond to that error. On the Response tab for the new alert you see both operators. You configure them to receive an email but when you click OK you receive an error message informing you that the operators do not have corresponding address information. What is the cause of this error? (Choose the best answer.)

    A. You cannot email two operators from a single alert.

    B. You have not configured an email address for at least one of the operators.

    C. The SQL Agent Mail is not configured correctly.

    D. The server is not currently accessible from the network.

    E. You have mistyped the email address for one of the operators.

LAB QUESTION

Objectives 9.01–9.04

You have been asked to automate certain administrative tasks on a SQL 2000 server. You need to perform the following tasks:

■ Back up several small databases to the local hard drive.

■ Prior to performing the backup, copy the pervious day's backup to a network share that corresponds to a particular day of the week (for example, \\netsrv\monday, \\netsrv\tuesday).

■ The backup job should run every week day at noon, and at 10 P.M. on Saturday and Sunday.

■ After the backup you want to send an email to the primary administrator for each database informing then that the backup either completed or failed.

1. How many jobs must you create to meet these requirements?

2. How will you perform the data transfer?

3. How will you notify the operators?

4. What rights do the operators gain on the system?

    You have also been asked by one of the database operators to create an alert on the products table that sends the product manager an email whenever the inventory level becomes equal to the reorder level. Users use a web-based application that updates the table every time a product is added or removed from inventory.

5. What steps must you take to create this alert?

6. What must you do to allow the error message to contain the name of the product and its current inventory level?

QUICK ANSWER KEY

Objective 9.01
1. **A**
2. **A** and **C**

Objective 9.02
3. **D**
4. **B** and **D**

Objective 9.03
5. **E**
6. **B** and **C**

Objective 9.04
7. **A, C,** and **E**
8. **B**

IN-DEPTH ANSWERS

9.01: Creating, Managing, and Troubleshooting SQL Server Agent Jobs

1. ☑ **A** is the correct answer because it requires the least amount of work to create and maintain. You can create multiple schedules for the same job. You must give each schedule a unique name, and you can specify recurrence during a particular period of time. Creating one single job with multiple steps is preferable because you can then control the execution. If the import sets fail you will have missing or incomplete data in the table when the stored procedure runs. For this reason you want to prevent the stored procedure from executing if any of the import jobs fail. This level of control is best achieved by creating a single multi-step job with each step quitting on failure.

   ☒ **B** is incorrect because you cannot have control extended between jobs. If one of the import jobs fails, you cannot prevent the stored procedure job from running. Furthermore, if it takes more than ten minutes for a particular import to take place, the stored procedure will be executed before all of the data is imported. **C** is incorrect because the SQL job steps can include active scripts including VBScript. **D** is incorrect because it contains unnecessary steps. This answer will meet the basic requirements, but it means you will need to maintain three jobs. If, for example, any part of the job steps or the operator responsible for the job changes, you will need to make the changes to all three jobs. You will also need to monitor the histories for all three jobs individually.

2. ☑ **A** and **C** are the correct answers. **A** is correct because the SQL Server Agent must be running in order for any automation job to run. It is the SQL Server Agent service that monitors the schedules and executes the jobs. **C** is correct because SQL Server will allow you to create a job to run when the processor is idle without the idle threshold configured.

   ☒ **B** is incorrect because you must be a member of the sysadmin role, not the server admin role. As a local administrator on the server, Jane is automatically a member of the sysadmin role. **D** is incorrect because there is no option to monitor for idle on the Server Properties sheet. This functionality is added automatically when you configure the idle threshold in the SQL Agent Properties sheet. **E** is incorrect because there is no `xp_set_idle_monitor` stored procedure in SQL Server.

9.02: Configuring Alerts Using SQL Server Agent

3. ☑ **D** is the correct answer. Jamie needs to be notified when the transaction log on *any* database fills. This includes the system databases (Master or MSDB in particular). By creating an alert that pages her whenever error 9003 is raised, it will ensure that she is paged if any database becomes full. Creating the second alert which pages the sales administrator only when error 9003 is raised on the sales database will ensure that the sales administrator is only paged if the transaction log for that particular database becomes full.

   ☒ **A** is incorrect because it is not possible to have a filtered phrase apply to only one operator in the alert. If you were to put **Sales** in the Error Message Must Contain This Text text box, neither operator will be notified unless the transact log that is full belongs to the sales database. This would prevent Jamie from being notified if any other database log was full. **B** is incorrect because you could not create a single alert that limited its response to two databases. The database option in the event definition window will only allow you to specify a single database (or all databases). Even if this were possible the answer would still be incorrect because Jamie would not be notified if the logs for the system databases became full. **C** is incorrect because it would involve more work to configure and maintain than answer **D**. It also would not notify Jamie if any of the system database logs become full.

4. ☑ **B** and **D** are correct. **B** is correct because it is the SQL Agent that monitors the counters. If the Agent is not running, no information will be retrieved from the performance counters and this alert will never fire. **D** is correct because this particular counter can have multiple instances. This means that Windows tracks the same information for multiple objects. In this case the different instances

are databases on the server. If you have not specified the westcoast_inventory database in the instance box, the alert will not execute.

☒ **A** is incorrect because performance conditions are not written into the Event Viewer. The Agent only reads the Event View application log for event-based alerts. **C** is incorrect because these logs are installed automatically as part of the SQL Server installation process. Furthermore, if for some reason this particular counter was not installed, it would not show up in the list of available counters in the Create Alert Properties sheet. **E** is incorrect because the SQL Server Agent does not require the Windows 2000 System Monitor. The System Monitor is included so that administrators can watch the output of these counters in real time. It is not required for internal processes.

9.03: Creating and Using User-Defined Event Messages

5. ☑ **E** is the correct answer because it has the least amount of impact on the existing system. With the trigger, you do not have to change the application in any way. Every time the users update a customer using their application, the trigger will fire and raise the error. Because you have specified the WITH LOG command, this error will also be written to the event log and therefore will be read by the SQL Server Agent. This will allow the alert to execute.

☒ **A** is incorrect because it would involve changing the application on each user's desktop. In addition, because it is writing the log before running the UPDATE statement, you cannot be sure if the update actually occurred, of if there was a SQL Server error that prevented it from completing. This may lead to false information being sent to the sales manager. **B** is incorrect because it does not include the WITH LOG command and therefore does not write the log into the Event Viewer. **C** is incorrect because it would force you to rewrite the application. It would also mean that you would have to confirm programmatically that the update was successful before issuing the RAISERROR statement. **D** is also incorrect because it would force you to rewrite the application. If you were building this system from the beginning, using a stored procedure in this fashion is actually preferable to using a trigger from a performance standpoint.

6. ☑ **B** and **C** are the correct answers. The `xp_logevent` does the same job as a RAISERROR with log. The only different between the two is that you can execute the stored procedure on its own rather than including it in a trigger or stored procedure the same way you would a RAISERROR statement. Remember that if the error message is not set to log automatically, you must include the WITH LOG command to write the error in the event log.

    ☒ **A** is incorrect because severity 18 will not cause an event to be automatically written to the log. If you set the severity between 19 and 25, it will register as an error and SQL Server will automatically write it to the event log. **D** is incorrect because setting the @with_log value to 1 would produce a syntax error. The correct syntax is to use the value "True." For example, the following statement will always write the message to the Event View when it is raised:

    ```
    sp_addmessage @msgnum = 50020, @severity = 10, @msgtext
    ='Write me to the Event Log' , @with_log = true
    ```

    Notice that True is not enclosed in single quotes. If you place quotes around it, it will generate an error when executed. **E** is incorrect because there is no `sp_logevent` stored procedure in SQL Server.

9.04: Configuring Operators

7. ☑ **A**, **C**, and **E** are the correct answers. **A** is correct because the SQL Agent must contact the mail server. If the Agent is not running it will be unable to contact and retrieve information from the server. **C** is correct because the SQL Agent Mail service uses the profile to find which mail server to connect to and how it should connect. (That is, what user account and password to send if necessary.) If any of this information is incorrect, SQL Agent Mail will not be able to connect to the mail server correctly. **E** is correct because the Agent must be using a domain user account in order to authenticate to the mail server.

    ☒ **B** is incorrect because you do not need to have a mail client running in order to connect the mail server, as you will be connecting through the Agent and not your own profile. **D** is incorrect because SQL Agent Mail requires a MAPI-compliant mail server. It does not necessarily require Exchange.

8. ☑ **B** is the correct answer. Whenever you specify a contact method for an operator, SQL Server checks the sysoperators table to make sure it has the contact information for the operator. If it does not find the information, it raises an error.

☒ **A** is incorrect because it is possible to have multiple operators defined on the same alert. You can only have one operator defined per contact method on a job. **C**, **D**, and **E** are incorrect because SQL Server does not attempt to make a MAPI connection until the alert is raised. All of these would prevent the alert from functioning properly, but would not cause any problems in configuring the alert. The only other time the connection is tested is when you click on the test buttons on the Operator Properties sheet.

LAB ANSWER

Objectives 9.01–9.04

1. You can meet all of these requirements with a single job. The job would consist of multiple steps. The first step would be to copy the previous day's backup to the correct network share. Because you need to programmatically determine the day of the week, you would need an Active X script job to perform the copy. If this step fails you would configure the job to quit reporting an error, since you do not want to overwrite the backup files if you have not moved them. The remaining steps would back up each of the databases. You would need two schedules: one for weekdays, and one for the weekend. You would configure the job to notify the operators on completion. This will include both successful and failed jobs.

2. The first step would be performed using an ActiveX script or a Windows CmdExec file to determine the day of the week and copy all of the files to the appropriate network share.

3. Because you want to notify multiple operators as part of a job, you will have to create an email alias and create a group operator that uses the alias as its email address.

4. Users do not gain any special rights on the server when they are configured as operators. The only effect of being made an operator is that SQL Server records your contact information in the MSDB database.

5. In order to configure this alert, you must first create a user-defined error. Next, you will most likely create an UPDATE trigger on the products table that compares current inventory levels against the reorder level and issues a RAISERROR WITH LOG if the reorder level is higher. After that, you will have to configure an operator for the product manager and then configure an alert that emails that operator whenever the error is raised.

6. To allow the error message to contain the name of the product and its current inventory level, you must put placeholders (use %s and %d) in the error message. You will then populate variables programmatically for each parameter and pass them into the RAISERROR statement.

MICROSOFT CERTIFIED DATABASE ADMINISTRATOR

10

Managing, Monitoring, and Troubleshooting SQL Server 2000

TEST YOURSELF OBJECTIVES

S QL Server systems can range widely in size and scale. SQL Server does not require very much manual configuration, allowing you to focus primarily on the hardware required to accommodate your workloads, and isolating and resolving application bottlenecks such as excessive locking or other problems that can lead to poor performance.

Various tools are available to monitor system performance, SQL Server database activity and also display information about the actions of SQL Server components such as the Query Optimizer. These tools are designed to assist you in isolating performance problems, and in some cases making recommendations to improve performance. This chapter will discuss the use of these tools for monitoring your servers and databases.

TEST YOURSELF OBJECTIVE 10.01

Optimizing Hardware Resources

For the purposes of this objective, you should ensure that you are familiar with the System Monitor tool and the various performance counters that can be used to isolate hardware bottlenecks. You should also be familiar with the configuration options available within SQL Server that can be used to control hardware resource usage.

While SQL Server does not require significant manual configuration to obtain optimal system performance under most circumstances, there are various opportunities for higher volume systems to improve performance by focusing on the hardware platform on which you run the product, and also controlling how SQL Server will use the various hardware resources available to it.

In cases where SQL Server will be running on the same system as other applications, it becomes particularly important to ensure that SQL Server has sufficient resources, without interfering with the operation of other processes running on the same system. Some applications with extensive and complex application logic running alongside SQL Server may, in fact, require more resources than SQL Server itself requires. In these cases, you can configure SQL Server to use fewer system resources, freeing them up for the other processes on the system. In cases where multiple instances of SQL Server run on the same system, (such as with Internet hosting companies), the various instances of SQL Server can be configured for optimal resource usage.

In these types of environments, SQL Server provides the capability to configure memory and processor allocation. These allocations can be changed via the system properties in Enterprise Manager or by using SP_CONFIGURE. The illustration on the left shows the Memory settings available, and the illustration on the right shows the Processor configuration options. Both sets of options can be accessed via the properties of the instance within SQL Server.

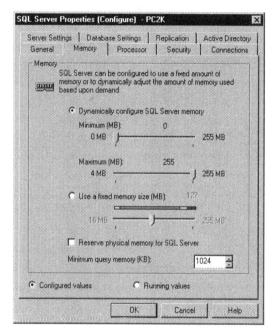 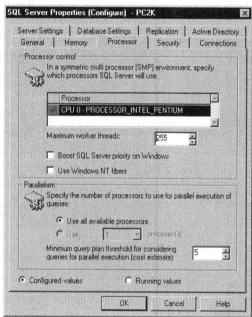

As shown in the preceding illustration, SQL Server can be configured with minimum, maximum, or specific fixed amounts of system memory. When using a fixed memory size, remember to change the value if you add or remove memory from a server.

Note: A side effect of using the Reserve Physical Memory For SQL Server option is that by preventing SQL Server memory pages from being swapped to disk, this will interfere with dynamic memory management, causing SQL Server not to release memory when it is needed for other processes.

It is generally recommended that SQL Server use the default Memory options. If necessary, you can configure an appropriate minimum or maximum value. It is not recommended that a fixed memory size be used.

It is recommended that the Minimum Query Memory option be left unchanged as it allows you to specify the amount of memory that should be allocated each time the

Query Optimizer requests memory. This option has been found to have little effect on performance in general.

Shown in the previous illustration are the Processor options available to SQL Server. On systems with multiple system processors, the system can be configured not to use some processors. When running multiple processes (or instances of SQL Server) on a system, this will prevent SQL Server from monopolizing processor resources. However, this is not normally necessary as the Windows kernel is quite adept at managing multiple processes and system processors. Enabling the Use Windows NT Fibers option configures SQL Server to use a Windows NT and 2000 feature that allows threads to be managed by SQL Server instead of Windows. Avoiding having to switch between User mode and Kernel mode code can save some additional processor time. Under heavy load, the reduced thread management overhead can provide a small performance boost of a few percentage points. This may not be a substantial gain, but it won't cost you anything. Enabling this on systems that are not operating under heavy loads is not recommended. Microsoft recommends enabling this value on multi-processor systems when processor utilization is completely maximized and the number of Context Switches/Sec reaches 8000.

On systems with many concurrent users, you may need to increase the Maximum Worker Threads value to allow more SQL client activity to occur simultaneously. SQL Server can use thread pooling to allow more than one database connection to share a worker thread, which works very well when users are often idle, but when running high-throughput transactions, this can lead to inefficiencies.

You can also specify the behavior for parallel queries on multiprocessor systems. Parallel query support allows the Query Optimizer to divide a query plan into multiple plans, which can be executed on different system processors. This is particularly useful for queries that require operations against multiple tables. Making multiple processors available to a single complex query can greatly improve performance, however attempting to break a simple query plan into multiple parallel plans will incur system overhead. This overhead may counteract the benefits of parallel query execution if the cost of building parallel plans exceeds the performance savings of executing queries across multiple processors. In order to ensure that only expensive queries are considered for parallel execution, you can modify the minimum query plan threshold value.

In order to build an effective I/O platform, you should keep these tips in mind:

- RAID-1 provides additional fault tolerance, with little performance impact.
- RAID-5 provides additional fault tolerance and improved read performance. Write performance is poor compared to RAID-0&1. Since RAID-0&1 does not require the parity calculations of RAID-5.

■ RAID-0&1 or RAID-10 provides additional fault tolerance with improved read performance and little additional write overhead. In fact, if configured using RAID-10, you would be using a stripe set of mirrored volumes. In this configuration, as many as half the drives can fail (assuming no two drives in the same mirror fail at the same time) and the volume will still be available. The major drawback to this approach is the cost of having a backup drive for every drive in the set. The I/O subsystem must also manage twice as many I/O operations. The integrated Windows software fault-tolerance features can be used to create RAID 0, 1, and 5 volumes (referred to as striped, mirrored and RAID-5 volumes respectively) but cannot be used to create a RAID-0&1 volume.

You should also keep in mind that different types of database data structures or objects have very different I/O patterns. Some tables may be very write-intensive, while other tables are written to rarely and are read frequently. Objects with similar I/O patterns can be grouped on the same disks, thereby ensuring that read operations do not interfere with write operations and vice-versa. The various database objects and the transaction logs all behave differently with regard to read/write activity. The following are examples of different I/O characteristics of SQL Server databases:

■ Transaction logs are write-intensive.

■ Indexes are generally read-intensive, although indexes must also be kept up-to-date when modifying data and this can affect write performance.

■ Tables may be either read or write-intensive and it is very important to be familiar with your databases to determine which will be the case.

QUESTIONS

10.01: Optimizing Hardware Resources

1. You are monitoring performance data on one of your multiprocessor servers. The system is running only SQL Server. Microsoft Search is not installed. The server seems to be running at near maximum capacity. All processors are running at or near 100% most of the time during periods of heavy system load. You have been asked to devise a strategy for squeezing additional processor

capacity out of the system in the easiest manner possible. You notice that processor queuing is occurring and the system is exhibiting very heavy context switching. Currently, according to the System Monitor, the average number of Context Switches/Sec is 9,500. Your database comprises multiple filegroups distributed across six RAID arrays controlled by several storage controllers. All RAID functionality is hardware-based. How can you easily free up additional processor capacity?

A. Install additional processors in the system.

B. Decrease SQL Server's priority using Task Manager.

C. In the SQL Server instance properties, configure SQL Server to run at a higher priority.

D. In the SQL Server instance properties, configure SQL Server to use fiber mode switching.

2. You are planning the integration of SQL Server with a new Enterprise Resource Planning (ERP) application that your organization is deploying. Due to the high level of user activity anticipated, it has been determined that to cut network traffic, the ERP package will run directly alongside SQL Server on the same system. In order to accommodate the heavy workload, the system will be upgraded to eight processors. What can be done to ensure that SQL Server does not interfere with normal operation of the resource-intensive ERP package?

A. Configure SQL Server to run at a lower priority via the system properties.

B. Configure the ERP package to run at a higher priority.

C. In the SQL Server instance properties, configure SQL Server to use only certain system processors.

D. Configure the ERP package to run on specific processors by setting the Affinity using Task Manager.

3. You are the administrator of a large data warehouse. Currently you are running SQL Server Standard edition on a four-processor system running Windows 2000 Advanced Server. You have recently implemented new data quality assurance guidelines dictating that database consistency checks must be run more frequently and you are concerned with the length of time it takes to complete the checks. Currently, it takes approximately 14 hours to run DBCC

CHECKDB against the database. You are concerned that the long run time for DBCC operations will interfere with scheduled reports. What can be done to decrease the length of time required for DBCC operations?

A. Run DBCC CHECKDB using the WITH_PARALLEL option.

B. Upgrade to SQL Server Enterprise edition.

C. Enable parallel query support.

D. Span the database across multiple RAID sets using filegroups.

4. You are using SQL Server as the data store for a mapping database. Most data is stored in SQL Server as coordinates and reference points. In order to improve response time, each of the users has a local copy of SQL Server Desktop edition to store their own personal map data. The mapping application is extremely resource-intensive and the local copy of SQL Server is generally idle. At certain times of the day, each local copy of SQL Server runs various tasks to validate and update mapping data. Occasionally, this will interfere with normal operation of the mapping application itself, which is unacceptable to your users. You would like to ensure that during these tasks, a minimum amount of memory is always available to the mapping application running on your client desktops. You want to prevent maintenance tasks in the local copy of SQL Server from interfering with the operation of the mapping application.

Which SQL Server memory configuration is most appropriate for this scenario?

A. Configure SQL Server to specify the maximum amount of memory that can be used.

B. Configure SQL Server to use a fixed amount of memory.

C. Configure SQL Server to reserve physical memory.

D. Decrease the Minimum Query Memory value.

5. You are configuring the filegroup layout for a large database. You currently have the following filegroup layout:

▓ The first filegroup, FG_TABLES, contains one data file. All database tables are stored in this filegroup.

▓ The second filegroup, FG_INDEXES, also contains one data file. All non-clustered indexes are stored in this filegroup.

- FG_TABLES is stored on drive D:, which is a RAID-5 volume with six disks.

- FG_INDEXES is stored on drive I:, which is a RAID-5 volume with eight disks.

- The database transaction logs are stored on drive L:, which is a mirrored volume.

Using the System Monitor, you are noticing an increasing amount of write queuing on the disks containing the FG_TABLES filegroup. The RAID set that contains the FG_INDEXES filegroup is not exhibiting any performance problems.

Which of the following could be used to improve write performance? (Choose all that apply.)

A.   Increase the Recovery Interval setting.

B.   Add disks to the RAID set for the FG_TABLES filegroup.

C.   Change the RAID type for the filegroup to RAID-0&1.

D.   Move some of the write-intensive tables to the disks containing the indexes.

TEST YOURSELF OBJECTIVE 10.02

Monitoring Hardware Using System Monitor

In order to monitor performance behavior of your system, the System Monitor can be used to either view performance data directly, or the system can be configured to log performance data to a file, which can be read later. This allows for easier long-term performance monitoring. You can configure the system to log during certain time periods or, when a specific performance condition occurs, a performance log can be started automatically using performance alerts in the Windows 2000 Performance tool. This operates independently of SQL Server performance alerts and allows monitoring of non-SQL Server performance counters. The next illustration shows the performance log properties.

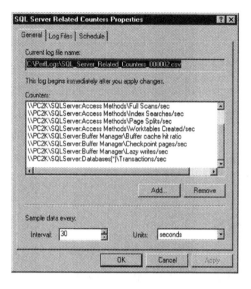

Performance alerts can also be configured to run a script or executable when triggered; this can be used to notify administrative staff of a potential problem, and can also be used to take remedial action, such as shutting down non-critical processes. The following illustration shows the alert action properties. When configuring performance alerts to run a program, you may need to modify the Command Line Arguments value if your program or script expects to get input parameters in a different order, or if it expects different command syntax.

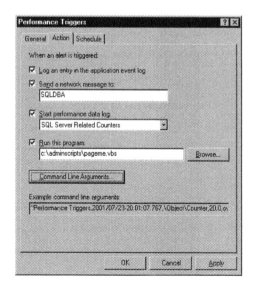

It is recommended that you monitor the following counters:

- Processor/% Processor Utilization should be less than 90% for each CPU.
- Memory/Pages/Sec should be less than five per second.
- System/Processor Queue Length should be less than two for each CPU.
- Physical Disk/Avg. Disk Read Queue Length and Physical Disk/Avg. Disk Write—Queue Length should be less than two (or one per disk in a RAID set).

Additional SQL Server-specific counters will be discussed later in this chapter.

QUESTIONS

10.02: Monitoring Hardware Using System Monitor

6. You are reviewing the performance of one of your systems. Users are complaining that in recent months, system performance has become very poor. Using System Monitor, you retrieve the following performance data from the system:

Counter	Monitored Value
Processor: % Processor Time	98%
System: Context Switches/Sec	3740
SQL Server Buffer Manager: Buffer Cache hit ratio	87%
System: Processor Queue Length	3
Physical Disk: Avg. Disk Write Queue Length	0
Physical Disk: Avg. Disk Read Queue Length	1

What should be done to improve the performance of this system? (Choose all that apply.)

A. Add an additional network interface.

B. Install additional memory.

   C. Install an additional processor.

   D. Decrease the number of worker threads configured on the system.

7. Users are stating that performance occasionally drops significantly for extended periods of time. The system is primarily used for decision support, and users are primarily report developers and savvy users who have taken to writing their own database queries and reports in order to get faster results. You have decided that it is important to implement a long-term monitoring scheme to plan for future user activity. In order to stay on top of performance issues on this system, you have found that you need to track a significant number of performance counters. The amount of data generated is difficult to manage, and you have decided that you would rather monitor certain strategic counters and enable additional monitoring when performance problems occur. You have decided to start with monitoring processor usage and will decide which additional counters to monitor after a short test period. How can this be done?

   A. Use a Windows 2000 performance alert. Define an alert on the Processor Usage object. Configure the alert to start a performance log.

   B. Create a performance condition alert on the Processor Usage object in the SQL Agent. Configure the alert to start a performance log.

   C. Use System Monitor to track the counters you need. Log performance data to a file.

   D. Create a scheduled job in the Agent to verify the processor utilization and notify you via XP_SENDMAIL.

8. You are reviewing the performance of one of your systems. You have configured the system to log all performance data to a log file. After loading the log file into the System Monitor, your performance counters show the following values:

Counter	Monitored Value
Processor: % Processor Time	76%
System: Context Switches/Sec	2896
SQL Server Buffer Manager: Buffer Cache hit ratio	95%
System: Processor Queue Length	0
Physical Disk: Avg. Disk Write Queue Length	4
Physical Disk: Avg. Disk Read Queue Length	1

The disk layout for your database is:

■ Operating system and SQL Server program files are on drive C:. The
database and transaction logs are on drive D:.

■ Drive C is a hardware based RAID-1 set. Drive D is a hardware based
RAID-5 set.

What should be done to improve the performance of this system? (Choose the
best answer.)

A. Add additional drives to the RAID-5 set.

B. Move the transaction logs to another set of disks.

C. Convert the RAID-5 set to a RAID-0&1 set.

D. Increase the amount of memory available to SQL Server.

TEST YOURSELF OBJECTIVE 10.03

Resolving System Bottlenecks by Using System Monitor

In addition to being able to detect and isolate hardware bottlenecks, you should also
be familiar with various performance counters and critical monitoring areas relating
specifically to SQL Server, such as the database Buffer Cache hit ratio.

Table 10-1 shows some examples of areas that need to be monitored within SQL
Server, and recommendations that Microsoft makes regarding the desired values for
these key performance indicators.

For purposes of the exam, you should be familiar with these performance areas and
ensure that you are aware of the recommended remedy for the various performance
scenarios.

You should also be familiar with SQL Server's connection pooling behavior. The
SQL Server Maximum Worker Threads value can be used to control how many
internal database operations can be performed simultaneously. On high-end systems
with large numbers of users, the default value of 255 may prevent SQL Server from

using all of the resources available to it; in cases when performance is poor, but resource usage is relatively light, you should consider increasing the number of worker threads available. After doing this, ensure that you monitor for new performance problems that can be caused by setting this value to high. Symptoms of this can include high processor utilization and excessive Lazy Writer activity.

TABLE 10-1	Counter	Target Value	Remedy
Collected Performance Data	SQL Server Buffer Manager: Buffer Cache Ratio	Over 90% in OLTP environments	Increase the amount of memory available to SQL Hit Server.
	SQL Server Access Methods: Page Splits/Sec	As low as possible	Decrease the FILLFACTOR value for indexes.
	SQL Server Buffer Manager: Lazy Writes/Sec	Low enough to prevent disk write queuing	If write queuing is occurring and this value is elevated, decrease the maximum number of worker threads.
	SQL Server Buffer Manager: Checkpoint Writes/Sec	Low enough to prevent disk write queuing	If write queuing is occurring and this value is elevated, increase the system recovery interval.
	SQL Server Locks: Lock Waits/Sec	As low as possible	Re-evaluate database indexing, re-design transactions.
	SQL Server Locks: Number of Deadlocks/Sec	As low as possible	Re-evaluate table processing order in transactions, redesign design transactions, re-evaluate database indexing.
	SQL Server SQL Statistics: SQL Compilations/Sec	Low enough to prevent heavy processor utilization	Re-evaluate use of stored procedures and query plan caching strategy.

QUESTIONS

10.03: Resolving System Bottlenecks by Using System Monitor

9. You have installed SQL Server with the default settings. Your database is used primarily for transaction processing and needs to support as many as 500 users simultaneously. In order to accommodate the heavy workload, the system contains four processors and is running SQL Server 2000 Enterprise edition on Windows 2000 Advanced Server. During testing using a client load simulation tool, you have noticed very poor throughput for client operations. Using System Monitor, you see no symptoms of poor performance. Average processor utilization is below 50%, and very little disk queuing is occurring. What should be done to improve performance on this system?

   A. Increase the Maximum Worker Threads setting.

   B. Increase the Max Async I/O setting.

   C. Decrease the Recovery Interval setting.

   D. Configure SQL Server to run at a higher scheduling priority.

10. You are monitoring your database performance during your routine monitoring duties. You notice that the number of Lazy Writes/Sec counter has doubled compared to your previously observed performance baselines and the Transactions/Sec counter is also quite highly elevated. What is this an indication of?

   A. More database transactions are being committed to the database.

   B. The system is unable to commit transactions to the database quickly enough.

   C. The SQL Server Agent idle threshold is set too low.

   D. The number of configured Worker Threads is too high.

TEST YOURSELF OBJECTIVE 10.04

Optimizing and Troubleshooting SQL Server System Activity Using the Profiler

The Profiler utility provides a wealth of functionality to track system behavior within SQL Server. While it is certainly useful to be able to track generic behavior in the system using the Performance tools, it does not provide enough data to be able to associate that performance behavior with the root cause. On the other hand, Profiler provides the capability to:

- Display SQL statements running against the database.
- Display extended system information regarding system behavior.
- Apply filters to include or exclude trace data to be displayed.
- Group trace data based on specific criteria.
- Save or import trace data to a file or table.
- Replay trace data against a database for testing.
- Use trace data as input for the Index Tuning Wizard.

For purposes of the exam, you should be familiar with creating and managing traces and should be able to interpret the data that is generated. It is also important that you be familiar with the Index Tuning Wizard.

In order to create a trace in the Profiler you must specify the logging options to use, the events and data that you wish to capture, and filters on the data to be captured. When creating a new trace, you will be presented with the following options:

- Whether trace data should be saved to a table or a file (a maximum size can be specified for both options).
- Whether a template should be used. Templates provide preconfigured trace settings for various scenarios. For example, the SQLProfilerTSQL_Replay template traces the necessary events and data to replay activity from one database against another database. (This can be only be used with SQL authentication, and not when using Windows authentication.)
- How long the trace should run.

■ The events to be tracked. Events represent user activity in the database. Events are organized into event classes such as Transact-SQL and Locks which allow you to trace Transact-SQL statements and system locking behavior. Other event classes include errors and warnings, which allow you to log errors that are occurring in your database, and the database event class, which allows you to view how user activity affects the database size.

■ The data columns to be included in the trace. The data columns allow you to add or remove detail from the trace, such as displaying information about the client such as the username or computer name or system information such as the permissions that were used to fulfill a client request.

■ Filters to include or exclude user activity based on specific criteria. Filters can be used to trace activity originating from a specific user or workstation for tracing very specific activity and you can also filter by application if multiple different client applications access your database but you are only interested in the behavior of specific applications. For example, by default, traces in Profiler will not trace database activity generated by the Profiler utility itself. (This can be disabled, if you are interested in investigating the operation of the Profiler.)

Once a trace has been created, it must be run. While a script is running it can be paused and resumed or stopped. If a trace is stopped and restarted, previous trace data will be lost if it is not saved.

Once user activity has been collected, the trace can be stopped manually or configured to stop at a specific time. Trace data can then be used to:

■ Generate a script of all the SQL statements (scripts can be generated to be either SQL Server 7.0 or SQL Server 2000-compatible) that can then be saved for testing or documentation purposes.

■ Generate a script for the trace. This can be used to create a scheduled job in the agent to run a trace on a schedule.

■ Bookmarks can be inserted into the trace to mark interesting activity.

■ The trace can be replayed against another server. When replaying a trace, breakpoints can be configured to stop processing the trace at specific points so that you can interrupt the replay to examine the state of the database or the response of the system at different points in a database transaction.

■ The trace can be used as input to the Index Tuning Wizard.

The Index Tuning Wizard will analyze the activity in the trace and recommend an indexing strategy for your database. It can report the estimated performance improvement for your system's worst performing queries and display statistics showing the number of queries that rank in specific improvement percentiles. The Index Tuning Wizard can also be used to implement the recommended changes. Implementing the changes can be scheduled to run at a later time, or the recommended changes can be saved to a script, which could then be run against another system. This could be used to test the new indexing strategy on a test server, before implementing the changes on your production server.

The Index Tuning Wizard can be run against either Profiler trace data or the currently selected block of a script in the Query Analyzer.

QUESTIONS

10.04: Optimizing and Troubleshooting SQL Server System Activity Using the Profiler

11. You have recently run the Index Tuning Wizard against your development server. You would like to implement the index changes recommended by the Index Tuning Wizard on your production server. What steps should you take? (Choose all that apply.)

   A. Using the trace file from the development server, run the Index Tuning Wizard on the production server.

   B. Re-run the Index Tuning Wizard using the saved trace file on the development server. Save the index tuning recommendations as a script. Run the script on the production server.

   C. Re-run the trace. Use the trace file as input for the Index Tuning Wizard on the production server.

   D. After running the Index Tuning Wizard on the development system, you should specify that recommended changes be run against the production system.

12. You would like to tune your database and have decided to review the performance of some of the longer running queries. You would like to find the queries that run the longest, and then review their query plans using the Query Analyzer. You would like the query plans output in text format so they can be exported for documentation purposes. What steps need to be completed to allow this? (Choose all that apply.)

    A. Create a new trace using Profiler. Create the trace using the SQLProfiler_TSQLDuration template.

    B. Run the Index Tuning Wizard. Save the index tuning recommendations as a script. Run the script in the Query Analyzer.

    C. Save the trace as a SQL script. Run the script in the Query Analyzer.

    D. Execute the SET SHOWPLAN ALL statement.

13. You are trying to determine the cause of high memory usage on one of your servers. Although you know that SQL Server's memory allocation increases at various times, due to heavy system usage, it is very difficult for you to determine what is causing SQL Server to require more memory. Which tools can be used to determine what is causing the increased memory usage?

    A. System Monitor

    B. Query Analyzer

    C. Profiler

    D. Enterprise Manager Current Activity window

LAB QUESTION

Objectives 10.01–10.04

You are the new database administrator for a medium-size company. You are supporting a database that is in production but that you are not familiar with. In order to help isolate performance problems you would like to set up a test server and run simulations of client activity.

You would like to take a sample of the queries being run against your production system in order to do drive client simulations. You are also interested in reviewing the indexing strategy for the database using the Index Tuning Wizard.

Required results:

- Trace all queries being run from a specific workstation that will be used for testing.

- Ensure that trace data can be imported into a SQL Server table.

Optional desired results:

- Generate output that can be replayed against another system using the Profiler or Query Analyzer.

- Ensure that trace data can be used as input for the Index Tuning Wizard.

Proposed solution:

- Create a new trace based on the SQLProfilerTSQL_Replay template.

- Configure the trace to login using Windows authentication.

- Configure the trace to log to a trace file.

- Configure a filter in the trace properties to only include the testing workstation.

What results will this solution produce?

QUICK ANSWER KEY

Objective 10.01

1. D
2. C
3. B
4. A
5. A, B, C, and D

Objective 10.02

6. C
7. A
8. B

Objective 10.03

9. A
10. A

Objective 10.04

11. B
12. A, C, and D
13. C and D

IN-DEPTH ANSWERS

10.01: Optimizing Hardware Resources

1. ☑ **D** is correct because SQL Server is causing the system to run at maximum capacity. Managing a single system thread per worker thread can cause the operating system process manager to become a bottleneck. When processor usage is near 100% and the number of Context Switches/Sec is approaching or over 8000, SQL Server can use it's fiber mode scheduling feature to manage worker threads, instead of having the threads managed by Windows. This reduces the occurrence of context switching and can improve performance. User connections are multiplexed into worker threads via connection pooling. Both these features can allow SQL Server to reduce operating system overhead, freeing up additional system resources for use by SQL Server.

   ☒ **A** is incorrect since it is not the easiest solution, although it would address the problem. **B** and **C** are incorrect because changing SQL Server's priority would have little effect on performances since SQL Server is not competing with any other processes for resources.

2. ☑ **C** is correct because specifying that SQL Server shouldn't use some of the processors in the system allows them to be used by the other application.

   ☒ **A** is incorrect because SQL Server can be configured to receive a priority boost in the system properties. Configuring SQL Server to run at a lower priority cannot be done using the SQL Server tools. It can be configured using Task Manager and other process control utilities, such as the START command. **B** is incorrect because raising the priority of an already resource-intensive process can cause performance to suffer if SQL Server is not given sufficient resources to accommodate the ERP package requests! **D** is incorrect because assigning processor affinity this way would only allow the ERP package to use one processor. This may lead to performance degradation.

3. ☑ **B** is correct because SQL Server Enterprise edition allows database consistency checks and index operations to take advantage of multiple system processors. When using this feature, the Parallel Query option must be enabled.

☒ **A** is incorrect because when using the parallel query feature with a DBCC check, no special options need to be used. **C** is incorrect because the system is not running SQL Server Enterprise edition. **D** is incorrect because DBCC execution time would not be cut substantially using multiple disk sets if DBCC execution is not being run in parallel across multiple processors.

4. ☑ **A** is correct because specifying the most memory that SQL Server can use will ensure that a sufficient amount of memory is always available to the rest of the system. Under most normal operations, SQL Server's dynamic memory management feature will be sufficient and have little impact on performance. In cases where both applications are running under heavy load, SQL Server and the application will compete for memory and the constant allocation and de-allocation of memory between the two processes will either cause heavy processor overhead or in many cases, swapping to the system pagefile.

☒ **B** and **C** are incorrect because SQL Server would not be able to release memory if it was needed by the application, and SQL Server would not be able to use additional memory that might not be needed by the application. **D** is incorrect because the Minimum Query Memory option is used internally to SQL Server and would not allow you to control the amount of memory available to the application.

5. ☑ **A, B, C,** and **D** are correct. Increasing the Recovery Interval will force the system to wait longer before committing transactions to disk.

This will increase the amount of memory required for SQL Server and only defers disk writing; it does not decrease the amount of data that must be written to those disks. However, this should free up the disks to accommodate more read requests. Adding disks to the RAID set will allow more I/O operations to be completed simultaneously, thereby preventing disk queuing. RAID-5 provides relatively poor write performance, which is a side-effect of the parity calculation used for data redundancy. Using RAID-0&1 (or RAID-10, which is a popular variant of RAID-0&1) for data striping with mirroring allows for improved write performance, due to the lack of parity calculation overhead. Moving some of the tables to the other filegroup should allow the load to be more evenly distributed across your storage arrays. This may interfere with index read performance and you should exercise caution when doing this to ensure you do not simply move the problem to another area of your database!

10.02: Monitoring Hardware Using System Monitor

6. ☑ **C** is correct because installing an additional processor will provide the system with more capacity for existing and future users. Heavy processor utilization and processor queuing are clear indications of a bottleneck.

    ☒ **A** is incorrect because there is no indication of the network interface being a bottleneck. **B** is incorrect because although the Buffer Cache hit ratio is slightly below the ideal, this is not an indication of a major bottleneck. **D** is incorrect because while decreasing the number of worker threads would reduce processor utilization, it would not improve system throughput or response time.

7. ☑ **A** is correct because performance logs and alerts are designed for this purpose, as well as long-term monitoring.

    ☒ **B** is incorrect because performance condition alerts in SQL Server cannot be used to start a system performance log without additional scripting. **C** is incorrect because this solution would not allow on-demand performance logging when processor usage is high. **D** is incorrect because it is a difficult and inappropriate solution. Collecting performance data through SQL Server is relatively difficult and is not recommended.

8. ☑ **B** is correct because the transaction logs for the database should be isolated from the rest of the database to improve transactional throughput. This should be the first response to this scenario.

    ☒ **A, C,** and **D** are incorrect because these other solutions would improve performance, but are not the best answer to this problem.

10.03: Resolving System Bottlenecks by Using System Monitor

9. ☑ **A** is correct because increasing the maximum number of worker threads will allow SQL Server to generate a larger workload and use more of the system's resources in cases where there are large numbers of users connected to the database. This can also be changed using `sp_configure 'max worker threads'`. Changing this value should cause an increase in processor and disk

utilization, but system throughput should be increased as well. If excessive processor or disk queuing occurs, decrease this value until queuing ceases.

☒ **B** is incorrect because SQL Server 2000 does not require this option to be changed manually, as in previous versions of the product. **C** is incorrect because it would not improve system performance since disk write activity is not interfering with other user activity. There is no need to override the system checkpoint behavior to defer disk writes. **D** is incorrect because SQL Server does not need to compete with other processes for CPU time, due to the fact that the system processors are relatively idle.

10. ☑ **A** is correct because this is not an indication of a bottleneck but simply a reflection of increased transactional throughput. You should check for resource queuing to see how the system responds to the increased workload.

☒ **B** is incorrect because high values for these counters do not indicate performance bottlenecks. **C** is incorrect. The Agent idle threshold is used to specify the threshold at which jobs that are configured to run when the system is idle will start. **D** is incorrect because high transactional throughput is not an indication of a configuration error.

10.04: Optimizing and Troubleshooting SQL Server System Activity Using the Profiler

11. ☑ **B** is correct because saving the tuning recommendations to a script allows the changes to be implemented on another system. They can also be used as documentation of the changes or to recreate the indexes if necessary.

☒ **A** is incorrect because running the Index Tuning Wizard on the production server will generate unneeded overhead when a test system is readily available. **C** is incorrect because re-running the trace on the production server is unnecessary, since a trace with all the needed queries is already available. Re-running the Index Tuning Wizard on the production server will also cause unneeded overhead in this case as well. **D** is incorrect because you cannot use the wizard to specify which system the changes should be implemented on.

12. ☑   **A, C,** and **D** are correct. Grouping Profiler trace data by duration allows you to isolate the longer running queries. The trace (or selected portions of the trace) can be saved as a script. The script can then be loaded into the Query Analyzer. Using the SET SHOWPLAN ALL statement will output the query plans instead of the normal query output.

 ☒   **B** is incorrect because the Index Tuning Wizard does not need to be run.

13. ☑   **C** and **D** are correct. The Server: Server Memory Change event can be added to a Profiler trace to watch this activity or the amount of memory used by a database connection can be viewed in the Current Activity window in Enterprise Manager. Unlike the Profiler, the only Transact-SQL activity that you can view in the Current Activity window is the last Transact-SQL batch submitted on each connection.

 ☒   **A** and **B** are incorrect. The System Monitor cannot indicate what user activity is causing heavy memory usage. The Query Analyzer cannot display memory utilization for all user activity—only the behavior of specific queries.

LAB ANSWER

Objectives 10.01–10.04

In this scenario, the proposed solution does not directly produce all of the results in question. The trace that is written to the log, using these options, cannot be used with the Profiler's replay functionality to run captured activity against a database. The Replay function will only work using SQL authentication, and does not support Windows authentication. The trace file can be used with the Index Tuning Wizard.

Filtering the trace based on the workstation name will allow you to trace only data from that workstation. This can be specified in the trace properties, via the Filters tab. You can also use this feature to simply filter out other hosts such as remote SQL servers participating in replication.

The trace can then be loaded into a table using the Profiler, using the File | Save As menu and selecting Trace Table.

The trace can also be saved as a Transact-SQL script. This script could be used to display execution plans for various queries or for documentation purposes.

Practice Exam

Q & A

QUESTIONS

1. Sue has configured linked servers with a number of different data sources. The data sources are a mix of SQL 2000, SQL 7.0, and SQL 6.5 servers, as well as Oracle servers and Access database files. She has added each server using `sp_addlinkedsrvlogin`. Users are complaining that they can execute distributed queries against some, but not all of the data sources included in the linked servers. Furthermore, the servers that are available seem to differ from user to user. What would likely account for this discrepancy?

   A. Sue has not set a security context for the linked servers. All of the users are connecting with pass-through authentication.

   B. Some of the users are authenticating with SQL Server login accounts.

   C. Some of the users do not have OLEDB installed on their local computers.

   D. Some of the users are using the wrong OLEDB provider to connect to the remote servers.

2. Stuart is the database administrator for the Bigcorp shoe company. He is planning to implement a SQL Server back-end for their e-commerce site. They are expecting to handle approximately 3000 transactions per hour. The specifications for the server are 6GB of RAM and 8 processors. This server must be available at all times and will most likely use Windows Cluster Service to create a clustered SQL Server implementation. Which version of SQL Server must he install to meet these requirements?

   A. Standard

   B. Developer

   C. Advanced

   D. Enterprise

   E. Datacenter

3. Gina is the administrator for a SQL server called WestData2. The server is installed on a Windows 2000 Advanced server also called WestData2. The server has a default SQL Server instance and a named SQL instance

called WestTestData2 installed. Gina has been developing a database in WestTestData2 that she now wants to move onto another production server. She plans to copy the data file and use `sp_attach_db` to attach the database to the new server. She has stopped WestTestData2. The database was created in the default file location. Assuming SQL Server was installed on the C: drive in the default path, where will Gina find the data files for her database?

A. c:\mssql8\data

B. c:\Program Files\Microsoft SQL Server\mssql\WestTestData2\Data

C. c:\Program Files\Microsoft SQL Server\mssql$WestTestData2\Data

D   c:\Program Files\ Microsoft SQL Server\WestTestData$Mssql\Data

E. c:\Program Files\Microsoft SQL Server\mssql$WestData2\WestTestData2\Data

4. James is attempting to install a SQL server. However, each time he runs the installation program it fails at the same point, just prior to the point where the server service is started. James is not sure what is causing the failure. Where would he go to locate the cause of the failure? (Choose all that apply.)

A. The application log in Event Viewer

B. The SQLstp.log file

C. The SQL Server Error logs in c:\Program Files\ Microsoft SQL Server\ Mssql\Log

D. The SQLInstallog.out file

E. The error logs in Enterprise Manager

5. Sam has installed a SQL 2000 server. He wants to configure some automatic tasks on the server, but the SQL Server Agent service will not start. He is using a domain user account to authenticate the service. He has confirmed that the account used by the service is installed and has confirmed that the password is correct. He has also confirmed that he can ping at least one Domain Controller on his network. What other factors may account for the service not starting? (Choose all that apply.)

A. He has not added the account to the server admin fixed server role.

B. The domain account has the **user must change password at next login** password property set on.

C. The server is running TCP/IP Sockets as its only network library.

D. The domain user account does not have administrative privileges on the local Windows 2000 server.

E. The account has not been granted the **logon as a service** user right.

6. James is planning to add a database to hold sports statistics for amateur sport teams. The database tracks the statistics for hundreds of teams in different sports. The local leagues will update the database constantly, via an Active Server page. Any player will also be able to query the database, again via an Active Server page. Because the service will be nationwide, there will be constant activity on the web site. The initial database size will be 200GB. The disk structure of the server is as follows:

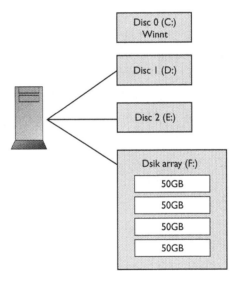

James is concerned with both performance and fault tolerance. How should James place the data files to provide the best possible query and update performance? (Choose the best answer.)

A. Place SQL Server on a separate disk from the operating system. Place the transaction log by itself on the third disk. Create a RAID-0 array on the hardware array. Place the database in one large data file on the array.

    B. Place SQL Server on a separate disk from the operating system. Place the transaction log by itself on the third disk. Create one data file on each disk in the hardware array.

    C. Place SQL Server on the same disk as the operating system. Create a RAID-1 array on the two single disks and put the transaction log on that disk. Create a RAID-5 array on the hardware array and place the database in five data files on the array.

    D. Place SQL Server on the same disk as the operating system. Create a RAID-1 array on the two single disks and put the transaction log on that disk. Create a RAID-0 array on the hardware array and place the database in a single data on the array.

    E. Create a RAID-5 set between disks 1, 2, and 3. Place SQL Server and the transaction log on that array. Create a RAID-5 array on the hardware array and place the database on that array on five separate disks.

7. You are the administrator for a SQL server database called Prod_data. Recently you have imported a very large number of rows into your table. These rows have now been deleted, but your data files are still quite large. Your database consists of three data files called prod_data1, prod_data2, and prod_data3. The database is currently 12GB is size (divided between the three files). However, 6GB of that data file is currently free space. You want to reduce the size of the database so that there is only 20% free space remaining. Which statement or statements would you use to reduce the database?

    A. `DBCC SHRINKFILE (prod_data1, prod_data2, prod_data3, 20)`

    B. `DBCC SHRINKDATABASE (prod_data, 20)`

    C. `DBCC SHRINKDATABASE (prod_data, 80)`

    D
```
DBCC SHRINKFILE (prod_data1, 20)
GO
DBCC SHRINKFILE (prod_data2, 20)
GO
DBCC SHRINKFILE (prod_data3, 20)
```

    E.
```
ALTER DATABASE
SHRINK DATABASE = 20%
```

8. Jim is designing several tables in a database that contains inventory records. In this system, whenever items are removed from stock, an entry is placed in the order_pick table that lists the productid of the item removed, the quantity and the order number for which the item was removed. When this row is inserted, a trigger modifies the in_stock column on the products table. The warehouse manager has complained that operators occasionally mistype productids and the inaccuracies are entering into the inventory list. What can Jim do to ensure that the productid entered in the order_pick table represents a valid product id with the least amount of overhead? (Choose the best answer.)

   A. Create a Foreign Key constraint on the productid column in the order_pick table that references the productid column on the products table.

   B. Modify the trigger so that it checks to see if the productid is valid before it attempts to update the in_stock column. Have it roll back the initial insert and return an error if the productid is invalid.

   C. Create a CHECK constraint on the order_pick table that checks to see if the productid exists in the products table.

   D. Create a RULE on the order_pick table that checks to see if the productid exists in the products table.

   E. Write a stored procedure to verify that the productid exists in the products table before it allows the value to be inserted into the order_pick tables.

9. Jim is the administrator for a SQL 2000 server. Recently his users have been complaining that access to the Customerorders table has been exceedingly slow, particularly when issuing INSERT statements. Jim runs the DBCC SHOWCONTIG statement on the table and gets the following result.

```
DBCC SHOWCONTIG scanning 'Order Details' table...

Table: 'CusomerOrders' (325345198); index ID: 2, database ID: 8

LEAF level scan performed.

- Pages Scanned................................: 3250

- Extents Scanned.............................: 440

- Extent Switches.............................: 539

- Avg. Pages per Extent.......................: 3.3
```

```
- Scan Density [Best Count:Actual Count].......: 33.33% [1:3]

- Logical Scan Fragmentation ..................: 20.00%

- Extent Scan Fragmentation ...................: 26.00%

- Avg. Bytes Free per Page.....................: 21.698

- Avg. Page Density (full)......................: 99.23%

DBCC execution completed. If DBCC printed error messages,
contact your system administrator.
```

The Customer orders table contains a clustered index that was originally created with a FILLFACTOR of 75%. What should Jim do to improve the performance of this table? (Choose all that apply.)

A. Run the DBCC INDEXDEFRAG statement and to reset the fill factor.

B. Issue an ALTER TABLE statement to reset the fill factor.

C. Issue an ALTER INDEX statement to reset the fill factor.

D. Issue a CREATE INDEX statement using the DROP_EXISTING option to re-index the table and reset the fill factor.

E. Run the DBCC DBREINDEX option to reset the fill factor.

10. You are configuring a database on your SQL server. This server will run a point-of-sale system for your company sales desk. Users will update tables in this database on a constant basis throughout the day. Every night, a DTS job will import all of the day's sales from a branch office. All of the sales will be added in a single operation. Which recovery model would you use to ensure recoverability while ensuring this insert does not have a significant impact on your system?

A. The full recovery model

B. The simple recovery model

C. The bulk-logged recovery model

D. The bulk-import recovery model

11. Your development team has approached you to move some tables from their test system to a production environment. They also want the data and any dependent objects (such as triggers and indexes) moved at the same time.

Which tools could you use to perform the move operations? (Choose all that apply.)

A. Use the DTS Designer.

B. Use bcp.exe.

C. Use the DTS Import/Export Wizard.

D. Use the script generator to script both tables and their dependent object. Run the script on the production server.

E. Use DBCC MOVETABLE.

12. You are the administrator for a database that stores scanned images. The database is over 500GB in size. Because of its large size, you have placed the database on five filegroups (FG1 to FG5). You backup one filegroup each night starting with FG1 on Monday and ending with FG5 on Friday. You also perform transaction log backups every 6 hours. Every Sunday, you perform a full backup. This backup takes 18 hours to run. On Thursday morning, one of the disks containing a data file in FG1 fails. What steps should you take to recover the database? (Choose all that apply. Each choice represents a partial solution.)

A. Restore the full backup.

B. Restored FG1 from the backup made on Monday.

C. Restore all of the filegroup backups from Monday to Wednesday.

D. Restore all of the transaction logs since the Monday backup.

E. Backup the current transaction log.

F. Restore all of the transaction logs since the Wednesday night backup.

13. Sam is the administrator for the Tor_sales database. The database consists of three data files and one transaction log file. Each file is on a separate disk. She has also enabled Torn Page Protection on the server. The server is accidentally disconnected from the UPN. When it is restarted, Sam notices that the Tor_sales database is marked as suspect in Enterprise Manager. What should Sam do to recover the database?

A. Recover the database from the most recent backup.

B. Run the DBCC CHECKDB statement with the REPAIR_ALLOW_ DATALOSS option.

C. Run the DBCC CHECKALLOC statement with the REPAIR_ALLOW_DATALOSS option.

D. Use `sp_configure` to turn the Recover In Inconsistent State option to 1 and manually repair the error.

E. Run the DBCC DBREPAIR stored procedures.

14. You are configuring replication for the servers in your environment. You have three warehouses that store their inventory information on a SQL server. They need to send their inventory lists back to a server at the head office; they also need to share their inventory lists with each other. The data on the central office server must be updated every hour. Data will only be updated at the warehouse that is maintaining the inventory. Data between warehouses must be updated every two hours. All of the offices are connected by an ISDN link. How would you configure replication to satisfy these requirements? (Choose two. Each selection represents a partial answer.)

A. Configure merge replication between all of the warehouses.

B. Configure snapshot replication between all of the warehouses.

C. Configure transactional replication between all of the warehouses.

D. Configure merge replication between each warehouse and the head office.

E. Configure transactional replication between each warehouse and the head office.

F. Configure snapshot replication between each warehouse and the head office.

15. You are the administrator of the HR database. You have 50 users in this department who need access to the database. You also have 20 HR managers who need all the access the HR users have, but will require additional rights on the server. All of the users are part of the corp.local Windows 2000 domain. What would be the best way to give these users access to the database?

A. Create a login for each user. Map that login to a database user account. Create two roles: HR and HR__mgr. Place the HR staff in the HR role and the HR managers in both roles. Assign appropriate permissions to the roles.

B.   Create two global groups in the Active Directory and place the HR users in one group and add the HR managers in the second. Place the HR managers group inside the HR users global group. Create one database login for the HR users group. Map it to a single database user account and assign that user account permissions all objects.

C.   Create two global groups in the Active Directory and place the HR users in one group and add the HR managers in the second. Place the HR managers group inside the HR users global group. Create a login for each group and map each login to two database user accounts, assigning the appropriate permissions to each user account.

D.   Create a global group for the HR users. Add all of the users and the managers into that group. Create one database login for the HR users group. Map it to a single database user account and assign that user account permissions to all objects. Create separate user logins for the HR managers and map them to database login accounts. Create a role on the database and add the managers to the role. Assign the appropriate permissions to the role.

16.   All of your company employee records are stored in a table called employees in the HR database. The employee table appears, as shown here:

One of the users in HR is responsible for mailing pension information to all of the users in the company. This user must be able to retrieve the mailing address of each employee. However, the HR manager does not want this user to have access to personal information (like salary, date of birth, or home phone number). What is the best way to make only address information available to this user? (Choose all that apply.)

A. Create a view that only returns the address information and employee name. Give the user permission to SELECT from the view but not permission to SELECT from the underlying table.

B. GRANT the user SELECT permission on the table, but DENY the user SELECT permission on all columns that contain sensitive information.

C. Grant the user SELECT permission on only those columns that contain mailing address information.

D. Create a stored procedure that returns the user mailing address using their employee id as an input parameter. Grant the user EXEC permission on the procedure. Do not give them any permissions on the employee table.

E. GRANT the user SELECT permission on the table, but REVOKE their access to the columns that contain sensitive information.

17. You are a member of the developer team for a new management system. All the members of the developer team are members of the db_ddladmin fixed database role for the database. You have created a tabled called Work_records. You have given George, another developer in your group, the SELECT permission on this table. George has created a view on the Work_records table and has given the SELECT permission on his view to another user. That user reports that she is not able to retrieve data from the view. What is the most likely reason why this user cannot access data through the view?

A. George did not create the view with dbo as the owner.

B. You have not given George permission to grant access to your table to others.

C. You did not give George the REFERENCES permission on the table.

D. The table and view have different owners.

E. George is not able to grant permission on his view.

18. You are the primary administrator for the sales database. Your database has been running for eight months. Since then, it has increased in size by 40%.

Recently, your users have been complaining that their queries are getting progressively slower. The database options are configured as shown here:

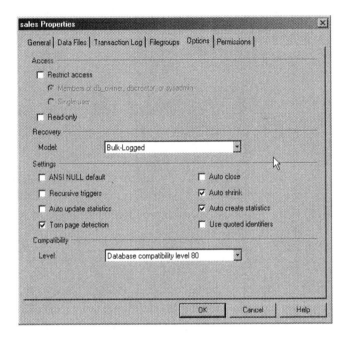

What could you do to speed up the queries? (Choose the best answer.)

A. Set the database into the simple recovery model.

B. Remove the Autoshrink option.

C. Turn off Torn Page detection.

D. Enable Auto update statistics.

E. Disable Auto create statistics.

19. You are the administrator for a SQL 2000 server. Your users report that periodically their applications run very slow. You suspect that there is a process that is causing excessive logging on the server. You are not sure where the process is originating from because by the time you are aware of the problem and check in the Enterprise Manager, the process has stopped running. You want to be notified by pager as soon as the SQLServer:Locks-Percent lock time

exceeds 30. How would you configure SQL Server to send you this notification? (Choose all that apply. Each answer contains part of the solution.)

A. Create an operator with your pager number.

B. Use the Windows 2000 Performance Logs And Alerts tool to raise an alert to the Windows application log whenever this counter exceeds the threshold.

C. Define a performance alert on the counter. Set the appropriate threshold for the alert.

D. Define an event alert that monitors for the errors raised by the Performance Logs And Alerts tool.

E. Create a job that reads the application log every 5 minutes.

F. Configure the alert to notify you by pager whenever the alert is raised.

20. You are configuring some automated maintenance tasks on the server. You are attempting to create a job that backs up your system databases and sends you an email if any step of the job fails. You have created the job successfully and have tested and scheduled the job. However you are having problems configuring the operator. You have entered your email address, but when you click the test button it fails to connect. You have even run the job and forced it to fail. The job history shows that the job has run unsuccessfully, but you did not receive an email. You have confirmed that a mailbox has been created on the mail server and that you are entering the correct email address in the New Operator Properties sheet. What may be preventing you from receiving email from your automated job? (Choose all that apply.)

A. The SQL Server Agent service has not started.

B. The SQL Server Agent service is configured to use the local system account.

C. You have not configured SQL Mail.

D. The mail profile used by the SQL Server Agent service is pointing to the wrong mail server.

E. You mail server is not MAPI compliant.

F. The SQL server is not on the same server as the Mail server.

21. You are the administrator of a SQL 2000 server. For security reasons, you have installed two instances of SQL Server on a server running Windows 2000 Advanced server. The server has 1GB of RAM. You want to configure the server so that one instance is not able to completely monopolize the memory resources on the server. What would you do to ensure that the two instances shared the memory resources evenly. (Choose all that apply. Each answer will represent a portion of the solution.)

    A. Use sp_configure to set the max worker threads to 512 on each instance.

    B. Use sp_configure to set the max server memory to 512 on each instance.

    C. Use sp_configure to set the max server memory to 512 on only the default instance.

    D. On the Memory tab of the Server Properties sheet in Enterprise Manager, set the Minimum Memory option to 256 on each server.

    E. Increase the Minimum Query Memory setting to 256MB.

22. Samantha is the administrator for a SQL 2000 server. She has added two new databases to the server and has been monitoring the performance on the server using the system monitor. She notices that the Buffer Cache hit ratio value is consistently low (between 25 and 35) and the Available Bytes counter is also consistently low (between 20 and 30). What must Samantha do to improve the performance of her server?

    A. Do nothing. These values are both in an acceptable range.

    B. Add more RAM to the server.

    C. Increase the size of the Windows page file.

    D. Move the Windows page file to another disk.

    E. Increase the size of the Buffer and Procedure cache.

23. Susan is the administrator for a SQL 2000 server. She is concerned that there are a large number of deadlocks occurring on her server. Which tool could she use to determine the amount of deadlocking that is occurring on her system? (Choose all that apply.)

    A. The SQL Server Profiler

    B. The Current Activity tool in Enterprise Manager

C. The sp_lock stored procedure

D. The System Monitor

E. The Windows Event Viewer

24. You have been asked to create a database for an order entry application that will be used by the telephone sales group. This system will consist of several lookup tables (for product lists, customers lists, etc.) and one large table that will contain order items. This table will be modified more frequently than any other table in the database. The lookup tables will be fairly static. The server where SQL Server is installed has four physical disks. Windows 2000 and SQL Server are installed on the first disk. What would be the best way to configure this database?

A. Create the database with two filegroups on separate disks. Place all of the lookup tables on one filegroup and put the order item table by itself on the second filegroup. Place the transaction log on the third disk.

B. Create the database with three filegroups on the three unoccupied disks. Place all of the lookup tables on one filegroup, put the order item table by itself on the second filegroup and place the transaction log in third.

C. Stripe the three disks together with RAID-0. Create two filegroups and the transaction log on the stripe.

D. Create a single filegroup that spans two disk. Place all of the lookup tables on one disk and place the order item table on the second file.

E. Create the database with two filegroups on two of the disks. Make the second filegroup default and create all objects on the default filegroup.

25. You have created a database on a server with three SCSI disks. SQL Server and Windows are installed on the first disk. The second disk contains the data file and the third disk contains the transaction log file. The data file has consumed almost the whole disk, and you need to expand the database to handle future growth. What would be the easiest way to expand the database? (Choose the best answer.)

A. Add a fourth disk and create a second data file on that disk.

B. Create a second data file on the disk that contains the transaction log.

C. Install a larger hard drive and copy the data file to the bigger hard drive.

D. You cannot expand the database once the disk is full.

E. Add a second disk and stripe the data file onto the second disk.

26. Which of the following statements cannot be issued on a linked server?

A. ```
GRANT select ON RmtServer.database.dbo.tablex
TO user1, user2
```

B. ```
UPDATE RmtServer.database.dbo.tablex
SET colx = 10
WHERE coly = 1
```

C. ```
CREATE VIEW rmtlist
AS
SELECT id, name, ext.
FROM RmtServer.database.dbo.tablex
```

D. ```
EXEC RmtServer.database.dbo.sp_help tablex
```

E. ```
SELECT a.id, a.name, b.deptid, b.location
FROM employee a INNER JOIN
RmtServer.database.dbo.department b
ON a.deptid = b.deptid
```

27. You are in the process of installing a SQL 2000 server. However, when you run the installation, it fails at a certain point. You rerun the installation and it fails a second time. You decide to look in the SQLstp.log file to find the source of the problem. Where would go to find this file (assuming Windows and SQL Server are installed on the C drive)?

A. `c:\Program Files\Microsoft SQL Server\80\logs\`

B. `c:\Program Files\Microsoft SQL Server\mssql\logs\`

C. `c:\Temp\`

D. `c:\Program Files\Microsoft SQL Server\mssql\binn\installogs\`

E. `c:\winnt`
```

28. Jim has installed Microsoft SQL Server 2000 on a Windows 2000 server called CorpData. He has written a trigger to email an operator using xp_sendmail whenever a record is deleted. However when he tests this trigger, SQL Server does not send the email. He has confirmed that the trigger is correct. He is also able to ping the Exchange server both by IP address and by host name. What might prevent the SQL server from sending mail?

    A. SQL 2000 does not support xp_sendmail.

    B. Jim must create a mailbox on the Exchange server for the local system account and assign this account appropriate access rights to this mailbox.

    C. Jim must use a domain user account for the mssqlserver service and create a mailbox for this account.

    D. Jim must add the local system account to the administrators local group on the CorpData server.

29. You have been asked to upgrade a SQL 6.5 server to SQL 2000. This server is still being used in production and must be available while you are performing and testing the upgrade. The computer that SQL 6.5 is installed on does not meet the minimum hardware requirements for SQL Server 2000 so you have purchased a new server. How would you upgrade this database while leaving it available for production?

    A. Install SQL Server 2000 on the new computer and use the Copy Database Wizard to copy all of the databases from the SQL 6.5 server.

    B. Use the DTS Object Transfer tool to copy all of the databases and users from the SQL 6.5 server to the SQL 2000 server.

    C. Stop the SQL 6.5 server and copy the device files for all of the databases from SQL 6.5 to the SQL 2000 server. Use the sp_attach_db stored procedure to add these files to the SQL 2000 server as new databases.

    D. Install SQL Server 2000 on the new computer and run the SQL Server Upgrade Wizard to migrate all of the databases and users to the new server.

30. You are the administrator for a database called Sales_Info. Your database has a table called sales_history that contains archival sales data used for historical comparisons. Data from the sales_details table is periodically moved into the table. You have recently added a CHECK constraint to the sales_details table and you also want to add the same constraint to the sales_history table.

However, you are aware of several older entries that will violate this constraint. How can you add the constraint to the sales_history table?

A. Include the WITH NOCHECK option when you create the constraint.

B. You cannot add the constraint if any of the data does not meet requirements of the constraint. You must remove or modify all non-compliant values.

C. Use the NOCHECK option in the ALTER TABLE statement.

D. Use the sp_maskdata stored procedure to conceal the older data from the new constraint.

E. Set the constraint_nocheck option on the database using sp_dboption.

31. You are the administrator for a database called Corpinfo. You initially created a non-clustered index on the lastname column of a table called Customers. However, you have found that your users often query the Customers table on the lastname and firstname columns. You want to alter the index so that it includes both columns. What is the best way to modify the index?

A. Edit the index definition in the sysindexes table.

B. Run the ALTER INDEX statement.

C. Use the DBCC DBREINDEX statement to alter the index definition.

D. Use the CREATE INDEX statement with the DROP_EXISTING option.

E. Drop the index with the DROP INDEX statement and recreate it incorporating both columns.

32. Your organization would like to move some decision support functionality to a web-based application. Although your users will not write their own queries, queries will be developed on the fly based on user input and your developers would like to ensure that queries can be generated dynamically in the easiest manner possible.

Which type of XML access should be used for this database?

A. URL queries

B. X-Path queries

C. Template queries

D. Ad-hoc queries

33. You are creating a DTS package that will be run daily. The package will need to transfer as many as 50,000 rows between two systems.

    Both servers are located in the same data center, and they are connected via Gigabit Ethernet.

    After building the package and executing it, you notice that throughput is very poor and that network bandwidth is not being heavily utilized. No other database activity is occurring during the package execution. You would like to improve performance of the package. How can this be done?

    A. Decrease the Fetch buffer size.

    B. Increase the Fetch buffer size.

    C. Turn on the Enable Identity Insert option.

    D. Turn on the Always Commit Final Batch option.

34. You have configured a linked server to another SQL Server 2000 system. Users are complaining that some of the data in various reports is sorting in reverse order. What can be done to resolve this?

    A. Specify an ORDER BY clause to force those columns to sort in the correct order.

    B. Enable the Collation Compatible option in the Linked Server properties.

    C. Disable pass-through queries.

    D. Disable the Collation Compatible option in the Linked Server properties.

35. You are configuring replication for a large organization. You need to replicate data from your head office to various locations throughout the world. You would like to reduce the amount of overhead that SQL Server generates on your production system and you would like to avoid having to cross trans-oceanic WAN links more than once for replication traffic.

    Currently, your international WAN backbone connects New York to London and Tokyo. All other networks link into one of these regional hubs for WAN connectivity.

    You will need to configure replication for the following cities:

    ▪ NORTH AMERICA

    ▪ NEW YORK (HEAD OFFICE)

    ▪ WASHINGTON

- CHICAGO
- EUROPE
- LONDON
- PARIS
- ASIA
- TOKYO
- BOMBAY

You must accomplish the following tasks:

- Replication overhead must be kept to a minimum.
- Data should not need to be replicated across trans-oceanic WAN links more than once.
- Data should not be updatable on subscriber systems.
- New subscribers should complete their initial synchronization from mailed backup tapes to reduce traffic load.
- You take the following actions:
- Configure a new SQL Server system to act as a distributor.
- Configure a new transactional publication for the data.
- Configure the new distributor to replicate to all the systems in North America.
- Configure the distributor to replicate with LONDON and TOKYO.
- Configure LONDON to replicate with PARIS.
- Configure TOKYO to replicate with BOMBAY.
- Specify that subscribers will synchronize manually in the publication properties.

Which of the following conditions are met? (Choose all that apply.)

A. Replication overhead on the publisher is kept to a minimum.

B. Data is not replicated multiple times across trans-oceanic WAN links.

C. Data is not updatable on subscriber systems.

D. New subscribers can complete their initial synchronization via backup tapes.

36. You execute the following script on a SQL 2000 server:

```
BACKUP DATABASE HRDATA

TO monday_backup

GO

BACKUP DATABASE HRDATA

TO monday_backup

WITH DIFFERENTIAL

GO

BACKUP DATABASE SALESDATA

TO monday_backup

WITH NOINIT

GO

BACKUP DATABASE SALESDATA

TO monday_backup

WITH DIFFERENTIAL

GO

BACKUP LOG HRDATA

TO monday_backup

WITH INIT

GO

BACKUP LOG SALESDATA

TO monday_backup
```

What will be the contents of the monday_backup after the script runs?

A. All of the backups in the script.

B. Only the backups to HRDATA.

C. Only the backups to SALESDATA.

D. Only the final two log backups.

E. All full and differential backups.

37. You have been asked to create a table that will hold customer information. Your company is currently only dealing with customers from the United States, Canada, and Mexico. You want to make sure that your operators cannot add customers from other countries into the table. What would be the best way of controlling the data within the table? (Choose the best answer.)

    A. Create an INSTEAD OF trigger that checks the values before inserting the row.

    B. Create an AFTER trigger that issues a ROLLBACK of the value in the country column if not one of the three allowable countries.

    C. Create a CHECK constraint on the country column that will only allow the three allowable countries.

    D. Create a rule that will only allow the three allowable countries. Bind the rule to the table.

38. You are responsible for a large order entry database. You have several developers working on different parts of the database. When the database is complete, you need to be able to easily move data from one table to another. You are concerned that there may be problems with data type inconsistencies (especially with telephone and fax numbers). You want to make sure that all developers use a char(10) data type for all telephone and fax number columns. What would be the easiest way to insure this data type is used? (Choose the best answer.)

    A. Create a rule to enforce the data type. Have the developers bind this rule to each phone number or fax column using the sp_bindrule procedure.

    B. Create a stored procedure that finds all telephone number columns and converts them to a char(10).

    C. You must enforce this rule manually by checking all tables.

    D. Create a user-defined data type called phone_no as a char(10) using sp_addtype. Have your developers use this datatype when creating columns to hold phone and fax number data.

39. You have created a stored procedure that accepts two price values and returns all products on the productlist table that fall between these two values. There are 50,000 products in the productlist table. When your users execute this stored procedure, they return a wide range of values (between 1% of the table

and 70% of the table). They are complaining that sometimes the procedure runs quickly and other times it runs very slowly. What could you do to improve this procedure? (Select the best answers.)

A. Alter the procedure and include the WITH RECOMPILE option.

B. Alter the procedure and include the WITH SCHEMABINDING option.

C. Use `sp_dboption` to set the cacheproc setting to false.

D. Use `sp_configure` to set the cacheproc server setting to 0.

40. You are responsible for a SQL 2000 database called TOR_SALES. You perform a full backup every Sunday night. You perform a differential backup each night and perform four transaction log backups (at 9:00 A.M., 11:00 A.M., 2:00 P.M., and 5:00 P.M.). At 1:10 P.M. on Thursday afternoon, one of your developers deletes the contents of your customer table, mistaking it for a table on a test server. The developer realizes that the delete statements have all been committed and contacts you at 1:15 P.M. How would you restore this database? (Choose the correct answers in order. Not all options will be part of the answer.)

A. Restore the full backup with NORECOVERY.

B. Place the database in READ ONLY mode.

C. Backup the current transaction log.

D. Restore all differential backups from Monday to Wednesday with NORECOVERY.

E. Restore the Wednesday differential backup with NORECOVERY.

F. Restore the 9:00 A.M. and 11:00 A.M. transaction log backups from Thursday, specifying RECOVERY.

G. Restore the 9:00 A.M. and 11:00 A.M. transaction log backups from Thursday, specifying NORECOVERY.

H. Restore the final transaction log backup using the STOP AT option to stop the restore at 1:09 P.M.

41. You are the administrator for a SQL server that has two instances. The default instance is called WestSrv and the second instance is called WestSrv\Sales. The disk containing all of your system databases for the WestSrv\Sales database has failed. You have backups of all of your system databases. You use rebuildm.exe

to rebuild Master and are able to start SQL Server. However, when you run the restore database statement, you receive the following message:

```
Server: Msg 3108, Level 16, State 1, Line 1
```

```
RESTORE DATABASE must be used in single user mode when trying
to restore the master database.
```

```
Server: Msg 3013, Level 16, State 1, Line 1
```

```
RESTORE DATABASE is terminating abnormally.
```

When you go into the Properties sheet for the Master database you are unable to change the database into single user mode. You are also unable to change to single user mode using `sp_dboption`. What must you do to restore the Master database?

A. Start the database with the net start command and include the /singleuser option.

B. Use `sp_configure` to enable the Allow Updates option. This will allow you to change the properties of the Master database and set it into single user mode.

C. Start SQL Server from the command prompt with the following statement: sqlservr.exe -c -m -s sales.

D. In the Properties sheet for the server, select the Start In Single User Mode option on the General tab and then stop and restart the server.

E. Click the Start In Single User Mode button on the SQL Services Manager and then restart the server.

42. Sam has been asked to configure the SQL server for an application that will run as a computer in the lobby of their office. This application will allow people to query the extension and office numbers for employees who work in the building. All of this information will be drawn from the Emp_info table of the Corpinfo database. Management also wants to make this utility available to all users in the company. All users have access to the server, but not all users have access to Corpinfo. How would you configure this server?

A. Create a SQL server login for the application and map it to a database user account. Give that account permission to the Emp_info table.

B. Give the guest account permission to select from the Emp_info table.

C. Create a Windows authenticated login for the Everyone group. Map a database user account to this login and give it the appropriate permissions on Emp_info.

D. Create an application role and give the role permission to query the Emp_info table. Create a generic login without any specific rights to the database. Use `sp_setapprole` in the connection string for the application.

43. The EMPLOYEE_DATA table is heavily queried to retrieve user contact information for the web-based employee directory. Users are complaining that contact lookups take too long and the HR department is claiming that their database activities take too long to execute. You would like to allow the address book query to proceed without interfering with the HR activity. The text of the address book lookup is:

    SELECT EMP_FNAME, EMP_LNAME, PHONE_NO FROM
    EMPLOYEE_DATA WHERE EMP_FNAME = @FNAME AND
    EMP_LNAME = @LNAME

    How can you allow the employee query to run more efficiently?

    A. Create a composite index on the EMP_LNAME, EMP_FNAME, and PHONE_NO columns.

    B. Split the employee table into two new tables.

    C. Use the READPAST locking hint in the employee lookup query to skip locked records.

    D. Set the transaction isolation level to READ UNCOMITTED for the HR transactions.

44. Jane is the administrator for a SQL server called Corpinfo. Recently, her users have been complaining that the server is running quite slowly. When she runs some tests on the server with Performance Monitor, she discovers that the %processor time is consistently above 97. What can she do to improve the performance on the server? (Choose all that apply.)

    A. Add more RAM.

    B. Add a second processor.

    C. Decrease the number of worker threads.

    D. Move any other applications running the server to another server.

45. You are concerned that statistics for new indexes are not being created. You would like to be able to monitor the system for missing statistics. How can this be done?

    A. Use Profiler. Add the Errors and Warnings: Missing Column Statistics event class to a new trace.

    B. Display the execution plan for the queries in the Query Analyzer.

    C. Use System Monitor. Add the SQL Server:Access Methods - Missing Statistics/Sec counter to a performance chart.

    D. Configure System Monitor to log SQL performance data to a file. Import the file into Excel for analysis.

ANSWERS

1. ☑ **A** is the correct answer because if you do not configure the security for the connection, the default is to use pass-through authentication. This means that whenever a user attempts to connect to a linked server, the local SQL server passes the logon credentials of the user to the remote server. If that user has a valid logon on the remote server, the user will connect; if the user does not have a valid logon on the remote server, the connection fails. The connections in this scenario are sporadic because different users have different rights on the network. You can alter this by using `sp_addlinkedsrvlogin` to alter the security context for the users. For example, you could create a login on the remote server and have all users connected through the linked server using that user account when they authenticate to the remote server. This allows you to have much more control over what a user is able to do when they connect to a linked server.

   ☒ **B** is incorrect because if the user had a valid SQL Server login on one of the linked servers, they would be able to connect. The local SQL server will pass the SQL login and password provided to the remote SQL server. Users who connect with SQL Server logins will not be able to connect to the Access or Oracle databases because only the SQL server information would be passed. **C** is incorrect because your users do not need to have OLEDB installed on their local computers to use a linked server. OLEDB is one means of connecting to a SQL server; the user could also be using ODBC or DB-Library to connect. Linked servers use OLEDB to connect to the linked server, so only the local SQL server requires OLEDB. **D** is incorrect because the provider that is used to establish the linked server connection exists on the SQL server holding the link—not the client computer.

2. ☑ **D** is the correct answer because it is the only version of SQL 2000 Server that will support clustering. To get support for 6GB of RAM and 8 processors, you would need a minimum of Windows 2000 Advanced server. Windows 2000 Advanced server is the minimum operating system requirement for installing SQL Server 2000 Enterprise server.

☒ **A** is not correct because the Standard version of SQL Server does not support failover clustering. You can install SQL Server Standard edition on a Windows 2000 Advanced server, but it will only support four processors and 2GB of RAM (regardless of the actual hardware supported by the OS). **B** is incorrect because the Developer edition cannot be used in a production environment. You can install clustering on the Developer edition and it will support the processor and memory requirements; however, to use this edition on your corporate web server would violate the Microsoft licensing agreement. **C** and **E** are not correct because there is no Advanced or Datacenter edition of SQL Server. These are both editions of Windows 2000. You would need to be running one of these two editions of Windows 2000 to install the Enterprise edition of SQL 2000 Server.

3. ☑ **C** is the correct answer. The default path for SQL Server installation is under the c:\Program Files\Microsoft SQL Server\ path. All of the files for the default instance are contained in a subfolder of this path called mssql. All files for any named instances are contained under a subfolder called mssql$instance_name where instance_name is the name given to the named instance. All of the administrative tools are stored in a subfolder under c:\Program Files\Microsoft SQL Server called 80. All instances of SQL Server share the administrative tools, and any changes made to a file within the 80 subfolder will affect all instances.

☒ **A** matches the form of the SQL 7.0 default path (c:\mssql7), which SQL 2000 does not use. Those familiar with SQL Server 7.0 should avoid this trap. **B** is incorrect because it is pointing to the path for the default instance. **D** is incorrect because it has inverted the placement of the named instance name. **E** is incorrect because it uses the full naming form for a default instance. When you reference a named instance in Enterprise Manager or Query Analyzer, the name includes the name of the default instance (and the server, since default instances always take their names from the server). However, in conjunction with the mssql$, only the unique name of the instance is included.

4. ☑ **A** and **B** are the best answers. Windows writes application errors into the Event Viewer application log. If the Installation utility raised any errors to Windows when it failed, they would be reported to this log. **B** is a better choice because SQL Server spools the output of each step of the installation program to the SQLstp.log file. The last line of this file would show you the last step the

installation program took before the failure. You can use this information to diagnose the cause of the failure. This file is creating in the Windows system root folder (usually c:\winnt).

☒   **C** and **E** are both incorrect because they both point to a set of log files that get created when the SQL Server services starts for the first time. Since the failure occurs prior to the service starting, these logs are not generated. Furthermore, you cannot view any server information in Enterprise Manager until the SQL Server service is started. **D** is false because this log file does not exist.

5. ☑   **B** and **D** are the correct answers. **B** is correct because the service has no mechanism for altering its password and Windows will not allow the service account to logon (and allow the service to start) unless it changes its password. **D** is correct because the agent account needs certain administrative rights to function. If the user does not have administrative privileges, the Windows will not allow the service to start.

☒   **A** is incorrect because the agent must be a member of the sysadmin role to function. Making the agent a member of the server admin role will not give the account any of the permissions it needs to function. **C** is incorrect because a TCP/IP socket is one of the three network libraries needed for Windows authentication (which the agent service will need to connect to the server). The other two are Named Pipes and Multiprotocol. **E** is incorrect because when you enter a domain user account as the authorizing account for any service, that account is automatically granted the logon as a service right.

6. ☑   **C** is the correct answer. Since he is concerned with fault tolerance, he should use RAID-1 (disk mirroring) to protect the transaction log from failure. He should also make sure to separate the log and data files and place them on separate disks. Using RAID-5 (disk striping with parity) will provide fault tolerance for the data file because it stores redundant data on each stripe and can continue functioning even if one disk fails. Furthermore, to improve performance he should create one data file per disk in the array. This will break up I/O across the members of the array.

☒   **A** and **D** are incorrect because you should avoid placing any SQL Server files on a RAID-0 array. RAID-0 (or disk striping without parity) does not provide any redundancy. In fact, because the failure of any one disk will invalidate the entire array, a RAID-0 array is actually more susceptible to data loss than having the data files on separate disks. **B** is incorrect because you do not provide any fault tolerance by placing a separate file on each disk. You are not providing any redundancy and if one disk is lost, the database will not be available. **E** will provide full fault tolerance on the database, but you will gain much better I/O performance if you separate the database into separate disks. If you make this separation, SQL Server is able to issue multiple I/O operations to run in parallel (one for each file). Since you have multiple disks in the set, you may have SQL Server writing to one disk while reading from another. With one data file, SQL Server will only process one I/O against the array at a time.

7. ☑ **B** is the correct answer. The command to shrink an entire database is DBCC SHRINKDATABASE. In this statement you must include the name of the database and a numeric value that is the percentage of free space that you would like remaining. Both of these values must be enclosed in single quotes.

☒ **A** and **D** are incorrect because you would not use the DBCC SHRINKFILE command in this scenario. The DBCC SHRINKFILE is used to shrink individual files. This command must be executed on a file-by-file basis, so the statement in **A** would return a syntax error. Also, the numeric value in the statement indicates the size (in MB) that you want the file after it has been shrunk. Both of these statements attempt to reduce the data file(s) to 20MB. This is smaller than the existing data and will also cause an error. **C** is incorrect because it would reduce the file to 80% free space. This is actually greater than the current amount of free space, and executing this statement would make no change to the file. **E** is incorrect because you cannot resize an entire database with the ALTER DATABASE statement. You can, however, reduce individual files with the SHRINKFILE statement.

8. ☑ **A** is the best solution because check constraints are evaluated *before* any inserts are processed. This means that if a user has entered an invalid productid, the insert operation will never take place (and therefore, no I/O or processor time will be expended).

☒ **B** and **E** will both solve the problem, but in both cases, there is an increased amount of processing involved. In **B,** the insert that calls the trigger will be processed, then the trigger. If the user has entered an invalid productid, then further I/O and processing time will be incurred to roll back the INSERTED row in order_pick. The stored procedure is better than the trigger but will still require increased resource use to execute. **C** and **D** are both incorrect because neither a CHECK constraint nor RULE are able to validate data in a column based on values from other tables.

9. ☑ **D** and **E** are possible answers. The DBCC DEREINDEX can be used to rebuild one or more indexes on a table. When it rebuilds, it can also reset the fill factor. Fill factor is space that is left free on the leaf level of an index to slow page splitting as data in inserted into the table. Fill factor is not maintained dynamically; as data is inserted into the table, the fill factor becomes less and less until the index pages are full. At that point splitting occurs. It is probably this index splitting that is causing the slowdown on the database (since the avg. page density values shows that the leaf pages are over 99% full). You can also recreate the index using the CREATE INDEX with DROP_EXISTING. This will rebuild the index and you can specify a new fill factor.

☒ **A** is incorrect because you cannot use the DBCC INDEXDEFRAG statement to reset the fill factor. This procedure will reorder pages on the leaf level of an index and will maintain the fill factor when removing free space, but it will not reset the fill factor if there is not enough room on the existing pages. This statement will not add more pages to the index. **B** is incorrect because you cannot modify indexes with an ALTER TABLE statement. The only exception to this is that you can use this statement to add and remove Primary Key and Unique constraints. These will add or remove indexes to the table. You cannot use this statement to set or reset fill factor. **C** is incorrect because there is no ALTER INDEX statement. To change an index you must drop in and recreate it, or run CREATE DATABASE with the DROP_EXISTING option.

10. ☑ **C** is the correct answer because the bulk-logged recovery model will log all activity during the day, but will not log each operation of the DTS job. Instead it will simply log the fact that the operation took place. You must be careful, however, to perform a backup after the bulk insert or SQL will switch to simple mode (because of the non-logged operation).

☒ **A** is incorrect because it would log a separate Insert statement for each row inserted by the DTS job. This may fill the transaction log. If the log fills, the transfer job will fail. **B** is incorrect because the simple model will remove all committed transactions from the transaction log whenever a checkpoint occurs. This means that you will not be able to use the log to recover activity during the day. **D** is incorrect because there is no bulk-import recovery log.

11. ☑ **A** and **C** are the correct answers. You would perform this activity using the DTS Object transfer. You can configure an object transfer using either tool. In the designer, you would create a source and destination object and then add the object transfer object to link the two together. The DTS Import/Export Wizard will allow you to perform object transfers, but only from one database at a time. You would need to run the wizard twice to move both tables. With the DTS Designer, you could add both transfers and have them run either serially or in parallel.

    ☒ **B** is incorrect because the bcp.exe is unable to move schema objects. This utility can only export data to text files, and import data from text files. **D** is incorrect because you cannot script the data using the Script Generator. It can create a script that contains all dependant objects. **E** is incorrect because there is no DBCC MOVETABLE statement.

12. ☑ **B, E,** and **D** are the correct answers. When recovering a filegroup, you only need to restore the filegroup that is corrupt. This is one of the advantages to creating filegroups. However, since the FG1 backup is now four days old, you will need to reapply your transaction logs to bring this filegroup up to date. To avoid data loss, this should include the current transaction log. You will start by backing up the current transaction log. Next you will restore the FG1 backup (makes sure to restore with the NORECOVERY option so that you can recover the transaction logs. You must then restore all transaction logs since the FG1 backup, ending with the transaction log backup you made before beginning the restore. When you restore this last transaction log you can restore the database using the RESTORE command.

    ☒ **A** is incorrect because, unlike differential or transaction log backups, you are not required to start this filegroup restore process with a full backup restore. **C** is incorrect because it is only necessary to restore the filegroup that has been damaged. Recovering all three will not prevent the database from being recovered, but will perform unnecessary tasks and prolong the restore process. **F** is incorrect because SQL Server will not allow you to restore only the logs from Wednesday's backup. The logs start when the FG1 backup ended. If the LSN (Log Sequence Numbers) are not correct, the restore will fail.

13. ☑ **A** is the best answer. The Torn Page detection detects when write operations are incomplete due to some interruption (like a power outage). SQL Server stores its data is 8K pages, however, these pages are actually written to

the disk in 16 512K sectors. The torn page occurs because SQL Server marks a page as written after the first sector is written. If the system fails before the 16th sector is written, the result is a torn page. Torn pages mean that data has been lost. To recover lost data, you must restore the database from the most current backup.

☒   **B** is incorrect because the DBCC CHECKDB statement is used to repair allocation and structural errors for all objects within the database. It will not, however, repair the data lost by a torn page. **C** is incorrect because the DBCC CHECKALLOC statement, like CHECKDB, only corrects allocation errors. It is not able to tell what part of a page has not been successfully written to disk. **D** is incorrect because there is no option that allows you to start a database in an inconsistent state. This is not something you would want to do anyway, because you would have no way of telling (internally) which page was damaged, since SQL Server thinks it's written. **E** is incorrect because the DBCC DBREPAIR statement is an older statement used to drop damaged databases. It is only available for backwards compatibility and has been replaced by the DROP DATABASE statement.

14.   ☑   **C** and **E** are the correct answers. In this scenario, transactional replication is the best solution in both instances. Because you are replicating with a relatively low latency (that is, the time between when a change occurs and when it is replicated), you want to choose a replication type that will only send necessary data. Transactional replication starts with an initial snapshot to create the schema of the publication on the subscriber. From that point on, only changes are sent from the publisher to the subscriber. This will also reduce the amount of traffic sent across the wide area network.

☒   **A** and **D** are incorrect because there is no justification for using this type of replication. Merge replication is most useful where there is a high degree of latency and both the publisher and the subscriber will be updating the data. In merge replication, SQL Server takes all changes from both the publisher and the subscriber and synchronizes the two databases. It also resolves conflicts. Conflicts are situations where the same field was updated on both the publisher and the subscriber. Since only the warehouse holding the inventory will be updating the database, there will be no need to use merge replication. **B** and **F** are incorrect because snapshot replication sends all data from the publisher to the subscriber. This means that every time replication takes place, the publisher will send all data across the Wide Area Network, even if that data already exists on the subscriber. Because you are replicating so frequently this would be a waste of network resources.

15. ☑ **C** is the correct answer. With Windows authentication you can create a single login for Windows groups. This allows you to manage the permissions for a large number of users as if they were a single user. In Windows 2000 you can also nest global group accounts inside other global groups. By nesting the HR managers group inside the HR users group, the managers will inherit any permission that you assign to the users. This meets the requirement that the HR managers must have the same permissions as the users. And you do not need to assign these permissions twice because the managers inherit them automatically. In addition, by creating a separate login for the managers, you can assign rights to the managers group that are not inherited by the users group.

☒ **A** is incorrect because it is not necessary to deal with each user individually when you have groups available. This would only be a valid solution if you did not have permission to create global groups in the Active Directory. **B** is incorrect because you have given the HR users and the HR managers the same login account on the server. This means that you cannot give the managers rights independent of the users. You must create a separate database user account (mapped to a separate login) in order to assign permission to the managers independent of the users. **D** is incorrect because, even though they are only a few, you should avoid dealing with users individually (even for logins) when you have a group of users with the same security requirements. If you manage security through groups, you do not need to make changes on the SQL server as managers join and leave the company. Security is managed entirely through group membership.

16. ☑ **A** and **D** are the correct answers. If you are the owner of both the table and the dependant object (either the view or the procedure), you can give a user access to that object without giving them access to the underlying table (or tables). This allows you to control access with a single permission. With stored procedures, when the procedure executes, it runs under the security context of its owner. This means that you can give a user access to your permissions by giving them the EXEC permission. However, you control what they can do when impersonating you through the code of the procedure.

☒ **B** and **C** are not the best answers because you should avoid assigning column level permissions. With the view or the stored procedure, you have to add and administer permissions only once; with column level permissions you multiply your administration by the number of columns affected. Technically, both of these answers will provide the correct permissions. **E** is incorrect because column level permissions are not equal to table level permissions; by issuing a revoke against the column you will only affect permissions that have been granted or denied on that column. Any permission granted or denied at the table level will not be affected by the column level revoke.

17. ☑ **D** is the correct answer because the problem relates to a broken ownership chain. As a db_ddladmin, both you and George have permission to create objects in the database. By default, when you create an object you become its owner and your user id is attached as the objects schema (you.yourtable). When George created his view, he automatically became its owner and it becomes attached to his schema (george.view). As creator/owner for your objects, both have the right to grant permissions on your objects to other. However, when a user accesses an object that is dependent on another object (such as a view dependent on a table) and the owners are different, SQL Server checks for permissions every time the owner changes. Therefore, the user has permission to select from george.view but not from you.yourtable. In order to access the view, therefore, the user would also need to have permission to access the table (which would make the view unnecessary). The only way to solve this is to have the same owner for both the table and view. If ownership does not change between depended objects, SQL Server only checks permission on the object being accessed. As a db_ddladmin, both you and George have the permission to create a job with dbo as owner (by specifying dbo before the object name in the CREATE TABLE or CREATE VIEW statement).

☒ **A** is incorrect because creating the view with dbo as the owner would only solve the problem if you had also created the table with dbo as the owner. **B** is incorrect because giving George SELECT permission is all that is required to allow him to create the view. Once he creates the view, he becomes the owner of that view and as owner has rights to assign permissions to the object to any database user. **C** is incorrect because the REFERENCES permission allows users to create Foreign Key constraints that reference a particular table. You would only place the references permission on a table if you wanted the user to be able to create the Foreign Key, but not query the table. **E** is incorrect because George is the creator/owner of his view and is automatically granted this right. It does not have to be explicitly granted to him.

18. ☑ **D** is the correct answer. Statistics are the information that the SQL Query Optimizer uses to determine the best execution plan for all SQL statements. In order to make the best choices, it needs to have an accurate understanding of composition of the data in the various tables. For example, it needs to know how many rows are in the table and the distribution of data. This allows it to determine, for example, how many rows a query will return and whether or not a particular index will be useful. Statistics can be created either manually or automatically. In the sales database, they are being created automatically. This means that whenever an index is created, or an un-indexed column is accessed, SQL Server will create the necessary statistics for that object. However, because the Auto Update Statistics option is not enabled, these statistics are not maintained. This means that as the composition of the data changes, the statistics do not reflect the change. This will lead the Query Optimizer to make less efficient choices than it might make if it had accurate statistics. This is why the query performance has been degrading over time.

☒ **A** is incorrect because the recovery option does not effect queries. It only affects how SQL Server logs transactions. **B** is incorrect because the Autoshrink process runs in the background and does not take resources away from the queries. **C** is incorrect because the Torn Page detection only slows Inserts and Updates (and even these are not greatly affected). Queries do not cause SQL Server to write data back to the disk and therefore does not cause SQL Server to flip the torn page bits that it used for Torn Page detection. **E** is incorrect because disabling the Auto create statistics will only make queries perform even slower. Without this option you must manually create statistics every time an index is created or a column is accessed for the first time. If you do not create these manual statistics, SQL Server will not use the indexes and will force full table scans on the tables.

19. ☑ **A**, **C**, and **F** are the correct answers. In order to receive this notification, you must first define an operator for yourself. You create the operator to provide SQL Server with information on how to contact you. You can provide an email address, pager information or a net send address. Once you have created an operator, you can define an alert to monitor the Lock Wait Time. A SQL Server alert has the ability to monitor either Windows events or

performance conditions. It is only able to monitor those counters that are added by SQL Server when it is installed. For each performance alert you can set a threshold value. Once this threshold value has been exceeded the alert is raised and any defined operators are notified. You must have the SQL Server Agent service running for these alerts to occur.

☒ **B** and **D** are incorrect because they add unnecessary steps that will delay the alert. It is possible to define an alert using this tool to write to the application log in Event View. However, by the time this message is written, and the Agent has parsed the log, determined that there is an Event alert configured for this error, and raised the alert, the problem application may have already ended. By contrast, if you set a performance alert, the Agent is monitoring this counter itself and will respond much faster.

20. ☑ **B**, **D**, and **E** are the correct answers. **B** is correct because you must use a domain user account to configure mail support. The local system account has no existence outside of the local server, therefore, the SQL Server Agent would be unable to authenticate the mail server. **D** is correct because the SQL Server Agent server uses the profile associated with its logon account to find information about the mail server. This information includes the name of the mail server and any required logon or password. If any of this information is incorrect, it may cause SQL Mail to fail. **E** is correct because the SQL Mail and SQL Agent Mail services require a MAPI-compliant mail server to send mail.

☒ **A** is incorrect because if the SQL Server Agent service was not running, you would not have been able to test the job. You require a running SQL Server Agent service to run any job, or to write any information to the job history logs. **C** is incorrect because the SQL Server Agent does not use SQL Mail. SQL Mail is used by the SQL Server service to send and receive mail (through xp_sendmail and xp_processmail). You must configure the SQL Server Agent Mail separately. It may be possible, however that both mail services share the same profile (if the SQL Server service and SQL Server Agent service share the same domain user account). **F** is incorrect because SQL Server doesn't have to be on the same server as the mail server. If fact, for performance reasons it is not a good idea to place the two applications on the same server.

21. ☑ **B** is the correct answer. SQL Server uses memory dynamically; this means that it will take available memory when it needs it and release the memory when it is not needed. If one instance was in a period of low activity and the

other instance went into a period of high activity, the second instance would grab all available memory. If later on, activity on the first instance increases, there will be no memory available. The second instance will hold all of the memory it has acquired until it is finished with it. To prevent this, you can configure each instance to take no more than half of the available RAM. This means that if this period of unequal activity occurs, the busy instance will not take all of the available RAM.

☒ **A** is incorrect because the number of worker threads affects the number of processes waiting for access to the processor; it has no bearing on memory use. **C** incorrect because if you only limit the default instance, there is nothing to stop the secondary instance from taking all available RAM at the expense of the default instance. **D** is incorrect because this means that each server will take a minimum of 256MB of RAM. There is nothing to prevent either instance from taking more than that amount. **E** is incorrect because this value has nothing to do with the use of memory as a whole—rather it looks at the amount of memory assigned to any given query. This amount is set in KB and the default is only 1024KB. If you assign 256MB to this value, SQL Server would assign 256MB to each query running on the server. This would make the query run very fast, but would only allow the server to run three or four queries at time.

22. ☑ **B** is the correct answer. The Buffer Cache hit ratio measures how often SQL server finds the data it requires in cache. An ideal Buffer Cache hit ratio would be consistently above 90. The Available Bytes indicate the amount of memory that is available for processes on the SQL server. The value is the total memory; it could indicate a memory shortage, or that one process was consuming the majority of the available memory. However, the Buffer Cache exists in physical RAM, so when both values are low, this indicates that there is a shortage of physical RAM on the server.

☒ **A** is incorrect because, ideally, both of these values should be high. **C** and **D** are incorrect because the problem cannot be solved with paged memory. Because the Buffer Cache exists in RAM, adding more space to the page file or moving the page file to another disk will not affect the this value. It will increase the Available Bytes value. Moving the page file to another disk won't actually improve either value. The only impact moving the page file would have is to speed up paging. If you move the page file to a disk that does not have a large number of I/O operations against it, the paging will run faster, which will increase performance to a certain degree on the server. **E** is incorrect because you cannot set the size of the Buffer Cache or Procedure cache. SQL Server dynamically sizes these caches depending on the amount of free (physical) memory.

23. ☑ **A** and **D** are the correct answers. Deadlocking occurs when two processes block each other by locking resources the other needs to complete their transaction. If SQL Server allowed deadlock to persist, they would not end until you killed one of the processes and allowed the other to complete. SQL Server manages deadlocks by choosing one process as the "deadlock victim." This process is killed so that the locks are not permanently held. The two tools you can use to monitor this behavior are System Monitor and the SQL Profiler. The System Monitor contains a counter that displays the number of deadlocks per second. This counter will not show which applications are causing the deadlocking, but it will show you the degree of deadlocking that is occurring on your server. The profile will show you all of the deadlocks that are occurring on the server. It will also show you what operations are causing the deadlocks and which application or users these operations are coming from. The Profiler is the better of the two for troubleshooting the cause of the excessive deadlocks.

　　 ☒ **B** is incorrect because the Current Activity in Enterprise Manager is a static list. It shows all processes running and will let you see if one particular process has a large number of processes waiting for it to release its locks. However, because SQL Server dynamically kills processes, dead locks will be removed before they show up on this list. You must constantly refresh to view deadlocks and most of them will be removed before the screen refreshes. The tool is best for looking for long running processes that are blocking other processes on the server. **C** is incorrect for the same reasons that **B** is incorrect. The sp_lock stored procedure returns a stick list of locks. It will only display deadlock information if you happen to run the procedure at the exact moment a deadlock occurred (and before SQL removed it by killing one of the two processes). **E** is incorrect because locking information is not written to any of the event logs.

24. ☑ **A** is the correct answer because it allows you to separate the main table in this database to its own disk. By placing this table by itself on a disk, it offers a performance benefit because this table is not contending with any other object

for disk access time. All of the disk's resources are made available to that one table. It also becomes possible to backup that table separate from the rest of the database. Because this table is updated frequently and the other tables are not updated as often, you may want to backup this table more frequently than the others. This is only possible if the table is in its own filegroup.

☒ **B** is incorrect because you cannot place a transaction log in a filegroup. Transaction logs are different than data files and are created individually on the database. **C** is incorrect because RAID-0 makes the system less stable. In RAID-0, data is written across two or more disks in 64KB stripes. RAID-0 is very fast, however, it does not protect your data; if one of the disks in the stripe fails, all of the data on all disks is lost. In addition, transaction logs write sequentially and do not gain any benefit from being striped (see Chapter 3, section 3.05 for more information on placement of transaction logs). **D** is incorrect because you cannot specify where a table is created without filegroups. SQL Server assigns disk space based on logical divisions. If you create one big file group with multiple disks, these disks are all considered part of the same logical grouping and SQL Server will spread the objects across all of the disks in the filegroup. **E** is incorrect because if you change the default and place all objects on the default, it will simply place the entire table on the second disk (the new default location).

25. ☑ **A** is the correct answer because it is possible for a database to have more than one data file. It is also possible for these files to be on different physical disks. When you add a new data file to a database, SQL Server simply adds the space in that new data file to the database. For example, if you had a 20GB primary data file and added a second 20GB data file, SQL Server would simply see this as 40GBs of available space and would place all objects and data within that space in a balanced manner. The database would not be considered "full" until both data files were full.

☒ **B** is incorrect because you should not place data files and log files from the same database on the same disk. If you need room for your database, and there is room on the disk containing the transaction log, you could, technically, create a second data file but this is not the best answer because it does not protect the database in the event of a disk failure. **C** is technically correct, however, it would be much more difficult to migrate the existing file to a bigger disk than to create a second data file. This move would involve stopping the server and moving the files. The new disk would also have to have the same drive letter as the original or SQL Server will not be able to find the data files. **D** is incorrect because it is possible both to expand an existing data file on the same disk and to increase the database size by adding secondary files. **E** is incorrect because you do not create a stripe when you add the second data file. Striping involves writing across both disks in even block sizes (or stripes) usually of 64KB in size. While SQL Server adds data to both files, it does not do it in as organized and consistent a manner as a stripe set.

26. ☑ **A** and **C** are the correct answers because you cannot issue DCL statements (such as a GRANT statement) or DDL statements (like CREATE VIEW) on a linked server. Both of these statements can only be run locally. **B** is incorrect because you are able to issue DML statements against tables on remote data sources. **D** is incorrect because you are allowed to execute stored procedures (including system stored procedures) on remote data sources. The procedures will always run locally. This means that you cannot use a stored procedure on a remote data source to return information about a local resource. **E** is incorrect because a linked server will permit you to join a local table and a table or view located on one or more remote data sources.

27. ☑ **E** is the correct answer. SQL Server creates the file in the system root folder for Windows (winnt). If you have given the system root folder a different name, SQL Server will still place the SQLstp.log file in this folder.

☒ **A** is incorrect because there is no log folder under the Microsoft SQL Server\80 subfolder. This subfolder contains the client tools that are installed with SQL Server. **B** is incorrect. There is a log folder in this path, however it only contains the SQL Server error logs and the SQL Agent error log. These files can be viewed in Notepad, or viewed through the Enterprise Manager. None of these files, however, deals with installation errors. **C** is incorrect. SQL Server writes a log to the c:\temp folder called SearchSetup.log if you have configured the Microsoft Search service. This log is only useful in troubleshooting problems with the Search service. **D** is incorrect because there is no installlogs subfolder under the binn folder.

28. ☑ **C** is correct, because in order to use `xp_sendmail`, your SQL Server service must be able to contact and communicate with a MAPI-compliant mail server (such as Microsoft Exchange). This requires a domain user account (that is, one which can validate itself to the Exchange server). The service will need access to the SMTP service in order to send mail.

☒ **A** is incorrect because `xp_sendmail` is fully supported in Microsoft SQL 2000. **B** is incorrect because you cannot access Exchange from the local system account. This account does not have any security context outside of the local server and you cannot create a mailbox for the account. **D** is incorrect because this account cannot be added to a security group. In any event, the account already has administrative rights on the local server, so adding it to the local administrators account on Windows would have no effect.

29. ☑ **D** is correct. The SQL Server Upgrade Wizard does not have to run on the SQL 6.5 server. When you run this wizard on the SQL 2000 server, it establishes a Named Pipe connection to the SQL 6.5 server. If you install SQL 2000 on the same server as SQL 6.5, the SQL 6.5 server will not be available while you are performing and testing the upgrade. However, if you run the upgrade from a different server (which effectively becomes a migration rather than an upgrade) the SQL 6.5 server will remain active and accessible by clients.

☒ **A** is incorrect because the Copy Database Wizard can only be used to copy databases from SQL 2000 or SQL 7.0 servers. It will not copy databases from earlier versions of SQL Server. **B** is incorrect because the DTS Object Transfer tool will also only move objects from SQL 7.0 or SQL 2000 databases. In fact, the Copy Database Wizard in SQL Server 2000 uses the DTS Object Transfer tool to transfer the database objects between servers. **C** is incorrect because `sp_attach_db` is unable to attach SQL 6.5 data files to SQL Server 2000. This stored procedure was introduced in SQL Server 7.0. It will take SQL 7.0 or SQL 2000 data files and "attach" them to the database by placing an entry corresponding to these data files in the sysdatabases table in the Master database. Because there are significant differences between the way that SQL Server 6.5 and SQL Server 2000 physically store data, the SQL 6.5 data storage type is not supported by this stored procedure.

30. ☑ **A** is the correct answer. If you use the ALTER TABLE WITH NOCHECK option to create the constraint, it will not apply the constraint to any existing data. It will only apply the constraint to subsequent INSERT or UPDATE statements. This option should only be used if the data is unlikely to change, because if you were to modify any column in one of the older data roles, all constraints are applied to the row.

    ☒ **B** is incorrect because the WITH NOCHECK option provides this capability. **C** is incorrect because the NOCHECK option is used to temporarily disable a constraint without removing it. **D** is incorrect because there is no `sp_maskdata` stored procedure. **E** is incorrect because you cannot turn off or modify constraint-checking behavior at the database level.

31.   ☑ **D** is the correct answer. The DROP_EXISTING option allows you to rebuild (and modify) an existing index. With DROP_EXISTING you can alter the columns in the index list, the fill factor or even the type of index. This is more efficient than dropping and completely rebuilding the index.

    ☒ **A** is incorrect because you should never modify an object directly in the system tables. **B** is incorrect because there is no ALTER INDEX statement. **C** is incorrect because the DBCC DBREINDEX cannot alter the definition of an index. It is used to reset fill factors and to rebuild the structure of the index tree. **E** is technically correct and will modify the index, however, it is not as efficient as using the DROP_EXISTING option.

32.   ☑ **A** is correct. Using URL queries, they can be dynamically generated as text strings and this provides the easiest way to programmatically create new XML queries.

    ☒ **B** is incorrect because X-Path queries are based on schema mapping, and this is not what is asked for. **C** is incorrect because Template queries draw their queries from files, which would be more complex to generate queries on the fly than using URLs. **D** is incorrect because there is no XML functionality called Ad-hoc queries, although XML queries can be submitted directly to SQL Server using the FOR XML AUTO operator. This is not recommended and is not the easiest method available.

33.   ☑ **B** is correct. Increasing the Fetch Buffer Size will allow more rows to be transferred at once. This will increase network traffic but can improve performance considerably.

    ☒ **A** is incorrect because decreasing the Fetch Buffer Size will reduce performance. **C** is wrong because enabling Identity Insert will have little effect in this example. **D** is incorrect because enabling the Always Commit Final Batch can improve performance in some cases, but only when it comes to error handling.

34. ☑ **D** is correct. By specifying that the collations are not compatible, all sort operations and comparisons can be executed locally in order to maintain consistency.

    ☒ It is not recommended that you ORDER BY in this case, as it will require additional work on the part of the developers to determine what sort of options should be used, and queries would need to be rewritten. For this reason **A** is incorrect. **B** is incorrect because using the Collation Compatible option on systems that do not have compatible sort orders will cause, rather than solve this problem. **C** is incorrect because there is no mechanism to disable pass-through queries (queries that use the OPENQUERY operator).

35. ☑ **A, B,** and **D** are correct. Configuring a remote distributor will reduce overhead on the publisher. Using publishing subscribers will reduce the number of times that WAN links must be crossed, and specifying that subscribers will synchronize manually will also cut network traffic.

    ☒ **C** is incorrect because, in this case, data should not be updated on the subscriber but no steps have been taken to prevent that. If data is modified on the subscriber, problems with data consistency will occur, as none of the data will be able to be sent back to the publisher in this configuration.

36. ☑ **D** is the correct answer because the last transaction log backup for HRDATA includes the INIT option. This option instructs SQL Server to overwrite the contents of the device. If you do not specify the INIT option, the default is to backup the database with the NOINIT option. NOINIT instructs SQL Server to append the backup to the current backups in the device.

    ☒ **A** is incorrect because the WITH INIT statement will cause the backup issuing the statement to overwrite the contents of the device. **B** and **C** are incorrect because you can have backups from different databases in the same device. The backup device is simply a storage file that is known to SQL Server. It is not bound to any particular database. **E** is incorrect because a backup device will hold all backup types including log backups. The devices (and SQL Server) do not differentiate between the types of backups.

37. ☑ **C** is the correct answer. In this question all of the answers will satisfy the requirements. **C** is correct because the constraint is check before the insert statement is processed. For this reason, it has the lowest cost to the server of all the options.

☒   **A** and **B** are incorrect because any insert or update statement must be processed before the trigger is fired. The INSTEAD OF trigger will be more efficient than the AFTER trigger, however neither is as efficient as the CHECK constraint. **D** is incorrect because SQL Server must lookup the rule in the metadata every time data is modified in the table. This lookup makes the RULE less efficient than the constraint.

38.   ☑   **D** is the correct answer. By creating a user-defined data type, you can control the type and precision for the column.

☒   **A** is incorrect because rules only apply to the data added to a column. The rule is not applied when you use the CREATE or ALTER TABLE statement. **B** may be possible, but it would certainly be much more difficult than using the stored procedure. **C** would ensure the correct data type was used, but is much more difficult than using the user-defined data type.

39.   ☑   **A** is the correct answer. When the procedure is first run, the execution plan that has been compiled for the procedure is stored in an area of memory called the procedure cache. When the procedure is executed a second time, SQL Server uses the cached execution plan instead of optimizing and recompiling the procedure. Normally this improves performance. However, because the procedure is producing a wide range of possible outcomes, the cached plan may not be the most optimal plan for all situations. When you include the WITH RECOMPILE option, SQL Server does not use the cached execution plan and optimizes and recompiles the procedure each time it is run. This will slow queries that match the cached criteria slightly, but will greatly increase the speed of queries that do not match the cached criteria.

☒   **B** is incorrect because the SCHEMABINDING option is not available for procedures. It is used to bind views to their underlying table objects and prevent the tables from being altered. **C** and **D** are incorrect because there is no cacheproc option at either the database or server level.

40.   ☑   The correct order is **C, A, E, G,** and **H**. The first thing you need to do is to capture all transactions since the 11:00 A.M. backup. Remember that the current transaction log will be dropped and recreated when the full backup restore is run. If you do not backup the log, you can only restore to the last backup (and you will lose 2 hours and 15 minutes worth of data instead of 5 minutes worth of data). Once the transaction log backup is complete you

must start with a restore of the full database backup, making sure not to recover the database. You only need to restore the Wednesday night differential backup (again specifying NORECOVERY). You must then restore each transaction log backup in chronological order, ending with the transaction log backup you made just prior to beginning the restore process. Because you are recovering from data corruption, you can use the STOP AT command to prevent the error from being applied when restoring the final log. This also helps to minimize data loss.

☒ **B** is incorrect because setting the database to read only will not prevent users from connecting. You should restrict access to members of db_owner, dbcreator and sysadmin instead. **D** is incorrect because the Wednesday night differential backup contains all of the changes from the earlier backups and is, therefore, the only differential backup that needs to be restored. **F** is incorrect because you should only recover the final backup in the set. If you were to recover the 9:00 A.M. transaction log backup, SQL Server would not permit you to restore the 11:00 A.M. log backup or the final log backup.

41. ☑ **C** is the correct answer. You need to start not only Master in single user mode, but the whole server. If you do not include the -c and -m options, Windows starts SQL Server as a service and the service account establishes a persistent connection with the Master database. In single user mode this connection is not established. Also, because you are starting a named instance in single user mode you must also include the -s switch to specify which instance to start.

☒ **A** is incorrect because the net start command does not have a /singleuser switch. **B** is incorrect because there is no configurable setting that places SQL Server into single user mode while it is running. The Allow Updates option will allow you to make manual changes to system tables, but will not help in this instance. **D** and **E** are incorrect because you cannot set the database into single user mode from either location. This check box does not exist on either location.

42. ☑ **D** is the correct answer because the application role will allow you to assign permissions to roles without having to give permission to the individual users. You would need to create a login for the application to use, but you would not have to give this login any specific access to any database. When

you execute the `sp_setapprole` stored procedure, your login's permissions are replaced by those permissions granted to the application role. This means that all users, whether they have access to the database or not, will be able access the Emp_info table through the application (but only through the application).

☒   **A** is incorrect because if you create a specific user account for the computer running in the lobby, it will be able to run the application but not the corporate users (particularly those users who do not have a database user account for Corpinfo). **B** is incorrect because you want to avoid giving access to users through the guest account, because guest is a member of the public role, and anything granted to public will also be granted to this role. Additionally, you would still need to create a login for the lobby computer. **C** is incorrect because SQL Server will not allow you to create a login for the Everyone group.

43. **A** is correct because it allows lock contention to be reduced, allowing the HR transactions to run, and also improves performance for the employee lookup since all data required for the query can be retrieved from the index. Performance could be further improved by placing the newly created index on another disk or RAID set. This solution may, however, produce a very large index.

    ☒   **B** is incorrect because HR transactions must still use this data, thereby not addressing the issue of I/O contention. It could also require changes to stored procedures, views and client code. **C** is incorrect because it will not improve performance for HR transactions and would also fail to retrieve any records existing but locked by the HR activity. **D** is incorrect because the HR transactions are not trying to view the data and the READ UNCOMITTED option will not provide any benefit.

44.   ☑   **B** and **D** are correct. The %processor time indicates the percentage of time that is being spent by the processor on active threads. You do not want this value to be too low (which would indicate that your hardware far exceeds your requirements). However, if this value is too high, then you may have a processor bottleneck. When this occurs, each process will have a longer wait time to access the processor. Adding a second processor (or a faster processor) will reduce the %processor use and thereby reduce the wait time. Also, this is the total processor usage for the server. If there are other processor intensive applications running on the server, you should move them (or SQL Server) to another server that has more processor usage available.

    ☒   **A** is incorrect because the %processor time is not affected in any way by memory. **C** is incorrect because worker threads are used internally by SQL Server to schedule user process access to the processor. Decreasing the number of worker threads will actually make the users processes run slow (because they must wait longer within SQL Server to gain access to the processor).

45.   ☑   **A** and **B** are correct. Using Profiler will allow you to see all queries that are missing statistics. You can use the Find feature in the Profiler to quickly locate any references to missing statistics in the trace output. Using Query Analyzer would allow you to verify this for specific queries, but would not monitor activity on the server. Query Analyzer can also be used to create the missing statistics.

    ☒   **C** and **D** are incorrect because you cannot monitor the creation of statistics with the System Monitor.

Glossary

A TO Z

Active/Active cluster   A configuration of servers in a Window Cluster where all servers are the primary nodes for one virtual server. These servers will have one of the other servers as its secondary node. (*See also* primary node and secondary node.)

Active/Passive cluster   A cluster configuration of servers in a Window Cluster where one server acts as the primary node and the other server is the secondary node. In this configuration, only one server runs the associated virtual server. (*See also* primary node and secondary node.)

Alert   An automated response to a pre-configured performance condition or SQL Server message. Alerts are raised by the SQL Server Agent service and can execute jobs or notify operators. In order for an alert on an error to be raised, the error must be written to the application log in Event Viewer.

ANSI   The American National Standards Institute. ANSI is the standards body for the SQL language. The current SQL standard is known as SQL-99 or SQL3.

Application role   A SQL Server role that can be used to provide access to objects based on permission given to the role rather than to the user. When you activate an application role, its security context replaces the security context of the connected user.

Auditing   The process of monitoring the activity on the server. SQL audits will capture activity created by users and automated processes. You can configure audits to capture successful actions, failed actions or all activity. For example, you can audit for successful or failed attempts to access the server or database objects on the server.

Backup device   A named storage location for SQL Server backups. You can use devices to automate SQL Server backups. You can also append multiple backups to the same device.

Buffer cache   An area of memory where data modification occurs. When you issue a modification operation such as an UPDATE statement, the pages updated are loaded from the data file into the buffer cache. They are then modified in the cache. Once the modification takes place, the pages are considered "dirty pages" because they contain data that is different than the data stored in the data file.

C2 Security   A U.S. government standard for computer security.

Checkpoint An event that causes dirty pages to be written from the buffer cache back to the data files. These events are recorded in the transaction log. Checkpoints improve the speed of recovery because SQL Server looks to the last checkpoint rather than the beginning of the transaction log.

Clustered index A clustered index is an index that orders the data in a table on the clustered key value. In a clustered index, the table becomes the leaf level of the index.

Collation The collation is a set of rules for character data. The collation setting includes the sort order, case sensitivity and the ASCII code page used by character data. In SQL 2000 you can set the collation at the server, database, and column level.

Constraint A constraint is a table property that dictates what data can be stored in a particular column or columns. For example, a check constraint will test any value added to a column against a set condition and reject all modifications that do not meet the condition. Constraints are check before an INSERT, UPDATE, or DELETE statement is executed.

Data page The page is the smallest unit of storage for a table. All data files are divided into 8k pages. These pages will hold 8060 bytes of data. One row of a table cannot span more than one page. A data page can only hold data from one table. To calculate how many rows of a table will fit on one page, divide the size of one row by 8060.

DBCC (Database Console Commands) These statements are used to check the logical and physical consistency of databases.

Dbo (Database owner) A built-in database user account that has full permission to perform all activities on a database. Each database has a dbo account, which cannot be deleted. Members of the sysadmin fixed server role are automatically mapped to this user account.

DCL (Data Control Language) The part of the SQL language that manages security. It includes the GRANT, DENY, and REVOKE statements.

DDL (Data Definition Language) The part of the SQL language that deals with object creation and manipulation. This includes all CREATE, ALTER, and DROP statements.

Deadlock   A situation in which two processes hold locks on resources needed by the other to complete a transaction. SQL Server automatically removes deadlocks. It does this by choosing one process as the "deadlock victim" and ending the process. When the victim process is ended, the second process is able to complete. The client application, which has run the victim process, needs to check for the error raised by this condition and resubmit the operation.

Differential backup   A type of backup that only records extents that have changed since the last full backup. Differential backups speed up both the backup and restore process (since they are faster to restore than a series of transaction log backups).

DML   (Data Manipulation Language) The part of the SQL language that deals with manipulating and retrieving data. This includes the SELECT, INSERT, UPDATE, and DELETE statements.

DSS   (Decision Support Server) A SQL server that is used primarily for running complex queries. The data in a DSS server changes less often than an OLTP server. DSS servers tend to be indexed more thoroughly and often contain computed or repetitious data.

DTS   (Data Transformation Service) A series of tools used to move and transform data to and from many different data sources. These tools include the DTS designer and the DTS Import/Export Wizard.

Event log   A series of logs maintained by Windows and viewable using the Windows Event Viewer. All servers have at least three logs—the system, security, and application logs. The system log stores information about services and Windows processes. The security log stores the results of auditing. The application log stores events and errors raised by applications. SQL Server is able to write its errors to the application log. In addition, the SQL Server Agent service parses this log to see if errors with alerts defined on them are raised. If errors are not raised to this log, alerts will not execute.

Extent   An extent is a group of eight contiguous pages. Extents can be uniform or mixed. A mixed extent contains pages from multiple tables or indexes whereas all pages in a uniform extent belong to the same object.

Filegroup   A logical grouping of one or more data files. You can use filegroups to backup portions of a database or to place objects on specific data files.

Fill factor   An index property that specifies how much data to place on each page of the leaf level. The remaining space is left free. For example, if you set a fill factor value of 70, SQL Server will place data on 70% of each page and leave the remaining 30% free to hold additional inserts. The fill factor is used to slow down page splitting in the indexes of heavily modified tables.

FTP   (File Transfer Protocol) A TCP/IP application used to move data to and from an FTP server (like the IIS FTP service).

Full backup   A backup that provides a baseline for other backup types. A full backup saves all data in a database including the locations of all data files. Differential and transaction log backups cannot be restored unless you first restore a full backup.

Global group   A Windows security group used to group users together. A global group can contain user accounts and other global groups from domains where the group is created. Global groups are created on Windows domain controllers.

Heap   The collection of pages that make up one table. Data in the heap is not stored in an ordered fashion. If you place a clustered index on a table, the heap is ordered and becomes the leaf level of the index.

Job   An automated operation containing one or more Transact-SQL, Active X script, operating system command, or replication tasks. Jobs can be scheduled and are executed by the SQL Server Agent.

Kerberos   A service that allows for mutual authentication between Windows 2000 users and services. Users connecting to a SQL 2000 server use Kerberos to authenticate their Windows logins to the local Windows server on which SQL Server is running.

Linked server   A defined link to another server. When you create a linked server, you include the connection information (such as which OLEDB provider to use and the server name). Once you have created a linked server you can access the server in SQL statements by including the server name in the fully qualified object name (that is, servername.databasename.owner.object).

Lock   A limitation on access placed by SQL Server to prevent concurrent operations from overwriting or otherwise conflict with each other. SQL Server can lock at the row, the page, the extent, the table, pointer, schema, or the database level. Locks are necessary for maintaining transactional consistency.

Metadata   Data that is stored by SQL Server about itself (for example, what databases the server contains or what objects are contained in a database). SQL Server stores metadata in the system databases and in system tables found in all user databases. These system tables are copied from the Model database when the user database is created.

MSX   (Multi Server Master) A server that is configured as a master server for controlling automation. A job created on the MSX master server can be configured to run on any registered target server. This allows you to centralize the automation of several SQL servers by creating the jobs on a master server and enlisting all other servers as targets (capable of receiving jobs from the master server).

MAPI   (Messaging Application Programming Interface) An API used to connect to messaging applications (such as Microsoft Exchange or Unix SendMail).

Master database   The main system database. SQL Server uses the Master database to hold such information as logins, listing of user databases, and system configuration settings. If the Master database is not available, SQL Server will not start.

Model database   Model is the template for all user databases. It contains all of the system tables needed by the user database to store metadata specific to the local database (such as database objects and users) and the dbo account. When you create a new user database, SQL Server copies Model to create the primary data file.

MSDB database   The system database used by the SQL Server Agent service. The MSDB database contains information about jobs, alerts, and operators. DTS packages can also be stored in MSDB.

Named instance   An installation of SQL Server, other than the default instance, that is given a unique name. SQL Server allows you to place multiple installations of SQL Server on the same computer. The first instance is the default instance and has the same name as the server. All subsequent instances are named instances and are identified with the server name and a unique name (for example, server\NewInstance).

Network library   An Inter Process Communication mechanism that allows applications to communicate across the network with a SQL server. SQL Server can have several network libraries installed. In order to connect to the server, the client application must be using one of the libraries installed on the SQL server. The available network libraries are TCP/IP Sockets, Named Pipes, Multiprotocol, NWlink IPX/SPX, Apple Talk, Banyan Vines, and VIA.

Non-clustered index   A non-clustered index is an index that references values the heap from the leaf level of the index (or the clustered index key value if the table also contains a clustered index). A non-clustered index does not change the placement of data in the table, but instead uses Row Identifiers (RIDs), or the clustered index key, to indicate where a particular value is located.

NULL   A specific entry for a field that does not contain a value. A NULL represents the absence of a value (and cannot, for example, be equated to 0 which is an actual value).

NWLink   Microsoft's version of the Novell NetWare IPX/SPX network protocol.

Object permission   Permissions governing how a user can interact with the various objects in a database. The permission to execute a stored procedure or select from a table or view are examples of object permissions.

OLEDB   A set of APIs that allow you to connect to multiple data sources. You require the correct provider to connect with the OLEDB data source, for example. The provider to connect to a SQL server is SQLOLEDB and the provider for Oracle is MSDAORA.

OLAP   (Online Analytical Processing) A system using the Microsoft Analysis Services to store and access data in such a way as to allow rapid processing of complex queries. OLAP databases are most often designed as data warehouses.

OLTP   (Online Transaction Processing) A SQL server that is used primarily for manipulating data. An order entry database that processes a large number of orders would be an example of an OLTP database.

Operator   Contact information (email address, pager e-mail, and/or net set address) for a user that is responsible for some aspect of a SQL server. When you define an operator, you can then have the SQL Server Agent service contact the operator when certain events occur (such as an alert executing or a job failing).

Primary node   The server in a Windows Cluster that actively processes requests. When a client sends a request to the virtual server, it is the primary node that responds to the request.

RAID (Redundant Array of Independent Disks) A hardware or software-based storage system that links multiple disks into a single logical volume. There are different types of RAID, which provide varying levels of I/O performance improvements and fault tolerance.

RAID-0 (Disk Striping without Parity) In RAID-0, two or more disks are striped together. This means that data is written evenly across all disks. RAID-0 greatly improves I/O, however, it does not provide any fault tolerance. If one disk fails, the entire array must be replaced.

RAID-1 (Disk Mirroring) A RAID-1 array keeps a mirrored copy of a volume on a separate disk. RAID-1 will slightly improve read I/O because SQL is able to read from both members of the mirror. Disk mirroring provides a high degree of fault tolerance because if the primary disk fails, the mirror can be used in its place.

RAID-5 (Disk Striping with Parity) Like RAID-0, RAID-5 writes data in stripes across all members of the array. However, unlike RAID-0, it includes a "parity bit" on each stripe. This is redundant data that can be used to replace any one disk in the set. RAID-5 provides improved I/O performance and fault tolerance. Because the parity bit must be calculated for each stripe, you may experience a decrease in write performance if you have too few disks in the RAID set.

RAID 10 (RAID-1&0) RAID 10 is a combination of RAID-0 and RAID-1. It involves mirroring two RAID-0 arrays together. This provides all of the I/O benefit of RAID-0 and the fault tolerance of RAID-1.

RAISERROR A statement that allows you to programmatically raise a SQL server error. If you include the WITH LOG option, RAISERROR will also write its errors to the application log in Event Viewer. It is important to raise errors to the application log if you intend to place an alert on the event. You can also use xp_logevent to raise errors to the event log. (*See also* Alert.)

Recovery An automatic process that is required to maintain transactional consistency. When the SQL Server service starts, SQL Server checks the transaction log for each database. It looks to the last checkpoint and rolls forward any committed transaction and rolls back any uncommitted transactions. Until a database is recovered, it cannot be accessed. You can also manually recover a database as part of a restore operation by including the WITH RECOVERY option.

Recovery model   A database property that determines how the database manages its transaction log. There are three models: full, bulk logged, and simple. In the full recovery model, all activity on the database is logged. In the simple model, the log is not maintained and all committed transactions are deleted when a checkpoint occurs. The bulk logged operation logs all operations except those generated by a bulk-loaded operation (such as a SELECT … INTO statement or a DTS bulk insert job).

Replication   An automated process for distributing data between servers. Replication has three logical parts: publisher, distributor, and subscriber. The publisher provides the data that will be distributed and the subscriber is the server that will receive the data. It is the job of the distributor to ensure that data gets from the publishers to the subscribers.

RID   (Row Identifier) A RID is a value that can be used to locate an exact row in a heap. The RID contains the file number, page number, and row offset value for each row in a table. Non-clustered indexes use RIDs to locate data.

Role   A security grouping that exists on the SQL server. There are three types of roles: fixed system, fixed database, and user-defined roles. Fixed database and server roles are created when SQL Server is installed and cannot be removed or modified. They are used to give users special permission to the server to an individual database. The sysadmin role is an example of a fixed server role. User-defined roles can be used to give permissions to a group of database users. These roles are useful when you have a number of users with similar security requirements and you are not able to create a Windows security group to assign permissions to the users.

sa   The built-in system administrator account. This account is created automatically when SQL Server is installed, and cannot be removed. You must be in mixed security mode to log on as **sa**. The **sa** account has become less relevant now that SQL Server includes the sysadmin fixed server role.

Secondary node   The redundant server in a Windows Cluster. The secondary node does not reply to requests from the virtual server. Instead it monitors the primary node and will step in (or fail over) to the role of primary node, if the existing primary node fails.

SID   (Security Identifier) A unique value assigned to each user and group by Windows. When a user account is dropped and recreated it is created with a new SID. When you create a Windows authenticated login, SQL Server records the SID of the user or group in the sysxlogins database. When you create SQL Server logins, SQL Server generates a SID for the login, which is only used internally.

SQL mail   The mail service used by SQL Server service. You must configure the SQL Mail service to allow SQL Server to send mail using the xp_sendmail stored procedure. If you plan to use SQL Mail, your SQL Server service must use a domain user account for authentication.

SQL Agent Mail   The mail service used by the SQL Server Agent service. If you want SQL Server to have the ability to email operators in response to jobs or alerts, you must configure the SQL Agent Mail service. If you plan to use SQL Agent Mail, your SQL Server service must use a domain user account for authentication.

Statement permission   Permissions governing the creation and manipulation of objects on the server. Statement permissions include permission to execute DDL statements such as CREATE or ALTER TABLE.

System database   Databases controlled by SQL Server that contain metadata. SQL Server uses these databases to store information about itself (such as the user databases or automatic jobs it contains). These databases are controlled entirely by SQL Server, and they cannot be dropped or modified. When you install SQL Server, it creates four databases that only contain metadata. These tables are Master, Model, Msdb, and Tempdb. If your server is a distributor, there will also be a distribution database. Tempdb does not store metadata, but is used by the SQL Server service as a temporary storage location.

System Monitor   A tool used to monitor Windows and SQL Server. With the System Monitor you can log and chart counters that show specific metrics about the computer (such as the percentage of memory or processor used by the server). SQL Server adds its own counters to the System Monitor, and the SQL Server Agent is able to monitor counters for alert conditions set on these counters.

TCP/IP Socket   One of the Network libraries on SQL Server. A TCP/IP Socket is available on a specific port number. The default port number is 1433, but this port can be changed. Any client connected to the SQL server must use the port number set in the Socket's Properties sheet.

Tempdb   One for system databases. Tempdb is used as a storage location for the SQL Server service. For example, if you create a temporary table, SQL Server may cache some or all of that table to Tempdb while the table is open.

Transaction   One or more Transact-SQL statements that must commit entirely or not at all. Transactions can be delimited using a BEGIN TRANSACTION and COMMIT TRANSACTION statement. If the system fails before a transaction is committed, SQL Server will roll back the transactions. You can also manually roll back a transaction by issue the ROLLBACK statement. Transactions can also be implicit. If you do not frame a transaction with a BEGIN and COMMIT TRANSACTION statement, SQL Server will autocommit each executable statement (such as an INSERT, UPDATE, or DELETE). Therefore you must use the BEGIN TRANSACTION statement if you want to have multiple statements in the same transaction.

Transact-SQL   The variant of the SQL language used by Microsoft SQL Server. Transact-SQL is based on the current ANSI SQL standard. Transact-SQL includes language elements that are specific to Microsoft SQL Server.

Trigger   A Transact-SQL script that is bound to a table or view. The script is executed by an activity that is programmed into the trigger. Triggers can be programmed to fire when an INSERT, UPDATE, or DELETE statement is executed against the table. SQL Server 2000 has two types of triggers: an AFTER trigger that executes its code after the INSERT, UPDATE, or DELETE has taken place, or an INSTEAD OF trigger that fires in the place of the INSERT, UPDATE, or DELETE statement.

View   A view is an object that derives data from an underlying table. Views are treated like tables (for example, they can have their own permissions and can be referenced in a FROM clause), however they do not contain data. Instead, views derive values by executing queries that were written into the view definition when it was created. Because views do not contain data, any changes to the underlying tables will be immediately returned when the view is accessed.

Virtual server   A creation of the Windows Cluster service that appears on the network as a real server. Virtual servers have their own IP address and name, however any requests to the virtual server are actually processed by the primary node in the cluster. The advantage of the virtual server is that the cluster service can fail over to the secondary node, but clients will still see (and connect to) the virtual server and will not have to be directed to the secondary server.

XML   (Extensible Markup Language) A markup language that uses tags (similar to HTML tags) to describe data. SQL Server can use XML to give web-based applications access to the SQL server.

INTERNATIONAL CONTACT INFORMATION

AUSTRALIA
McGraw-Hill Book Company Australia Pty. Ltd.
TEL +61-2-9417-9899
FAX +61-2-9417-5687
http://www.mcgraw-hill.com.au
books-it_sydney@mcgraw-hill.com

CANADA
McGraw-Hill Ryerson Ltd.
TEL +905-430-5000
FAX +905-430-5020
http://www.mcgrawhill.ca

**GREECE, MIDDLE EAST,
NORTHERN AFRICA**
McGraw-Hill Hellas
TEL +30-1-656-0990-3-4
FAX +30-1-654-5525

MEXICO (Also serving Latin America)
McGraw-Hill Interamericana Editores S.A. de C.V.
TEL +525-117-1583
FAX +525-117-1589
http://www.mcgraw-hill.com.mx
fernando_castellanos@mcgraw-hill.com

SINGAPORE (Serving Asia)
McGraw-Hill Book Company
TEL +65-863-1580
FAX +65-862-3354
http://www.mcgraw-hill.com.sg
mghasia@mcgraw-hill.com

SOUTH AFRICA
McGraw-Hill South Africa
TEL +27-11-622-7512
FAX +27-11-622-9045
robyn_swanepoel@mcgraw-hill.com

**UNITED KINGDOM & EUROPE
(Excluding Southern Europe)**
McGraw-Hill Education Europe
TEL +44-1-628-502500
FAX +44-1-628-770224
http://www.mcgraw-hill.co.uk
computing_neurope@mcgraw-hill.com

ALL OTHER INQUIRIES Contact:
Osborne/McGraw-Hill
TEL +1-510-549-6600
FAX +1-510-883-7600
http://www.osborne.com
omg_international@mcgraw-hill.com